Plato's Socrates as Educator

SUNY Series in Ancient Greek Philosophy

Anthony Preus, Editor

Plato's Socrates as Educator

Gary Alan Scott

State University of New York Press

Published by
State University of New York Press, Albany

© 2000 State University of New York

All rights reserved

Printed in the United States of America

No part of this book may be used or reproduced in any manner whatsoever without written permission. No part of this book may be stored in a retrieval system or transmitted in any form or by any means including electronic, electrostatic, magnetic tape, mechanical, photocopying, recording, or otherwise without the prior permission in writing of the publisher.

For information, address State University of New York Press, 90 State Street, Suite 700, Albany, N.Y. 12207

Production by Michael Haggett
Marketing by Michael Campochiaro

Library of Congress Cataloging-in-Publication Data

Scott, Gary Alan, 1952-
   Plato's Socrates as educator / Gary Alan Scott.
   p. cm.—(SUNY series in ancient Greek philosophy)
   Includes bibliographical references (p.) and index.
   ISBN 0-7914-4723-5 (HC : acid-free paper)—ISBN 0-7914-4724-3 (PB : acid-free paper)
     1. Socrates. 2. Methodology—History. 3. Philosophy—Study and teaching—History. 4. Plato. Lysis. 5. Plato. Symposium. 6. Plato. Alcibiades I. I. Title. II. Series.

B318.M48.S36 2000
183'.2—dc21
                                                         00-027112

10 9 8 7 6 5 4 3 2 1

For my parents,
Leila and Harold,
with love and appreciation.

Socrates From this point of view do you see any salvation that will suffer the born philosopher to abide in the pursuit and persevere to the end? Consider it in the light of what we said before. We agreed that quickness in learning, memory, courage, and magnificence were the traits of this nature.

Adeimantus Yes.

Then even as a boy among boys such a one will take the lead in all things, especially if the nature of his body matches the soul.

How could he fail to do so? he said.

His kinsmen and fellow citizens, then, will desire, I presume, to make use of him when he is older for their own affairs.

Of course.

Then they will fawn upon him with petitions and honors, anticipating and flattering the power that will be his.

That certainly is the usual way.

How, then, do you think such a youth will behave in such conditions, especially if it happens that he belongs to a great city and is rich and wellborn therein, and thereto handsome and tall? Will his soul not be filled with unbounded ambitious hopes, and will he not think himself capable of managing the affairs of both Greeks and barbarians, and thereupon exalt himself, haughty of mien and stuffed with empty pride and void of sense?

He surely will, he said.

And if to a man in this state of mind someone gently comes and tells him what is the truth, that he has no sense and sorely needs it, and that the only way to get it is to work like a slave to win it, do you think it will be easy for him to lend an ear to the quiet voice in the midst of and in spite of these evil surroundings?

Far from it, said he.

And even supposing, said I, that owing to a fortunate disposition and his affinity for the words of admonition one such youth apprehends something and is moved and drawn toward philosophy, what do we suppose will be the conduct of those who think that they are losing his service and fellowship? Is there any word or deed that they will stick at to keep him from being persuaded and to incapacitate anyone who attempts it, both by private intrigue and public prosecution in the court?

That is inevitable, he said.

Is there any possibility of such a one continuing to philosophize?

None at all, he said.

Do you see, then, said I, that we were not wrong in saying that the very qualities that make up the philosophical nature do, in fact, become, when the environment and nurture are bad, in some sort the cause of its backsliding, and so do the so-called goods—riches and all such instrumentalities?

No, he replied, it was rightly said.

Such, my good friend, and so great as regards the noblest pursuit, is the destruction and corruption of the most excellent nature, which is rare enough in any case, as we affirm. And it is from men of this type that those spring who do the greatest harm to communities and individuals, and the greatest good when the stream chances to be turned into that channel, but a small nature never does anything great to a man or a city.

      Plato, *Republic,* Book VI (494a–495b; Shorey trans.)

Contents

Acknowledgments	xi
List of Abbreviations	viii
Introduction	1
Chapter 1 Socrates and Teaching	13
Section 1.a Why Socrates Denies Being a Teacher	15
Section 1.b Conventional Athenian Assumptions about Teachers and Teaching	24
Section 1.c Socrates as Student: The Contrast between a Market and a Gift Economy	27
Section 1.d The Meaning of "Teaching" in the *Gorgias*: "Additive" versus "Integrative" Models	37
Section 1.e Conclusion: The Socratic *Paideusis*	43
Chapter 2 The *Lysis*: Limits and Liberation in Socrates' Encounter with Lysis	51
Section 2.a The Threshold Imagery in the Dramatic Setting and Prologue (203a1–206e2)	59
Section 2.b Socrates' First Conversation with Lysis (206e3–211b5)	62
Section 2.b.1 Step One—The Unsettling: Disturbing What Is Familiar	63
Section 2.b.2 Step Two—The Arousal: Fanning the Flames of Desire	66
Section 2.b.3 Step Three—The Chastening: Reimposing Limits	69
Section 2.c Conclusion: The Positive Results of the *Lysis*	74

Chapter 3 The *Alcibiades I*: Socratic Dialogue as Self-Care   81
  Section 3.a Disarming Alcibiades: The Preliminary Contest   86
  Section 3.b Introduction to the Problem of Taking Trouble
    over Oneself   91
  Section 3.c The Meaning of Taking Trouble over Oneself   93
  Section 3.d Practices for "Taking Trouble": *Gumnastikē*
    and *Mathēsis*   98
    Section 3.d.1 *Gumnastikē* and Dialogue   99
    Section 3.d.2 Learning What Needs to Be Learned   113
  Section 3.e Conclusion: The Ominous End of the *Alcibiades I*   116

Chapter 4 The *Symposium:* Eros, Truth Telling, and the
    Preservation of Freedom   119
  Section 4.a Alcibiades' Motive in the *Agōn* with Socrates   121
  Section 4.b Alcibiades' Attempt to Dominate Socrates   126
    Section 4.b.1 Eros and *Thumos*   131
    Section 4.b.2 The Vindication of Socrates' Approach to Others   134
  Section 4.c Irony and Inebriation: Two Ways of Telling the Truth   138
    Section 4.c.1 Six Points of Emphasis in Alcibiades' Speech   140
    Section 4.c.2 Inebriation and *Parrhēsia* in Truth Telling   145
  Section 4.d Conclusion: Adjudicating the *Agōn* over Truth Telling   152

Chapter 5 Dramatic Failure and the Gift in Socratic *Paideusis*   159

Notes   179

Selected Bibliography   235

Index   245

Acknowledgments

I am indebted to several colleagues and friends who graciously provided comments on earlier versions of this book. Their suggestions and criticisms have been invaluable, calling my attention to any number of errors and offering helpful ideas for improvement. Each comment has enriched the resulting product in some way, although of course any shortcomings the book still manifests belong entirely to me. I thank Ron Polansky, Nick Smith, Bob Madden, and Bill Welton for their perspicuous criticisms of an earlier draft of the manuscript. Their comments alerted me to some of the broader questions triggered by the issues I was examining, and their conscientious readership helped me anticipate possible objections from various quarters. Even where we may disagree about Plato, each has helped clarify my thinking about the dialogues and complex issues surrounding their characterizations of Socrates.

Many others have offered generous criticisms on one or more parts of this book. Each deserves individual thanks here: Mauro Bottalico, Daniel Conway, Lisa O'Neill, Gerald Press, David Roochnik, Hilde Roos, Tom Schmid, and Joanne Waugh. Finally, I appreciate the thoughtful comments by Anthony Preus, editor of the SUNY Series in Ancient Greek Philosophy, and by several anonymous readers during the editorial review process. I heartily acknowledge here other people at SUNY Press who played key roles in bringing this book to fruition. I am especially grateful for the meticulous copy editing of Michele Lansing. Her efforts improved my prose at innumerable places and her keen eye saved the book from many mistakes. Michael Haggett, Production Editor, was conscientious and attendant to all details as he shepherded the book, and guided me, through the various stages of production. Thanks also to Jane Bunker, Acquisitions Editor, James Peltz, Senior Acquisitions Editor, and

Katy Leonard, Acquisitions Assistant, for their support and encouragement. Other specific intellectual debts are acknowledged where appropriate throughout the book.

Several sections of this book have been published previously as journal articles, and I thank the editors and publishers of each journal for permission to reprint the revised articles here. Sections 2.a and 2.b appeared, in an earlier form, as "Setting Free the Boys: Limits and Liberation in Plato's *Lysis*" in *disClosure: A Journal of Social Theory* 4 (Winter 1994–1995): 24–43; an earlier version of parts of Section 4.c appeared as "Irony and Inebriation in Plato's *Symposium:* The Disagreement between Socrates and Alcibiades over Truth-Telling" in *The Journal of Neoplatonic Studies* 3, No. 2 (Spring 1995): 25–40; and an earlier version of Sections 4.c.2 and 4.d appeared as "Games of Truth: Foucault's Analysis of the Transformation from Political to Ethical *Parrhēsia*" in *The Southern Journal of Philosophy* 34, No. 1 (Spring 1996): 97–114. Finally, a revised version of Sections 4.a and 4.b, co-authored with William A. Welton, appeared as "An Overlooked Motive in Alcibiades' *Symposium* Speech" in *Interpretation: A Journal of Political Philosophy* 24, No. 1 (Fall 1996): 67–84. I am grateful to *Interpretation* for allowing me to use this material here.

Last, but by no means least, I express my profound appreciation to my wife and partner in life Hilde for her unfailing support and boundless encouragement during the research and writing of this book. She assisted me in countless ways, and she never complained about being enrolled temporarily in the Philosophy Widows' club, whose membership extends all the way back to Xanthippe, the wife of Socrates and mother of the philosopher's three abandoned children.

List of Abbreviations

PLATO'S DIALOGUES

Alc. I	*Alcibiades I (or Major)*
Alc. II	*Alcibiades II (or Minor)*
Ap.	*Apology of Socrates*
Charm.	*Charmides*
Crit.	*Critias*
Cri.	*Crito*
Euthyd.	*Euthydemus*
Euthyp.	*Euthyphro*
Grg.	*Gorgias*
Hi. Ma.	*Hippias Major*
Hi. Mi.	*Hippias Minor*
La.	*Laches*
Lys.	*Lysis*
Men.	*Menexenus*
Parm.	*Parmenides*
Phd.	*Phaedo*
Phdr.	*Phaedrus*
Phil.	*Philebus*
Pol.	*Statesman*
Prot.	*Protagoras*
Rep.	*Republic*
Soph.	*Sophist*
Symp.	*Symposium*
Tht.	*Theaetetus*
Tim.	*Timaeus*

WORKS BY ARISTOTLE

Eud. Eth.   *The Eudemian Ethics*
Nic. Eth.   *The Nicomachean Ethics*
Pol.   *Politics*
Rhet.   *Rhetoric*

Introduction

Despite his ceaseless efforts to purge his fellow citizens of their unfounded opinions and bring them to care for what he believes are the most important things, Plato's Socrates rarely seems to succeed in his pedagogical, or "psychagogical," project with the characters he encounters in the dialogues.[1] More often than not, his target interlocutors leave their conversations with the philosopher wholly unchanged by the experience, hence it is doubtful whether, in Plato's depiction of him, this divinely appointed physician of the soul could ever be judged to have had a measurable, lasting effect on another person. If some kind of noticeable turnaround in a character's way of life is the standard by which one is to assess Socrates' ultimate effect on those with whom he converses, it could be argued that this great gadfly never succeeds in improving any of his would-be pupils in the conversations that Plato dramatizes.[2] In fact, it might be concluded from evidence about the later careers of historical characters such as Charmides and Alcibiades that more young men were made worse than made better by this philosopher's counsel.[3]

Indeed, it remains one of the enduring enigmas surrounding Plato's characterization of Socrates, that the Socrates who speaks and acts in these dialogues is so much less successful—as either a teacher or a student of the characters he meets—than the historical Socrates appears to have been with the people *he* encountered. After all, the historical Socrates could have claimed at least to have engendered the careers of Plato, Xenophon, and several other writers of Socratic conversations whose works have not survived, to have given rise to a number of what would later be called Socratic schools, and to have constituted enough of a political threat to cause himself to be put to death by the city that he spent his life trying to serve. What is more, Plato's literary Socrates fails to turn souls toward a life of philosophical self-examination, despite being far better outfitted with argumentation—to say nothing of the arsenal of other, extraargumentative devices with which he is equipped as a result of Plato's decision to present his philosophy in dramatic dialogue form, and especially as a result of his decision to write the *kind* of dialogues he writes—than any flesh-and-blood philosopher could have been. And Plato's Socrates experiences with his targets only the faintest hint of the success in the drama of the dialogues that this same Socrates has had on their audiences for nearly 2,400 years.

Recognizing the peculiar disparity between this literary character and the historical Socrates, one is immediately faced with a set of interrelated questions: Why does Plato choose to portray his Socrates as so dramatically less successful than the historical Socrates may be presumed to have been? Did he mean for his audience to regard his Socrates as a complete failure in his ordained roles as gadfly and midwife in the dialogues? If not, in what sense, and to what degree, does Plato think his Socrates succeeds in benefitting or improving others, something he has the philosopher criticize Pericles (and others) for failing to do? How would his Socrates improve the young, and what will be his new kind of educational strategy, or *paideusis*? In what sense does Plato think Socrates is engaged in teaching, and in what sense is the philosopher just not supposed to be viewed as a teacher? The audience of these dialogues also cannot help but wonder to what extent Socrates is genuinely optimistic that he will learn from his interlocutors, and to what extent the philosopher is just trying to draw out his more reticent conversation partners. And further, one wonders, to what degree is failure in the argumentation and dramatic action of the dialogues necessary as a way for Plato to succeed on another level with his own audience?

Many recent interpreters have stressed the need to take seriously the dramatic dialogue form in which Plato presents his philosophy, arguing that its form is inseparable from the content of Platonic philosophy and from Plato's conception of how philosophy, in general, should be practiced. That Plato's dialogues create and show as much as they *assert* necessitates that we strive to grasp a dialogue's meaning on several levels.[4] In addition to working simultaneously on discursive and dramatic levels, a specific conversation between Socrates and an interlocutor may have at least three distinct audiences, and what is said and done in the primary conversation may therefore need to work in as many as four different senses at once:

1. between Socrates and his target interlocutor;
2. between these primary interlocutors and any third parties gathered and "listening in";

3. between the primary conversation (in 'real time') and anyone who might hear about the conversation or hear it rehearsed, or who might be rehearsing it themselves later;
4. between Plato and his audience.

The *Symposium* furnishes an illustrative example. When Socrates cross-examines Agathon after the latter has delivered his rhetorical *tour de force*, the primary conversation is occurring between Socrates and Agathon. Phaedrus, Pausanias, Eryximachus, Aristophanes, and Aristodemus would all be examples of third parties, in sense #2. Apollodorus, as our narrator, is rehearsing (for the second time in a few days) the framed dialogue, related to him by Aristodemus. Both Apollodorus and Aristodemus then, along with their future auditors, would be third parties as meant in sense #3. Anyone who ever heard Plato's *Symposium* read or performed, or who read it themselves, would be the audience in sense #4. Now in several dialogues Socrates is alone with his interlocutor. In such cases, the dialogue only needs to work in sense #1 and sense #4, but all of the dialogues involve at least these two levels. This book will be primarily concerned with what happens on the first level, on the level of the dramatic action and the arguments presented therein. The goal of this focus, however, shall be to determine how what happens on the level of the dramatic action is supposed to be construed and judged by Plato's audience.

In an attempt to locate signs of the philosopher's success with a targeted character within the drama of the dialogues, I endeavored to find examples in which Socrates achieves some positive outcome in his role as pedagogue or psychagogue to others. Leaving aside for the moment the question of whether he purports to be, Socrates is not greatly successful with his targets. He plainly achieves more satisfactory results in his role as teacher with Meno's slave boy than he does with Meno himself, even though the latter is the philosopher's main concern in the dialogue bearing his name. Like Euthyphro and others, Meno proves to be unteachable, because he never acknowledges that he has anything to learn, and this conceit of wisdom bars him from learning from the philosopher. With other highly combative interlocutors—such as Callicles and Polus—Plato's audience will not even have its hopes aroused for the character's psychic improvement. Callicles cannot maintain the pretense of being amicably diposed toward Socrates as long as he clings to his desire to win the argument at all costs. He must either drop the veil of friendliness or abandon the attempt to dominate Socrates.[5] Toward some promising characters—Glaucon, Adeimantus, Simmias, and Cebes, for instance—Socrates does not directly aim his well-honed arrows, for he does not really engage these characters in one of his patented psychic examinations. And since examining their lives directly is not his main objective, encounters such as these furnish scanty evidence concerning the philosopher's overall effect on his target interlocutors.[6]

Moreover, while there is surely a group of followers—including Apollodorus, Aristodemus, and perhaps Hippocrates—portrayed as self-anointed disciples, Plato is surely not holding out these characters as laudable examples of the effectiveness of Socrates' educational methods.[7] Such characters seem to imitate only the philosopher's superficial mannerisms and eclectic idiosyncrasies, and they appear dedicated to the hortative aspect of his practice, to the exclusion of its other dimensions. As one commentator writes of Apollodorus, "He lacks only the placard with the message 'The day of judgment is at hand.'"[8] The zeal displayed by such disciple types provides no evidence either of Socrates' beneficial effect on others, and Plato seems to have therefore disqualified this class of characters from receiving more sustained or more substantive attention from the philosopher.

This book is a study of two exceptional cases, Lysis and Alcibiades, characters who are featured in dialogues belonging to a special class of conversation in which Socrates *does* enjoy some degree of success in bringing about a dramatic turnaround in his target. In each of the dialogues in this group—*Lysis*, *Alcibiades I*, and *Charmides*—the ugly, old philosopher sets out as the pursuing lover of a beautiful young man, only to end up as the beloved object of the youth's adoration by the end of the conversation. Perhaps more than in any other type of dialogue, these "erotic" conversations demonstrate how literary and rhetorical tools are used to augment, enact, or complicate Socrates' arguments in his cross-examinations of unsuspecting characters. What is more, these few dialogues exhibiting the erotic reversal dramatize Socrates' first encounters with the most vulnerable interlocutors he engages anywhere in the Platonic corpus; and before these youths, Plato has Socrates unveil the full arsenal of weapons at his disposal. So these cases afford us perhaps the best glimpse of Socratic education in practice, for in them the target interlocutors receive a dramatic lesson from Socrates.

The initial approach to these young men will be seen to involve a seductive arousal and a powerful chastening aimed at desires specific to each of them. To arouse and chasten them, Plato fashions for Socrates a strategy constructed around a whole cornucopia of dramatic and rhetorical devices: from irony and hyperbole to Socrates' sometimes outrageous sounding claims; from the philosopher's uncanny ability to assess an interlocutor's character to the *ad hominem* challenges to that character; from his citations of the poets to his own opportunistic introductions of myths and stories; and from his use of narrative to his attribution of ideas to dreams, oracles, and divination. Plato's strategy in these few extraordinary dialogues appears designed to show Socrates "seducing" these young men as a way of galvanizing them into taking an active role in their own self-improvement. Socrates attempts to disclose to these ambitious youths an aperture to their own freedom. Therefore, these dramatic portrayals of his approach have the further effect of exemplifying a rare, positive outcome of an encounter with Socrates.

The way in which Plato has the wily philosopher approach these ambitious, aristocratic, beautiful, and promising young men is at once interesting and problematic: interesting because Socrates deploys a distinctive kind of Eros to accomplish the striking role reversal with these boys, and problematic because some of the tactics he uses to complete his extraordinary seduction of them are at least questionable. These are curiously—but by no means incidentally—erotic conversations, with interlocutors who would seem to fulfill all of the prerequisites to serve as good subjects for Socrates' philosophical approach: they are nobly born and gifted, well-educated, handsome, and seemingly teachable youths when Socrates first encounters them. And they have not yet had to commit themselves to a particular way of life, although each one aspires to a position of power and authority. Socrates encounters them at just the right time for his approach to have a chance of succeeding. And last, each is suddenly smitten with Socrates in the course of his initial conversation with him. In this way, these dialogues show how normally passive and conceited youths could be transformed into active (and sometimes quite aggressive) pursuers of Socrates. If his educational approach was ever going to be successful in improving a target interlocutor in some discernible way, then the dialogues exhibiting the erotic reversal between Socrates and a beautiful boy—*Lysis Alcibiades I*, and *Charmides*—seemed like the best places to look for evidence of that success.

In other cases, the main characters lack one of the essential traits for teachability, or else something clouds the reader's view of Socrates' effect on them. Some characters are recalcitrant or incorrigible; others, such as Laches, Nicias, and Crito, are old or not beautiful, and thus Socrates' conversations with them lack the vital, erotic subtext exhibited by the dialogues studied here.[9] Even if he had been successful with them, Socrates' improvement of people who were already some kind of expert or presumed expert (in the arts, for example, or in rhetoric or mathematics) or of people who were already older and set in their ways would not be so easy to detect. In contrast, his young partners in these erotic conversations are ambitious aristocrats, well-educated heirs to political office in the city. They all aspire to become rulers, and they are therefore likely to be drawn to the Sophists, those itinerant teachers of rhetoric and practitioners of eristic disputation who are criticized by Socrates and cast by Plato as the irresponsible intellectuals of the day. The philosopher's approach to these young, promising men presents them with an alternative path to knowledge and excellence (*aretē*) at a most opportune time.

Now, following a period of twenty-seven years, during which Athens was at war almost constantly, and on the heels of the postwar overthrow of Athenian democracy by a group of thirty oligarchs, some of whom were relatives of Plato, it is not difficult to imagine a heated debate raging within the city about its future direction and about who should bear responsibility for the events of the immediate past. At least part of Plato's objective in writing his dialogues would have been to contribute his response to this debate and hopefully, thereby, to vindicate Socrates and philosophy in the face of antiintellectualist forces and rampant scapegoating. In the face of events that Plato must have regarded as a stain on the city sufficient to tarnish its former greatness, the debate over how to tell the story of these past events must surely have grown heated and acrimonious in the late fifth and early fourth centuries B.C.E. After Socrates' death, the question "Who improves the young?" would have sparked considerable debate over the question concerning how the city's youth were to be educated. Should Athens institute greater discipline, such as that that existed in Sparta, or is martial courage not to be regarded as the most essential element in the education for citizenship? Could Athens commit itself anew to traditional values, in light of the tragedies of its recent past, or had it suffered a loss of innocence, straying so far from its own ideals that even another Pericles could not restore it to its former greatness? In the wake of Athens' losses in the war and the subsequent debate about what went wrong and where to go from here, Plato's view of education and politics must have formed in response to these turbulent events of his young adult life. Questions such as these would not have been simply matters of intellectual curiosity but issues of vital concern that would have been passionately debated before and after Socrates' death. People would have asked, to whom should Athenian parents send their sons for the vital education in citizenship and virtue that defines the *paideia* of a free person? To the poets? To the Sophists? To the generals? To the politicians? To the businessmen? What would be the form of the new *paideusis*, and what would be the leading values it would attempt to confer?

If Plato had wanted to exhibit the differences between the various paths to knowledge and excellence available at this time, he might have crafted his dialogues to contrast the practices of the irresponsible intellectuals with those of his own alternative type, personified by Socrates, the paradigmatic practitioner of the fledgling vocation called philosophy. And since all of his dialogues are set in the past, this historical dimension—which includes, at least, dramatic dates, settings, and his self-conscious employment of anachronism—creates a debate between the quasihistorical settings and characters of these dramas and what his audience would have known about the individual histories of the various personae featured in them. It is therefore impossible to appreciate fully Plato's dialogues without familiarizing oneself with the social and intellectual climate within which he is writing and the specific historical periods within which his dramas are set. In view of his project of conspicuously engaging in the cultural battles over the history of the period, it is inevitable that Plato's philosophical beliefs will be embedded within a set of social and intellectual concerns that today would be reserved for the social historian. In contrast, it is important to appreciate how thoroughly Plato's notion of philosophy is woven into the interdisciplinary fabric of his world. Hence the erotic dialogues to be explored here promise to be especially revealing for the sharpness with which they set in relief Socrates' peculiar behaviors and practices, and for the way in which they differentiate both his philosophizing and brand of education from the approaches of the competition.

Two of the three target interlocutors in these conversations exhibiting the erotic reversal meet additional criteria that make them exceptional. Most striking of these is that Socrates' success with Lysis and Alcibiades is more pronounced than it is with Charmides. Both of them experience the perplexity (*aporia*) that is the potentially positive outcome of a Socratic refutation; both are revealed to have grandiose ambitions (at least commensurate with their noble birth and education), and most important, both pledge, more or less explicitly, to learn what needs to be learned in order to become self-ruling, prudent individuals. In all of the dialogues, only Lysis and Alcibiades manifest such a marked turnaround at the end of their very first conversations with the philosopher. Therefore, they will be the characters in the narrow class to be isolated and focused on in this book. These two young men seem to make perfect targets for Socrates' methods, appearing to meet all of the conditions necessary for the philosopher's approach to work well. And since each experiences a dramatic turnaround through his interaction with the erotic Socrates, a more thorough inspection of these conversations should be most helpful in clarifying the philosopher's overall objectives with those best and brightest youths that he approaches in conversation. Examining these two cases in detail should allow the results of his educational strategy to be evaluated under the most propitious conditions.

Unlike Theaetetus, for example, whose natural inclination toward mathematics predisposes him toward knowledge, and who is characterized as resembling Socrates in important ways already, Lysis and Alcibiades display no such predisposition or likeness. They will have to be enticed or provoked into entirely new pursuits. When Socrates first approaches them, they are barely able to suppress their desire to rule the world, regarding themselves as capable, ready, and entitled to do so. Their naive arrogance makes Socrates' chastening fairly easy to effect, and this humbling moment within each dialogue secures a crucial foothold on the way to the eventual erotic reversal. More decisive than the simple reversal of roles, however, is that, by the end of these conversations, Socrates succeeds in evoking from both boys acknowledgments of their ignorant, slavish condition and pledges to follow his advice. Each boy seems to recognize that he is ill equipped to attain his lofty goals without further preparation. Each is chastened by the older, wiser philosopher, responds well to the humbling lesson, and is then praised by Socrates for the philosophical nature that he exhibits, before positively affirming his readiness to follow Socrates. This certifies in each case that, at least during one conversation, these young men experience an appreciable benefit from the erotic turnaround. And that in itself makes Lysis and Alcibiades exceptional in Plato's dialogues.

The restrictive focus of this book means that its primary concern will not be with Socrates' adversarial conversations with Sophists or rhetoricians. What follows instead is an examination of the philosopher's methods with his most vulnerable interlocutors in all of the dialogues, because these encounters provide both the clearest view of these methods and the best opportunity to see growth or improvement in the characters he targets.[10] Through this exploration, it will be possible to disclose how Socrates' "extraargumentative" devices both augment and complicate the philosopher's argumentation. The results of these case analyses will then enable me to speculate about what Plato wants to illustrate through the qualified success of Socrates' approach in these two extraordinary instances. From this investigation, it should be possible first to ascertain and then to assess the philosopher's overall purpose with at least the teachable characters he encounters in the dialogues. The dramas to be examined here supply good reasons for suspecting that Socrates' ultimate effect, not only with Lysis and Alcibiades, but perhaps with all of those "best and brightest" young men he engages in conversation, may be to facilitate something similar to what modern philosophers will call *empowerment*, though this is not a term that Socrates or Plato would have used. The examination of Socrates' first approach to each of them will show how Socrates attempts to confer a kind of freedom upon these two youths.

To interpret Socratic Eros, in general, and Socrates' unconventional tactics in these two specific cases, Socrates' conversational practices will have to be situated against the background of the dominant conventions that they appear designed to counterpose and place in question. Two of these conventions will be shown to be especially anathema to the philosopher's approach: the first is the market economy governing teaching as the Sophists practiced it, and the second is the conventional ethos of freedom. By contrasting Socrates' own behavior in these dialogues with other practices dominant at the time, we can see how the philosophical concepts emerge through these contrasts when they are carried out through reasoned inquiry. I believe that such an approach to these dialogues is vital to any attempt to determine what Plato may have thought or believed. Perhaps it is just by having Socrates act against the background of the contemporary social order without adopting the prevalent intellectual currency that Plato thought he could throw the philosopher's uniqueness into sharpest relief and thereby move his audience from its conventional understanding of certain concepts and practices to a more philosophical understanding of them.

In addition to the way Socrates' behaviors in the dialogues call into question both the conventional notion of teaching and some assumptions about freedom that were prevalent in the late fifth and early fourth centuries, his way of practicing philosophy calls into question a host of traditional Athenian assumptions about sex and gender. The conventional conception of gender roles prevalent in Socrates' time can be seen not only in the dialogues of Plato—especially *Lysis, Charmides, Alcibiades I, Symposium*, and *Phaedrus*—but also in the writings of Aristotle, in the playwrights, and in the extant speeches of various orators. Throughout this examination of these two cases, we shall contrast the alternatives that might be adduced from Socrates' own behavior with the conventional behaviors that the philosopher's practices seem designed to supplant. Although it will not be possible to explore Greek homoerotic practices fully within the scope of this book, the analysis to follow will make reference to aspects of these practices that illuminate something vital about why Plato has his characters act as they do.[11] It will be the conventional ethos governing the homoerotic distinction between lover and beloved that underwrites the context for the dramatic action in the conversations with Lysis and Alcibiades. However, it is worth reminding ourselves in advance that Plato can have Socrates enact a reversal of traditional homoerotic roles only because the ethos governing these roles would have been well known, even taken for granted, by his fourth-century audience. In Plato's dramatic twist on the conventional practice of *sunousia*, the ugly, old philosopher slowly becomes the object of love by these youths, while the formerly complacent boys are somehow animated and transformed into active lovers through their encounter with him.

The lines along which classical Athenian social relations were stratified provide other essential information for interpreting the words and deeds of Plato's characters, especially Socrates. It is a striking feature of social interaction in Plato's time, and one that will be most relevant for the present investigation, that even among citizen-men of relatively equal age, wealth, and education, there seem nevertheless to have been ample opportunities for assessing one's relative advantage vis-à-vis others. Where a modern reader might assume a virtual equality (*isonomia*) among Athenian citizens, there persists a tendency on the part of the characters populating the literature, history, and philosophy of the period to place greater stress on the asymmetry in human relations than on the relative equality in them. Plato's dialogues are no exception, as we shall see. This social milieu, within which the distances between people are constantly being measured in various ways, permeates the dramatic action of the dialogues, and Plato is able to illustrate important dimensions of the issues under discussion by having his characters behave in one way rather than another. Hence Socrates is sometimes depicted inverting, sometimes contravening, and sometimes merely modulating aspects of conventional behaviors and practices. Context will be crucial in determining what Plato might be trying to show his audience in any particular instance. This principle will guide our interpretation of specific problems or questions. It might, however, be helpful to outline in advance some other distinctive features of conventional Athenian social roles that will be central to our study.

It is by now a commonplace to say that in Athenian society men enjoyed far greater privilege than women, citizens than non-citizens, free persons than slaves, and adults than children. This social stratification furnishes the basis for further distinctions applied among citizen-men. It seems to have made a great difference, for example, whether one acted like a free man or a slave, like a man or a woman, like an adult or a child. But social relations were further stratified to such a degree that even among men sharing the same status conditions, it would matter further whether one behaved in their roles as a lover (*erastēs*) or a beloved (*eromenos*), an active agent or a passive recipient, a manly man or a soft man, a benefactor or a beneficiary. Whether one was beautiful or ugly provided another significant point of contrast and that Socrates was ugly (famous for being short and pot-bellied, having a thick nose, a bulging forehead, and protrusive eyes) is about the only feature common to the varied portraits of him by the several authors of Socratic conversations. It was of no small importance, either, whether one acted honorably or shamefully (nobly or ignobly), and with courage or like a coward. Clearly, within such a matrix, one of the two ways of behaving is always celebrated while the other is disparaged. To determine Plato's own views on the many topics discussed in the dialogues, the ways in which his characters act will need to be viewed and interpreted against the background of contemporary Athenian behaviors and practices. The contrast between Socrates' behavior in his first approach to Lysis or Alcibiades, for example, and the behavior of a typical Athenian *paiderastēs* should illuminate something vital about Plato's conception of the philosophical Eros, about his assessment of the Socratic form of education, and about his estimation of the manner in which classical Athenian principles were actually instantiated in practice.[12]

Chapter 1 establishes the context for the examination of the two specific cases by providing a working conception of Socratic education, exploring how it is supposed to function and contrasting its goals with other models of pedagogy. Any investigation into Socratic education is immediately faced with the question of whether, or in what sense, Socrates can properly be called a teacher. The analysis in Chapter 1 begins by testing Socrates' suitability for the roles both of teacher and student while attempting to provide a coherent interpretation of his most prominent disclaimers that he is (or has ever been) anyone's teacher. Even if one restricts the definition of teaching so that Socrates' actions toward others in the dialogues would not qualify him for the job as it would have been conceived by his jurors, it seems unmistakable that Socrates is engaging in an educational process of some kind with many of his interlocutors. Since the dispute inevitably turns on how one defines "teaching," Chapter 1 examines several possible definitions on the way to assessing the suitability of various terms as a description of how Socrates acts as an educator and a student. That Plato places Socrates' practice of philosophy outside of the prevalent market economy will be shown to be key to the demarcation of Socratic education from the Sophists' brand of teaching, and of philosophy, in general, from sophistry. Chapter 1 concludes that keeping Socrates' educational approach free from economic exchange is central to Plato's characterization of Socrates' distinctive practice. This stance also will be crucial for establishing the pre-commercial context within which Plato seems to think philosophy can be best undertaken. Where Athenian conventions prescribe elaborate rituals for giving and receiving gifts—from offerings to the gods to payments and bribes to the city's leaders—Socrates is framed by Plato as someone who gave a gift to those with whom he conversed without accepting anything in return. He is portrayed at his trial both as a gift to the city and as one who eschews gifts, fees, and payments for his conversations. Now if human relations in fifth-century Athens were conceived, for the most part, within such a cultural milieu of gift or market exchange, contrasting these practices with those of Socrates' should illuminate important conditions for the proper practice of philosophy, in Plato's view. Comparing and contrasting a Socratic model of education with professional teaching based upon a market model will establish essential parameters for understanding Socrates' behavior in the dialogues to be studied here.

Chapters 2 through 4 evaluate the three texts that furnish the evidence for Socrates' effect on the two characters who are the focus of this study: (1) Socrates' conversation with Lysis; (2) the inaugural conversation with the young Alcibiades in *Alcibiades I*; and (3) Alcibiades' speech in praise of Socrates in *Symposium* (*Symposium* 212d–223b).[13] The specific means by which Plato keeps Socrates' practices free from market relations turn out to be central also to a new conception of freedom. Socrates will be seen to refuse not simply payments and gifts but any diminution of his self-sufficiency or self-mastery, anything that would undermine his *sophrosunē* (sound-mindedness) and cause him to *transact* philosophy out of a desire for gain, honor, or anything else that would reduce his conversational activity to a mere instrumental good. Since freedom, in a sense similar to the modern notion of empowerment, will be shown to be one of the key results of Socrates' first encounters with Lysis and Alcibiades, and since Socrates' behavior in the dialogues also seems designed to illustrate a conception of freedom quite different from the conventional Athenian one, Chapter 5 returns to the problem of freedom in connection with Socratic education to reevaluate the successes and failures of Socrates in the dialogues.

The emergence of freedom as a practice (*askēsis*) requiring training (*taxis*) around which Socrates' conception of philosophy revolves leads one to wonder about the apparent incompatibility of this freedom with certain kinds of social and political relations. Does Socrates' concern with maintaining his freedom cause him to assume his precarious political posture? Does the indomitable philosopher perfect his freedom at the price of intimacy or friendship, as commentators such as Gregory Vlastos and Martha Nussbaum have charged?[14] Will Socrates be able to square the care of the self with the concern for the city? More implausible still is the way that Socrates' devotion to the practice of freedom, coupled with his repeated counsels to others to take more trouble over themselves, positions him as a paradoxical caretaker of others. The philosopher cuts an unlikely figure as a philanthropist. And many learned scholars have entertained the sobering possibility that Socrates did not really care for the improvement of other people's souls.[15] This concluding chapter offers some final reflections concerning Socrates as a teacher and suggests reasons for Plato's decision to depict Socrates as he does, and through the character and example of this philosopher, to portray an alternative model for human relationships.

Chapter 1

Socrates and Teaching

Any investigation into Socrates as an educator would seem obliged at the outset to decide whether, or in what sense, Plato's Socrates may properly be called a teacher. It cannot simply be assumed that every reader of the dialogues will construe Socrates' words and deeds, or Plato's ultimate judgment on his educational methods, in the same way. For on the one hand, the philosopher is famous for announcing that he has "never been anyone's teacher" (*Ap.* 33a5) and on the other hand, he will stand in for the paid pedagogues of Lysis and Menexenus, as we shall see in the next chapter. Now surely Socrates is not supposed to be taken as a pedagogue in the ordinary Greek sense of the term, where it signifies a sort of superintendent or master of a youth whose job it is to see to it that the youth does what he is supposed to do. Socrates is no mere chaperon or guardian, and he is not placed in a supervisory role with his associates. Plato's Socrates is no more a pedagogue in this sense than he is a slave to anyone, as might perhaps be inferred from the fact that the pedagogues in ancient Athens often were slaves. Here, as elsewhere, Plato utilizes the contrast between Socrates' behaviors and practices and those conventional in his day as a way of underlining important differences of both approach and purpose, means and ends.

No, Socrates is obviously not a pedagogue in the ordinary Greek sense, but neither is he a "teacher" in the manner of the Sophists. Against the Sophists' claims to teach, Socrates will be ever anxious to contrast his own mode of philosophical inquiry.[1] He is no more a "teacher" in a sophistical sense than he is "pious" in a conventional sense, or a "lover" in the pedestrian sense, or possessed of wisdom as the many think of it. To contrast his own duty to the god with conventional piety, his own "small wisdom" with genuine knowledge, his approach as a lover with the feigning, pseudo lovers, and Socratic *paideusis* with professional teaching, for example, Plato often has Socrates refuse conventional labels for his philosophical practices. At other times, he has him expand a conventional term to serve a philosophical purpose, as he does with the concept of Eros in the *Symposium*. Moreover, the dialogues seem to show example after example in which the philosopher differentiates his methods and objectives from those of other practices prevalent in his day. In this way, Socrates' behaviors often exhibit an alternative conception of whatever topic is under consideration in the dialogue's argumentation. This strategy allows Plato's audiences to *see* important differences in a term or in ways of acting, and to judge matters for themselves.[2]

In the *Lysis*, the philosopher sets out to show Hippothales how a genuine lover should act, in preference to the feigning and ridiculous way Hippothales acts as a lover. The *Laches* contrasts the demonstrations of courage by experts with a Socratic examination of courage. In the *Apology*, Socrates speaks differently and separately to his "true jurors" than he does to the pseudo-jurors who turn out to be in the majority. And the Delphic oracle story contrasts—for the most part implicitly—several kinds of conventional knowledge with a more Socratic understanding of what would be required for genuine knowledge and, more broadly, contrasts the wisdom the gods have with a human kind of wisdom. At *Gorgias* 521d, Socrates tells Callicles that he is the only one of his contemporaries who practices the *true* political art. In *Republic* VI, Socrates contrasts the out-of-place educator with a more appropriate educator such as himself. The *Phaedrus* contrasts bad rhetoricians with "the true rhetorician," and the *Sophist* contrasts sophistry, as it was ordinarily practiced, with a "sophist of noble descent." And Socrates uses his chance to speak in *Symposium* to recall how Diotima characterized the *true* lover in terms of characteristics associated with Socrates, thus contrasting a philosophical kind of Eros with conceptions of it advanced by previous speakers in the dialogue. Indeed, it becomes increasingly difficult to distinguish the "*true* lover," "*true* statesman," the "*true* rhetorician" and the "sophist of noble descent" from the philosopher, at least if what is meant by this is a philosopher such as Socrates. In fact, in each contrast, I suspect that the positive alternative can be shown to harmonize with Socrates' way of philosophizing as Plato depicts it in the dialogues. These contrasts, taken together, might even furnish a kind of composite sketch of Plato's exemplary philosopher. But demonstrating this would require a separate study. What I will try to exhibit in the contrast that follows are the many ways that

Socrates differs as a teacher from the professional teachers of his day, and how his *paideusis* will differ from other models of education.

To begin with, the difficulty in characterizing Socrates' role as an educator derives chiefly from apparent inconsistencies in what he says from one place to another, sometimes even within a single dialogue. Consider, for example, what he says in his defense speech. In the very same speech in which he proclaims, most emphatically at 33a, that he is not a teacher, we shall see that Socrates tells his jurors that some of his associates imitate him, applying what they have learned. Furthermore, what they have learned by observing his approach to others and from talking to and imitating him seems to be something concrete and demonstrable. Plato's rendition of the philosopher's legal defense clearly goes on to identify the actions of these imitators as a chief cause of the criminal indictment against him (17c; 23d–e). So he may not *intend* to teach people things, but some people nevertheless seem to have learned things from him. These ambiguities enshrouding Socrates' role as a teacher pose unavoidable questions for our investigation. This chapter attempts to establish a working conception of Socratic education, and its exploration of the meaning of the term *teacher* as a label for one of Socrates' key roles in the dialogues shall begin in what seems like the most obvious place—with the philosopher's own defense of his life's work in *Apology*.

After Section 1.a examines the reasons Socrates denies being a teacher at *Apology* 33a, Section 1.b offers a brief sketch of how Socrates' jurors would have understood the activity of teaching. Section 1.c uses the preliminary exchange between Socrates and Thrasymachus at *Republic* 337c–d to show that there is an analogous ambiguity enshrouding Socrates' role as a student in the dialogues. These first three sections raise the question about what Socrates thinks teaching entails, thus Section 1.d draws upon James King's helpful contrast between two models of teaching, teaching as the Sophists claimed to do it, and teaching, as Socrates says in the *Gorgias* that it should be conceived, to determine the meaning of teaching that might be most fittingly associated with the philosopher's practice. Section 1.e elaborates on the account of Socratic education and offers a fuller characterization of the teacher-student relationship as Socrates is shown engaging in it in the dialogues.

SECTION 1.A WHY SOCRATES DENIES BEING A TEACHER

Plato's *Apology of Socrates* dramatizes the seventy-year-old philosopher's arguments against charges of impiety and corrupting the youth of Athens. In his defense, Socrates also reviews the daily philosophical activities in which he attests to having been engaged for his entire adult life, providing his jury of at least 500 dicasts, and a (presumably) large audience of observers, with an account of his distinctive philosophical practice in the city. He attempts to prove that he has never acted unjustly to anyone. In this context, the accused philosopher utters these oft-cited lines:

> I have never been anyone's teacher (*didaskalos*). If anyone, young or old, desires to listen to me when I am talking and dealing with my own concerns, I have never begrudged this to anyone, but I do not converse when I receive a fee and not when I do not. I am equally willing to question the rich and the poor if anyone is willing to answer my questions and listen to what I say. And I cannot justly be held responsible for the good or bad conduct of these people, as I never promised to teach them anything and have not done so. If anyone says that he has learned anything from me, or that he heard anything privately (*idia*) that the others did not hear, be assured that he is not telling the truth. (*Ap.* 33a5–b8, Grube trans.)

What precisely is Socrates denying in the first sentence cited above? He is denying being a *didaskalos*, that is, one who is a master or instructor of others. Socrates has no *didaskaleion*, or school, and he claims no expertise or mastery of any particular art or science, as would have been conventionally thought to be a prerequisite for one to instruct (*didasko*) others. A *didaskalos* should be able to instruct others on the various subjects he has mastered; hence Socrates is denying having ever purported to be anyone's master or instructor. In whatever sense Socrates may be characterized as a teacher, then, he is not a teacher of any specific subject on which he regards himself as an expert. He has no art or science that he considers himself able to teach to others. He is not associated with any school (*didaskaleion*), and he has no formal pupils because he charges no fee for conversing with people. What is more, his methods are not didactic, a word that derives from the Greek word *didasko*. He does not teach by means of an exposition that aims to persuade or demonstrate, in the manner of a Protagoras, for example. Perhaps Socrates would accept that he is an educator if one means something quite different than would have been connoted by the term *didaskalos*.

Some interpreters claim that the above passage must be taken "literally," and they cite Socrates' denial here as a reason for enjoining others against referring to what Socrates does as teaching in any sense. Those who interpret the passage in this way claim to be taking Socrates' statements at face value. Yet, precisely what "face value" does this passage have? For the "literal" approach, Socrates' unequivocal denial is the end of the story, rather than grounds for comparison and contrast.[3] But far from being a merely literal rendering of the statement, this allegedly *prima facie* way of interpreting the passage requires, in fact, that one ignore its broader context within the dialogue and within history. If we make the effort to situate these apparently categorical denials within their larger dramatic, historical, and discursive contexts, we shall see that Socrates' statement here is far from obvious or unambiguous. The broader context supplies a wealth of information that must be taken into account if an interpretation is to fully explicate, and fairly evaluate, the accused philosopher's denial. Socrates' disclaimer must be heard in light of the wider political and legal objectives he might be supposed to have had for saying what he says and for saying it in the way that he does. And situating his disclaimer within the dialogue as a whole will reveal that Socrates qualifies and clarifies, elsewhere in his speech, what he says in the above-cited passage. So although Socrates' denial at 33a5 sounds unequivocal, the assertion never to have been anyone's teacher will turn out to be a much more restrictive claim than it first appears to be.

Let us first adumbrate the immediate context. The philosopher's denial to be anyone's teacher must, of course, be construed as part of a legal, if plainly spoken, defense for a capital crime. His defense (*apologia*) is delivered before the largest crowd to whom Socrates ever speaks in Plato's dialogues, and because this public setting is so extraordinary—and the occasion so monumental—it is of utmost importance to clarify what would seem likely to have been his leading objectives in addressing his jury. Ascertaining his larger purpose here will illuminate much about why Socrates stresses here the particular issues he does.

In the first place, Socrates' denial ever to have served as anyone's teacher establishes the cornerstone for his legal defense against the charge that he corrupted the youth of Athens. This defense is based upon the principle that before a person can be held responsible for corrupting another, a causative relationship between the teachings or practices of the alleged corrupter and the faults of the ones allegedly corrupted must be demonstrated. In this case, a link would need to be shown between the actions or words of Socrates and the future actions of people with whom he had associated. Since Socrates had no custodial relationship over his companions, such as parents have over their children or masters over their slaves, he must next attempt to convince his jury that he also had no contract or agreement of service with the people with whom he conversed. In cases where associations are bound by a contractual agreement or an implicit warranty of service between the parties, it would seem fairly easy to establish the necessary causal link between them, and thereby to hold one party accountable for the faults of the other. However, a lack of evidence for such a contractual agreement between the parties—in the form of any contract or implied warranty of service (which might be thought to result from the payment of a fee)—would seem to make it far more difficult to prove this legal charge against Socrates.[4]

During his trial, Socrates would surely have been well aware that the transgressions of some of his former associates would be weighing heavily upon the minds of his jurors as he speaks to them. Indeed, the philosopher has fraternized with some characters from whom he might like to unhinge himself as far as possible in the present context. It is reasonable to assume that his attempt to distance himself from these people would need to go beyond simply making a case against the concrete charges pending against him. But just who are "these people" referred to in the passage cited above, the putative students Socrates asserts he has not promised to teach and to whom he has not taught anything? Just prior to the passage quoted, Socrates had related to his jury the story of defying the illegitimate order of the Thirty Tyrants in the matter of Leon of Salamis. He goes on to ask the infamous question concerning whether his jurors think he would have survived as long as he has had he led a more overtly political life in the defense of justice. And then he asserts:

> Throughout my life, in any public activity I may have engaged in, I am the same man as I am in private life. I have never come to an agreement with anyone to act unjustly; neither with anyone else, nor with any one of those who they slanderously say are my pupils (*mathētas*). (*Ap.* 33a1–5, Grube trans.)

There are at least three different kinds of former associates who might have been perceived as pupils of Socrates and whose association with the philosopher may have been used to slander him publicly. These are the kinds of former associates from whom Socrates would have wanted to distance himself in the present circumstances, and he may have had one or more of them in mind when denying above that he was the *didaskalos* of any person:

a. *The Rogues.* These are characters of disastrous historical consequence.
b. *The Imitators.* These are his regular companions in the streets of Athens who mimic his method of cross-examination and perform refutations on prominent citizens.
c. *The Disciples.* These are the most extremely devoted of his associates who act like those characters in the dialogues who are portrayed as fawning over Socrates, adopting his style of dress, and making it their business to know everything Socrates says and does.

Let us look briefly at each of these three groups in turn.

a. *The Rogues*. Perhaps the philosopher's most brilliant protege, Alcibiades, betrayed Athens about sixteen years prior to Socrates' trial, in the middle of the Peloponnesian War. His defection to Sparta most likely shifted the balance of power against Athens, contributing significantly to its ultimate defeat at the hands of the Spartans. Along with Alcibiades, Phaedrus, who is featured in the *Protagoras, Symposium,* and *Phaedrus,* also was implicated in the mutilation of the Herms and banished from Athens sometime around 415. Some eleven years later, in 404, two other people with ties to Socrates—Charmides and Critias—were involved in the uprising against the city by the so-called Thirty Tyrants before, in 403, the oligarchs were overthrown and the democracy was reinstated.[5] It would not have been possible for Plato's earliest audiences to forget these facts, given that this insurrection occurred just a few years prior to Socrates' trial. Socrates must expose and rebut the attempt to hold him guilty by association for the crimes of these former associates. By writing his *Apology of Socrates,* Plato's version of the defense speech is presumably offering Socrates' first and only public account of his actions with respect to these momentous political events. Hence, in declaring, "I have never been anyone's *didaskalos,*" Plato is, in the first place, making Socrates respond to quite concrete circumstances and very recent political events. What the philosopher is denying is playing the role of mentor or advisor to anyone, since if he never advised anyone at all, he could not have been a mentor or an advisor to the thirty oligarchs.

This public perception of Socrates as providing political counsel to oligarchs might explain why only in the *Apology* does Plato have Socrates speak about his interlocutors and about his philosophical practice in such inclusive terms, asserting three times (29d, 30a, 33a–b) that he will talk to anyone and everyone. This leads Vlastos to conclude that Socrates is a "street philosopher" who will talk to "all and sundry."[6] In fact, the kinds of characters with whom Plato has him converse are not just anybody and everybody. In the dialogues taken as a whole, Socrates seems to be far more selective than he claims to be when apologetically stressing his civic concern and the egalitarian nature of his practice. Alexander Nehamas has shown that what he is claiming in his defense is made even more narrow, and far from indiscriminate, when he explains his divinely appointed mission to examine only those who believe they are wise.[7] This selectivity is probably necessary. After all, Plato's dialogues provide only about two dozen examples of a Socratic conversation, while Socrates had a career that spanned nearly forty years during which, according to his testimony in *Apology,* he spent every day in conversation. Now if the philosopher had talked to just one person a day, he could have conversed with nearly 15,000 people by the time of his trial. Whether Plato's two dozen cases of such philosophical dialogue attempt to present a cross-section of the kinds of people with whom the historical Socrates conversed, or whether Plato blends features culled from the tens of thousands of conversations Socrates might have had into two dozen or so composite philosophical dialogues with characters he finds most interesting for some reason, we can only conjecture. Yet judging from the *kinds* of characters with whom Socrates is depicted in conversation, it seems clear that, on the one hand, Plato does not take the philosopher to be indiscriminate about the people he approaches, as Vlastos claims, and yet, on the other hand, Socrates *does* talk to people who are not presumed to be wise. The cases of Lysis and Alcibiades will illustrate that his objectives are not as narrow as Nehamas would have us believe.[8] Socrates seems to be motivated by broader concerns than simply searching for a kindred spirit, another good person like himself, even though this purpose might well explain the thrust of a dialogue such as the *Theaetetus*. When he is not portraying him going toe to toe with some kind of expert, Plato chooses to depict Socrates in conversation with some of the very best and brightest youths in Athens (including his own brothers).

His disclaimer above, of having been anyone's *didaskalos*, is uttered in response to a specific charge, but it is a charge fueled by a much larger set of historical and political developments. This helps clarify why Socrates insists that these people have not learned anything from him and why his chief objective in the *Apology* seems to be to try to disabuse his jury of the confused idea that he is either a *didaskalos*, a Sophist, a nature philosopher, or a peculiar amalgam of all three. His seemingly broad assertion never to have been anyone's *didaskalos* will be qualified further in the next part of his argument by what Socrates says to adumbrate his point.

Socrates continues by denying that he plays the role of *didaskalos* or that he has ever been employed as a professional *didaskalos*. In this context, the philosopher is reserving the term *teacher* for the established professionals. If he were a "teacher," then he would receive payment for this service; and since he does not collect fees or payments from anyone, as his poverty attests, he cannot be a *didaskalos*. Since he is not a *didaskalos*, he cannot justly be bound by any implied warranty of service. As a layperson, he did not have the kind of professional relationship with his associates that would justify the expectation that he was going to deliver something to them. Therefore, as he himself concludes, he "cannot justly be held responsible for the good or bad conduct" of people who talk with him or hear him talking to others about his own affairs.[9] If he were paid for his services, the fee payment of itself might provide evidence for holding that some kind of contract or implied warranty had indeed existed between Socrates and those rogue associates who brought deep suspicion upon the philosopher's practice in the city. In such a case, he might rightly be held liable for their later actions. In sum, Socrates' denial that he is anyone's *didaskalos* is here made for a quite straightforward and immediate purpose: to vitiate the conditions that would evidence a contract of service, and thereby the implied warranty, which must be presumed, and should be established, if he is to be convicted of corrupting the youth. The philosopher must flatly deny being a *didaskalos* in order to challenge any possible legal basis on which he could be held responsible for the crimes of some of his former associates.[10] Precisely what *kind* of teacher he denies being, and the differences between Socrates' educational approach and the practices of the Sophists, will be examined later.[11]

Notwithstanding the legal reasons underpinning the philosopher's reliance on a conventional definition of "teacher" for his disclaimer here, however, Plato's audience might imagine many people learning a variety of things from partaking in or listening to Socratic conversations. In particular, some aspects of his method of cross-examination—what has come down to us as "the Socratic method" (see Introduction, note 10)—appear to have been amenable to imitation and appropriation by his young followers. These imitators furnish another reason for Socrates to rely on a conventional definition of teaching at this point in his defense.

b. *The Imitators.* Socrates says at 23c that others were mimicking his techniques of cross-examination with some success:[12]

> Those young men who follow me around of their own accord
> (*automatoi*) . . . take pleasure in hearing people questioned; they
> themselves often imitate (*mimountai*) me and try to question others.
> I think they find an abundance of men who believe they have some
> knowledge but know little or nothing. The result is that those
> whom they question are angry, not with themselves but with me.
> (Ap. 23c2–8, Grube trans.)

Whether or not Socrates *intended* to teach them anything, this group of followers seems to have learned something from its frequent association with the philosopher, and it seems to have become quite skilled at the refutational part of Socrates' approach to others by imitating his manner of cross-examination. It is precisely this skill at cross-examination and refutation that has landed Socrates in his current difficulty.[13] The philosopher immediately goes on, following the passage cited above, to identify the delight that his associates take in debunking those citizens who arrogantly imagine themselves to be wise as the moving cause of the hostility against him, the main motivation for the prosecution of the case (23d–e). Thus, these imitators of Socratic refutation constitute an important second group of followers whose actions seem to have reflected badly on his practice of philosophy in Athens.

But whereas Socrates clearly attempts to distance himself from the future actions of his rogue associates, his relationship to the young followers who have appropriated some of his methods is more ambivalent. On the one hand, Socrates might say, "Cross-examination and refutation are practiced by many people, so they could have learned such techniques from any one of them just as readily as from me." On the other hand, however, he wants to argue that he provides a moderating influence, for these youths are like young cubs at play. It is not that their actions are wrong or inherently destructive; it is that at present their *paideusis* is incomplete, and without the guidance the philosopher alone can furnish, it may never find its proper completion. Socrates is suggesting that he is the only one who can provide the necessary limit and direction to the actions and aspirations of these youths. Without him, they are likely to become only more wild and unruly, or lapse into misology and misanthropy, skepticism and cynicism. So he seems to be both distancing himself from these followers—by exposing their lack of refinement and maturity—and linking himself with them, by arguing that he is the only one who can show them how to put their distrust of authority to good philosophical use. At 39c–d, he sternly warns the jury that certain aggressive young associates will take revenge on those who have convicted him, in the absence of the restraining influence he now provides. Socrates is warning his jurors that they cannot inoculate conventional wisdom against criticism; intellectuals and youths will always question traditional authorities and challenge common sense. For his part, Socrates has lived his life on the threshold between living an overtly political life and living an entirely private one. He is neither a *politikos* nor an *idiotēs*. His life is a public service, though he avoids customary political channels. But his young followers have not yet attained the delicate balance that kept the mature Socrates out of trouble up to this point, hence they may do foolish and harmful things. To deny being a *didaskalos* in the way that he does is also to deny being responsible for the actions of these passionate practitioners of cross-examination and refutation. After all, these associates are the ones whose actions Socrates had already pinpointed (at 17c and 23d–e) as prompting the legal indictment against him. There is yet a third kind of associate whose identity should help Plato's audience understand better both Socrates' denial of being a *didaskalos* and the motivation for the corruption charge against him.

c. *The Disciples.* The disciple types comprise a third group of followers—some of whom also may belong to the second group—from which Socrates may be seeking to distance himself in denying that he is a *didaskalos* who ever taught anyone anything. Aristodemus and Apollodorus, in the *Symposium*, furnish Plato's audience with luminous examples of such self-appointed understudies. They imitate the philosopher's appearance and his mannerisms, and they seem most passionate about the protreptic dimension of Socrates' practice of philosophy. Their performance as narrators of the dialogue is at once incomplete and indispensable. They would appear to have been the most visible and most laughable of Socrates' followers. It is exactly his affiliation with characters such as these that Callicles excoriates in his condemnation of the philosophical life at *Gorgias* 485d–e, saying, "[He lives] the rest of his life sunk in a corner and whispering with three or four boys, and incapable of any utterance that is free and lofty and brilliant" (Woodhead trans.). Callicles, of course, charges that philosophy emasculates these boys who are lured by Socrates away from civic life and into a life of idle talk. The public behaviors of these "disciple" types must also have reflected badly on Socrates' practice of philosophy. (Perhaps Plato considered this public perception of philosophers a sufficient reason to found a formal school, since by removing the philosopher from the city streets, he would thereby be freed from constant public scrutiny.)

Given the actions of these three kinds of followers, it is little wonder that Socrates wants to insist to his jury that anyone who claims to have "learned" anything from him is lying. Socrates' declaration here would be most implausible if he were not taken to mean "learn" in a very narrow and conventional sense, too, as conventional as his sense of "teaching" is in the context of his defense, where it means to carry out formal instruction for a tuition about subjects of which one is master or in which one has technical expertise. We have seen that his conception of teaching is conventional here because, in the *Apology*, Socrates is concerned primarily with contrasting what he does in his philosophical conversations with the behaviors and practices of the Sophists, those professional rhetoricians who *were* paid to be someone's *didaskalos* in Socrates' day.

In his "Socrates versus Sophists on Payments for Teaching," David Blank reminds us that the kinds of discourses for which the Sophists were notorious were rendered even less estimable in the minds of noble Athenians as a result of the tuition charged for them. The Sophists' practices appear to have given negative connotations to all professional teaching in the minds of Socrates' fellow Athenians.[14] And after all, they were the ones who had laid first claim to the title of "teacher," and their policies were the ones with which the conversational street philosopher's would be most easily confused in the minds of his jurors.[15] Now that we have briefly clarified Socrates' primary motives for issuing his blanket denial ever to have been anyone's *didaskalos*, let us attempt to state more precisely what kind of teaching he is disclaiming at his trial.

Section 1.B Conventional Athenian Assumptions about Teachers and Teaching

At *Apology* 33a, Socrates quite clearly seems to say that he is not a teacher, according to the definition of a *didaskalos*, as his audience would have understood it. Just what does his Athenian audience seem to think teaching is, and what does it think a *didaskalos* does? In addition to being connected to a school, we have seen that a *didaskalos* seems to be someone who meets the following four criteria:

1. A *didaskalos* is someone who claims to be able to instruct others in a specific subject about which presumably the pupil does not know and about which she or he presumably does.
2. A *didaskalos* is someone who accepts money for this instruction.
3. A *didaskalos* is someone who instructs *only* when payment is made.
4. A *didaskalos* instructs through expository speeches and demonstration in private lessons to the one who is paying the tuition. In addition to identifying the primary mode of instruction as lecturing or speech making, this implies that he or she speaks differently (or reveals more) to a paying customer within the school than he or she would in a public forum that might include nonpayers.

It is at least possible that Socrates would agree with the city in holding that anyone who meets conditions #2 and #3 might justly be held responsible for the misdeeds of his customers, as a result of the contractual warranty such a tuition-instruction arrangement would imply. (But it is another question indeed whether Socrates really thinks that the Sophists fulfill all four of these conditions—as they claim to do—and it is a further question still whether these four conditions add up to a good definition of teaching.)

It is important to recall that the philosopher's argument in the present context is designed to convince his jury that he cannot justly be held responsible and therefore *should not be* held responsible for the actions of others, whether or not they claim to have learned from him. He does not deny conversing with people, interrogating them, and offering *logoi* of his own to which they must be willing to listen. He says he begrudges no one the chance to listen or converse with him (33a), but he also seems to be fully aware that he has no control over what either his interlocutors or third parties will do or say about what he has said or about what they suppose they have learned from him. What he *does* deny is being anyone's *didaskalos*, that is, he denies ever taking a fee, and thereby entering into a professional, contractual relationship with any of his interlocutors that would entail a set of expectations that he is not prepared to meet. This nuance, as we have seen, is important to his defense, because it is aimed at vitiating any legal basis for holding him accountable for the actions of others. It is at least partly in order to avoid the expectation of a *quid pro quo*, which is implied whenever one accepts a fee for services, that Plato's Socrates approaches his interlocutors in the stubbornly ignorant, relentlessly interrogatory, and consistently *pro bono* way that he does.

Early in *Apology*—within the first three Stephanus pages—Socrates has already begun framing the contrast between his practices and those of the Sophists'. In the following passage, he links teaching with fee taking, making evident that being a professional, who can persuade others to pay a tuition to learn what the *didaskalos* knows, is central to what he means by "teaching" from the very beginning of the argument he presents in his defense.

> If you have heard from anyone that I undertake to teach (*paideuein*) people and charge a fee for it, that is not true either. Yet I think it is a fine thing to be able to teach people (*paideuein anthropous*) as Gorgias of Leontini does, and Prodicus of Ceos, and Hippias of Ellis. Any of these men can go to any city and persuade the young. (*Ap*. 19d8–e5, Grube trans.)

Plato's audience is led immediately to wonder, does Socrates really think the Sophists teach in a genuine, philosophical sense? One need only recall Socrates' long discussion with Adeimantus in *Republic* VI to discover an answer to that question. There, Socrates likens the way the Sophists "teach" to the handling of a wild beast. The Sophists are said to master the desires and aversions of the many, so they can give the large beast exactly what it wants. And worse, Socrates says, they call this knowledge of the beast's likes and dislikes *wisdom*. The Sophists are obliged to learn what pleases people and then learn how to dazzle them while delivering what the audience craves, if they are going to be successful in the way that Socrates describes above. One can infer from what he says here that Socrates does not believe that the student will be the best judge of what he or she needs to learn, nor of when and how this learning should transpire. The genuine teacher knows that fee-based teaching forces one to pander to the extent that making the student feel good about the session is necessary if the teacher expects to generate repeat business. In their discussion in *Republic* VI, Socrates and Adeimantus agree that political education, the *paideusis* appropriate to the requirements of *politikē*, must not be carried out without regard to what is just or good or true, as is the case in the system of education practiced and promoted by the Sophists. Therefore, Socrates and Adeimantus conclude at 493d7–8 that one who "teaches" like the

Sophists do would be strange or "out of place" (*atopos*) as an educator (*paideutēs*).[16] Socrates proceeds directly to contrast this *atopos* kind of *paideutēs* with someone like himself, someone we might call the "true *paideutēs*." It should be clear from this cross-reference to *Republic* VI that it is the pseudo-educator from whom Socrates wants to distinguish himself and, by implication, his kind of *paideusis*, from the very outset of his trial.

The philosopher underscores his restrictive, conventional definition of teaching here when he says that the Sophists he names "can go anywhere and persuade the young," which means that they can find enough youths willing to become clients to allow them to make a living wherever they go. Whether this is because the Sophists are truly good instructors or merely good salesmen, whether the young are just gullible, or the Sophists are shameless and supremely skilled at persuasion and deception, Socrates does not say here. He leaves these matters for his jury to ponder. But the definition of teaching that emerges from these contextual considerations of Socrates' defense speech suggests that, from the beginning, when he speaks about "teaching" or being a *didaskalos* in the *Apology*, Socrates has in mind the conventional conception of the Sophists' fee-based instruction. What is crucial to my argument here is that Socrates elsewhere explicitly contrasts a strange or an "out of place" *paideutēs* with an appropriate *paideutēs*, thus he allows for the possibility of genuine educators. We should conclude that in the *Apology* it is the *pseudo* kind of teaching, not the genuine alternative, that Socrates testifies to being neither able nor willing to engage in.

The leading motivations for Socrates' denial at 33a should now be clear enough: he needs to refute the charge of corrupting the youth, and to accomplish this, he must exhibit the differences in form and substance between his lay practice in the city and the Sophists' professional activities. Plato may have had still other reasons for having Socrates deny being a teacher in the way he does at his trial. Perhaps Plato stresses this in his account in order to temper his own audience's expectations for the philosopher's success with the characters he targets in the dialogues. Plato also surely knew that the ability to convince or persuade depends on the skills of one's interlocutors, in this case, his jury. Hence, also, no one can really *teach* another something the other is not prepared to learn, just as no one can ever really convert someone else, since the turning around entailed by both pedagogy and "psychagogy" must take place *within* one's own person. This is surely one important reason why learning is explained as a kind of recollection in various places throughout the dialogues. Socratic education is incompatible with a conception of the education process as some kind of knowledge transfer and of the teacher as a mere "content provider." Hence the question concerning whether, or in what sense, Plato's Socrates can aptly be regarded as a teacher continues to puzzle readers of the dialogues.[17] Yet this is only one side of the perplexing problem. The ambiguity in Socrates' role as a teacher is complemented, and perhaps compounded, by the ambiguity in his role as a student. And since "teacher" and "student" are correlative terms, perhaps our investigation shall benefit from a brief examination of the way Socrates acts when he is positioned on the other side of the relationship.

SECTION 1.C SOCRATES AS STUDENT: THE CONTRAST BETWEEN A MARKET AND A GIFT ECONOMY

In Plato's Socratic dialogues, the larger-than-life philosopher seems superior to every interlocutor with whom he converses, and although he always appears eager and willing to learn from those he examines in conversation, he never seems to learn much of substance, if anything, from his interlocutor about the topic under discussion. Yet these conversations are supposed to exemplify the exercises through which Socrates says his character and his beliefs are tested and strengthened.[18] These discussions define the Socrates we know, an interlocutor without equal in the dialogues. He is perceptive and adroit on his feet, as only one whose words have been carefully scripted can be. Now Socrates regularly declares that he expects to learn something from these conversations, and he clearly regards his practice of cross-examining others as strengthening him. But the great examiner seems only to gather additional evidence with which to support his already thoroughly tested beliefs. At most, he could be said, if one can draw inferences from these representative conversations, to gain inductive evidence about the various types of human character and about possible arguments and their entailments for various positions. Moreover, these conversations provide him with the opportunity to perfect strategies for the best approach to different kinds of interlocutors. But he appears to learn little or nothing about the subject matter during these conversations. As the master of his conversational craft, Socrates seems to learn only how better to assay the character of his interlocutors, to identify their fundamental beliefs or the structure of their desires, and to anticipate them in argument. He claims thereby to be learning about himself, caring for himself, and perfecting his character.

Moreover, Socrates is rarely portrayed in the role of student, just as he is rarely shown being interrogated in the way he interrogates others. Only twice in the dialogues (*Prot.* 338c–339d and *Grg.* 462a–467c) is he cross-examined at length. And only twice does he really seem to be depicted as learning something of substance from another person and positioned in the role of a student, and both times it is with a woman, with the mysterious priestess Diotima in the *Symposium* and with Aspasia, Pericles' longtime companion, in the *Menexenus*. In many dialogues, he appears to be merely taunting or toying with his less able interlocutors. This feature of Plato's characterization of Socrates regularly frustrates first-time readers in introductory philosophy courses.[19] Students often are annoyed that Socrates refutes the positive efforts of everyone else without seeming to put forth anything constructive himself. Not only does he sometimes seem to be refusing to assert any of his own ideas about the matters under discussion, however, but often when he professes his expectation that he is about to learn from an interlocutor who appears self-satisfied and ready to teach him something, this turns out to be Socrates' way of drawing the other person out, while exposing to onlookers the would-be teacher's misplaced conceit. And in a few cases, such as with Thrasymachus in the opening book of the *Republic*, Socrates' profession that he expects to learn from such a boastfully self-confident teacher leads to the unveiling of the philosopher's most offensive kind of irony, the overly humble, self-deprecating standpoint he sometimes occupies. Whether this is just a way for the clever cross-examiner to provoke a reticent interlocutor into saying what he really thinks or believes, or whether Socrates truly has nothing to say, the same ambiguity that characterizes Socrates' role as a teacher also inheres in his posture as a student.

With Thrasymachus, we shall again see that Plato uses Socrates' behavior to illustrate key differences between a conventional concept and his novel alternative. The precarious stance occupied by the philosopher is threatened in the opening book of the *Republic*. When Thrasymachus finally jumps—like a wild beast—into the conversation that Socrates has been having with Polemarchus, I, the Sophist ridicules the philosopher for not being much of a teacher,' giving nothing himself and just profiting from the wisdom of others (338b). He begins by charging Socrates with being a poor excuse for a teacher, but he ends up accusing him of being an unsatisfactory student as well, alleging that the philosopher is willing to give neither praise nor payment in recognition of the benefits he receives from those who teach him. Thrasymachus' defiant questions levy the familiar critique against Socratic interrogation:

> What is this nonsense that has possessed you for so long, Socrates? And why do you act like fools making way for one another? If you truly want to know what the just is, don't only ask and gratify your love of honor by refuting whatever someone answers—you know

that it is easier to ask than to answer—but answer yourself and say what you assert the just to be. (*Rep.* 336b–c, Bloom trans.)

Socrates responds ironically, professing incompetence and suggesting that Sophists such as Thrasymachus should pity him rather than treat him harshly; Thrasymachus exclaims (scoffing) that he knew Socrates would be ironical. For Thrasymachus, Socrates' legendary irony comes as no surprise, and he charges that the philosopher will say anything rather than offer his own answer (336e–337a). Socrates' irony turns to sarcasm as he calls Thrasymachus "wise" before chastising him for forbidding any of the possible answers that he might have been inclined to give. Socrates is only able to hint that one of the proscribed answers might have been his "opinion upon consideration" (337c), before Thrasymachus issues this challenge:

> "What if I could show you another answer about justice besides all these and better than they are?" he said. "What punishment do you think you would deserve to suffer?"
> "What else than the one it is fitting for a man who does not know to suffer?" I said. "And surely it is fitting for him to learn from the man who knows. So this is what I think I deserve to suffer."
> "That's because you are an agreeable chap!" he said. "But in addition to learning, pay a fine in money too."
> "When I get some." I said.
> "He has some," said Glaucon. "Now, for money's sake, speak, Thrasymachus. We shall all contribute for Socrates."
> (*Rep.* 337c–d, Bloom trans.)

Socrates takes offense at the accusation that he is ungrateful for what he learns from others and that he never gives thanks. Because he has no money, he says, he cannot pay a fee, but he claims to be willing to give praise whenever he learns from others. Now Socrates probably does not expect to learn much that is new about the nature of justice from Thrasymachus. He might have suspected that the Sophist would define justice as the advantage of the stronger. Hence, it could be argued, Socrates does not expect either to have to suffer the humbling antidote of being "taught" by Thrasymachus or of having to pay him a "fine." But if Socrates is really to be regarded as a genuine student, if he is capable of learning from others and is willing to do so, then it must be assumed that he enters into such agreements in good faith, sincerely hoping to learn from others. Yet notice how quickly the philosopher begins to distance himself from his conversational companions. At 338a, he commands

Thrasymachus, "Gratify me by answering and don't begrudge your teaching (*didaxi*) to Glaucon and the others." What he means by "teaching" here is the lesson or instruction, in the form of a shower of words, that he expects to be forthcoming now that Thrasymachus has stipulated his demand for a conditional "fine." "Teaching" here signifies the mere *quid pro quo* required of the Sophist by the promise to pay the fee. It seems clear enough that Socrates does not consider himself a student of the Sophist's "teaching" in the same sense he thinks his friends are. And perhaps Socrates does not think that Thrasymachus will tell him anything about justice that he does not already know. The answer he awaits will, as Thrasymachus rightly fears, "gratify" Socrates, because it will provide the philosopher with a positive view that he can begin to examine and put to the test. But we should note that the Sophist's instruction is being requested only by Socrates' friends, not by Socrates himself.

What is especially interesting here is that Thrasymachus knows that Socrates has no money, yet he persists in demanding a payment from him. His persistence on the money issue, when he is aware of the futility of demanding payment from Socrates, indicates that he is attempting to extort some kind of capitulation from the philosopher. Thrasymachus surely cares less about the money than about getting Socrates to play his game, to conceive of learning in general and conversation in particular as a "knowledge business." He seems at least to want to bring Socrates to admit to being a freeloader who never pays his own way. He evidently regards him as more of a parasite than a gadfly in the city. This contrast between their respective approaches to education makes plain the fact that Socrates is unwilling to participate in the market economy in which sophistical teaching is rooted. What is important, I think, is that it is from the commercialization of the learning process, not from the role of student per se, that Socrates is withdrawing in the above-cited passage.

One suspects that Thrasymachus would like to provoke Socrates into confessing that he merely *plays* the student, just as he merely *plays* at being a *didaskalos* in the Sophist's opinion. For Sophists such as Thrasymachus, the teacher's role consists of making speeches for money, and the student's role is to pay and praise. His attack on Socrates voices his complaint that the philosopher does not uphold this simple obligation, commonly considered incumbent upon one aiming to learn. Thrasymachus assumes that Socrates cannot be a "real" teacher, because he is not a professional; and he cannot be a genuine student, because he pays no tuition. The argument here calls to mind a confusion of cause and effect in the popular portrayals of Socrates.[20] Socrates did argue in the *Apology* that since he had no knowledge, he could not claim to teach anybody anything. He also points to his poverty to prove that he had never been a fee-based teacher. But Thrasymachus' view echoes the common opinion that since Socrates is poor, he cannot be wise.[21]

On another level, this contest illustrates something important about Plato's conception of philosophy. It has been argued that Plato was the first Western thinker to organize a specific method and set of concerns under the heading "philosophy," but it has not been sufficiently emphasized how crucial it seems to be to his conception of the newly delineated field that its practice be carried out at a pre-commercial level of human relations.[22] This is a prominent, though seldom stressed point of this long, preliminary contest between Socrates and Thrasymachus.[23] In addition to establishing the appropriate pre-commercial context for the discussion of justice to follow in the *Republic*, the above exchange between Socrates and Thrasymachus provides grounds for differentiating practices dependent upon a market economy from practices that are not.

Throughout the Socratic dialogues, even when it causes Socrates' behavior to seem implausible, callous, or superhuman, Plato ensures that Socrates' incorruptibility is secured.[24] Indeed, he makes the philosopher's incorruptibility—by money, gifts, honors, and even sexual favors, as the encounter with Alcibiades, to be discussed in Chapter 4, will illustrate—a vital, prominent feature of his characterization of him. This way of depicting Socrates and, by extension, philosophy, as Socrates is shown practicing it, appears to be extremely important to Plato's portrayal. This stance also is critical to his characterization of the philosopher's role as a *paideutēs*, a lover, and a gadfly in the city. It should be no surprise then that Plato has Socrates argue in his defense that, far from benefiting personally from his practice in the city, he has neglected his own affairs in order to do the god's work, always refusing to accept a fee (or to enrich himself in any other conventional way) for his services (cf. *Ap.* 23c, 31c). This stance is vital to his philosophical practice, because it keeps Socrates uniquely free in several important respects: to converse with whomever he wishes, to be able to speak the truth, to be unconstrained by his interlocutor's evaluation of him or any need to make him feel good, to be mastered by no one, and to be in no one's debt. What is more, this curious philosopher casts himself as God's gift to his city, proclaiming himself the greatest of benefactors to the Athenian people (see *Ap.* 30a, 30d–e, and 36c–d). In precisely what sense Plato conceives him as a "gift" and the "greatest benefactor" to his city will be one of the ongoing issues with which our analysis of his first approach to Lysis and Alcibiades will be concerned. What is important here is that Plato not only keeps Socrates from being beholden to anyone, he also portrays him as a gift to his city and as someone who confers a great benefit upon others. We will see that Socrates gives a gift to others while consistently refusing to allow his gift to be reduced to an item of exchange.

There are many ways in which an economy can operate as an exchange economy. All of the forms of market transactions, including sales of goods and fee for service transactions as well as barter, are obvious forms of economic exchange. Human interaction is sometimes conceived on a model of economic exchange too, and one may think of other classical forms of exchange—exchanging blows in battle, exchanging trophies in the heroic epics, exchanging speeches in rhetorical contests, and exchanging "knowledge" for a price, as the Sophists claimed to do.[25] Human beings also exchange gifts. A complete account of the conventional ethos governing Athenian practices of gift exchange in the last half of the fifth and first half of the fourth centuries B.C.E. would require a different kind of study, constructed around a much more detailed examination of a wide array of ancient sources for historical and philological evidence than can possibly be brought to bear here. What I shall do instead is take Aristotle as a source and adduce from his writings on benefaction a framework for grasping prevalent Athenian beliefs and practices at the time Plato would have been writing his Socratic dialogues. Aristotle's analysis will be augmented by a brief survey of ethnographic evidence concerning the meaning and function of the gift. Before turning to Aristotle, let us briefly construct a general framework within which to interpret his discussion.

In his pathbreaking study on the gift, Marcel Mauss showed that gift exchange is different in important respects from the ordinary exchange of goods or other market-based economic transactions; but Mauss also argues that while the notion of a gift seems to require no reciprocity (what I am calling, in general, "exchange"), gift giving actually involves three interconnected obligations: giving, receiving, and reciprocating.[26] When one person gives a gift to another, this act of giving a gift or benefit is rooted in a whole ethos governing how such a gift exchange is to be properly practiced. Such an ethos stipulates what is fair in these relations, what type of behavior is expected in which circumstances, what kinds of gifts are appropriate for what occasions, and much more. Mauss' study showed that practices surrounding the gift can constitute the very foundation of social relations, involving core issues of honor, freedom, sexual reproduction, and religious observation. The gift was shown to entail an ethos that intersects and regulates in myriad ways the whole spectrum of human behaviors and practices.

Mauss' analyses of potlatch cultures exhibit how one person can place another in debt through the conferral of a gift or benefit. The recipient of the benefit incurs an unspoken debt to the benefactor until an equal or a greater benefit is given in return. Though the return is not explicitly commanded, and this distinguishes it further from commercial contracts and other forms of market exchange, Mauss found that beneficiaries will nonetheless be obliged to make a return in order to escape feelings of indebtedness to their benefactors. This results from the gift's tendency to oblige recipients to reciprocate. When gifts function in a reciprocal way between two people, this is a "restricted" or "limited" gift economy.[27] For the most part, only a (more or less equivalent) *quid pro quo* is expected of a beneficiary or recipient of a gift within such an economy. As long as the scales roughly balance out over time and neither party ends up giving very much more than the other, this gift economy continues to operate as a restricted or limited one.

When a recipient of a gift or benefit repays more than is owed, the excess causes the scale of obligation in the relationship to shift, not only liquidating the existing debt by settling accounts but adding a benefit that carries with it a new obligation, placing the other person in the position of beneficiary. The gift, then, also can function as a means of economic redistribution. The tendency to escalate into one-upmanship, in which each party tries to outdo the other in beneficence, is a constant threat. Employing the gift as a weapon for waging war was shown by Mauss to be characteristic of potlatch cultures. Such an economy with similar conventions also flourished in classical Athens, as can be demonstrated from a brief survey of Aristotle's account of the benefactor-beneficiary relationship in his ethical writings. Aristotle explicates the principles governing the ethos of benefaction that would have been operative in Plato's time. Grasping these principles will contribute to our appreciation of Plato's characterization of Socrates.[28] A few illustrations will help illuminate the prevalent conventions that underwrite the dramatic action of the dialogues. This is essential for appreciating the richness of Plato's depiction of Socrates as someone who gives a gift to his city without accepting fees or gifts in return.

For Aristotle, the benefactor-beneficiary relationship constitutes one of the fundamental models in terms of which social interaction can be conceived, along with the model of ruler and ruled. His direct discussions provide a philosophical basis for grasping key principles of what Sir Kenneth Dover called "Greek popular morality."[29]

The benefactor-beneficiary model is prominent as the background for Aristotle's reflections on asymmetrical friendships. In the following passage, he seems to take the structural form of ruler/ruled and benefactor/beneficiary as models for many other kinds of human relations:

> Into this class falls the relation of father to son and of benefactor to beneficiary; and there are varieties of these again, e.g. there is a difference between the relation of father to son, and of husband to wife, the latter being that of ruler to subject, the former that of benefactor to beneficiary. (*Eud. Eth.*, Bk. VII, Ch. 3: 1238b22–26)[30]

In his discussion of greatness of soul, Aristotle articulates another basic principle governing the benefactor-beneficiary relationship, illuminating the traditional identification of benefaction with superior nobility and freedom.

> And he [the great-souled man] is the sort of man to confer benefits, but he is ashamed of receiving them; for the one is the mark of a superior, the other of an inferior. And he is apt to confer greater benefits in return; for thus the original benefactor besides being paid will incur a debt to him, and will be the gainer by the transaction. (*Nic. Eth.*, Bk. IV, Ch. 3: 1124b10–13)[31]

Benefaction is connected to activity, which is noble, at *Nicomachean Ethics* IX, while the beneficiary's role is passive and hence may be called advantageous but not noble. Aristotle characterizes the benefactor's relationship to the beneficiary as analogous to the relationship of a mother to her child or a poet to his works. If benefaction, being active and noble, renders one free and superior, receiving benefits, being passive and lacking in nobility, positions one as indebted and enslaved.[32]

> At the same time to the benefactor that is noble which depends on his action, so that he delights in the object of his action, whereas to the patient there is nothing noble in the agent, but at most something advantageous, and this is less pleasant and lovable. (*Nic. Eth.*, Bk. IX, Ch. 7: 1168a9–12)

For this reason, the benefactor is thought to love the beneficiary more than the beneficiary loves the benefactor. Aristotle explicitly denies that the reason for this is simply that the debtor wishes to see his creditor disappear. This suggests that, for Aristotle, conferring a benefit is most appropriately analogized to *poiesis* ("making" or "creating"). It is clearly imbued with deep significations for human relations (see especially *Nic. Eth.*, Bk. IX, Ch. 7: 1167b16–1168a9; *Eud. Eth.*, Bk. VII, Ch. 8: 1241a35–1241b11).

In cases of extreme generosity, where the benefit cannot be repaid, Aristotle says that the beneficiary must acknowledge and honor the beneficence. Honoring one's benefactor displays one's abiding gratitude when no form of repayment is possible or adequate. Aristotle even wonders how one can repay another for bestowing an immeasurable benefit, since such a benefit is incommensurable with ordinary ones.

In *Nicomachean Ethics*, Book VIII, Ch. 13, he illuminates the difficulty in affixing a value to such incommensurable benefits within this restrictive, conventional framework:

> In a friendship based on virtue each party is eager to benefit the other, for this is characteristic of virtue and of friendship; and as

they vie with each other in giving, and not in getting benefits, no complaints nor quarrels can arise, since nobody is angry with one who loves him and benefits him. But on the contrary, if a person of good feeling, requites him with service in return, the one who outdoes the other in beneficence will not have any complaint against his friend, since he gets what he desires, and what each man desires is the good. (*Nic. Eth.* 1162b6–13; Rackham trans.)

Two chapters later (Book IX, Ch. 1), reflecting on how beneficiaries of gifts should repay their benefactors, Aristotle writes of incommensurable gifts:

But in cases where no agreement is come to as to the value of the service, if it is proffered for the recipient's own sake, as has been said above, no complaint arises, for a friendship based on virtue does not give rise to quarrels; and the return made should be in proportion to the intention of the benefactor, since intention is the measure of a friend, and of virtue. This is the principle on which it would seem that payment ought to be made to those who have imparted instruction in philosophy; for the value of their service is not measurable in money, and no honor paid them could be an equivalent, but no doubt all that can be expected is that to them, as to the gods and to our parents, we should make such return as is in our power. (*Nic. Eth.*, Bk. IX, Ch. 1: 1164a33–b7, Rackham trans. See also *Nic. Eth.*, Bk. VIII, Ch. 13: 1163a10–23; 1165a21–25; *Pol.*, Bk. III, Ch. 15: 1286b9–11).

Although this last passage helps illustrate the sense in which Socrates' gift to others is incommensurable with material, political, and other conventional rewards, we shall see that Socrates' gift is not confined to the kind of limited or restrictive economy of gift exchange that is the background for Aristotle's account. It is, however, most likely the matrix within which ordinary gifts would have circulated, therefore, Plato makes it the background against which Socrates' precarious stance as a benefactor to Athens is contrasted. So it is from a logic such as that operative in Aristotle (and Xenophon) that the nature and function of Socrates' gift will have to be distinguished. Mauss helps by making explicit what was only implicit in Aristotle, namely, that the gift used as potlatch can function as a veiled form of interpersonal warfare that produces effects across the entire spectrum of social relations. This excursus into the gift helps locate the source of conflict between Socrates and Thrasymachus in the above-cited example, and we shall see in Chapter 4 how this economy of gift exchange sheds light also on the struggle between Socrates and Alcibiades.

Returning to the *Republic*, in addition to sharpening the distinction between the gift economy in which philosophy transpires in Plato's dialogues and the market economy in which the Sophists operate, the encounter between Socrates and Thrasymachus forces the audience to reflect upon the philosopher's dual role as teacher and student. Readers will likely have sensed already that the philosopher is no more a "student" in Thrasymachus' sense—paying, praising, and applauding the masterful display of rhetoric—than he is a "teacher" in the sophistical sense. But Socrates can honestly regard himself as a student of many matters, even if he is not a student of any master, and even if his most pivotal lessons—the disenchantment with the nature philosophers that caused him to embark on his "second sailing" (*Phd.* 97c and following) and his conversation with Diotima concerning the art of love (*Symp.* 201d and following)—were lessons learned some forty years before his trial. That Socrates should be regarded as a student of many matters might explain how, even if he were far superior to his interlocutors in knowledge about the specific topics discussed, this unequaled philosopher still could be said sincerely to benefit from dialogue with others. His daily conversations also provide him with a means of remaining vigilant against false conceits, of scrutinizing the unexamined presuppositions lurking behind his provisional conclusions, even concerning matters he has discussed many times, and of being open to seeing things from other perspectives, as he continues to work on himself.

Plato, in the *Gorgias*, has Socrates take a different route toward this same end of contrasting his methods with other available approaches. There, Socrates sets out to refute the claim that the Sophists teach. The contrast is drawn between Socrates' conception of what teaching *should* do and what the Sophists, who claim to teach, actually do. Examining this contrast will further clarify the differences between Socrates' methods of education and the Sophists' methods, and it will show why Socrates does not think that the Sophists teach, even when judged by their own standards. Note that Socrates will deny in this context what he had avowed in *Apology*, namely, that the Sophists are teachers. Put another way, he is anxious to refute in the *Gorgias* what he had let stand in the context of the *Apology* on the way to making the case in his defense. This is because his main objective at his trial was to say, "The sophists are the teachers, not me; I'm a philosopher." Since in the *Gorgias* he is talking face-to-face with three Sophists, however, his objective is to call into question whether the Sophists, in fact, actually teach, a point that he will not simply grant here.

Section 1.D The Meaning of "Teaching" in the *Gorgias:* "Additive" versus "Integrative" Models

I shall draw here upon a concise and an illustrative account of the many differences between the Socratic manner of teaching and the Sophists' method of teaching. In "Nonteaching and Its Significance for Education," James King uses the discussion between Socrates and Gorgias about the persuasion of rhetoric and what it produces in the listener to sketch key points of contrast between what teaching should be able to do, according to the standard Socrates holds up to Gorgias, and what rhetoric actually does.[33] King recalls the key points that Socrates puts forth against Gorgias in an attempt to refute the notion that the rhetoricians are teachers. Socrates is attempting to show conclusively that rhetoricians cannot be said to teach, even when measured against their own conceptions of teaching. King draws out the following six points that combine to explicate the sophistical view of teaching underwriting the rhetorician's profession. First, "teaching" requires that the speaker be knowledgeable. Second, this knowledge can be directed only at those who do not presently have such knowledge, presuming that the learning process begins as an unequal relationship between a knowledgeable speaker and an ignorant auditor. Third, the teaching process entails bringing to the listener the knowledge the speaker has. Fourth, teaching produces a total increase in knowledge, since the knowledge spreads from one to two or more persons. Fifth, the equalization process, as knowledge is distributed, results in a community of knowers. Sixth, the teacher must aim at the truth and not be deceitful or reticent, so that both parties come to see that the goal of the process has been fulfilled.

Now Socrates argues repeatedly throughout the dialogues, most notably in *Gorgias, Protagoras,* and in the context of explaining the origin of his mission in *Apology*, that rhetoricians do not have knowledge. Although they are persuasive and skilled at the art of oratory, they are in fact ignorant of their subjects. They tend to care more for the effectiveness of their techniques of persuasion than for the truth of any matter. Hence, Socrates would say, they are required to deceive prospective clients right from the start about what they do and do not know and about what they can and cannot do in the capacity for which they are paid a fee.[34] Now since they have no knowledge of their own but instead merely give their customers what the customer desires (or thinks he or she needs) in advance, the customer cannot really be said to have gained in knowledge. In the end, as King summarizes Socrates' conclusion, the prospective student remains as ignorant as he or she was at the beginning. Because there has been no genuine epistemic gain, the original inequality between speaker and listener remains, and the two parties never experience a shared community of knowledge. The only thing that *does* get distributed (or transferred) on this model is money. So even measured against their own standards, as King recounts the arguments Socrates presents to Gorgias, it is shown that rhetoricians do not actually teach.

King then goes on to compare and contrast Socrates' pedagogical practices in the dialogues and the model of education implied in them with the conception of teaching the philosopher had employed to make his argument against the rhetoricians' claims about teaching. He reminds us that Socrates does not usually claim to have knowledge, incessantly professing his ignorance.[35] Moreover, he notes, Socrates' interlocutors do not openly declare their ignorance or desire to be educated at the beginning of their conversation with him—though of course many come to do so during the course of their discussion—and because Socrates adheres steadfastly to his profession of ignorance, he cannot claim to have conferred knowledge upon others or to have formed a community of knowers with them (though King points out that he and his interlocutors often form a makeshift community of inquirers). This leads King to conclude, "Both from Socrates' own testimony and from a Socratic theory of what is involved in teaching, . . . Socrates indeed was not a teacher" (224).

This conclusion seems hasty. Granted that Socrates is not a *didaskalos,* and granted that the philosopher's own practices may not be able to stand up to the criteria to which he holds the rhetoricians in the *Gorgias* any better than those of Gorgias do, one must still ask: Are these the only possible models of education available? What grounds do readers have for holding that Socrates truly thinks teaching is best defined by the conditions he employs to show Gorgias that the rhetoricians do not really teach? Why should one accept either the definition of teaching that Socrates utilizes to refute Gorgias or the conventional conception of the *didaskalos* from which he distinguishes himself in the *Apology*? Why should the criteria for judging whether Socrates is some kind of teacher be restricted to the two sets of standards he employs to criticize the bad teachers of his day? There is a fallacious and an unexpressed premise in King's argument, namely, that any standards Socrates uses to refute his competitors must be standards that he believes he himself could meet. Yet what if he is merely accepting his opponents claims in order to use them against them? Do we, as readers of the dialogues, agree that the definitions of the education process derivable from these two models fit well the art of teaching as *paideusis,* as Socrates himself conceives of and engages in it, especially in view of his explicit contrast in *Republic* VI between an appropriate and inappropriate *paideutēs*? Should we not attempt to discern what Socrates, in general, thinks genuine teaching and learning entail, and then try to construct a model of the true *paideusis* from his own words and deeds in the dialogues?

King concludes that although Socrates is not a teacher in the strict sense he uses with Gorgias, his behaviors and practices do not fit the description of a rhetorician either.[36] He describes what Socrates does as a *tertium quid* between what the rhetoricians do and what teaching should do according to the conception of teaching Socrates uses in the discussion with Gorgias. King gives one additional point of contrast between Socrates and the rhetoricians, and it is the sharpest one: People who listen to an orator or a master rhetorician derive pleasure, but those who converse with Socrates are most often pained.

This contrast suggests once again that, under Socrates' direction, the learning process will be neither facile nor entirely comfortable, because genuine learning involves confusion and possibly even a radical unsettling of much, if not all, that is familiar. A true *paideutēs* will be the one whose methods of education cannot expect and should not aim to make students feel good, because this would only make evident the fact that the teacher is merely validating and reinforcing the student's comfortable conceits and preconceptions without challenging him or her to take risks and to grow. In contrast, conversing with Socrates, or even just really listening to him, would appear to have been painful to many interlocutors in the dialogues.[37] Yet without this unsettling phase, there could be no *paideusis*. For real learning to take place, there must be challenge, risk, and sometimes even pain, at least the pain that issues from an impasse or a profound perplexity through which one must struggle to find one's way again. It should not be a surprising claim then that for Socrates, as for any good educator, the student will not be deemed the best judge either of what she or he needs to learn or of when it should be taught; nor will students be the best judge of a teacher's pedagogical methods. Socrates seems to believe that when education becomes a popularity contest, as it inevitably will if the educator is obliged to guarantee that students will *feel* good throughout the education process, there can be no genuine education. What is more, if the student—now cast in the role of customer—does not perceive the value of each lesson and judge it worthwhile, he or she can merely withhold payment or fire the unsatisfying teacher.

That Socratic education does not aim to make students feel good is largely due to the fact that Socrates took very seriously his realization that genuine education fundamentally involves the necessary unlearning of false beliefs and unjustified opinions, since these are the conceits of wisdom that stand in the way of learning and render some students unteachable. Plato also shows how such a pretense of wisdom, even if only about one's proposed course of study or action, can lead to unjust, impious deeds, such as the examples of Euthyphro and Meletus seem to illustrate. He also knew that it is just these familiar and deeply held opinions and beliefs to which people are most passionately attached. In a most Socratic aphorism, Josh Billings, a contemporary of Mark Twain, used to say, "It ain't that people are stupid; it's that they know too much that ain't so." For his part, Socrates seems far more concerned about what people know that "ain't so" than he does about the areas in which they remain completely ignorant. Genuine learning begins with a challenge to what one thinks one knows prior to learning, that is, it involves the unlearning of comfortable conceits and the exposure of presuppositions. One would not start to build a house on an inadequate or an unstable foundation; one would first raze the old structure and begin by laying an adequately solid foundation prior to building the new house.

This is why refutation is so indispensable in Socrates' kind of education; becoming aware of one's ignorance is an essential first step in the process of gaining intellectual clarity, so it is his leading objective with every new interlocutor. This awareness of ignorance is pictured in the *Meno* as the all-important first step in the learning process. And in the *Apology*, this knowledge of one's ignorance is deemed an important kind of wisdom, even though it is merely human wisdom. With respect to Socrates' method of refuting others, it is well to remember that the rhetorical procedure of first presenting a serial critique of other positions has a venerable history in Greek literature and culture, from the Parmenides to Aristotle. And in Plato's hands, a Socratic refutation may come in many forms: an argument, a counter-example, a myth, or even some dramatic event that undermines or belies an argument being made. But in whatever form it is presented, refutation is crucial, to Socrates' approach, because it aims to spur on the interlocutor toward a deeper understanding, leading him or her to see the inadequacy not only of this or that *doxa* to which he or she is attached, but of all opinion or belief, inasmuch as all *doxa* falls short of genuine knowledge and is thus susceptible to deception and falsehood.

The highlight of King's short essay is the contrast it draws between two models of learning—what he calls the "additive" model, on which the sophistical kind of teaching is based, and what he calls the "integrative" model, which he says is the model of Socratic education implicit in the dialogues.[38] On the additive model, knowledge is presumed to transfer from the one who has it to the one who does not. (This also could be called the "knowledge-transfer" or "hydraulic" model.) The additive model assumes that learning is defined by an increase in the sum of the factual information at one's disposal, and so, from this view, new information is merely added to whatever knowledge one previously had, like new data is added to a data bank or inventory is added to a warehouse. Socrates does not think teaching is a matter of conferring facts upon others or showering them with speeches, in large part because he does not subscribe to the "additive" view of the learning process. He refuses to conceive of education as a knowledge transfer (cf. *Symp.* 175d–e and 217a).

With the integrative model of education, however, new knowledge is thought to be substituted for, or integrated with, old knowledge or belief in such a way that both the content and form of one's knowledge might be said to be fundamentally reconstituted. With this model, the incompatibilities and inconsistencies in the various beliefs and opinions one holds must be reconciled, and some of them must perhaps be discarded before new ideas can be appropriated or assimilated to the old. Here one's knowledge must be thoroughly reformulated, reconstituted, or reconfigured, with as much attention to its form as to its content. In many of the "What is X?" dialogues, for example, the philosopher's interlocutors do not so much learn a new definition of X as they learn what kind of answer would be adequate as a definition of any term such as X. Throughout the dialogues, Socrates seems to denigrate the additive model while embracing the integrative one.

With this conception of teaching, the student will need to unlearn before he or she can learn, just as, King says, unless one is already naked, one must get undressed before one can get dressed. Little wonder then that being questioned by the philosopher-diagnostician would have felt to some characters like being forcibly disrobed for examination by a trainer. King argues in sum that Socrates is a model pedagogue with much to teach us about teaching.[39] However, since the "integrative" model requires so much unlearning, he concludes that Socrates must be taken literally when he says that he is not a teacher. King ends up calling Socrates a "nonteacher," since the philosopher's primary mode of teaching is this process of unlearning. But perhaps it is simply the case that since "unlearning" is the chief task in which any educator on the integrative model will be engaged with new people he or she encounters, and since Plato devotes more attention to showing the philosopher's approach to new characters than to showing what he would do if he were to spend sustained effort on those he has previously brought to an admission of *aporia* (perplexity or confusion), this "negative" or "purgative" aspect of Socrates' method receives far greater attention in Plato's depiction of Socrates' philosophical activity than does its positive, constructive side.

While King prefers to call Socrates a "nonteacher" and his practice "nonteaching," I see no reason to concede the word "teaching" to the additive, "knowledge-transfer" model of learning, or the word "teacher" to the paid professionals of the day. On the basis of the two narrowly technical definitions of teaching used by Socrates (the latter's key points reconstructed above from King's analysis of the *Gorgias*) to demarcate what the philosopher is *not* doing, no one has the requisite knowledge about the most important things, and no one could qualify as a teacher of them. Outside of the context of distinguishing himself from the Sophists or rhetoricians, of what use would be a definition of either teaching or learning that simply renders the two activities, in any meaningful sense, impossible? These are especially strange definitions for us to expect Socrates to endorse: both are based on a model of pedagogy that neither Socrates nor modern education theorists would countenance. In fact, to accept one or both of these definitions of teaching—the one that Socrates relies upon in his own defense in the *Apology* and the one he employs to refute Gorgias in the *Gorgias*—is perhaps to accept a definition of teaching according to which no one will ever be able to teach anyone anything (or at least anything philosophically important).

This is primarily because knowledge in what Aristotle would later call the "practical sciences" does not admit of the high degree of precision that is possible in, for example, geometry. Politics and ethics, indeed any study that involves the discussion of values, entail highly contingent and variable circumstances to which one's knowledge must be adaptable and within which it must be fluid or "context sensitive"; hence knowledge in these areas, and indeed in any area devoted to critical examination of normative theories, cannot be reduced to something formulaic, at least if one hopes to learn anything other than the teacher's own ideology. And while craft knowledge, or "know-how," may lend itself well to being transmitted from an expert to an apprentice, neither Socrates' practice of philosophy nor his conception of education can be reduced to a set of techniques for performing concrete, technical skills. Technical skill does not therefore furnish an adequate model either for Socratic education, nor can it provide a suitable basis for teaching for many other fields of study.

Perhaps this is why Socrates lays bare the pretensions to knowledge claimed by all groups of people that enjoyed a reputation for wisdom in his city. The Delphic Oracle story (*Ap.* 20c–23a) underscores Socrates' conviction that knowledge is neither just the art of persuasion nor the ability to speak well on subjects about which one has no real concern, as the orators and politicians do. Nor is knowledge merely the poet's ability to write beautifully, inspired by the muses, without the ability to give an account of what one knows. And although Socrates admits that he does not have the technical skill the craftspeople demonstrate, and he does regard this as a kind of knowledge, he still does not consider such know-how, or skill, alone to be wisdom. Technical skill is expertise in one specific area without any necessary comprehension of how the part is related to the whole. Worse still, it seems to seduce those who have it into believing that they know more than they do, satisfied that their expertise in one specific field qualifies them to speak as experts on any and every subject. Put as simply as he puts it, they are led to believe that they are truly wise when they are not. In disclaiming the role of teacher, Socrates is announcing—at one time to Gorgias the Sophist and another time to the crowd gathered to hear his case in court—that he does not think he possesses a *technē* that he can teach to others, least of all a *technē* for teaching virtue (*aretē*).

SECTION 1.E CONCLUSION: THE SOCRATIC *PAIDEUSIS*

Teaching and learning have been shown to consist in quite different things for Socrates and the Sophists. We have seen that the philosopher does not accept fees for his conversations, and his practice of conversing on a *pro bono* basis has been shown to entail other crucial differences from the sort of instruction engaged in by the Sophists. For not only does fee-based teaching situate the educational process within a framework of market relations, commercializing the teacher-student relationship and embedding the learning process within an economy of exchange, it also cannot help but engender the expectation that something tangible, even formulaic, will flow from the one who is paid to the one who is paying. All discourse on this model becomes merely instrumental to the end of transferring some measurable knowledge from one party to the other, and the teacher is reduced to an information provider. In contrast, not taking a fee keeps Socrates free of such expectations and of the implied warranty rightly presumed by a payment for services rendered. Moreover, his practice of conversing *pro bono* effectively safeguards the inherent value in dialogue by refusing to subordinate the activity of conversation to any material gain or body of content it may yield. It would also, therefore, seem to support a novel conception of teaching consistent with a conception of learning as an end in itself.

Socrates' principle of conversing exclusively on an informal, nonprofessional basis keeps the philosopher free to talk to whomever he wishes and to tell them the truth when he does. In contrast with the Sophists, he will not have to treat his interlocutors as customers, and he will not have to be constrained by the fear that, as customers, his interlocutors might refuse to pay him if he says anything offensive. This policy, as we have seen, frees him from having to pander to his interlocutors to make them feel good. In sum, not taking a fee keeps Socrates from having to traffic in knowledge, and to this end he refuses, over and over again in the dialogues, to "transact" philosophy according to any form of exchange, as we shall see from the examination of specific dialogues in the chapters that follow. The *pro bono* basis for his practice has the additional consequence of relieving Socrates of the burden of supplying the answers in his conversations.[40] This allows Socrates to philosophize as he does, without the presumption of expertise and without making education a one-way street.

Socrates teaches primarily by asking questions and inducing his interlocutors to answer. Conversation, for him, is more than just a means to a tangible and useful benefit, as he stresses in dialogues such as the *Euthydemus;* it is an activity valuable and good in itself. Plato too seems to believe the activity of philosophical inquiry is best pursued through the question-and-answer method, as evidenced by his choice of the dialogue form for the presentation of his philosophy. As he has Socrates explain in various places, this method has several important advantages over lectures or speeches.[41] First, in the question-and-answer method, the same person can act as both speaker and listener, pleader and judge, in joint deliberation or inquiry. In dialogue, one listens and speaks in the same activity; every remark contains within it the solicitation of a response. Second, the question-and-answer method is easier to follow than long speeches. The opportunity to interrupt and ask questions in order to gain further clarification is always available along the way. Third, in the question-and-answer method, each participant is more thoroughly persuaded as a result of giving voice to a position herself or himself than she or he would be by merely hearing someone else assert it. Fourth, through question and answer, the other's assent can be obtained step by step, building upon previous understanding to minimize confusion and identify clearly the points of disagreement or uncertainty between the parties. New ideas can be appropriated and tested on the spot. Finally, this mode of shared inquiry or deliberation has the intrinsic benefit of exercising the analytic, argumentative skills of both conversation partners, allowing them to give further shape to their own respective positions in and through the process of talking something through in dialogue (*dialegesthai*). Hence dialogue is an activity capable of molding character, not only by explicitly forming and shaping one's opinions and beliefs but also by the more subtle and practical means of the constant probing and yielding that occur in the activity of conversation.

The question-and-answer method permits Socrates to teach through the communal endeavor of "taking counsel together" (*koinē bouleuesthai*), "placing in question," or "talking through" (*dialegesthai*) rather than by just advancing claims or counterclaims that he will go on to support. In this way, dialogue establishes its own kind of community, and Plato's audience is allowed to see these ad hoc communities of inquiry being formed in the course of many dialogues. Socrates can frequently be heard inviting a prospective interlocutor to join him in this shared endeavor by saying, "Consider with me" or "Let's put our heads together." In the dialogues to be studied here he is shown befriending Lysis and Menexenus and enrapturing the young Alcibiades. Rather than by offering demonstrations or answers through declarative assertions that he is obliged to back up with great emotional fervor, the philosopher uses his style of argument to hypothesize or place in question the matters to be considered. The *aporia* experienced by characters in many dialogues also works well as a strategy through which Plato can give full range to the consideration of the "What is *X*?" question or whatever issue is being discussed. Often he will have the interlocutors entertain contrary hypotheses about the various definitions advanced.[42] In this way, these conversations provide an example of Socratic placing in question. The burden of supplying hypotheses to be tested in response to Socrates' questions usually falls to the interlocutors, at least initially, in their shared interrogation of a problem. Not only does this tactic have the effect of binding the interlocutor to her or his answers, it becomes a way of tethering philosophy to character; it is a way for Plato to show his audience how beliefs and opinions are connected to the particular people who hold them and to the particular way of life that each leads.

In his role as leader of the discussion, Socrates does not typically summarize the conclusions at the end of the dialogues, nor does he often assert his own views, except in response to what various specific interlocutors say. This reticence may be partly a pedagogical device, designed to encourage the interlocutor to formulate his or her own ideas or to state without reservation whatever opinion or belief she or he might hold on the topic. But more importantly, Socrates' approach forces his conversation partner to think and express his own thoughts prior to hearing what the much more thoughtful and experienced philosopher has to say on the subject. In this way, Socratic questioning promotes what is today called *active learning*. Plato knew that the kind of activity involved in thinking is sustained to a much greater degree when one is conversing than when one is just listening passively, and here it seems obvious that Plato's desire to get his audience thinking outweighed any temptation to let his philosopher-protagonist have the last, authoritative word. Also, sometimes Socrates' leading questions seem indispensable, especially in conversations with younger or less astute target interlocutors. Socrates is obliged at the outset of his discussion with any new interlocutor to ask questions, if only to ascertain the specific approach he should use with each person. Since education is not a one-size-fits-all affair, Socrates, like any good teacher, has to establish the background and level of his interlocutor so he can tailor a customized approach to him.

Yet to say that Socrates' reticence in the dialogues serves his own as well as his author's educational strategy well and to hold that there may be several senses in which the Socratic practice of asking questions rather than furnishing answers functions as a pedagogical device designed to place the priority on questioning over answers is not to claim that Socrates' reticence is always merely a deliberate holding back on the philosopher's part. In fact, it seems contrary to the spirit of his kind of *paideusis* to conclude that Socrates is just playing with his interlocutors by being reticent. To assert that Socrates' reluctance to put forth straightforward and positive views of his own is simply a trope designed to deceive his interlocutors into the truth, as Vlastos, for example, claimed, underestimates the complexity of Socratic irony and minimizes the important anti-hubristic principle at the heart of the Socratic manner of philosophizing, as Nehamas has argued. In the end, Vlastos's interpretation of Socrates—as Nehamas rightly concludes—makes him not only manipulative but dogmatic, because it is based on the assumption that Socrates is withholding what he suspects, believes, or knows from his interlocutors.[43] Not only do such interpretations rest on the assumption that the philosopher usually knows more than he is admitting, they also seem to be based on a methodological imperative that appears to require that, in any pedagogical relationship, the one further along in knowledge must tell everything she or he knows or be deemed guilty of manipulation. If one takes seriously Socrates' repeated professions of ignorance about the most important things, then it cannot be supposed that the philosopher might just as easily have supplied an answer himself as asked his string of questions. Finally, if an important aspect of the learning process is to undertake for oneself philosophical reflection on questions both of method and content, then the fact that Socrates regularly puts on his interlocutor the burden of initiating the direction a conversation will take must be grasped as an essential part of the experience of practicing philosophy, as Socrates and Plato conceive it.

Still, it also is true that Socratic ignorance is not ordinary or simple ignorance. To qualify as a teacher, in the Socratic sense, Socrates, who remains "positively" ignorant, must also be able to recollect the knowledge within him. Socratic *paideusis* assumes that knowledge, as well as ignorance, exists within everyone, and this is another reason why Socrates never teaches merely by inculcating his own views in those with whom he converses. His educational approach is not designed to instill in others something that was entirely absent before, as the "additive" or "knowledge-transfer" model of pedagogy presumes to do. In his role as teacher, this philosopher knows that he can only nourish seeds that are already within his students. He is depicted in the dialogues as teaching primarily by guiding and questioning, leading others to pay attention to, to recollect, what is in some prephilosophic way already within them. His teaching is designed to evoke something unique and quite personal *within* his interlocutors rather than to implant his own ideas in them. As long as it is understood in this way, then the term *teaching* may, I think, still be aptly used as a generic description of what Socrates does with many characters.

Socratic education is based on the principle that both the teacher and the student harbor knowledge as well as ignorance within themselves. Knowledge never exists without ignorance, therefore, even the teacher must qualify any claim to authoritative knowledge. Yet in conversation, the teacher can appeal to the knowledge buried within the student, striking a chord in him or her and causing a bond to be forged between them. Such resonance arises from within the student. In this view of education, which attempts to be faithful to the concept of Socratic ignorance, knowledge and ignorance are mysteriously commingled in both the teacher and the student. What the teacher says can be understood only by students who are ready to "recollect" its meaning, that is, those who are able to find its purport in themselves. Hence what the teacher endeavors to keep in memory and express in any teaching, is something the student knows also but has forgotten.

Thus teacher and student respond to one another now as two dancers, and now as two wrestlers do: the student's process of recollection guides the teacher, and the teacher's prodding and questioning leads the student further along the path of learning. The teacher learns both from self-scrutiny and from the contribution of the student, and it is important that neither controls the process, even if one leads the other. Viewed more broadly, both are students who have subordinated themselves to something greater than them, and yet what is greater than them courses through them, so they are both capable of teaching too. They end as they begun, in this in-between condition, neither completely ignorant nor thoroughly wise, yet they are no longer precisely at the same point at which they began; something immeasurable has been gained through the ensuing exercise. For this reason, the open-endedness in which the Socratic dialogues often end is not nothing; it is a reminder of the provisional, presumptive character of human wisdom, and this is far from being just ordinary ignorance. And the *aporia* that one character or the other may have reached along the way is shown to be what furthers human wisdom. It is important to see also that this *aporia* is just a momentary impasse and not a permanent roadblock. Thus the tentative or inconclusive ending of a dialogue should not be taken as leaving Plato's audience in *aporia*, for often a possible way forward is indicated explicitly or foreshadowed in some way.

In addition to the "negative" kind of knowledge implied by Socratic ignorance, that is, *not having* genuine knowledge, Socrates seems to have amassed a tremendous amount of empirical evidence from his daily conversations over a lifetime of philosophizing, and this evidence seems to have led him to a few basic inductive conclusions.[44] His thoroughly tested beliefs and opinions may not qualify as genuine knowledge, but they nonetheless add positive content to his mere knowledge of ignorance. He also appears ever willing to reopen an investigation at any time in order to reexamine one of his well-considered opinions or beliefs. Thus the Socratic educational process, as it is dramatized in Plato's dialogues, remains ever philosophical, and philosophy is shown to be a method of education guided by an erotic striving in which both teacher and student become co-seekers (*sunerastēs*) after truths which are sure to be difficult to express and which turn out to be harder still to discover. Rooted in the world of becoming, and yet seeking after truths not subject to becoming and change, the philosopher-teacher also will always remain a student in this important sense. In Socratic education, neither teacher nor student can ever abandon the in-between condition proper to Socratic ignorance, hence the act of recollection is no solitary, final act wherein one acquires indelible or complete knowledge. As Socrates (recalling Diotima's explanation) puts it in the *Symposium*, "What we call studying exists because knowledge is leaving us, because forgetting is the departure of knowledge, while studying puts back a fresh memory in place of what went away" (208a, Nehamas and Woodruff trans.). For this reason, the condition of Socratic ignorance, this being in-between genuine wisdom and sheer ignorance, which is the hybrid condition of the philosopher, never seems to yield knowledge in the strongest sense, or truth with a capital "T," but it never ceases to strive for it either.

No matter how far the roles of teacher and student are enriched and intertwined in Socratic *paideusis*, however, the two roles remain distinguishable as a result of the asymmetry between Socrates and his interlocutors. He remains still the teacher, the interlocutor still the student. In a typical Socratic conversation, both parties seem to be left in a kind of ignorance, yet each also has learned through the inquiry. What is this learning? If Socrates is presented as the paradigm, or the exemplar, of the philosophical life, and yet he remains ignorant, so that he cannot be said to have acquired authoritative knowledge, then what may we suppose is gained through the conversational inquiry that is the heart of Socratic education? Through their conversational inquiries, Socrates and his interlocutors, as students and teacher, give shape and clarity to the world of Becoming, while experiencing fleeting glimpses of Being. This conversational practice, through the question-and-answer method, results both in greater self-knowledge and greater knowledge of the other. Since Socrates and his interlocutor are engaged in an activity that resembles most closely wrestling or a dance, an activity in which each participant modulates certain aspects of herself or himself in relation to the other, each comes to know the other, and at the same time greater definition is given to her or his own character through this cooperative probing and yielding. Each has become more familiar too with the character of the matters discussed, gaining with respect to them a greater familiarity, even an intimacy, such as that which exists between two old friends.

Before evaluating the overall success of Socratic education, as we have come to understand it, we must examine closely the two cases in the dialogues in which the philosopher-teacher seems to enjoy his greatest degree of success in turning around his target interlocutor: his encounter with Lysis (Chapter 2) and his first encounter with Alcibiades (Chapter 3). Then, in Chapter 4, we shall explore the follow-up case to Socrates' initial conversation with Alcibiades provided by the latter's infamous speech in *Symposium*. Finally, in Chapter 5, we shall be in a position to evaluate the overall effectiveness of Socratic *paideusis* on its subjects.

Chapter 2

The *Lysis:* Limits and Liberation in Socrates' Encounter with Lysis

The *Lysis* is a rich but vastly underappreciated dialogue. It offers a positive example of Socratic education, and it thus substantiates the effectiveness of the philosopher's erotic strategy toward young Athenian men. In the *Lysis,* at least one of the two main characters appears to receive a tangible benefit through Socrates' intervention with him. For this reason alone, then, this dialogue warrants close attention. Resurgent interest in philosophical treatments of love and friendship has inspired readers to revisit the *Lysis*' thorough, if embryonic, line of argumentation for other reasons. For too long, the *Lysis* has been interpreted in the shadow of Plato's so-called mature works, *Phaedrus* and *Symposium*.[1] Its express topic is *philia* rather than Eros, and Socrates reinforces one of the chief differences between the two terms by beginning his questioning of Lysis with the example of parental love. Eros is not commonly thought of as applying to the feelings one has for one's parents or children. Moreover, Eros can be one-sided and unrequited, applying even to things that cannot love us back, whereas *philia* seems to imply mutual, reciprocal relations between two people. Thus, even though the *Lysis* seems to cover some of the same ground as *Phaedrus* and *Symposium,* and though it shares with these dialogues the intertwining issues of love and rhetoric, it does not seem justifiable to read the *Lysis* as merely an incomplete or inconclusive account of the nature of love or passionate desire.

Often, too, this dialogue has been regarded as merely laying the groundwork for Aristotle's various discussions of friendship in his works on ethics. To be sure, Aristotle draws upon the *Lysis* at several key points in his ethical writings. The *proton philon* argument of the *Lysis* covers much of the same terrain as parts of Book I of the *Nicomachean Ethics*.[2] Aristotle's treatment of friendship in Books VIII–IX too, owes a great debt to the *Lysis* for its schematization of the problem of friendship (*philia*).[3] Yet the *Lysis* deserves attention in its own right, for reasons that are not nearly as well known. As is the case with many of Plato's dialogues, the express topic of the *Lysis* does not exhaust the subject matter broached in it. In addition to outlining the philosophical issues involved in the question of friendship, it is a dialogue that explores—both in argument and through its dramatic movement—the similarities and differences between *philia* and Eros and the connection between freedom and limits of various kinds.[4]

Lysis and Menexenus are the two characters generally thought to be Socrates' youngest interlocutors in any dialogue. They are probably about twelve or thirteen years old.[5] That Plato chooses to have Socrates talk to very young characters has two main effects: (1) It underscores a necessary limit to the depth of the treatment of love and friendship in the argumentation;[6] and (2) It provides an opportunity to see how Socrates' approach to the boys contrasts with a panderer's such as Hippothales in conventional Greek homoerotic practices.[7] The first implication should temper in the audience any expectation of a seasoned treatment of the dialogue's themes. Their young age furnishes an explicit reason for the inconclusiveness of the dialogue's argumentation, and this apparent inconclusiveness forces Plato's audience to piece together the undeveloped strands of argument in order to discover the important philosophical problems at issue. One can expect the arguments in the *Lysis* to go only as far as the philosophical maturity of its young characters allows. One should not expect from this dialogue an elaborate taxonomy of friendship, though the broad outline for a more penetrating study is, I believe, finely sketched and a general, positive account of friendship can be constructed from Socrates' refutation of the first three theses about the friend considered in the *Lysis*, as Section 2.c will demonstrate.

The first three theses are: (1) Like is attracted to like; (2) Only the truly good are friends; and (3) Opposites attract. Socrates exposes problems with each of these three possible accounts of friendship in the course of their conversation. He accomplishes his refutations by offering the boys extreme definitions—for example, taking the Good to mean completely good, and thereby self-sufficient—and by introducing principles that he does not actually argue for in this context, for example, the view that the wicked cannot be friends to anyone or anything. But the refutations of the extreme positions produce a final thesis—"that the intermediate alone is truly friend to the Good"—and a reorienting notion concerning what is akin (*oikos*). Whatever else can be positively reconstructed from the leftover pieces of these arguments will be discussed in Section 2.c.

Why does Plato select such young interlocutors for this dialogue? If older characters are necessary in order for Socrates to explore the question of *philia* in all of its richness, why would Plato handicap the discussion by making the philosopher talk to such young characters? One can only assume, I think, that he did not regard this choice as handicapping him at all in carrying out his objectives in this dialogue, and thus that he casts these youths here to illustrate something else. What does their youthfulness allow him to exhibit? In addition to the uncritical trust that binds the friendship between Lysis and Menexenus, the dialogue seems to have as one of its goals the exhibition of the effectiveness of Socrates' erotic approach through a positive example of Socratic education with Lysis. Unlike the many cases in which he is not successful in teaching his interlocutors anything, unlike those cases in which he is spectacularly unable to transform another's view of the world, the *Lysis* offers a dramatic enactment of a successful Socratic lesson. And Lysis' age is essential to the result. Thus the *Lysis* demonstrates just how Socrates' erotic approach to promising youths produces in them a kind of "empowerment," while aiming at their ultimate liberation.

Implicit in this interpretation of the *Lysis* will be the contention that the choice to feature a main character named Lysis—whose name means "loosing" or "setting free"—for this dialogue is not accidental: "loosing" names the critical result of Socrates' appeal, the outcome of his encounter with Lysis; and the nickname *Lusi*, by which Socrates fondly refers to the boy, is a stem used to form many compound words connected to such a setting free.[8] This name supplies a word for the act of releasing—in a dual sense of freeing and of turning around—which is the first step of the learning process. The process of *psychagogia* involves the turning around of the whole person, the turning around Plato depicts allegorically in the Cave story in *Republic* VII. The buildup to Socrates' meeting with this youth, in which the erotic philosopher agrees to position himself as a panderer in order to show Hippothales how to speak effectively to a beautiful beloved, is coupled with the boy's name to engender the expectation that this conversation will exhibit dramatically a successful example of the Socratic approach, and thereby illuminate an emancipatory function within his kind of *paideusis*.[9]

Socrates will attempt to set Lysis free in two ways: he will "loose" in Lysis a desire to improve himself, and he will disclose to him what he needs to do to complete his self-improvement. But beyond the knowledge of his limits and the heightened desire to possess good sense he gains from Socrates, Lysis receives another unexpected benefit from the encounter when he is shown the path to his freedom. It may turn out that the greatest benefit Socrates gives to others is less a formulaic, transferable set of information, or even a "method" or set of procedures for obtaining knowledge, than something such as empowerment, since the philosopher's approach seems to be designed to impel youths like these toward their freedom. Now any discussion of ethical issues, and all prescriptions for right action, must necessarily presuppose freedom, since without the presumption of choice, it would make no sense for Socrates to speak of what one ought to do or not do. Without choice, there can be no ethics. Hence there is a fundamental sense in which a concern for freedom must precede any discussion of ethical matters. It is the cornerstone of Plato's portrait of him that Socrates believes he is carrying out the god's command by making it his vocation to exhort people to lead examined lives and to become as good and as just as possible. So it should not be surprising that Socrates also will have much to say about freedom in these conversations.

Plato does not explicitly advance his conception of freedom through arguments in these erotic dialogues; rather, he provides a kind of paradigm case through the dramatic example of Socrates, which allows the audience to witness how the practice of philosophic freedom will differ at key points from the conventional ways in which it would have been understood and exercised by Plato's contemporaries.[10] Socrates' own behaviors and practices throughout the dialogues show that the proper *ethos* of freedom includes at least three features: self-mastery (*enkrateia*), *sophrosunē* (soundmindedness and self-knowledge), and self-sufficiency (*autarchia*), where self-sufficiency characterizes not the person but the activity, as it does in Aristotle's discussion of happiness in *Nicomachean Ethics* I.7. In Plato's characterization of the philosopher's activities, these three traits are thoroughly interwoven. His erotic approach, his way of contravening the economy of exchange, and his habit of spending his time exercising himself in conversation all turn out to be indispensable expressions of this philosophic freedom, as Socrates is shown practicing it.

Now if Socrates is regarded as truly exhibiting the cardinal components of freedom as his author conceives it, must not the traits constitutive of this freedom be capable of being acquired by others? Or is the kind of freedom Socrates exercises available only to the philosopher? We shall see how the *Lysis* illustrates that the philosopher's kind of freedom seems capable of being shared with others, and as the action of the dialogue unfolds, Socrates is shown attempting to bequeath a share of freedom to Lysis. To show the youth what kind of freedom he has in mind, and why it is better than mere license, the philosopher first removes, or brackets, Lysis' unexpressed and perhaps unimagined limits with the goal of pointing the boy in the direction of genuine freedom.[11]

Although I am not claiming that Plato constructs a "theory" of freedom (nor does he devote any dialogue expressly to a discussion of it), I am arguing that one can plausibly infer from Socrates' actions how Plato's conception of freedom would be exercised in practice. While it is not made an explicit theme of any dialogue, I suggest that a coherent, comprehensive account of Plato's view of freedom can be adduced from Socrates' behaviors and practices in the dialogues. So not only do I claim that it is possible to sketch a conception of freedom's proper practice from Socrates' own dramatic example, I argue further that Plato's notion of freedom also is what undergirds Socrates' approach to his target interlocutors. One of the goals in this chapter then is to show that freedom, in the sense of something close to our modern concept of "empowerment," is also a less conspicuous aim of the Socratic *paideusis*, one of the intended consequences of the philosopher's erotic approach, as dramatized by Plato. Hence, despite the general neglect of freedom as a philosophical issue in antiquity,[12] and despite its rare appearance as a problem in the secondary literature on Plato, a coherent model of freedom *does*, in fact, emerge from the dialogues.[13] Thus to suppose that Plato is not concerned with the issue of freedom, just because he dedicates no conversation exclusively to it, would be to overlook a crucial theme in his philosophy. Questions about the meaning of freedom go to the heart of the Platonic vision of the good life, and they also are central to the dialogues' reflections on the best form of government.

If my thesis is correct, and Socrates is attempting to point the way to freedom for these young interlocutors, then a conferral, through which a kind of empowerment occurs, should take place in these conversations and be made evident to the audience. In fact, this chapter will attempt to show that the conferral of such a benefit on his interlocutor is nowhere more apparent than in these dialogues characterized by the erotic reversal. By closely scrutinizing his approach to Lysis and Alcibiades, the chief features of Socrates' practice of freedom will be adumbrated in the context of showing specific places at which this alternative kind of freedom is exhibited in the dramatic action. This also will permit us to delineate the steps that Socrates sets forth for his new initiates, revealing the regimen that the philosopher lays down for a coherent, sustainable practice (*askēsis*) of freedom.

Since freedom, for Socrates, has been said to consist of self-mastery, soundmindedness, self-knowledge, and the relative self-sufficiency of his activities, rather than emancipation from all limitations, it should not be surprising that the Socratic setting free of Lysis will aim toward a decisive shift in the way that Lysis thinks about limits and, hopefully thereby, his relation to limits. Through his methodical approach, Socrates moves his target interlocutor to a perspective from which the natural boundaries inherent in things can be grasped as something other than a constraint upon his liberty.

Distinguishing limits from forms of subjugation, this more mature perspective will recognize that limits are not simply impositions of authority upon individuals but combine to produce one's character, forming and shaping one as a person. In other words, this means that limits are not merely negative and restraining but also are positive and productive. By unearthing the connection between limits and philosophic freedom and by differentiating external from intrinsic limits, the *Lysis* discloses how limits *as such* are crucial to one's character and necessary for the formation of any civic identity at all within the *polis*. The dialogue's hypothetical bracketing of external constraints and conventional boundaries permits the limits inherent in things, as natural or intrinsic limits, to emerge as one of the *Lysis*' recondite themes.

This chapter will examine key components of Socrates' way of philosophizing to show how these tactics are integral to his strategy with the vulnerable young interlocutors with whom he converses in the *Lysis*. Here, as in many dialogues, Socrates seems to display an uncanny ability first for detecting and then for disclosing blind spots in the character or argumentation of others. These disclosures make explicit to Plato's audience, if not always to the interlocutor in question, the existence of, within every person, a level of trust or reliance, first and foremost upon some basic set of opinions and beliefs, which has been simply taken for granted and which therefore has remained hidden from view. Socrates may provoke the exposure of such beliefs by highlighting some aspect of one of the opinions that his interlocutor holds that has not been thoroughly examined. In other cases, he sets out to demonstrate the incompatibility between two or more of the beliefs that his interlocutor holds. And in still other cases, he attempts to disclose how some latent belief or opinion produces an inconsistency between a character's words and deeds, a disharmony that the philosopher rarely fails to illuminate for his unsuspecting interlocutors. In sum, although I do not think that Socrates has one uniform, overarching method of interrogation or refutation, he usually seeks to disturb his interlocutors in one or more of the following ways: to disclose to them their unexamined beliefs; to cause them to question the structure of their desires; to expose the contradiction between their actions and the beliefs or opinions they hold; and to illuminate some character trait that unwittingly rules them.

In the cases we are considering, the philosopher discloses the influence of deep-seated presuppositions in the form of beliefs or opinions of which the interlocutors are thoroughly unaware. These unacknowledged beliefs and opinions, these most basic assumptions at the core of human character, usually turn out to be connected to the person's chosen way of life and usually remain wholly latent until Socrates intervenes to make them explicit. With both Lysis and Menexenus, Socrates seizes upon such a key belief and utilizes it in an attempt to spark a heightened self-awareness in the boys.

He proceeds by pursuing clues that he has elicited from these boys about the things in which they trust. By making what each boy takes for granted the fulcrum of his approach, Socrates reveals how, at the level of character, unexamined opinions or beliefs (*doxa, pistis*) function as the analog of philosophical presuppositions. Worse, character limits have a way of chaining common sense to unexamined principles, just because they are what is most familiar. Hence, what is closest to each human being is what is hardest for him or her to see, because what is taken for granted or presupposed is further camouflaged through processes of typification. The philosopher is well aware that people trust most what is congenial to them, and that their latent beliefs predispose them to certain philosophical standpoints (and to certain types of friends). This kinship for what is most congenial, or most akin, is connected to the ancient notion that like is attracted to like, a notion that will later be examined briefly as one of the three main theses about the friend.

Though these impressionable adolescents may have an easier time acknowledging what they have taken for granted than Socrates' recalcitrant, adversarial interlocutors do, such latent beliefs reside innocently, but just as surreptitiously, in the promising youths that Socrates targets in the *Lysis*. Socrates will first diagnose the two boys and then attempt to carry out the purgative step in the process through which the two boys are disabused of some problematic conceit. Accomplishing the disclosure of such latent beliefs—raising to the level of a problem something that his interlocutor takes for granted—will be seen frequently to require that he take this two-pronged approach, combining arousal and chastening. These two components comprise the critical nucleus of his erotic strategy with these characters. One side of this carrot-and-stick approach fans the flames of his interlocutor's passions to heights that would be unimaginable without his intervention, while the other side chastens the interlocutor, undermining the possibility for acting on the outrageous desires that Socrates' questioning has just awakened without first addressing the task of self-improvement.[14]

To assess the volatility inherent in some of his educational tactics with these youths, three questions will guide our investigation in this chapter of Socrates' first approach to Lysis and Menexenus and in the next chapter to Alcibiades:

1. How does Socrates identify his interlocutor's fundamental beliefs and fashion his arguments to unsettle what the young men rely upon?
2. How does Socrates' erotic approach inflame his interlocutor's passions, targeting for arousal the latent structure of their desires without inciting therewith less laudable forms of spiritedness or appetitiveness?

3. Does Socrates succeed in chastening these youths, leading them to admit their ignorance and disclosing to them the need to take more trouble over themselves without engaging in unseemly tactics? If not, are such methods justified or unjustified by the results the lesson produces?

Nowhere is the explosive admixture of incendiary arousal and follow-up chastening set in greater relief than in his first exchange with Lysis.[15] We shall see that the dialogue depicts Socrates first inflaming Lysis' passions, provoking his desire for freedom and power, and then following this arousal with a powerful humbling. This strategy appears to be designed to move the youth toward a breakthrough in self-understanding. Concentrating on these two emblematic features of Socrates' erotic approach should prove advantageous for discovering what is unique about the philosopher's Eros and for determining and evaluating the function of this Eros in Socratic *paideusis*. Perhaps in no other context except the *Alcibiades I* does Plato allow the positive effects produced by Socrates' tactics to be seen so clearly. By disclosing the trust to which his targeted interlocutors are predisposed, Socrates will be seen to teach at least Lysis something crucial about the nature of the friend while having a remedial effect on the boy's character. He awakens in him both the desire to know and the possibility for greater self-sufficiency.[16] Therefore, scrutinizing his approach to Lysis in this chapter will illustrate the positive results of Socratic education.

On the surface, Socrates seems to be seducing his young, ambitious interlocutors into believing that their best hope of fulfilling their grandiose desires depends upon further association with him. This line of seduction is employed with both Lysis and Alcibiades. And in the *Lysis*, the qualms to which Socrates confesses after his presumptive "capture" of the boy (at 218c) cause one to suspect that the philosopher knows he is, at the very least, overstating his case. Plato seems to want to alert his audience to the possibility that a thinly veiled hubris[17] may have led Socrates to exaggerate his own efficacy in order to accomplish his worthy ends.[18] But is this dramatic device, in which Socrates uses the narrative frame to supply information directly to the audience, supposed to function also as a hint about why his educational efforts in general seem ultimately to fail?

We are led to wonder this: Does the fault in Socrates' dramatic failures to improve his interlocutors lie primarily with the interlocutors for misconstruing or misappropriating his words to them? Or does it lie primarily with Socrates for inflaming the passions of such youths in the first place, since this arousal might seem more likely to engender a tyrannical character than to lead people to dedicate their lives to philosophy? Are Socrates' erotic methods any more prone to being misappropriated or misconstrued than other pedagogical approaches? Will Socratic *paideusis* be more just, and therefore more legitimate, than the old forms of *paideia*?

Precisely how Socrates' two-pronged strategy accomplishes the profound and particular disclosure of Lysis' desire-structure is revealing. The lesson plan will be seen to proceed through a careful excavation of Lysis' trust, which brings the boy face-to-face with the limits (*paras*) of his character. This is in accordance with Socrates' general strategy of exposing some deficiency in the nature of an interlocutor's desires or present state of knowledge that would sabotage his ability to fulfill his aspirations. With Lysis, as with Alcibiades and others, Socrates follows the purgative first step of his approach by attempting to provide some positive knowledge, the most important aspect of which is not abstract, theoretical knowledge but a highly particular, highly personal self-knowledge.[19] We shall see how the philosopher sparks this reflexive knowledge in Lysis by serving as a mirror to the boy and making him more acutely aware of his present character limits.

Framed as the enigmatic *erastēs* (lover) in the *Lysis*, Socrates ends up bequeathing something invaluable to his young pupils, something that promises to transform them and to unlock their potential for both *sophrosunē* and self-sufficiency.[20] Hence, the *Lysis* demonstrates the degree to which the Socratic *paideusis*, at least with Lysis, is designed to culminate in a kind of liberation of the youth, guided by the beguiling Eros of Socrates' approach.[21]

SECTION 2.A THE THRESHOLD IMAGERY IN THE DRAMATIC SETTING AND PROLOGUE (203A1–206E2)

This section explicates some of the interpretive clues that Plato places in the dialogue, paying special attention to the suggestive threshold imagery with which the *Lysis* opens. It shows how the dialogue's setting frames dramatically the question of limits or boundaries, foreshadowing not only this theme but also the dialogue's central question concerning who is the friend. Plato's audience is placed in the role of judge and is challenged to assess which of the two erotic approaches—Hippothales' or Socrates'—is most appropriate. Socrates narrates this entire dialogue, and the audience learns that the conversations that he rehearses took place during a religious holiday, the festival of the Hermea.[22] The holiday setting signals a hiatus of everyday practices, indicating that this conversation is made possible by somewhat unusual circumstances, the suspension of the everyday. This suspicion is confirmed by the exceptional state of affairs inside of the wrestling school. Boys and men mingle while playing games, attired in their holiday dress, and the younger boys are unsupervised by their pedagogues, who are said to be gathered together drinking. When Hippothales and Ctesippus first encounter Socrates, he is between the Academy and the Lyceum (203a), on his way from one gymnasium to another. He is walking along the city wall, outside of the wall, but only just outside of it. In fact, the Palestra in which the dialogue transpires is constructed within the city wall (203e).[23] The bounded conflict characteristic both of wrestling and of a battle of wits with Socrates thus takes place on the threshold of another boundary, the limit, symbolized by the wall, that demarcates the *polis* from nature, and also Athens from other polities, the *agora* from the Piraeus, and the ordered from the chaotic. The wall itself symbolizes both the visible limit of the city and the way in which its citizens are bound together from birth and connected to a particular place (*topos*). Law, in turn, represents a concrete kind of limit, but only the most overt one in the realm of human behavior. Many more unwritten laws and unspoken conventions govern everyday life.

In the framed series of conversations that Socrates is recalling in the *Lysis*, the philosopher is neither collared, as he is at the beginning of the *Republic*, nor driven by any internal need to enter the place and action of the dialogue. Neither does he merely enter the discussion out of an unreflective agreement with, or trust in, the acquaintances who solicit his participation, however. That the opening scene is set at the threshold between several oppositions—nature and convention, the everyday and the exceptional—first introduces the issue of limits or boundaries. What is more, Socrates does not simply follow Hippothales and Ctesippus out of some naive trust, even though he is evidently more interested in what is going on inside of the Palestra than in talking to these two acquaintances. Socrates clarifies at the outset the terms upon which he will claim his share of the speeches. From 203b to 204b, he establishes several important things: where he is being asked to go, who is gathered there, that those gathered are spending their time in conversation, whose school he shall be entering, what expectations his hosts might have of him, and who is the most beautiful boy among them. Before passing through the final dramatic threshold, the gate of the wrestling school itself, Socrates explicitly questions the terms upon which he will come inside (204b). Socrates' decision to enter the Palestra thus situates the initial context for the *Lysis* within a framework in which limits are negotiable between two or more parties to an agreement. Its overtly consensual basis supplements the main character's name to foreshadow the fact that the *Lysis* will, directly or indirectly, have something to do with the question of freedom. This is already suggested by the way that the conversation is founded upon an explicit agreement entailing choice. And as to the terms of the agreement into which Socrates enters, it is important that he does not promise Hippothales and Ctesippus more than he can be sure to deliver. In this way, when he ends up not only fulfilling Hippothales' original request to demonstrate how a lover might endear himself to his beloved but also succeeding in "capturing" Lysis, this is an unexpected benefit rather than an obligation required of him by his initial agreement, as we shall see.

Limits are something that Socrates understands well. There are precious few areas in which this philosopher professes to have knowledge, and Eros is, in fact, the only domain in which he boldly claims to have *epistēmē*. Socrates' knowledge concerning erotic matters entails the knowledge of limits, because Eros is said to be for what we lack, and it acts as a go-between (*metaxu*) or messenger between human beings and the objects of their desires, and between mortals and gods, just as Hermes himself was known to do. (See, for example, *Symp.* 201d–204a.) Moreover, Sacrates' knowledge of his own limits is the key feature that distinguishes his "human wisdom" from the kind of wisdom the gods presumably have and his "Socratic ignorance" from simple ignorance (*Ap.* 23a-b). Socrates claims, in the *Lysis*, to have been given by a god the power to "recognize both a lover and a beloved" (204c).[24] Socrates' awareness of limits may perhaps also explain why the argumentation about love, friendship, and desire in the *Lysis* goes only as far as it does: there are inherent limitations upon human knowledge in the complex, contingent domain of interpersonal relationships. With regard to friendship, we will see how difficult it is to have precise knowledge of the good as the ultimate philosophical locus of *philia*, or ultimately to explain why one person becomes the friend or lover of another. Hence, the *Lysis* often seems to succeed only in demarcating important limits surrounding these topics: the limits that separate Eros, *philia*, and *epithumia*; the limit that distinguishes *philia* between human beings from *philia* in a broader, cosmic sense; the limit that differentiates the "in-between" philosopher from what is wholly good or thoroughly bad; the limit separating that "for the sake of which" something is loved from that "on account of which" it is loved; and the limit that distinguishes philosophic friendship from friendships based on utility or simple pleasures. Indeed, the conversation itself seems to straddle a kind of threshold, as it leads its audience increasingly to wonder how long the dialogue's ad hoc community of friends can remain intact.

The above qualifications about the dialogue's argumentation should not lead readers to suppose that Lysis and Menexenus can teach us nothing about friendship. On the contrary, these youths illustrate much that is important in the topics under discussion. The friendship between them is the friendship of schoolboys. It is fickle, competitive, and one-dimensional, derived most likely from their de facto association as neighbors and playmates growing up together; they probably became friends because they were thrown together into a situation. Among other things, this draws attention to the fact that one is always already experienced at some level with friendship or love before considering these topics as themes for philosophical reflection. One task of philosophy will be to move youths such as Lysis toward an increasingly explicit understanding of what they already know, in some way, implicitly.[25] For the moment the friendship between Lysis and Menexenus is at the level of companionship; it exemplifies only a nascent stage of friendship. When Socrates marvels at their association and calls on the testimony of the boys as experts (at 212a–b), it may be that what strikes him most about their relationship is its unreflective, trusting character.

It is this simple faith in others that Socrates himself is so far from having.[26] His relentless questioning makes such unreflective allegiance impossible for him. His critical distance from others—some have said his lack of friends[27]—is one consequence for Socrates of philosophy being the process of subjecting his beliefs, and the beliefs of others, to continuous scrutiny. Only by disengaging himself from the conventional coordinates of the many can the philosopher discharge—in himself and in others—the conceit of wisdom about the most important matters and begin to render formerly unacknowledged presuppositions more and more explicit. This process of making assumptions explicit, challenging presuppositions, and questioning established doctrine is part of the critical, anti-authoritarian role of philosophy as Socrates practices it. Not surprisingly, though, this role places him at a distance from others. We turn now to Socrates' first approach to Lysis to scrutinize the strategy through which he attempts to confer a benefit upon him. There are three steps Socrates takes to engender a positive change in Lysis, and Sections 2.b.1, 2.b.2, and 2.b.3 treat each of these three steps in turn.

SECTION 2.B SOCRATES' FIRST CONVERSATION WITH LYSIS (206E3–211B5)

Once inside of the wrestling school, Socrates takes the place of the boys' paid pedagogues. In the dramatic action of the *Lysis*, then, Socrates is made to stand in as pedagogue to the boys, while the actual pedagogues are celebrating the Hermea by drinking together.[28] Attention to the dramatic action thus presents us with Socrates positioned as a substitute teacher of some kind, even if he is not a card-carrying member of the established knowledge business. And here as elsewhere, Socrates' educational approach is able to succeed only to the degree that his interlocutors are teachable. Meno, for example, appears to be unteachable, and Socrates shows him that, for this reason alone, the slave boy is closer to knowledge than he is. Meno's slave is unobstructed by any presumption to know geometry, that is, he does not cling to the presumption of wisdom to which Meno holds fast.

In the *Lysis*, it is not simply the age of the boys that makes them teachable; Menexenus is about the same age as Lysis is, but he does not show the degree of promise that Lysis does, nor does he display the signs of undergoing the substantial transformation that his friend experiences at the hands of the philosopher. Charmides also was young when Socrates tried to cast his spell over him, but he is not changed as dramatically by his conversation with Socrates as Lysis appears to be. Yet if youth is not a sufficient condition for a teachable pupil, it certainly appears to be a necessary one. Socrates directs his efforts toward the youth of Athens, it would seem, because it is easier to kindle in them a sense of wonder or to drive them to perplexity, causing them to admit their ignorance more readily. Not yet hardened by experience or heavily invested in a particular way of life, Lysis is a promising student, and the dialogue bearing his name depicts the kind of setting free that is possible under such extraordinary conditions as these. That he does seem willing to learn makes Lysis an exceptional character in Plato's dialogues. It is not only because he is extremely young and noble then that Socrates will call him "best of men" (*ariston*).

But first Socrates has to unsettle the complacency in which Lysis presently rests, disturbing what he takes for granted and uncovering the most deeply held beliefs and opinions that subtend his way of living. This psychic purgative prepares the way for the Socratic arousal. In the second step, Socrates will employ his erotic strategy to inflame Lysis' desires and arouse his enthusiasm prior to showing him that these desires must be limited and properly directed. The third step is designed to bring on the discomforting, even painful, realization that Lysis' present condition renders him ill equipped to actualize his desires.[29] In this phase of the approach, Socrates severely undercuts any conceits that Lysis might still have about his present ability to fulfill his desires. Having done this, Socrates can go on to indicate which steps the boy must take next to further his goals.[30] The next three sections will clarify the three steps in turn. Socrates initially unsettles what Lysis takes for granted to bring the youth to acknowledge his present inadequacies and to confirm his willingness to learn.

Section 2.b.1 Step One—The Unsettling: Disturbing What Is Familiar

To adumbrate the context for Socrates' exchange with Lysis, it will help to recall the pretext for this conversation. Hippothales had asked Socrates to demonstrate how he might speak in a way that would endear him to the beautiful boy he loves from afar. Socrates did not promise to show Hippothales how he might inspire Lysis to desire him but only how he needs to speak to the young boy in order to humble him and make him easier to catch.[31] The series of questions that Socrates asks Lysis then is intended ostensibly to show Hippothales how to subdue the beautiful Lysis, rather than infusing him with pride and vainglory, as Hippothales does through his lugubrious praise. Hence, the philosopher is positioned as a kind of procurer in this encounter. Ctesippus had recounted the ridiculous extremes and ignominious deeds to which Hippothales is prone in his manic pursuit of the beautiful boy. Socrates takes it as a rule of thumb that no hunter who makes his prey harder to catch can truly be called a good hunter. As exemplar to Hippothales, Socrates goes on the hunt, and the rest of the dialogue enacts dramatically the philosopher's unusual brand of huntsmanship.[32]

The philosopher's incisive cross-examination begins unsettling Lysis, delivering the boy from his trust by calling into question the love his parents have for him. This will require the subversion of the belief that being happy means being permitted to do whatever he desires, free from the constraints of any limit. In Socrates' first exchange with Lysis (206e–211b), this commonsense view of happiness intersects the commonsense view of freedom as the liberty to do whatever one wishes. It turns out, of course, that Lysis' parents do not let him do whatever he pleases. They do not let him take the reins of the chariots in the races, they do not let him whip the mules, they do not let him conduct himself to and from school. Nor does his mother let Lysis play with her weaving implements. At school, additional masters rule over Lysis. Therefore, either Lysis is obliged to conclude that his parents do not love him, he is not free, and he is wholly unable to pursue his own happiness, or else the common understanding of happiness and freedom must be raised to a philosophical level and must be reexamined.

Now it happens that there are certain areas where Lysis *is* allowed to do as he wishes, specifically: reading, writing, and playing his lyre. Lysis supposes that he understands (*epistamai*) these disciplines and not others (209c2), but of course he is still not free to defy all limits in the practice of these arts. He may have slightly greater liberty when writing, to put the letters in whatever order he desires, than he has when he is reading words already formed before him. Likewise, he may have some leeway in the tightening or loosening of the strings of his lyre or in varying his manner of plucking it, but some intrinsic limit must still obtain for there to be harmony among the strings. In the first set of examples that Socrates utilizes, the boy supposes that he is constrained by various authorities because of his age. With the examples of activities in which Lysis has some knowledge, he seems to grasp slowly the internal, or natural, limits inhering in any art or skill, no longer imagining that once the external constraints are lifted, he will be able to pursue his desires and pleasures without restriction. Lysis needed to have his trust unsettled so his present limits could be made evident to him. Only in this way could he be aroused from his complacency. Through his questions, Socrates shifts the emphasis from limits that constrain extrinsically to limits that restrain intrinsically or naturally, thereby replacing Lysis' conception of freedom as the liberty to do whatever he wishes with a notion of freedom as the positive possibility for taking hold of himself, a freedom concerned precisely with the issue of limits. Knowledge, as well as maturity, requires that one comes to see limits as inherent in all things. Socrates must show Lysis why limits are necessary if he is to be successful in making concrete to him something pivotal about his character.

To accomplish this, Socrates shows Lysis that there are many kinds of limits, some of which, like illiteracy, emanate from the individual and some of which, like the laws governing the age of majority, are externally imposed. But if Lysis were to believe that if these conventional restraints would be lifted, he would be entirely free, Socrates also shows him how these limits are only the most overt kind of constraint upon his desires; many other more subtle limits, in fact, hold Lysis back from attaining his goals. Therefore, the first answer to the question "From whom or from what is Lysis being cut loose in the *Lysis*?" is the surreptitious limits that covertly bind him. Socrates attempts to emancipate Lysis from the subtle dominion of the most covert kind of trust that presently constrains him. Lysis needs to be cut loose from his customary moorings because, in his present circumstances, his reliance upon familiar authority constrains him much more completely than does his pedagogue or any external master.[33] It is precisely this cutting loose from latent trust in the familiar, through the hypothetical occlusion of various kinds of external constraints and conventional practices that would normally be operative, that is the purpose of Socrates' careful subversion of every important kind of authority in his initial approach to the boy. Socrates will make problematic Lysis' trust in familial, political, religious, and poetic authority.

Now since one's latent beliefs predispose one to take for granted certain behaviors, persons, and arguments, reliance upon what is familiar not only characterizes the act of trusting, it also is the linchpin undergirding such acts of trust, the affinity or kinship that disposes people to trust what they do. At this level, trust explains the attraction of like by like. It is this most basic, unreflective level of trust, the predisposition toward what is, pre-philosophically, most congenial or most kindred, that Plato masterfully unearths in Socrates' first encounter with Lysis. This covert dimension of trust is what people take the least trouble over or have the least concern for in their lives.[34] Even though Plato does not employ any technical expression for this distinction in the dialogue—no form of the word trust (*pistis*) is even used here—[35] the *Lysis* delineates three levels of trust—entrusting (placing something in another's care), explicit trust (presupposed in any act of entrusting), and wholly latent trust, of which one is completely unaware—evidencing important ways in which trust is precisely what is assumed by the climactic argument to Lysis.

Section 2.b.2 Step Two—The Arousal: Fanning the Flames of Desire

As his examples with Lysis become increasingly outrageous, Socrates appears to be awakening in Lysis the natural human desire for "the more" (*to pleion*), the desire to get the better of everyone and the most of everything.[36] Socrates begins to inflame the powerful reservoir of passions in Lysis, for insofar as Lysis overlooks the intrinsic harmony and order that function as a limit in reading, writing, and music, he may be led to abandon himself to the insatiable desire born of spiritedness and acquisitiveness. Socrates arouses the boy's desire for "the more" still further when he proclaims that on the very day that Lysis becomes knowledgeable, his father will turn over all of his affairs to him. Socrates not only asserts that the father will place Lysis in charge of his household, he tells the youth that after his father trusts him, his neighbors, the city of Athens, and even the Persian king will all entrust him with their affairs as well.

The hyperbolic promise that Socrates holds out to Lysis is that when the boy acquires prudent knowledge, his legitimate claim to authority will be recognized by everyone, and his ascension to power will follow automatically. But if Socrates possesses such knowledge himself, contrary to his frequent claims to be ignorant, then his conviction by a jury of his countrymen might provoke doubt that the many will esteem knowledge or lovingly prize the usefulness of those who possess it. And if he does not himself possess such knowledge, how can he give it to Lysis? Even more peculiar is the intimation that only the kind of knowledge Socrates offers is likely to equip Lysis to fulfill his teeming desires.[37] Plato's audience also will recall the ambiguities and paradoxes in Socrates' professions to lack knowledge himself and to be unable to teach formulaic knowledge to others.[38] It also might wonder that the redoubtable Socrates exhibits no desire for the kind of authority that Lysis aspires to wield.

Socrates embellishes the hyperbole by arguing that Lysis' rightful dominion will extend seamlessly from his father's household to his neighbor's, to Athens, and finally to the Persian empire. He clearly begs a host of questions concerning the difference between useful kinds of knowledge (*technai*) and Socratic wisdom. He also glosses over the mendacious assumption that prudent knowledge alone is a sufficient condition to inspire strangers to turn over their affairs to Lysis. This is interesting, because prudent knowledge (*sophron*) is exactly what Socrates claims here to possess in the greatest proportion vis-à-vis other men. The dialogues often show the philosopher comparing himself to others who lack self-knowledge or self-restraint, both of which are implied by the Greek notion of *sophrosunē*, or soundmindedness. And we shall see from the analysis of Alcibiades' *Symposium* speech in Chapter 4 that Socrates is portrayed as a paragon of *sophrosunē*. The emphasis on prudence with Lysis provokes one to wonder to what extent his own soundmindedness is linked to his self-knowledge, specifically to his prudent disdain for political office or material possessions. It would surely seem that his utter lack of concern for modes of political and material exchange places Socrates beyond the reach of corruption and bribery in his dealings with others. He is not a slave to anyone just because he is always the master of every situation; rather, he is not a slave because he does not care for the material and political things by which men in classical Athens commonly appraised one another. It will become increasingly apparent how his behavior in this conversation also contravenes the prevalent subjugation/domination paradigm for social relations.

In his argument to Lysis, Socrates pretends to overlook the bivalent trajectory of a *technē* that can be either combined with the excellences of character to produce good ends or divorced from those excellences and directed toward bad ends. It is a recurrent theme in the dialogues that the arts admit of contraries, thus the doctor who can heal also is the one who can harm most efficiently, albeit not strictly speaking in his capacity *as doctor*.[39] In the *Lysis*, Socrates and Lysis, in their imaginary roles as doctors, may rub ashes in the afflicted eyes of the Persian king's son, and, as cooks, they may throw handfuls of salt into the king's soup, but the ethical ambiguity inherent in the arts makes it likely that those in positions of authority will value someone they trust more than someone they do not, even if the latter is more competent. People tend naturally to entrust their affairs to someone in whom they have a prior trust. Socrates sidesteps this difficulty entirely when he asserts that he and Lysis shall be permitted to replace the king's own son in supervising the food preparation. Here Socrates is pushing his examples to a comic extreme in administering his lesson to the gullible young Lysis.

By this point, Plato's audience will no doubt look askance at the extent of Socrates' hyperbole with the innocent, ebullient Lysis. Taking this exchange seriously compels one to question what the argument presupposes here, namely the trust that is a precondition for any act of entrusting. Rather than simply begging the question of trust,[40] however, Plato spurs his audience to contemplate the movement from Lysis' implicit trust to the unacknowledged trust that is patently necessary for Socrates' examples to be plausible. By hypothetically and imaginatively eliminating all extrinsic limits, Socrates brings Lysis face-to-face with his own character limits, the most basic *trust* in whatever is akin (*oikos*) to him, just because it is familiar. This is a limit that every person takes for granted; indeed, the act of taking for granted itself is at the heart of all processes of typification, and this seems to be grounded in the principle of affinity, of the attraction of like by like.

At this point the impassioned Lysis could understandably be carried away by excitement over the intoxicating possibilities that Socrates has entertained to him. Had Socrates left the matter here, he would arguably have done more to propagate Lysis' *pleonectic* desires than to actuate his recognition of limits. Leading the discussion to the subject of the friend, though, interjects another kind of limit into the conversation, with the aim of deflating Lysis' unbounded desire. For not only do relations with others cultivate an awareness of, and respect for, limits, modulating those spirited ambitions to "get the better of" everyone and everything, but the way Socrates introduces "the friend" leads the discussion first through the issue of knowledge.[41] Socrates claims that only knowledge renders one useful and free. With regard to those things about which they acquire prudence, Socrates says:

> everyone . . . will entrust them to us; we will do in regard to these matters whatever we wish, and no one will voluntarily obstruct us. Rather, we ourselves shall be free in regard to them and rulers over others, and these things will be ours, for we shall profit from them. (*Lys.* 210b–c)

Socrates goes on to insist that if Lysis does not acquire good sense, no one will entrust anything to him. He will not rule over others, but he will be subject to them. Rather than gaining profit, he will be disenfranchised. Assuming the role of prolocutor for Lysis, Socrates concludes that if Lysis does not attain wisdom, he will be entirely useless. He will be loved, even by his parents, only insofar as he is useful. The argument concludes that no one is a friend to anyone, and no one loves anyone, who is useless.[42]

Socrates is taking more and more for granted as his humbling of Lysis nears its climax. Interchanging prudence, or "good sense" (*phronoumen*), with both skill and wisdom, he frames Lysis' alternatives in extremes that admit no middle ground. Moreover, he seems to allow the commonsense understanding of freedom as doing whatever one desires to stand; he emphasizes the profitable element of skill rather than the possibility that it may lead progressively to "good sense" and wisdom; he makes utility the basis of all friendship and love, even parental love (which seems most unselfish of all); and, most noticeably, he abandons the essential condition of trust that he had stipulated earlier.

Socrates supplies a qualification for the father to entrust (*epitrepsein*) the management of his household to Lysis (209c). The father must be convinced (*egestai*) that his son's thinking is better than his own. Lysis' neighbor applies the same criterion as the father (209c–d). The Athenians need only "perceive that you think capably," Socrates tells Lysis (209d). The Persian king will want a demonstration of their culinary talents before entrusting his food preparation to Lysis and Socrates (209d–e). But this same king is ready to turn over to them the care of his son if he merely assumes that they are skilled in the medical art (210a). When he generalizes from these examples to make his argument to Lysis (210b), Socrates omits any conditional term that would establish the grounds for trust in the boy. He fails to stipulate that one who would entrust his affairs to Lysis needs to be convinced, or to perceive, or to receive a demonstration, or at least to suppose, that Lysis possesses a particular skill. What is more, possessing this skill would not ensure that Lysis possesses either the proper prudence (practical wisdom), or a good ethical disposition.

Section 2.b.3 Step Three—The Chastening: Reimposing Limits

The learning process both transgresses existing limits and uncovers new ones. To become knowledgeable is to push back one's previous limits. Yet knowledge simultaneously unveils limits that were heretofore wholly latent or not yet present at all. When Lysis becomes as skilled in other matters as he is in reading, writing, and playing his lyre, others may come to value his expertise in those areas. But knowledge also will make him aware of the natural boundaries inherent in any art or skill. Socrates is willing to overlook all of the difficulties raised by his hyperbolic argument to Lysis in order to isolate the problem of limits and the unexamined connection of limits to trust in the familiar. Through such isolation, the trust that was previously presupposed is now set in relief for Lysis. With regard to knowledge, Socrates suggests that *technē* combined with practical wisdom (*phronesis*) may evolve into genuine wisdom, as Lysis begins to embrace the whole of knowledge. When he attains good sense in this way, people will have sufficient reason to trust him. And only when people trust him will they entrust the management of their affairs to him.

The turn toward knowledge transfigures Lysis' focus from the perspective of a subjugated individual to a vantage point from which limits can be conceived as immanent in all things. In this way, Plato has Socrates reorient Lysis with respect to his own limits. Whereas he first believes that restrictions are placed upon him as a result of his age, now he understands that these restrictions are imposed on him because he lacks understanding or knowledge. The investigation of limits in this way reveals something pivotal about Lysis' freedom. This shift that Socrates effects transports Lysis beyond the restricted viewpoint of the superintended individual, for whom all limits appear as a constraint. From his new vista, Lysis may be able to grasp how such boundaries not only restrict him but shape his character and self-understanding. Socrates shows Lysis how various limits combine to forge his character and civic identity, illustrating how limits form and produce what Lysis is. Thus the various boundaries around him must be seen as having the positive, constructive effect of molding him. Of course, some kinds of limits are more pliable than others. Certain invariable human boundaries, such as those imposed by time and space, may be less amenable to alteration than the kinds of limits belonging to specific individuals in particular circumstances. What is more, even when an individual's limits cannot be permanently altered, they may occasionally be transgressed. Perhaps this explains why Socrates begins his capture of Lysis by appearing to transgress established authority. To conventional wisdom, every placing in question of established authority is a transgression. So when Socrates hypothetically removes the limits constraining Lysis, this might have appeared as a transgression of traditional authority.

Socrates completes the humbling by telling Lysis, in effect, that he has no right to think highly of himself inasmuch as he is not yet thoughtful at all. He has already (208e–209a) led the boy to the conclusion that he will derive no benefit from his possessions, his noble rank, or his body if he does not acquire good sense, thereby disabusing the youth of any conceit that he might still harbor with respect to his natural gifts. In a manner reminiscent of the way Socrates upbraids Meno and others, he tells Lysis here that he is no better than a slave, since he is not able to do anything he wants to do and rules over no one, and that various hirelings are placed over him.[43] In this humbling that borders on humiliation, the inflammatory aspect of Socrates' erotic approach has given way to the concomitant chastening of Lysis. The humbling targets Lysis' passivity and connects this condition to his glaring lack of self-sufficiency. Lysis not only supposes that all limits constrain his freedom, he assumes that all limits are externally imposed upon him by others. The incisive questioning that Socrates carries out is designed to produce a disruptive effect, one way or another, in the youth.

Lysis reacts positively to the provocation; he does not display anger or despair. He is not dishonored by Socrates' strong antidote, although the reproach in front of others must surely have been painful. In the chastening of Lysis, we can see why refutation plays such an important role in Socrates' first approach to many interlocutors. Why is refutation so critical to his strategy? What should the positive outcome be of a successful refutation? Perhaps the clearest formulation of the desired result is given in the *Sophist,* when the visitor tells Theaetetus that *sophrosunē* is the desired outcome of a cross-examination and refutation (*elenchos*) for the cleansing of the soul, explaining why this purgative step is so vital:

> The people who are being examined see this [their inconsistencies] get angry at themselves, and become calmer toward others. They lose their inflated and rigid beliefs about themselves that way, and no loss is pleasanter to hear or has a more lasting effect on them.... [T]he soul, too, won't get any advantage from any learning that's offered to it until someone shames it by refuting it, removes the opinions that interfere with learning, and exhibits it cleansed, believing that it knows only those things that it does know, and nothing more. (*Soph.* 230b–d, White trans.)

Lysis confirmed that he learned something from these examples when he offered a more thoughtful response in his second attempt to explain why his parents entrust reading, writing, and music to him while forbidding him to do the other things that Socrates enumerates. Lysis explained, "I suppose ... it's because I understand (*epistamai*) these things, but not those" (209c2). He had, of course, first attempted to explain why so many people rule over him by saying, "That's because I'm not yet of age, Socrates" (209a4). Socrates wasted no time in expressing his doubt that this was the reason for the restrictions placed upon him. Lysis' more thoughtful response here prompts Socrates to ratify his achievement with the appellation "best of men" (*ariste*), and later he will refer to the youth's "love of wisdom (*philosophia*)" (213d7).

It is instructive to consider the way in which Lysis behaves during the balance of the dialogue. He is not the dominant interlocutor; Menexenus talks more than Lysis does. As Menexenus returns to the conversation, Lysis urges Socrates to perform on his comrade the same procedure that had unsettled him. But Socrates exhorts Lysis to try to recall the steps of the argument himself and to imitate him by rehearsing these steps to his friend, soliciting help from Socrates later only if he cannot remember everything. The philosopher exhorts him by declaring that Lysis had listened attentively throughout their conversation, thus Socrates considers him capable of questioning his friend as he himself had just been questioned by the philosopher. Socrates' remarks to Lysis here strongly suggest, quite surprisingly, that he thinks this young character is capable of carrying out a Socratic cross-examination after just one brief encounter. In his tutorial way, Socrates is encouraging Lysis to become an active participant in his own self-improvement rather than to remain merely a passive object of others' affection. His erotic approach to Lysis is shown to culminate in the exemplification of something that can apparently be appropriated and employed by the youth. This seems to be Socrates' belief, even though the boy is very young and even though their conversation has been quite short. Chapter 3 will show that he takes the same approach with Alcibiades.

Through such encounters, Plato's audience is permitted to see the synergistic effect of Socrates' erotic strategy on boys like Lysis. Once subdued, Lysis becomes an animated auditor of Socrates' contest with Menexenus. He is so absorbed in the discussion that he blurts out the answer to a question that Socrates has directed to his friend. Lysis' eagerness to defend his friend causes him to blush with embarrassment over his own impropriety.[44] But this blush betokens a new self-awareness in Lysis. At the beginning of their next exchange, Lysis is much more circumspect and cautious with Socrates. In this, his second and final exchange with the philosopher, a discussion that begins with an exploration of the conflicting stories poets tell about friendship, Lysis demurely equivocates in his answers to Socrates and becomes more tentative as the dialogue progresses.[45] Unlike the hostility that Meno displays toward the bewitching "torpedo-fish"[46] Socrates, Lysis is sobered by the disquieting experience that he has undergone in this pedagogue's hands, clearly exhibiting the optimal benefit from the humbling described in the *Sophist*.

Apparently, Lysis and Menexenus would rather stay with the philosopher at the end of the dialogue than leave with their pedagogues. With this intimation in its final scene, the *Lysis* depicts the complete role reversal between Socrates and his interlocutors. The hunter has become the hunted, while the hunted have been captured and set free. Whereas the feigning lovers—such as Hippothales—purport to teach virtue and wisdom, in exchange for a little pleasure,[47] Socrates shows himself to be the one from whom the boys can truly learn. That Plato does not show Socrates "going all the way" in his homoerotic game with these boys makes it easier to see what the boys get from Socrates than what Socrates gets from the boys.[48] Though Socrates first had to pursue them, entering their schoolyard and seducing them in conversation, breaching and transforming their view of the world, one imagines that after he has empowered him, Socrates will be hounded at least by Lysis, his new, knowledge-hungry associate.

The *Lysis* is one of several examples of this dramatic reversal. In the *Lysis*, Socrates both wins Lysis' favor and supplants him as the object of adoration in the dialogue. What does Socrates give to boys like Lysis that makes this ugly old man so endearingly attractive to them? Socrates offers himself as the paradigmatic example of freedom, and this is an exciting and a desirable quality in the eyes of these young men. The philosopher attempts to utilize Lysis' enchantment and his philosophical nature to trigger the process of self-rule in him, offering him a mode of access to his own capacities. Given this effect, it is no wonder that Socrates sparks explosive reactions in certain interlocutors because of his self-sufficiency and idiosyncratic self-mastery. The philosopher's tactics are designed to spark the discovery of untapped potential or unacknowledged conceit in them, and this is not always well received. It is interesting that the key features exhibited in Socrates' example of philosophic freedom seem to be qualities that he can share with others without any consequent diminution of his own share of them. This result illustrates the essential difference between the competition for material goods and the competition for excellence and goodness. Whereas the competition for material goods is often a zero-sum game where only one person wins and the others lose, in the competition for the good things Socrates is holding out, everyone wins, because everyone is enriched through the process of competing for them. Perhaps this is also one good way to distinguish the "gift" that Socrates offers from things that can be transacted or acquired for a price. His gift must not be conceived within a market or an exchange economy, because it is incommensurable with material goods. The philosopher's gift to others is not reduced by sharing it. Likewise, his own power, like his wisdom, might be intensified rather than lessened through his empowerment of others.[49] His conversational practice enriches him while rendering him increasingly capable of conferring benefits upon others. This may be one meaning of his claims to be benefitting and perfecting himself through his daily conversations.

Contrary to the accusation that Alcibiades will make in *Symposium*, the *Lysis* shows that Socrates' erotic approach has more in common with an act of seduction than with any kind of an assault. In a seduction, the other is mobilized subtly through an arousal that converts passivity into activity. Socrates seduces others by getting them to begin an unfamiliar process. He does this by arousing aspirations that the other scarcely realizes he has. By beginning with the exaggeration of their own desires and then proceeding through his incendiary arousal, Socratic seduction makes youths think that it is their own desires that first necessitate such a transformation. But does not all seduction in some way involve this complicity? Hence, even though seduction is often predicated on a disproportion in power, it requires cooperation from the one being seduced that is not present in the act of sheer domination, such as, for example, in the sexual assault for which the satyrs were renowned.

However, to some of Socrates' interlocutors, this nuance may have seemed of little consequence. When Alcibiades compares the philosopher to the Sileni (*Symp.* 215a–b), it is to highlight the propinquity between Socrates' methods and the brutal offenses for which the satyrs were noted.[50] But, in fact, Socrates' behavior in carrying out the seduction of boys such as Lysis would have been viewed as even worse than the exploits of the satyrs, for since seduction entails an aspect of complicity, it was viewed as more egregious than rape in classical Athens. Dover argues that an Athenian of the late fifth century or the early fourth century would perceive the difference between the two acts in terms of the offense to the "guardian" of the victim. Since it is the affront to the citizen-steward and not to the feelings of the victim that determines the severity of the injury, seduction, because it implies some acquiescence, was a worse offense than rape.[51]

Some of the most important lessons of the *Lysis* concern the problem of freedom. The dialogue exhibits the Socratic practice of philosophic freedom as a counterweight to the prevalent ways in which it was exercised. In these dialogues in which his role reverses from hunter to hunted in the game of Eros the philosopher plays with youths such as Lysis, it is worth stressing that Socrates' erotic strategy does not appear to perpetuate the endless cycle of escalation that characterizes contests for honor, wealth, and power. The kind of self-rule that Socrates shows Lysis navigates a middle course between ruling over others and being a slave to them.[52] So the enticement of Socrates' erotic approach does consist of a kind of liberation, but the freedom he confers upon Lysis entails the awareness of necessary limits.

SECTION 2.C CONCLUSION: THE POSITIVE RESULTS OF THE *LYSIS*

The experts seem to disagree quite fundamentally about the chief results of the *Lysis*.[53] If Plato scholars find the *Lysis*' argumentation unwieldly and inconclusive, then its generalist readers may rightly wonder what sense Socrates expected these boys to make of the sometimes confusing and often free-ranging argumentation through which he leads them. These arguments comprise more than half of the dialogue. The combative exchanges with Menexenus in particular appear to contain so much eristic that some early commentators were led to conclude that the *Lysis* was a spurious work.[54] It is crucial to remind ourselves here, however, that a failure at the level of the dramatic action or the inconclusiveness of an argument may be consciously crafted in this way by Plato to create a vehicle for learning by his audience.

Plato's audience can learn a great deal by paying close attention to Socrates' refutations of the various attempts by the boys to provide a comprehensive account of friendship. Aristotle surely did. It may be that the dialogue provides an adequate treatment of friendship only when considered as a whole, none of its definitions being adequate on their own. Socrates refutes three attempts to lay down a thesis about friendship, and something positive can be concluded by the conversation's larger audience from each of them.

The philosopher first refutes Menexenus, in the course of investigating the eristic question, "When someone loves someone, which one becomes a friend of the other, the one who loves of the loved or the loved one of the lover?" (*Lys.* 212a–b). It is striking how differently Socrates behaved with Lysis than he did with Menexenus in the adversarial contest he initiated with Lysis' friend. We have seen that their respective propensities for trusting different things necessitate the divergent approaches to the two boys. Whereas Lysis trusts in his natural gifts and in traditional authorities—his parents, his religion, his city, and the poets[55]—Menexenus tends to rely heavily upon argumentation, especially arguments of the eristic kind, for which the Sophists were notorious.[56] He has, we learn, already developed quite a reputation for being "contentious," or *eristikos* (211b7).

This inaugural question attempts to distinguish the active and passive members of a friendship, so that the investigation can decide whether the friend or the befriended is truly the friend. The account of friendship that emerges from this question does not explore in sufficient detail how one becomes the friend of, or is befriended by, another, so in the end it is unable to clarify sufficiently how both parties can be called *philos*. Since an account of friendship would seem obliged to clarify the meaning of "friend," the investigation with Menexenus appears to be ultimately inadequate. Socrates' refutation of the boy's argument, though, also forces him to differentiate the love of entities that cannot reciprocate from the love of beings that can. Philosophy, of course, belongs to the class of things that one can love that cannot love back. This first line of inquiry seems insufficient, because what is truly *philos* is never adequately determined.

Socrates continues the conversation with Lysis, refuting two opposing hypotheses about friendship: the thesis that like is attracted to like and the thesis that opposites attract. By denying that two wicked people can ever truly be friends because they are not in harmony within themselves, Socrates is able to introduce the idea of the Good into the discussion of friendship. This causes a modification of the first thesis. Since the wicked are incapable even of being friends with themselves, according to Socrates, it would seem that only two people who are alike in goodness can truly be called friends. But because Socrates assumes here an extreme sense of good (i.e., that which is wholly or perfectly good), the modified first thesis also appears inadequate. Socrates holds that it is equally unlikely that "like is attracted to like," that is, that two people who are both good can be friends, since he takes goodness in the strictest sense, entailing that each person is self-sufficient, already thoroughly good. He suggests a way out of the impasse by maintaining that friendship arises out of desire, which is a lack or a need for something that one does not, at present, have. This leads the discussion to the third thesis, that "opposites attract." But this thesis fails the test on logical grounds, violating the law of noncontradiction, which is the most fundamental principle of rational discourse. For it would mean that the just and the unjust, the good and the bad, are friends. Since it would make the enemy a friend and the friend an enemy, says Socrates, this definition is untenable.

Socrates has to show that friendship can be motivated by a lack or a desire without that lack entailing complete need or lack, complete badness, if he is to point the way out of this next difficulty. So when he introduces an intermediate or an "in-between" state between full possession of the Good on the one hand and complete corruption or wickedness on the other hand, a solution to the problem emerges. This in-between state will be the place that he locates both the philosopher and the true friend or lover, enabling him to complete his seduction of Lysis. The notion of the intermediate or "in-between" state offers the most promising solution to the dialogue's problem, and something Socrates says near the end of the conversation suggests that Plato's audience will have to go back and examine the whole conversation again, substituting *oikos* (the akin or kindred) for *philos* in order to grasp a possible sense in which it may be right to say that like is attracted to like or that good people may be friends. Socrates says, "It appears, then, Menexenus and Lysis, that passionate love (*Eros*), friendship (*philia*) and desire (*epithumia*) happen to be for what is akin (*oikos*), as it seems" (221e). The positive implications of this substitution may now be adumbrated.

Whether or not Lysis or Menexenus can construct a coherent, comprehensive account of friendship out of the various strands of argumentation that their conversations with Socrates left dangling, it is incumbent upon us to attempt to do so. Recall how Socrates illustrated the in-between state between pure goodness and absolute badness, which alone was said to be a friend to the Good (216e). To clarify this in-between position, he used the example of coloring Lysis' hair to show that something can be present in a thing without changing the thing's nature. Another way of "being present" to it might alter its nature permanently and irreversibly, just as Lysis' hair could become white either because of dye or because of age. In the realm of human character, when "badness" is present in the first, remediable sense, Socrates calls this position "in-between." For someone in this in-between state, neither good nor bad itself, the bad is present in it without it being present so thoroughly as to corrupt the person's character. Rather than obliterating any desire for the Good, the presence of the lack in this sense spurs a desire for the Good one lacks (217e). Being in the intermediate position, human beings are denied complete possession of the Good, but they are permitted an occasional glimpse, hint, or intimation of it for guidance, as Diotima's speech in the *Symposium* suggests (see, especially, 212a–b). Socrates' suggestion here accomplishes two things:

(1) it posits that only this intermediate can be truly a friend to the Good and Beautiful, allowing the several hypotheses and lines of inquiry left unexplored after Socrates' refutations of the earlier arguments to be rehabilitated,[57] and (2) it positions Socrates, as the philosopher, in this in-between state to complete the "capture" of Lysis.

But here, as Francisco Gonzalez and Aristide Tessitore stress, a problem may arise for all of the human relations in the dialogue.[58] If one in this intermediate position desires only the Good, what is most *philos* cannot be any living person per se. It may have seemed at first that the doctor became a friend due to disease and for the sake of health, but the present argument reveals that it had been health all along, rather than the doctor, that had been the most desired friend, the ultimate good. This may be why Socrates professes to desire a friend more than anything else in the world (211e). His desire can never be fulfilled completely by any mere human relationship because, for him, all desire is ultimately a desire for the Good and the Beautiful that animates and shines through the particular person one calls "friend." Socrates' ignorance impels him toward wisdom, and in this in-between position, he is neither fully wise nor wholly ignorant. He is portrayed as someone who is committed to being a friend to wisdom, for this defines his practice of philosophy, and this constant relationship with wisdom may sometimes threaten to supersede interpersonal friendships, yet this results more from the shortcomings of the particular friends than from any failure in the notion of friendship. The *Lysis* ends up showing that, far from being exclusive of interpersonal relationships, philosophy is an activity most conducive to true friendships. Paradoxically, it is only when human friendships are grasped as in service to the Good and, therefore, perhaps, as instrumental to the activities for the sake of which they are directed, that it seems to become first possible for humans to treat others as more than mere tools or instruments to be manipulated for their own ends. In pointing toward the Good as the ultimate object of all human striving, including the desire for friendship and love, Socrates is suggesting that philosophy is the activity best capable of furnishing the basis for all genuine human relations. In this way, the *Lysis* displays an alternative to the subjugation/domination framework for conceiving human interaction.

What is the Good and the Beautiful toward which the philosopher, as the truest lover, maintains a constant relation? The *Lysis* shows that the truly beautiful and good that the friend loves is something ultimately beyond it, for the sake of which the first something is loved. The argument in the *Lysis* culminates with the notion of a *proton philon,* that is, an ultimate friend for the sake of which all other good things are loved (219c). This *proton philon* turns out, of course, to be the source of friendship that Socrates has been seeking all along. The ultimate inconclusiveness of the dialogue results mainly from the present inability of Socrates' two young interlocutors to go further in the process of clarifying this Good that has now been identified as the ultimate object of desire. Yet it would seem difficult, if not impossible, even for the philosopher to say why the Good is desired, or to explicate the source of desire itself. The most Socrates himself can offer here is the notion of the "akin," and this late suggestion holds the key to the entire argument. Human beings desire what they lack, but what they lack belongs to them in some fundamental way (221e). Thus human desire announces both a sense of having and of not having whatever it is seeking. Socrates further distinguishes what is akin (*oikos*) from what is like, since he has refuted already the notion that friendship is of like for like. The suggestion he offers—unexplored here, but argued for in other dialogues, most famously in the "band of thieves" example in *Republic* II—is that the Good is akin to all things, while the Bad is alien to them. Socrates explains that only that which is in the intermediate state between the Good and the Bad can be truly friend to the Good. This final hypothesis, along with the notion of the akin, clarifies the entire discussion. Those who are in an in-between state, analogous to Socratic ignorance, and capable of experiencing true friendship, desire the Good that belongs to them, but on which they presently have only an insecure hold. This desire impels one toward the Good by the presence of the Bad, motivated by the sense of lack one experiences because one's badness is not yet so complete as to overwhelm any desire for the Good.

As Gonzalez rightly notes, the sense in which one can "possess" the Good is quite different than the sense in which Lysis wanted to possess those good things he desired when Socrates first questioned him.[59] In contrast to their first exchange, where the philosopher insisted that only by attaining a kind of technical expertise would Lysis be able to possess what is *oikos*, here he says that what is akin has been taken from human beings and, therefore, it is this that humans ultimately desire. This should make clear that the Good at which Socrates' search aims cannot ever be fully possessed in the way that Lysis hoped to be entrusted with those material possessions that will one day rightfully be his. It becomes clear that the way Socrates seemed to conflate technical knowledge and wisdom in his argument to Lysis was necessary to prepare the youth for this slide in the meaning of *oikos*. The Good belongs to the one "in-between" without its being amenable to complete possession or mastery. In the same way, with Plato's model, the genuine beloved "belongs" to his friend without being possessed or mastered. Neither friend can fully possess the ultimate, yet this need not undermine the friendship or produce strife as long as both friends maintain their kinship with the Good. Even quite asymmetrical friendships seem possible as long as the inequality between the friends is ameliorated by the recognition of both parties that neither can claim to possess the Good completely and securely.

Notwithstanding the pronounced gulf that separates their relative progress along the path toward the Good, Socrates and Lysis may still enjoy a kind of friendship based on this model. Even though Socrates seems close to the end of the path and Lysis is just starting out, each may maintain himself, as a friend of the other, in this intermediate state. This will require a constant vigilance against false conceits and ignorance in its various forms. The ongoing awareness of ignorance entails that one be equally vigilant regarding the knowledge of one's other limits and limitations. By completing the circle, the *Lysis* allows readers to grasp the connection that Socrates has been forging between limits and freedom. Philosophy not only explicates this knowledge of limits, it cultivates further the desire for the Good that sustains, through practices such as these conversational inquiries, the one in the in-between state. Socrates' practices in the dialogues exhibit how one can maintain an ongoing relationship to the Good, even though it can be neither known nor possessed completely.

In another sense, however, the *Lysis* presents an account of true asymmetrical friendship. Unlike the more equal friendship between Lysis and Menexenus, Socrates displaces Hippothales, the pseudo lover, becoming the true lover who is most akin to the boys. In true friendship, the lover (*erastēs*) is akin to the beloved (*eromenos*) and should be loved by him in return. The true lover differs from the feigning lover, because the true lover seeks to benefit the beloved rather than endeavoring simply to possess or use him in some kind of transaction or exchange. Friendships need not always be equal, but one way of acting as a superior can enslave by leaping in and taking over for the other, and another way of behaving as a superior can strive to liberate the other for his or her own freedom.[60] Socrates is clearly superior to these boys in age, experience, and wisdom, but he does not exploit his advanced station to possess or manipulate them in any unseemly way. Such a relationship, if genuine, would be most "useful" and beneficial to the one inferior in power and wisdom. This realization adds importance to the qualms to which Socrates gives voice after having ensnared the handsome Lysis. These qualms communicate to Plato's audience that the philosopher has reached the apex of his erotic lesson with the boy and will go no further.

If true friendship no longer depends upon likeness or possession, Socrates' way of practicing philosophy with noble and beautiful youths such as Lysis, exhorting them to their utmost potential in an attempt to confer on them a kind of freedom, is itself an act of friendship. Rather than making true friendship something that can be enjoyed only by people who are already good and wise, the *Lysis* seems to ascribe friendship to those who are "in-between" in goodness and wisdom. The philosopher turns out to be the one who is most *philos*, just as in the *Symposium* the philosopher is the truest lover, even made to replace Eros as the object of praise in the dialogue's dramatic action. The philosopher is the one in the in-between (*metaxu*) position, hence we should perhaps conclude that philosophy transpires as well in this in-between realm.

That Lysis has grown quite fond of Socrates by the end of the dialogue makes clear that he finds the philosopher's seduction much more useful and beneficial than Hippothales' obsequious, sycophantic approach. When the old philosopher includes himself as a friend to the boys at the end of the dialogue (223b), Socrates suggests that some kind of symmetry, if not full reciprocity, exists between them. In the end, the three inquirers seem "ridiculous," because they have been unable to say who the friend is, but they themselves have become friends through the attempt to do so.[61] It is their perplexity about these questions that now secures the bond between them. Since Socrates was able to awaken Lysis' wonder, and because Lysis has become an inquirer and a friend to the Good through his encounter with Socrates, he and Socrates have been transformed into co-lovers (*sunerastēs*). And though the new friends may seem ridiculous to others, as a result of their inability to give a simple definition of friendship or clarify the notion of the Good, they have located the friend in the human realm, in between true goodness and utter wickedness, the realm in which philosophy dwells and the realm wherein the ultimate Good remains akin to them.

Chapter 3

The *Alcibiades I:* Socratic Dialogue as Self-Care

Important similarities connect the *Lysis* and the *Alcibiades I*. Most notably, the reversal of roles between Socrates and the young Alcibiades in this dialogue replicates the pattern of the *Lysis*. Alcibiades, like Lysis, is not only young, noble, handsome, and promising but his desires also resemble those of Lysis' in their immodestly political nature. The yearning for power arouses both characters, and here again, Socrates utilizes a youth's unabashed desire for dominion as the catalyst in his approach. In both dialogues, the philosopher struggles to interject a limit into the desires of these aspiring rulers, prescribing certain prerequisites as essential for their political success. And in both cases, Socrates makes his assistance a precondition for the boys to attain the power they seek. Finally, by the end of both dialogues, Socrates supplants the beautiful, ambitious youth as the locus of the conversation's erotic undercurrent. By trading roles with these young men, who are accustomed to being the object of all forms of attention and praise, Socrates intervenes to attempt to prepare them for their future careers.

He enchants both boys with powerful inducements, inducements exceeding their wildest dreams; but he gives them only provocation, chastisement, and the chance for greater self-awareness, in place of the gifts of power and recognition they feel entitled to receive. And when each boy in turn exhibits his readiness to attend to Socrates like a doting lover, willing to gratify the philosopher's wishes in the role of compliant beloved, Plato has his unconventional lover intensify the humbling. This tactic functions dramatically to go further in purging each youth of his conceits, and on another level it allows Plato to contrast Socratic Eros, and its employment for educational purposes, to the practices of a panderer who is interested only in a homoerotic exchange. Recall the rationale at the heart of Pausanias' argument at *Symposium* 180c–185e for the distinction between a "heavenly" and "common" Aphrodite, that is, between a noble and right way to engage in the sexual aspects of *sunousia*, and the base and wrong way to engage in them (see also Ch. 2, Note 41).

The purpose of Plato's strategy in these dialogues will be shown to extend far beyond simplistically vitiating political life or pointing out its hazards. His Socrates is doing more than striving to dissuade these well-groomed sons of noblemen from entering politics. As a result, the *Lysis* and the first *Alcibiades* are, in key ways, the most extreme of Plato's Socratic dialogues—extreme because of the hyperbole in which Socrates engages, extreme because of the complete reversal of Eros he effects, extreme in virtue of the desires Socrates incites to tantalize his targets, and extreme because of the claims he makes about the nature and extent of his knowledge and efficacy. The *Alcibiades I* is extreme in two additional ways—first in its intensity of focus upon Socrates' appeal to Alcibiades, without any embellishment of the setting (we never learn when or where this conversation takes place) or anything else peripheral to the substance of the conversation itself, and second because Socrates has to spend so much time lecturing Alcibiades before he finally brings the youth to an admission of *aporia*. Ancient commentators on the *Alcibiades I* gave it the subtitle "On the Nature of Man" as a mark of its richness and scope. One of its most important contributions to the composite picture of the philosopher's approach to others is its discussion of "taking trouble over oneself." Clarifying this notion will be the main objective of this chapter, but before turning to an examination of the Socratic counsel, a few preliminary remarks about this dialogue are necessary.

In his perspicuous essay on the *Alcibiades I*, Paul Friedländer argues that the *Alcibiades I* is unique in the Platonic corpus.[1] He sketches several ways in which he believes it is unparalleled. Three distinctive features he stresses are especially worthy of reiteration here. First, noting that, as in the cases of Charmides, Lysis, and Theaetetus, Socrates appears on the scene just when the noble young Athenian boy is ready for him, Friedländer points out that the dramatic impact of this device in the *Alcibiades I* is accentuated by Socrates' first words to the youth.[2] Socrates explains that, until the present moment, the opposition of his divine sign had prevented him from talking to the boy he had long admired and observed from a respectful distance.[3] Plato's audience learns that the god prohibited Socrates from approaching sooner the youth he loved, because any earlier meeting would have proved futile. Socrates senses that the very strangeness of his loyal attendance to Alcibiades, his self-assurance, and his apparent ability to know what he thinks and believes will ensure an attentive audience in the now curious young man.[4]

Second, Friedländer emphasizes that, unlike the *Lysis, Charmides,* and *Euthydemus,* the conversation does not take place in the company of others.[5] Socrates, he notes, is not put in the position of vying with other participants and onlookers for the affections of the one superlative youth. The conversation with Alcibiades, in contrast, is most private, and this reinforces the expectation that their discussion will be open and direct, free of the posturing that an audience might occasion. Rather than having to prove himself a worthy lover in the face of a swarm of rival suitors, Socrates solemnly tells him that he is his truest lover, all the other lovers having run away (cf. *Alc. I* 103a, 134c, and especially 131c–132b).

Third, Friedländer sees the similarity between the beginnings of the *Lysis, Charmides,* and *Alcibiades I.* In all three contexts, the nobility and beauty of the boys is highlighted, and the conversation arises in response to a telltale characteristic of the targeted boy. Friedländer recalls that each dialogue concludes with a cautionary reminder that the process begun in it must be continued beyond the preliminary result it achieves in this one conversation. But whereas the other two dialogues entail a search for definitions that terminate inconclusively, Friedländer writes: "In the *Alkibiades* . . . the great movement of the dialogue is of an entirely different kind. The Socratic–Platonic principle of the state and *paideia* prevails against the hostile forces of tyranny here manifesting themselves in Alkibiades."[6] This leads him to conclude that whereas Charmides, for example, "bears a celebrated name as if by accident, . . . in the *Alkibiades* . . . the historical person himself comes to life in his character and fate" (Friedländer, *Plato,* 2:232).

Despite the brilliance of his insight into this extraordinary dialogue, Friedländer surprisingly conceives its dramatic movement to be unparalleled. He clearly notices the reversal of roles that the three dialogues share and the similarity of their openings, but he does not perceive that Socrates' effect upon Alcibiades resembles, in significant detail, his success with Lysis. He cites the *Charmides* and the *Gorgias* in support of his claim that, in contrast to the *Alcibiades I,* the target interlocutors in these dialogues are not substantially changed by their conversation with Socrates. In Friedländer's view, Charmides and Callicles are only more rigidly ensconced in the condition in which they began: Charmides is only more fond of Socrates, and Callicles is only more subdued, at the end of their conversations. Omitting any mention of the *Lysis* in this connection, Friedländer asserts that the change that Alcibiades undergoes during the course of his conversation with Socrates is unique in Plato's dialogues. This judgment overlooks the transformation, even if only a provisional one, that Lysis experiences through his memorable encounter with Socrates.

This chapter shows that Socrates' initial conversation with the young Alcibiades closely parallels his first encounter with Lysis in important and interesting ways. Most obvious of the parallels between the two dialogues is the way in which Socrates and Alcibiades switch places as "lover" and "beloved" through their conversation. This fact is made explicit at the dialogue's close. In his penultimate remark to Socrates, Alcibiades pledges, "From this day forward, I must and will follow you as you have followed me; I will be the attendant, and you shall be my master" (*Alc. I* 135d). This reversal of roles, effectuated by Socrates' erotic strategy, and familiar from the *Lysis*, will be shown in Chapter 4 to force Socrates to equivocate when Alcibiades attempts to seduce him. The *Symposium*, as Chapter 4 will confirm, provides much greater detail about the relationship between Socrates and Alcibiades than we have in the case of Lysis. I argued in Chapter 2 that a turnaround in Lysis can be justifiably adduced from the signs of his increasingly circumspect, more attentive comportment. That Socrates provokes a change in Lysis is clear from their one meeting, even though there is no evidence about Lysis' future life and fate. (A determination of the long-term outcome of Socrates' effect on him is not required to prove that Lysis undergoes a turnaround through their conversation, which is all that I am claiming.)

In the *Alcibiades I*, Socrates is shown effecting a beneficial transformation also in Alcibiades' self-awareness, convincing him that he must take more trouble over himself if he desires to advise the city about its affairs.[7] To inspire the several oaths and to elicit the promissory pledges he obtains from Alcibiades, Socrates once again employs his finely tuned erotic appeal, complete with the daring inflammation of the passions he believes embolden Alcibiades and the calculated humbling of the contumacious character that this fledgling tyrant displays. But whereas the much younger Lysis succumbs to the philosopher's appeal fairly quickly, with Alcibiades it takes Socrates more than half of the dialogue to finally subdue him, making the change much more noticeable to Plato's audience. And whereas in the *Lysis* it was far from clear what Lysis was supposed to do immediately and concretely with his life, once he became receptive to philosophy and aware of the limitations in his character, here Socrates spells out the central tenets of the *paideusis* that Alcibiades must follow if he truly wishes to improve himself. That Socrates elaborates the practices that comprise the care of the self, first explicitly linking the art by which human beings take trouble over themselves to his conversational method, and then connecting this activity to self-knowledge, points to the highly promising depths of this dialogue.

Once again in this dialogue I focus on Socrates' approach to the target interlocutor. Hence my concern in this chapter will be, first, to elucidate the parallels between Socrates' approach to Lysis and Socrates' approach to Alcibiades, and then to examine closely the positive steps that Socrates spells out concerning the educational regimen that Alcibiades must follow. Initially it will be necessary to trace the main lines of the contentious first part of the dialogue, but it will not be analyzed in detail since what it primarily discloses—Alcibiades' spirited character and his conventional conception of justice—will be issues that will need to be recuperated and developed in the next chapter to clarify Alcibiades' *Symposium* speech. One kind of interlude within the preliminary contest will prove especially illuminating for the broader evaluation of Socrates' educational methods, namely, Socrates' reflections about the prerequisites and ground rules for fruitful dialogue. The great interrogator is often most forthcoming about what makes a good conversation partner in those dialogues in which he confronts the most obdurate interlocutors. Forced by a character's obstinacy to explicate and justify some of his methodological precepts, dialogues such as *Meno* and *Gorgias*, along with *Laches*, *Crito*, *Euthyphro*, and most notably the *Alcibiades I*, afford Plato's audience valuable insights into how Socrates thinks a dialogue should proceed.

The main goal of our examination of this exceptional conversation will be to elaborate the meaning of Socrates' notion of "taking trouble over oneself" or "taking care of oneself" *(epimelesthai sautou)*.[8] With somewhat unusual forthrightness, Socrates begins his appeal in this dialogue purporting to be his first substantive conversation with the young Alcibiades by exhorting him to take more trouble over himself (*Alc. I* 124b–d). This leads to an inquiry into the difference between taking trouble over what belongs to one and taking trouble over oneself (128a–129a). After a brief excursus into the nature of "the self itself" (129b–130d), Socrates supplies a poignant metaphor for self-knowledge—the image of the eyes of the other as a mirror to one's own soul (133a–c). He has already cleared the way to fuse this image to both *sophrosunē* (131b) and conversation (130d–e). Here we reach the heart of the dialogue. "Taking trouble" is said to yield self-knowledge, which implies soundmindedness *(sophrosunē)*, and this self-knowledge is now said to be achievable through dialogue. With this, Socrates brings together his central lines of argument to Alcibiades. It does not seem accidental either that the simile he uses also is an image charged with erotic energy. Steven Forde finds it remarkable that Plato opens the *Alcibiades I* by having Socrates communicate his erotic attachment to the youth, and then depicts, through their conversation, how the philosopher's distinctively erotic quality is imparted to Alcibiades. This would certainly seem to provide evidence of a benefit being conferred by Socrates' efforts. At the end of the Royal Tale (124b), Socrates will declare that Alcibiades too has become erotic (or at least *more* erotic), as the dialogue reaches its apex with a most suggestive analogy for self-knowledge. Let us see how Socrates accomplishes this.

SECTION 3.A DISARMING ALCIBIADES: THE PRELIMINARY CONTEST

The philosopher approaches Alcibiades just when the young, brilliant nephew of Pericles is on the verge of reaching the age of majority. He will soon assume his rightful position alongside other Athenian citizens in the assembly and begin to advise them about the city's affairs. Socrates boldly initiates their first conversation by claiming to know just what Alcibiades thinks.[9] As was the case in his approach to Lysis, Socrates' elaboration of what Alcibiades thinks opens the deeper issue regarding what the young man believes and what he trusts most profoundly.[10] Socrates says that he knows how great Alcibiades' ambition is; it is so fantastic that if a god were to place any limits upon his extravagant desires, Alcibiades would surely prefer to die instead of living under such fetters. Bringing to bear upon Alcibiades his now-familiar tactics for fanning the flames of passion, Socrates incites the gifted youth by declaring that he will not be able to fulfill his aspirations without the help that the philosopher alone (though always aided by the god) can provide (*Alc. I* 105e).

In the first part of this dialogue, Socrates adopts the role of the combative cross-examiner, the petulant "gadfly," which he claims at *Apology* 30e to be his divinely appointed vocation in the *polis*. The role of gadfly as Socrates explains it to his jurors turns out to include at least the following three functions: (1) exhorting others to care more for *aretē* than for the other goods (money, pleasure, honor), that is, to get their priorities in order; (2) examining (or putting to the test) those who say they do care; and (3) exposing any lack of proper care that his examination reveals (cf. *Ap.* 29d–30b). With Alcibiades, Socrates says that he has clearly detected, through prolonged observation, the inflated opinion that Alcibiades has of himself, but he has only now been released to speak to him. The accuracy of his appraisal and the directness of his overture take Alcibiades by surprise. Socrates not only unmasks Alcibiades' grandiose aspirations, he confronts him with the disheartening news that the future statesman has been poorly trained and is thus inadequately prepared to meet his ultimate rivals in the political arena.

Socrates argues that politics is directly concerned with matters of justice and that Alcibiades has not begun to raise these issues for himself. There never appears to have been a time when Alcibiades was not cocksure about the nature of justice, so Socrates wonders how he could have learned what he assumes he already knows. Socrates wonders further how he can purport to advise others about such momentous matters at the ripe old age of nineteen. He asks Alcibiades, "How, then, is it likely that you should know the just and unjust things, when you are in such uncertainty and have plainly never learned them from anyone nor discovered them yourself?" The philosopher adroitly pits Alcibiades against the many, appealing to his sense of superiority and nobility. He brings the aspiring statesman to see that whoever cannot teach trivial matters—as the great statesmen of the day seem unable to do—cannot be presumed able to teach matters of the greatest importance. Alcibiades' spiritedness is manifested at once in his desire for victory and honors. Having Socrates trigger the confident young man's spiritedness is one way that Plato drives home the point to his audience about the proximity of Eros to *thumos*. Socrates seems to want to bring Alcibiades to see this too, by bringing him to see that, until he grasps that Eros does not try to get the better of everyone in everything, he cannot really become erotic. From the opening lines of the dialogue, Socrates also has been trying to bring him to see that his self-conceit is out of place.[11] We have seen already that this is precisely the purpose in general of the humbling experiences to which these young men are subjected by Socrates' refutations.

Alcibiades' resolve at 112d is beginning to wear down. Socrates has argued that the many are not unanimous in anything, and being of different minds about matters of justice provokes them to do each other the greatest harm. What follows next is an intriguing digression that casts light on Socrates' question-and-answer style of philosophizing. Alcibiades responds to Socrates' confrontational question about the just and unjust things by reluctantly conceding, "From what you say, it is not likely" (112d10). Socrates then asks if he realizes that this is not well spoken, to which Alcibiades retorts, "Why? Do you not say I have no knowledge about the just and unjust things?" When Socrates answers, "No, indeed," Alcibiades is lost. Socrates asks him whether two is greater than one and by how much. When Alcibiades answers, Socrates unveils the point of his lesson with a follow-up question: "Then which of us is the one saying that two is greater than one?" (112e10–11).

Alcibiades admits that he is the one saying this. Socrates leads him through a series of similar questions designed to convince Alcibiades that in the interrogatory method, the one answering the questions is the one saying something. Supposing that Alcibiades is finally ready to take responsibility for his beliefs, Socrates moves to tether Alcibiades to his answers, concluding, "And what was spoken was that Alcibiades the fair, the son of Kleinias, does not have knowledge concerning just and unjust things but supposes he does, and is about to go to the assembly to advise the Athenians on things he knows nothing about?" (113b8–11). Socrates, the questioner throughout, quotes Euripides and declares to Alcibiades, "You have heard 'from yourself these things, not from me'" (113c2–4).

The humbling of the young, would-be statesman should now be complete. But Alcibiades cannot yet bring himself to defer to Socrates. He still cannot imagine what he possibly needs to learn and tries to weasel out of his predicament. He thinks it is enough to know the expedient, leaving aside the question of justice. Socrates reproaches Alcibiades for not seeing that he is pretending to have the same kind of knowledge, about something he has neither learned from anyone nor discovered for himself, that led him into a quandary about the nature of justice (113e5–114b3). Here Socrates presents an alternative to him: "If you wish, question me as I did you, or present your own argument yourself."[12] When Alcibiades expresses his doubt that he could present a convincing argument, Socrates tells him that if he imagines himself capable of persuading people in the Assembly, he should be able to persuade his one particular interlocutor in the present context. Socrates pretends to discern no difference—and Alcibiades is not savvy enough to realize any—between making speeches to the Assembly and submitting to the one-on-one examination of a Socratic interrogation.[13] Alcibiades threatens to cease answering Socrates' "insolent" questions, and Socrates explains to him that to be genuinely persuaded, he must certify the argument by expressing it himself. This can only be accomplished by answering Socrates' questions, learning through his own attestation what he really thinks.[14]

Socrates presents another argument, which concludes by showing that the just and the expedient come down to the same thing. The philosopher constructs this argument to demonstrate that Alcibiades does not even know the expedient, since what is advantageous or expedient is intimately connected with the question of justice. This impasse, and the need to bring Alcibiades to see that the question "What is justice?" and "What is expedience?" may amount to the same question, has furnished Socrates with an opportunity to illuminate the requisite grounds both for effective persuasion and for a constructive conversation. After rehearsing his arguments to assure the youth that he does not know "the expedient" or "the advantageous" any more than he knew the just and the unjust, Socrates finally brings Alcibiades to the experience of *aporia* (at 116e2–4), causing the now-chastened youth to swear again "by the gods." Socrates gently explains to him the nature of his perplexity, reassuring him that such confusion is necessary to expose the conceit of wisdom, a condition that arises from the mistaken belief that one knows something when one does not. The young man's conundrum is due in greater measure to his arrogance of wisdom (the conceit that he knows when he does not) than to sheer ignorance. The way in which Socrates here explains the nature of Alcibiades' perplexity will become important in Chapter 4 for the evaluation of the philosopher's long-term failure with him.

It should be clear by now that bringing them to an admission of *aporia* cannot be the philosopher's only objective with youths such as Lysis and Alcibiades. For although each is brought to confess confusion, this moment neither concludes their conversation with him nor signals the end of the philosopher's attempt to benefit them. Refuting them is not an end in itself, thus it is important to pay attention to the direction a dialogue takes after the admission of perplexity has been reached, as this interpretation shall attempt to do. Whether or not one allows the philosopher's subsequent strategy to qualify either as teaching or giving counsel, the persistent Socrates certainly seems to exert a yeoman's effort to lay down a prescription for what Alcibiades must do to prepare himself for rulership after the youth here declares that he does not know anymore what he thinks.

Just when Socrates has spelled out for Alcibiades that the argument, as well as his own tongue, has accused him of the greatest ignorance, namely, of believing himself to be wise when he is not, the still haughty Alcibiades detects another loophole. If the demos is as ignorant as Socrates claims, Alcibiades imagines that he will easily be able to get the better of the many without any further training (119b–c). Socrates laments this supposition, both for Alcibiades' sake and on account of his love for him (119c5). He realizes that Alcibiades' intractability mandates something extraordinary. But, interestingly, what Socrates produces next is not another argument, but a *muthos* (myth) to complete the refutation of Alcibiades. What Forde calls the Royal Tale (120a–124b) fashions opponents for Alcibiades who are no longer mere mortals but are rather the mythical sons of the kings and queens of Persia and Lacedaemonia who have been superbly trained in the arts of self-care and in the cardinal, Socratic excellences. Forde reads the tale as "an exhortation to virtue" which, he says, is designed "to use Alcibiades' ambition to get him to care earnestly for his self-perfection" (232). He points out that the challenge the tale holds for Alcibiades is to rediscover his own excellence in some other aspect of himself besides his innate powers or brute force.[15]

Very early in the dialogue, when Socrates curiously cites Homer as the pedagogue of the many, his references to Odysseus and Achilles intimate that the common counsel about what justice is somehow points to a kind of erotic longing.[16] Here, Socrates not only needs to validate Alcibiades' sense of his own worth, following the humbling lesson he has just meted out to him, he also is trying to relocate his sense of excellence in something other than love of gain or victory, fueled by an acquisitive *thumos* that seeks to get the better of everyone and everything. Having heard Socrates' story, Alcibiades is at last ready to learn what trouble has to be taken in order to achieve greatness. Socrates tries to get Alcibiades to supply the answer to his own question. He asks him to say in what matters he will be called upon for counsel by the Athenians. The philosopher succeeds in eliciting from him that these matters will have to do with their common business as citizens; the young man says that these will be the same matters about which the wisest gentlemen will deliberate. Alcibiades seems to grasp that this involves the proper function of each person within the city and the perpetuation of concord. But when he is pushed to say what kind of friendship (*philian*) or concord (*homonoian*) it is, about which a ruler will need to be wise, Alcibiades resorts to the model of the family, as Forde shows.

This answer only accentuates the dialogue's tension between the care for oneself and the care for the city. This tension is between opposing trajectories in Alcibiades' concern, one centripetal and the other centrifugal. It also epitomizes another tension within Alcibiades, a tension between Eros, even if in his case it is only for fame and honor, and spiritedness, which drives him to seek victory and gain as ends in themselves. The former is erotic, the latter merely contentious. Alcibiades' understanding of what binds together a healthy city, as Forde explains it, seems to continue to be underwritten by spiritedness, hence it is not yet an adequate basis for concord or friendship within the city. Perhaps Socrates' declaration that Alcibiades has become erotic is uttered too soon. But the philosopher, as Forde rightly argues, has at least induced Alcibiades to become a lover of the renown which arises from excellence rather than remaining passionate only about his possessions and about winning his contest with Socrates. Forde underlines the fact that this is Alcibiades' last attempt to define the healthy city (233) and that from this point (127d) on, the initiative in their conversation shifts entirely to Socrates (234).[17]

It is at this juncture in the dialogue that Plato's audience begins to benefit most from the positive, almost programmatic, schema that Socrates will sketch for "taking trouble over oneself." The balance of this chapter explores this notion and attempts to answer two questions: (1) What does Socrates mean by "taking trouble over oneself"?; and (2) What are the specific practices that must be developed for proper self-care? We will see that Socrates classifies these under the headings "exercise" (*gumnastikē*) and "learning" (*mathēsis*). The answers to these two questions will help clarify how taking care of oneself is related to self-knowledge. Socrates repeatedly links self-knowledge to *sophrosunē* (compare 131b, 133c), and he will show self-knowledge to be, at least partly, gained through the give and take of philosophical conversation. So dialogue must be regarded as furthering both self-knowledge and soundmindedness, according to Socrates.

Before the *Alcibiades I* embarks upon an exegesis of the meaning of "taking trouble over oneself," the philosopher first has to demonstrate to Alcibiades what it means to take care of a particular thing. More than half of the dialogue is concerned with securing this foothold by provoking the brash Alcibiades to realize that he has failed to take the trouble to learn what must be learned prior to embarking on his political career.[18] In the absence of any obvious teachers of justice, Alcibiades' failure consists of not having investigated the problem for himself, instead assuming that he knows already what justice is. Once Socrates gets him to relinquish the conceit of wisdom, the certainty that he already knows what he needs to know, he can at last begin to show the youth what will be required for proper self-care. But first let us see how the issue of "taking trouble" arises in the dialogue.

SECTION 3.B INTRODUCTION TO THE PROBLEM OF TAKING TROUBLE OVER ONESELF

Ironically, the first time the expression "taking trouble" (*epimelesthai*) is used in the dialogue (104d3), Alcibiades is the one who uses it. After Socrates finishes his opening remarks, Alcibiades wonders why Socrates makes such a nuisance of himself, accusing him of "always taking such trouble to be present wherever I happen to be" (104d1–5). Socrates does not employ the expression himself until he believes he has succeeded in humbling Alcibiades, after their preliminary exchange about justice and its relation to expediency. At that point, Socrates asks whether Alcibiades is ready to begin taking trouble over himself (119a8–9). It is in response to this question that Alcibiades wriggles through the escape hatch with which he hopes the ignorance of the demos will provide him. Socrates marshals the Royal Tale to persuade Alcibiades that his present assumptions about his political opponents add up to an insufficient justification for forsaking his education and training. In this story, Socrates takes aim at what Alcibiades trusts, weaving the expression "taking trouble" into the fabric of his mythical narrative at several critical points.

He tells Alcibiades that before embarking on his political mission, he must look to the bad leaders who use barbarous speech and still show signs in their souls of their slavish origins. This leads Socrates to wonder whether Alcibiades would "take more trouble" if he believed his opponents to be fearsome than he would if he did not judge them to be worthy of fear (120d3). Later in the Royal Tale, Socrates has the Spartan queen say that only two things are a fitting basis for trust: "taking trouble" and "wisdom (*sophia*)" (123d2–4). The wise queen proclaims further that nothing will allow the Greeks to prevail over the barbarians except "taking trouble" and "skill" (*technē*) (124a1–b3). Here, just after Socrates has finished spinning his refutational *muthos*, Alcibiades finally asks, "What trouble has to be taken, then, Socrates?" (124b7–8).

His long-awaited receptivity provokes Socrates to borrow another phrase from Alcibiades. Socrates begins, "We must put our heads together" (*koinē boulē*) to stress that they must deliberate in common, or "take common counsel," about precisely what is required to become as excellent as possible.[19] Socrates' answer to Alcibiades' question takes up the final third of the dialogue. Plato's audience does not even get the first positive indication of an answer until 127c–d, and it is only after this crossroads is reached that Socrates begins to elaborate his answer. First he effectively aligns himself with Alcibiades in the search to follow by saying, "For indeed, I'm not speaking only of you when I say it is necessary to be educated, and not of myself, for I do not differ from you at all" (124c1–3). If Alcibiades were as shrewd as he takes himself to be, he would realize the interminable nature of the Socratic project of self-care. If Socrates is only marginally further along the path than Alcibiades is, the Socratic training will involve much more than an isolated lesson or an occasional conversation. He might find it worrisome, given his political ambitions, that Socrates has no time left for concerning himself with the things of the city (cf. *Ap.* 23b). If he were really astute, Alcibiades might ask Socrates how the focus upon his own betterment would prepare him for political life rather than divert him from it.

Alcibiades has little chance to reflect upon Socrates' admission before Socrates intensifies his initiatory arousal. Socrates' assertion in the passage cited above from 124c continues: "Unless it is one respect . . . My guardian is better and wiser than yours—than Pericles." Socrates proclaims his guardian to be "the god, the very one who did not let me converse with you before today and in whom I place my trust when I say that you will gain prominence through no one but me" (124c8–10). However Socrates defines "taking trouble" for Alcibiades, the fantastic buildup to it has piqued the young man's interest. "You're joking, Socrates," he says. "Perhaps," replies Socrates, "but what I say is true—that we need to take trouble, or rather that all human beings do, but most particularly the two of us" (124d2–3).[20]

That Alcibiades appears convinced that Socrates is right allows Socrates to become more stern with regard to the rules for their conversation. Early in the dialogue, Alcibiades often concedes a point to Socrates begrudgingly, acquiescing only to hear what more strange things the philosopher has to say. Socrates does not entreat him to say what he really thinks, nor does he eschew answers that Alcibiades offers merely to placate him. Now that Alcibiades is finally a full participant in their conversation, however, Socrates warns, "There must be no begging off or hanging back comrade." Reiterating that they must "consider in common," Socrates plunges right in and begins cross-examining Alcibiades about just which excellence they are looking for. This long prelude to Socrates' more direct answer confirms that the excellence of the ruler is what they are seeking, and this distinctive excellence within the city must be justice. Alcibiades' own attempt to pinpoint the source of this excellence falls short; he is unable to see beyond the family model of justice, and at 127d, he confesses his total inability to elucidate what he means.

Socrates assuages Alcibiades by assuring the young man that he still has time to rectify the inadequacy he has noticed in himself. If he were fifty years old instead of nineteen, the time for improvement might have passed; fortunately, the aspiring leader has discovered the need to take trouble just when it is most opportune to observe it. Alcibiades asks Socrates a second time what can be done once this need is perceived. Socrates gives a short, definitive answer that illuminates the direction any further answer will take: "Answer the questions, Alcibiades. If you do this, and god is willing—if we should put any trust in my divination—both you and I shall be in a better state" (127e6–7). Notice that Plato has made Socrates soften the pretentious promise with which he twice before tantalized Alcibiades. Not only did Socrates cite the god as his patron when he first spoke to Alcibiades, he promised earlier that only with his help and that of the god could Alcibiades attain the power and station he desires. With the deprecation here of his "divination," Plato's audience is duly warned that an element of chance remains in the project of Alcibiades' betterment, even if the youth were willing to put in the required effort and answer all of Socrates' "annoying" questions. What is more, Plato's audience is permitted to see that the philosopher's calculated exaggerations earlier in the conversation actually assert rather less than they appeared at first to be claiming.[21]

SECTION 3.C THE MEANING OF TAKING TROUBLE OVER ONESELF

The search for the meaning of "taking trouble" now begins explicitly and directly (128a). Socrates waxes metaphoric when he says to Alcibiades: "Come then, what is it to take trouble over oneself—lest it often escape us that we are not taking trouble over ourselves while supposing that we are? And when does a human being do this? When he takes trouble over his own things, does he then take trouble over himself as well?"

This last question becomes the immediate focus of their joint search. Alcibiades is not sure of the distinction that Socrates is attempting to draw between taking trouble over oneself and taking trouble over one's own things. Plato's audience might regard this as a premonitory device designed to evoke the memory of the historical Alcibiades' fickle allegiance; his own sense of what belongs to him seems to have been partly to blame for his political fate.

The question also indicates that Socrates is well aware of the high regard in which Alcibiades holds his possessions, including his natural gifts. Whatever it should mean, trouble is taken correctly when it improves the object of this care. Socrates uses the example of shoes to illustrate his point. It is a different kind of concern that takes trouble over footwear than that which takes trouble over the feet. And the art that takes trouble over the feet is the same art that takes trouble over the whole body, that is, gymnastics. Likewise, gymnastics takes trouble over the hand and the body itself, while the ring cutter and the weaver take trouble over what belongs to the hand and the whole body, respectively, that is, rings and clothing. Since different arts take trouble over oneself and what belongs to one, taking trouble over one's belongings does not amount to taking trouble over oneself. It will not be enough that Alcibiades esteems his possessions and prizes what belongs to him.

Before they can piece together an answer to the question about which art takes trouble over the self itself, the need to define the self arises. Socrates ruminates about how human beings can know themselves, wondering whether the inscription on the temple at Delphi was chiseled there in an act of meanness. Is self-knowledge truly available to everyone (129a)? Without determining how self-knowledge can be attained, the search for the self may have to be abandoned. Socrates enlists his companion in a preparatory investigation with the solicitation: "Come then, in what way might the self itself (*auto tauto*) be discovered?" (129b1–3).

Socrates abruptly shifts gears and poses a series of questions designed to demonstrate that it is Alcibiades himself who is conversing with Socrates. They are using speech to converse, but their persons are not, strictly speaking, defined as speech. They are the users of speech, just as Socrates would have Alcibiades believe that artisans are the users of their tools, hands, and eyes. While human speech is not really parallel to a craftsman's tools—and perhaps this is why Socrates drops this analogy from subsequent arguments—he is trying to bring Alcibiades to see that if the user and what is used are to be differentiated, and if the craftsman uses his hands and eyes in the performance of his art, then his body too is something he only uses; it is not constitutive for who he is. Thus, at 129e, Socrates concludes with the assertive question, "A human being is different, therefore, from his own body?" Introducing the notion of the soul to assist Alcibiades in proffering a definition of man, Socrates proposes that either human beings are essentially body, essentially soul, or both together in equal parts. Now Socrates leads Alcibiades through a proof devised to convince him that the self itself is coextensive with the soul (130b*ff*). The first part of the proof demonstrates that humans are not equivalent to body. The body cannot rule itself; the body is ruled; we are not seeking what is ruled but what rules, therefore, humans are not body. The second part of the proof shows that human beings cannot be both body and soul. Human beings cannot be (essentially defined as) both body and soul unless both elements rule equally; they are not co-rulers, therefore, humans can be both body and soul least of all. Since humans are neither body nor equally body and soul, the self itself must be defined as soul (130c1–3).

After a little equivocation over whether these proofs have been sufficient or precise enough[22]—they have certainly served Socrates' purpose—Socrates returns to the image of the two lovers conversing, not face-to-face but soul to soul. Socrates says his speech is directed toward Alcibiades' soul (130e3–5). In this way, the philosopher translates the injunction "Know thyself" into the requirement to become acquainted with and to work to improve one's soul.[23] The more remote one's concerns are from this acquaintance with the soul, the less one knows oneself. Insofar as they only know the body, doctors and trainers, for example, do not know themselves. The concerns of money makers are even further removed, since they do not even tend to their own things. Because *sophrosunē* entails self-knowledge, everyone who lacks self-knowledge necessarily lacks *sophrosunē*.[24] Therefore, the doctor, trainer, and money maker, qua human beings, all lack self-knowledge, but insofar as self-knowledge implies the ordering of the various parts of a person, they also lack soundmindedness.

The dialogue now quickly approaches its erotic height. Socrates is Alcibiades' truest lover, because he cares for the young man's soul and not merely for his body. This kind of Eros will not fade when the bloom of youth has passed. Alcibiades implores Socrates not to depart like the others, and Socrates bids him to become as beautiful as possible. In so doing, Socrates unites the qualities attributable to Alcibiades' physical beauty with the beauty manifested in a well-ordered individual.[25] It is *sophrosunē* that characterizes the orderliness of the parts of an individual's soul in accordance with its nature. Socrates often highlights the beauty perceptible in this order. In the *Republic*, Socrates celebrates the harmony of a beautiful body and a well-ordered soul, calling it "the most beautiful spectacle for anyone who has eyes to see."[26] In telling Alcibiades to "strive to be as beautiful as possible," Socrates is leading the young man to see that his physical endowments, on their own, are not what makes him beautiful; rather, his physical properties only serve to render him beautiful insofar as he makes himself beautiful in his whole person.

Here Socrates inserts the first qualification of his enduring love for Alcibiades. His profession of loyalty and love turns out to be conditional and, in stipulating its conditions, Socrates, for the first time, foreshadows Alcibiades' tragic weakness. He says, "And now, if you are not corrupted by the populace of Athens and become baser, I will not give you up" (132a1–2). He goes on to say that he fears most that Alcibiades will become a lover of the demos and goes on to prescribe a Socratic antidote: "Exercise yourself first!"

(*gumnasai proton*, 132b1).[27] This advice is underscored by the counsel to learn (*mathē*) what needs to be learned so that he will be armed with a powerful antidote (*alexipharmaka*) against suffering harm. This advice will be explored further in the next section of this chapter.

At this point, Alcibiades asks a third time in what way they might "take trouble" over themselves (132b4–5). Socrates recapitulates what they have agreed upon thus far about the nature of the self, and he introduces the analogy of sight to explain how self-knowledge is to be achieved. He has already prepared Alcibiades for this analogy by his earlier mention of conversing soul to soul. Just as the eye "sees itself" through its reflection in something—most reciprocally when it sees itself reflected in another's eye—so too the soul knows itself only when it fixes its gaze upon that part of another's soul in which its excellence consists, and this is wisdom (133b7–10). Socrates makes no attempt to justify the analogy between the eye and the soul, vision and self-knowledge. He merely continues to press his case. It is obvious, in the case of sight, that the eye will not see itself reflected in any part of the other's body except that part in the center, the pupil, which permits one to see. Likewise, in the case of knowledge, one cannot know oneself except by attending to the part of the *psuchē* that enables one to know. For this is the active, ruling part, not the irrational part. Therefore, it is by concerning oneself with the most divine part of the human being, the center of knowing and thinking, that one discovers what is divine in mankind and therewith what the human being essentially is. This is how one knows oneself. Without this kind of self-knowledge that has discovered its likeness to the divine, which is also to say, without justice and *sophrosunē*, it will be impossible to know what parts of ourselves are good and what parts are bad (134c–e).

There is a seemingly unavoidable circularity in Socrates' explanation to Alcibiades. It is the circularity of Meno's paradox, this time complicated by the reflexivity of the question of self-knowledge. If the excellence of another is to be discovered in the *psuchē* and, more precisely, in the aspect or characteristic in which the highest human excellence consists, then this is wisdom. One then can learn about the most excellent part of oneself only through the wisdom of another person. The circularity arises when one asks, "Which other person?" For one needs first to know, in some sense, what wisdom is to know whether or not the person to whom one entrusts one's chance for self-knowledge is in fact wise. So at least two prior conditions must be fulfilled: one must realize one's lack of self-knowledge, that is, one must know enough to know that one is ignorant, and one must already possess sufficient wisdom to recognize those who can further one's search for it.[28] For it will not simply be someone with technical expertise, someone who knows a certain craft or skill, or someone who is knowledgeable about some particular art or science alone who is needed. Rather, a person who can facilitate one's self-knowledge will be required, someone who can serve as both a lightning rod and a touchstone for another's self-awareness and self-understanding.

But here a second problem arises. This also must be someone who can help to improve us, for this would be the only criteria by which to evaluate the ability of those who would be midwives to our self-understanding. People who are inferior in wisdom and goodness are not likely to improve their superiors, though they may make them *feel* wiser. This would seem to mandate that all people must seek a superior in wisdom. But then why would the superior person be interested in staking her or his chance at self-knowledge on a less worthy interlocutor? In any relationship, indeed in any dialogue, how will the less capable partner—presumably the one inferior in wisdom—facilitate the self-knowledge of the wiser person?

One answer seems to be that within human communities, there must exist a few exemplars of the highest human activity. And such people must be willing to become benefactors to others, attempting to nourish and improve their fellow citizens, as Socrates does. These will not be masters of the persuasive arts but persons good at genuine teaching. These should be educators in the Socratic sense, not only because their task is to serve as a mirror to another's self-understanding but also because such people must be superior in wisdom and goodness if improvement is to result from their efforts. Perhaps no such people can be found, or perhaps they are unwilling, or perhaps no mere mortal is truly capable of filling this role. What then?

Socrates has a second answer. Here he introduces for Alcibiades the idea that when one communicates to the best part of another with the best part of oneself, namely, the ruling part of the soul, one is in fact communicating with the element of the divine in the other. With the notion of "the Self itself," perhaps Socrates means to suggest that human beings are never without recourse for a paradigm for this ruling part of the soul; one can always look to the heavens, to everything divine, as a guide. Whereas earlier it appeared as though one needed only a friend or a lover to engage in a soul-to-soul conversation productive of self-knowledge and self-improvement, Socrates' introduction of the divine element here suggests that even relationships between friends or lovers must be guided by something beyond the two lovers or friends if improvement is truly and continuously possible.

Now Socrates modifies something the two inquirers had agreed upon previously: he spoke loosely in saying that those who lack self-knowledge can know their own things and things even more remote. Socrates asserts now, however, that self-knowledge is the necessary condition for knowing these secondary things. If the lack of self-knowledge precludes knowing one's own things, one surely cannot know the things of others without it. Socrates now brings the conversation full circle, showing Alcibiades that he cannot rule a household, much less the city, without the requisite self-knowledge.

Socrates has contrasted practicing something well with practicing it badly throughout the dialogue (see, e.g., 116b and 134a). Forde reminds us that implicit in this contrast are two related distinctions: one between good and bad practices and the other between prosperity and not faring well. Here Socrates utilizes the ambiguity in the phrase *eu prattein*, which can mean either to act well or to prosper (do well), to suggest that if one's practices are good or "one practices well," this will result in prosperity.[29] Now, at 134a–b, all of these related meanings converge in Socrates' statement about happiness. He posits that *sophrosunē* and goodness are the preconditions for happiness. Under these conditions, it seems that only if Alcibiades makes the people more excellent can he be truly thought to practice well the things of the city. The only way Alcibiades can impart such excellence to others is by cultivating it in himself. Thus the acquisition of this excellence is the first goal of "taking trouble" over oneself, and it is only on the basis of this that one can properly take trouble over the affairs of others. It is noteworthy that Socrates asserts to Alcibiades that the need to take trouble over himself is the precondition for taking care of the affairs of the city, that is, for political life as such. Four steps can be delineated in Socrates' overall argument:

1. Taking trouble over oneself is necessary to attain excellence in oneself.
2. Excellence in oneself is necessary before one can take care of the affairs of the city.
3. The principal objective of the political art is to improve the citizens.
4. Only by taking trouble over oneself can a ruler impart excellence to those ruled.

In arguing for an isomorphic relation between taking care of oneself and properly taking care of the city, Socrates also couples individual excellence with the greater excellence of the city.

Section 3.d Practices for "Taking Trouble": *Gumnastikē* and *Mathēsis*

What is the outcome of Socrates' advice to Alcibiades about "taking trouble over oneself"? It will help if we recapitulate what has been learned thus far from his counsel to the aspiring statesman.[30] "Taking trouble over oneself" has been spoken about in two different ways: it has been referred to as exercise (*gumnastikē*) or training (*taxis*) and as connected to broader learning (*mathēsis*) of "what needs to be learned." Socrates refers consistently to this more general education as *mathēsis*, while variously referring to the other kind of preparation as "exercise" (*gumnastikē*), "training" (*taxis*), and practice (*askēsis*). Through an early and a sustained regimen, one receives the necessary foundation for formal education. Habituation toward the right disposition of the appetites is the precondition for *mathēsis* and precedes it in the general education of the young. Clearly, then, formal learning alone is not sufficient to prepare Alcibiades to rule the city; he must first exercise himself.

All forms of exercise combine to promote "order" (*kosmos*) in the individual and self-mastery in one's dealings with others. The specific forms that Socrates will explicate for Alcibiades further promote the character traits constitutive for the new conception of freedom that Plato seems to be adumbrating in the dialogues. Plato has the Athenian in the *Laws* explain that an undisciplined (*agumnastikos*) person will be overcome by his desires and unable to exercise dominion over himself.[31] Hence the same practices that prepare one to rule oneself prepare one to rule others well. This means that the person who is master of herself or himself is more likely to be judicious and equitable in the treatment of those she or he rules.

Socrates tells Alcibiades to "practice (*askein*) what requires practice" (120b8). This indicates the kind of preparation necessary for political life. As the dialogue unfolds, Socrates formulates his advice to the youth in various ways. He tells him to "take trouble" over that part of himself that is the source of thinking and knowing and, more immediately and concretely, to "answer the questions." His rigorous lesson is reinforced by periodic prodding and occasional guidance, punctuated with admonitions aimed at assisting Alcibiades in submitting to a Socratic cross-examination. How do the different instructions fit together? Precisely what kind of exercise is Socrates talking about, and what are the practices around which these exercises revolve? What can be discerned about how the improvement of the self itself is connected to the management of the things of the city? And what are the more formal subjects that Alcibiades needs to learn?

Section 3.d.1 *Gumnastikē* and Dialogue

All indications about what Socrates means when he exhorts Alcibiades to "exercise himself" point to the kind of regimen entailed by Socratic cross-examination. He seems to be indicating to Alcibiades something broader than the mere exercise of the body and *musikē* for the soul in which Athenian *paideia* has long consisted (cf., e.g., *Rep.* 376e). It becomes immediately clear that he is talking about a kind of exercise in which his conversational practice plays a central role, and he has taken pains in the preceding arguments to stress that it is not Alcibiades' body but his soul that is doing the talking. Socrates immediately distinguishes dialogue from the need to "learn what needs to be learned" (132b1).[32] It becomes clear that the *gumnastikē* to be set forth here fundamentally involves dialogue.

The exercises under the heading *gumnastikē* are called exercises because they involve the routine practice of certain skills. These often involve repetitive or tedious drills that slowly engender incremental growth in the particular skill or art. This can readily be seen in examples from military training, sports, martial arts, music, and learning a foreign language. But the only concrete example that Socrates gives of it in this dialogue is conversation. Of course, Socrates' notion of conversation here is not that of a freewheeling, open-ended "talking through" (*dialegesthai*) of the type one might imagine if the conversation were between two people who were relative equals; rather, conversation here seems to consist of one person (Alcibiades) submitting to relentless questioning in a cross-examination by another (Socrates).

Socrates initially asks Alcibiades if it will trouble him to answer a few simple questions (106b). Some of the guidelines the philosopher dispenses about how to participate in this exercise are quite instructive. Socrates tells Alcibiades: "Try to imitate me. For presumably what I answered is, what is correct in every instance" (108b5–7). Alcibiades is thus directed to look for the rule rather than for the exception, to look for universals that apply in general in order to advance the inquiry. In a search for the general principles of an art, Socrates coaches Alcibiades to use the mimetic art to learn the art of conversational investigation. This guidance makes plain that *mimēsis* will be one of the indispensable techniques in gymnastics.

During the interlude about who is speaking when one person asks questions and the other supplies answers (112e–113c), Socrates poses a quasi-eristic question to Alcibiades: "Come then, say in a single speech: when there is question and answer, who is the one saying something, the questioner or the answerer?"[33] While on one level, the answer is obvious—both are saying something—Socrates highlights the sense in which a Socratic dialogue bears little resemblance to a conversation in the everyday sense. He says that it is the respondent who is saying something. If only the answerer is speaking, it would be more apropos to call this an interrogation, inasmuch as it is a tightly constructed series of questions intended to squeeze information out of the reserved respondent. Later Socrates commands Alcibiades to "Just answer my questions," explaining that the youth will be more persuaded if he hears himself saying "the matter stands thus." Just as one learns better any skill by practicing it rather than merely by observing others, one is more persuaded when one gives voice to something oneself than when simply hearing another say it. This is especially true if one is to persuade oneself that one is, in fact, committed to a certain belief. Socrates' view of this interrogative process suggests that only by phrasing what they think or believe do human beings own up to that belief and become genuinely convinced that they think or believe it. Once an interlocutor owns up to his or her fundamental beliefs by stating them sincerely, these beliefs and opinions can be subjected to further testing by the philosopher.[34] When Alcibiades relents and says, "I don't suppose there is any harm in it," Socrates quips, "You are skilled at divining" (114e10-115a1). What could Socrates mean by this? One suspects that Alcibiades has no idea of what could happen to him under the weight of Socrates' methodical questioning.

Alcibiades' premonition of possible harm comes later. Explaining the nature of perplexity to him, Socrates asks Alcibiades how he would answer someone who wondered whether he had two eyes or three. Socrates says, "Do you suppose . . . that you would answer a certain way at one time and a different way at another, or would always answer the same thing?" Alcibiades prefaces his response by disclosing his trepidation: "I am already afraid for myself" (117a1). Socrates drives the point home: "As for the things where you involuntarily answer in opposite ways, it is clear that you do not know about them." Socrates refers to this condition in which Alcibiades finds himself as "wandering about in his soul." Socrates rallies Alcibiades' resolve with the words "Don't become weary of answering" (126d11–126e1). Finally, Alcibiades (at 127e) receives Socrates' imperative "Answer the questions" to his second request to know how he might take trouble over himself.

The examination of his approach to Lysis made clear that Socrates' use of the explosive combination of arousal and chastening is designed specifically to provoke disclosure of the interlocutor's character flaw. Such a provocative strategy is most necessary when the simple demand for the truth or for a sincere statement of deeply held beliefs is not enough. In many cases, it is not. Typically, Socrates has to whip his conversation partner into shape. In certain dialogues, all of his efforts must be directed toward getting a resistant character to admit his ignorance. The great lengths to which he has to go to elicit a satisfactory performance from Alcibiades are displayed for Plato's audience. His two-pronged strategy, arousal and humbling, again comprise the vital, dynamic tools for Socrates' approach, alternately seducing his interlocutor and breaking him down.

Chapter 2 also showed that Socrates employs his erotic methods to achieve the disclosure of something key to his interlocutor's character. He must first diagnose and then locate his interlocutor, situating him with respect to the subject matter and the pretext for the conversation in order to know which maneuvers have a chance of succeeding with a particular character. Every interlocutor will embody or propound some viewpoint, adopting a position that defines him in relation to Socrates, usually one that mirrors the position he has adopted in relation to the world in general. That a character, like people in general, speaks differently to different interlocutors and presents different aspects of himself in virtue of the varied roles he takes is not merely a dramatic device, however, it follows from the processive nature of the search for knowledge and is especially the case in relation to self-knowledge, as Socrates' image of conversing soul to soul suggests. Dialogue continually repositions one, redefining and relocating one in relation to others, to the *logos*, and to the dialectical process that Socrates seems to think propels sincere inquiry forward.[35] Understood as fundamentally relational, the character and self-understanding of the interlocutors also is always a presumptive, provisional one; all self-improvement is based on the possibility of modifying one's character in the process of practicing the excellences.

This means that the Socratic practice of freedom must perforce include the freedom to transform oneself through one's practices, that is, it is the freedom to become, in some sense, a different person. Clearly, no fixed or invariable character identical through time will be an adequate bearer of this kind of freedom. It is precisely the issue of the interlocuters' identity, the givenness of their agency as free citizens, that Socrates makes a problem for them, provoking these young men to wonder how they will establish themselves in their various roles as fathers, husbands, masters, citizens, friends, soldiers, and statesmen. He holds out to the characters studied here the opportunity for a radical transformation in their previous goals, desires, and preferences, even if it is not obvious to them that he is doing so. In this way he offers them a conception of "positive freedom" or "freedom for," which entails a metamorphosis of who or what they presently are.

It is through the promotion of self-care then that, somewhat paradoxically, Socratic freedom succeeds in altering the original goals, preferences, and desires of its practitioners. In fact, the care for the self, as Socrates' prescription for the proper exercise of freedom, consists chiefly in the alteration of oneself according to the proper form of governance. There are two basic ways in which this Socratic, or philosophic, freedom is to be exercised, hence there are two ways in which self-transformation might be thought to occur through its practice: one way develops the concrete activities by which one exercises and works upon oneself, and the other way carries out a critical examination of the beliefs and opinions that influence, or even structure, the ways in which one thinks and acts. As exemplified, or enacted, by Socrates in the dialogues, these two spheres of freedom's activity cannot be dissociated.

For an interlocutor to equate his character with any particular, transitory viewpoint and assume that this is the immutable "real" self augurs against further learning and growth. Not surprisingly, the interlocutors in the dialogues who seem most teachable are those who are willing to relinquish their previous standpoints, while the most intransigent are those whose self-image appears calcified. Thus to take oneself as identical with one's present viewpoint has dangerous consequences both for self-knowledge and for the possibility of dialogue. The consequence for self-knowledge is hubris, the belief that one's present perspective has the status of absolute truth and that one's present self is in fact the Self itself. This view rests on the unjustified presumption that there is a true and an immutable human self that remains unchanged throughout its manifold relations in the world of becoming.[36] The consequences for dialogue follow from the consequences for self-knowledge. One sense of hubris is this failure of self-knowledge, which issues in an arrogance that forecloses the possibility for learning. A degree of pliability of character is clearly presupposed by all forms of education, and it is certainly presupposed by any attempt to effect a marked turnaround in a person's life. Hubris causes the interlocutor to assume the position of one who does not think he has anything to learn. Moreover, as Daniel Anderson argues, believing that the surrender of his provisional identity portends the annihilation of the self as such, the interlocutor then clings ever more steadfastly to his present coordinates, becoming identified with his current, rigid viewpoint.[37] It is to breach the identification of the interlocutor's self with his unexamined viewpoints (beliefs and opinions) that Socrates undertakes his sometimes antagonistic cross-examinations.

Yet if it is only the one who answers questions that is saying something what does Socrates get out of these encounters? The most beneficial, concrete results he would appear to receive from these daily conversations are an increase in his (already uncanny) acumen for assessing his interlocutors' character and the chance to exercise his (already insuperable) skills in argument and interrogation. By engaging the best and the brightest youths, renowned orators, notable Sophists, and countless Athenian gentlemen, Socrates both hones his debating skills and sharpens the exceptional acuity that he already possesses as a diagnostician of human character. Taking Socrates at his word about the nature and purpose of his conversational practice leads to the further conclusion that what knowledge Socrates does gain from these frequent conversations includes most importantly a knowledge of himself. What the philosopher's own example teaches about how this knowledge is to be sought is mainly that his conversational practice is indistinguishable from the exercises through which he takes care of himself. The more one exercises oneself, the more one knows one's capabilities, weaknesses, limits, and ultimate limitations. Hence the more Socrates exercises himself in philosophical discussion, the more knowledge and freedom are bound together with self-care. It is in this way, by dramatizing the appropriate behavior of a free person through the character and example of Socrates, that Plato issues his most momentous counterweight to conventional Athenian practices and depicts his alternative to the subjugation/domination model of human interaction.

As Plato's chosen medium for conveying this idea of freedom, the drama of the dialogues continually reminds the reader that, at every moment, a character's identity is shaped differently by various situations and toward particular people. This highlights the need to tether philosophy to character. And Plato's choice of the dialogue form preserves both the fluidity and the situated character of human life, making particular features more readily perceptible by allowing the audience to observe various interlocutors interacting with one another at the same time it is permitted to listen to what they say. The fluidity of character is integral, not only to the dialogue form but also to the philosophical content of the Socratic strategy toward others. Socrates appears always able to identify the key belief or opinion that his interlocutor holds most dear, and this contributes to his decided advantage in argument. That the interlocutors tell the truth, stating their own sincerely held beliefs, will be essential for the success of a Socratic interrogation. It may, in fact, turn out that the apparent failures of Socrates' approach are sometimes simply the result of an interlocutor's unwillingness to participate fully. With Alcibiades, the demand to participate sincerely and completely climaxes in the struggle over truthfulness, as we shall see in Chapter 4, Section 4.c.

In another context, Meno poses a hypothetical question to Socrates, asking him how he would have responded if someone did not know color, which Socrates had just used to define shape. There Socrates seizes the opportunity to differentiate explicitly between eristic and dialectic argumentation and implicitly to distinguish philosophical inquiry from sophistry. In his answer, the philosopher provides some insight into the demand that his interlocutor be truthful. Socrates says that his answer would be "a true one" and continues:

> The more dialectical way, I suppose, is not merely to answer what is true, but also to make use of these points which the questioned person concedes that he knows. And this is the way I shall now try to argue with you. (*Meno* 75d, Jowett trans.)

"Telling the truth" or "saying what is true" does not mean that one already knows something, that it has been thoroughly investigated, and that a certain conclusion has been reached. The exhortation to tell the truth does not, for Socrates, signal the end of the discussion; it is rather a precondition for entering into genuine dialogue with the philosopher, the essential starting point that allows any sincere inquiry to get underway, even though Socrates does not always insist on this demand. For Socratic refutation to work, for the ensuing conversation to be fruitful, the interlocutor cannot simply utter any opinion or belief; he must disclose his own deeply held opinion or belief.

Yet, sometimes Socrates must be content to converse with a "straw man." For it often turns out that the belief or opinion first expressed by an interlocutor is later shown to be *not* truly his own, although the character may think it is. The beliefs or opinions initially proffered are often later revealed to be not the interlocutor's own in two senses: (1) in the sense familiar from our discussion of the notion of what is *oikos* in the *Lysis*, that they are not what is most "kindred," that is, they do not truly belong to one, and they are therefore not consonant with one's character and actions; and (2) in the sense that the ideas they express do not originate with the interlocutors but are merely repeated from other sources. Many times the belief or opinion expressed simply parrots conventional wisdom, or the interlocutor appropriates some aspect of a popular interpretation of the poets, or the ideas expressed are disclosed as being the doctrines of the interlocutor's *didaskalos*. An essential aspect of Socrates' task as an educator with such interlocutors is to teach them how to learn. But before he can teach them anything of substance, he must first teach them how to recollect in the right way. Merely regurgitating someone else's view is not the recollection in which Socrates elsewhere says learning consists. Implied in Socrates' demand for a sincerely held view is that the interlocutor must be committed to the view he expresses, that he must occupy some definite standpoint. This is because refutation is not possible when the interlocutor just does not care about the view he is propounding or the actions he is taking. It is not possible either when the interlocutor is inconsistent, waffling and wavering in his position. Adopting a definite position or having a firm standpoint also is vital to any attempt to measure an interlocutor's progress and Socrates' benefit to him.

Whether Socrates refutes his interlocutor with an argument or in some other manner, whether the premises for Socrates' refutations are taken from the interlocutor's initial answer, adduced from popular opinion, recuperated from a previous argument, or obtained in some other way, there is no more objective standard for the truth of the beliefs expressed at the outset of Socrates' discussions with others than that the interlocutor holds them as true.[38] It is enough that an interlocutor maintain a sufficient degree of internal consistency and own up to his opinions and beliefs in conversation with Socrates, if the discussion is to succeed. In the *Gorgias*, Socrates repeatedly insists that Callicles say what he really thinks. The philosopher is well aware that he may as well dialogue with himself (as Callicles tells him to do at

Grg. 505c–d) if the recalcitrant Sophist is going to hide his own convictions behind a mask. When Socrates cannot require or has not yet ascertained from an interlocutor either the admission of ignorance or a genuine desire to learn, this gadfly philosopher does his utmost to hasten it. Once he determines that the interlocutor has fulfilled the prerequisites, as characters such as Meno do only too reluctantly and belatedly, the inquiry may begin in earnest.

Hence a Socratic conversation is a kind of exercise. It not only trains one for future encounters, sharpening one's wits and refining one's ability to think on one's feet, it assays one's beliefs and ultimately one's character and way of life. Socrates tells his jury that the kind of interrogation he conducts with his fellow citizens is an *elenchon toū biou*, that is, an examination of one's life.[39] This is one important reason it is so crucial to the success of Socratic interrogation that one says what one really believes. Socrates is not interested in what the many think or even in what learned opinion holds; he wants to know what the particular interlocutor himself thinks, for it is only with the one person with whom he is conversing that Socrates can have any efficacy. The conversation with Alcibiades tests the mettle of both interlocutors; it seriously tests Alcibiades' greatest aspirations while gauging his present character; and it tests the extent of Socrates' persuasive powers, forcing him to invoke both a *paideutic* myth and some extraordinary pretensions in order to get Alcibiades to play the game. Socrates also must warn him against backsliding—retracting something he has said before—and whining or crying out that he just does not know. In fact, the philosopher chastises Alcibiades most sternly when the youth compels him to repeat arguments about the expedient that are exactly parallel to the ones he had earlier presented concerning the just.

So speech may indeed be only something human beings *use*, if we are to accept Socrates' earlier argument (129d–130b) at face value, but it is a supremely important tool for shaping human character. It is so singularly important that Plato's paradigmatic philosopher commits his whole life to the practice of self-care through dialogue. How this practice is best undertaken is exhibited in the present context through the various guidelines and reprimands that Socrates gives to Alcibiades. And when he tells Alcibiades, "Exercise yourself," he has demonstrated no other procedure for him except how to be the subject of a Socratic interrogation. Alcibiades has not really learned how to be a good conversationalist or how to dialogue with an equal, even when he and Socrates are "seeking in common"; he has learned only how to answer questions put to him by the philosopher. But by attending to the requirements that Socrates lays down for him, it may be possible to determine the benefits Socrates thinks are produced when one exercises oneself in dialogue.

Socrates' method of cross-examination, or *elenchos*, derives from earlier forensic usage, and it is one of the primary tools he employs in the process of refuting his target interlocutors. Of course, *elenchos* is not the only way he carries out a refutation, as should already be evident from the example of the mythical tale he fashioned to refute Alcibiades when arguments alone failed to convince. Although a thorough and comprehensive examination of Socratic interrogation and refutation is beyond the scope of this book, it is important to outline briefly some of the apparent purposes for which Socrates employs cross-examination and refutation in the dialogues being examined here. That Socrates believes that the question-and-answer method confers a benefit on those who engage in it, and that these daily conversations are central to his *asksēsis* of philosophy in the city, is evident throughout the dialogues. Sometimes the most important attestations to the benefits of his approach come when Socrates is conversing with a character whose way of life is most unlike his own, or a character who is reluctant to engage in a philosophical conversation.[40] In these exchanges, Socrates solicits the participation of the other by claiming that the other's compliance in answering his questions will result in a benefit to him, the inquisitive philosopher asking the questions. With Alcibiades in the present context, he insists that answering the questions will benefit Alcibiades, thus the regimen of dialogue constitutes the principal form of exercise that he prescribes for the youth under the heading gymnastics.

The question-and-answer method then somehow benefits both participants, the questioner and the one being questioned. It is surely easier to see how the inferior partner in such conversations will be benefitted, however, than how the older and wiser Socrates will be. Their conversations with Socrates shape in important ways how these characters conceive of themselves. But Socrates insists that a benefit accrues to both parties, even where there is a great disparity in their age, skills, and degree of wisdom. Now it follows from this shared benefit that his commitment to spending every day in dialogue with his fellow citizens amounts to an attestation that not only is Socrates expressly committed to examining the lives of others through his arguments in an effort to determine the best way to live, he is just as committed to examining himself. And the means that he employs are the same for both ends.[41]

He tells his jury (*Apology* 28e4–6) that the god stationed him in the city to "examine himself and others," and he makes the infamous declaration (38a5–6) that the "unexamined life is not worth living for a human being." Commentators are right to insist that Socrates thinks this applies to him as well as to others.[42] Yet since Socrates himself rarely submits to the sustained questioning characteristic of a Socratic interrogation,[43] and since he tells several interlocutors—most notably Critias (*Charmides* 166c–d)—that he expects to benefit from their compliance in answering his questions, one can only believe that Socrates conceives of the activity entailed by these cross-examinations as a regimen for examining, and thereby improving, himself at the same time they are supposed to benefit his interlocutors (see Note 40 above).

Socrates prescribes nothing for Alcibiades that he does not himself practice. His interrogations of others also may serve to confirm his inductive conclusions about the best way to live, as the preponderance of evidence builds in one direction or another; but these inquiries also exercise their practitioner in the examination of philosophical topics, forming and shaping its practitioner. Inquiry is available for use in purging any conceits that might arise unwittingly, and thereby dialogue furthers the attempt to know oneself. Through the process of cross-examination, one discovers what one does and does not know. Discovering one's ignorance vastly diminishes the likelihood that one will cling to the pretense of knowledge. To come up against the limits of knowledge, one must determine what one really believes. In this way, Socratic questioning reveals to his interlocutors the frontiers of their knowledge, minimizing their propensities toward hubris, increasing their degree of *sophrosunē*, and fueling their desire for wisdom.[44]

With Alcibiades, however, Socrates is still trying to bring about the initial turnaround in the youth through cross-examination. Presumably the reason he repeatedly tells Alcibiades to "answer the questions" is that he believes the youth himself will derive some benefit from doing so. Thus in addition to understanding how his cross-examinations benefit Socrates, we will see briefly how submitting to the philosopher's questions in this particular case is supposed to benefit Alcibiades. Whatever other objectives he has with Alcibiades, the following objectives are surely part of his aim: provoking him to take these matters seriously, reproaching him for prematurely setting out in pursuit of power, purging him of his prior conceits, and exhorting him to take more trouble over his way of living.

Socrates' counsel to Alcibiades draws upon the isomorphism between taking trouble over oneself and taking trouble over the affairs of the city. The link between these two domains of concern is secured through *sophrosunē* and can be stated in the form of a principle: only one who practices *sophrosunē* with respect to his or her own desires can be rightfully entrusted with the management of the city. This is because, as we have seen, the ability to rule oneself, ordering the various parts of one's person according to the right *logos*, establishes the basis for the proper rule of others. Socrates attempts to show youths such as Alcibiades how the kind of power one exercises over oneself is isomorphic with, and the precondition for, the proper exercise of power over others. As Michel Foucault stresses, this means that the *form* of power that one exercises in these two cases is the same; the power one has over others must be applied first to oneself, because it develops and regulates the form of rulership in general.[45] The development of *sophrosunē* perfects the power that a free person in Socrates' Athens is supposed to exert over himself, a power that, Socrates here seems to be suggesting, is precisely parallel to the form of power one wields over others. In Socrates' view, it is in virtue of the same excellence that one achieves self-mastery and properly exercises rulership over others.[46]

The philosopher's effort to refute the bold Alcibiades was aimed at inaugurating the practices that will promote *sophrosunē* in the young man. For not only does the extent of one's *sophrosunē* evidence the degree of one's freedom, confirming that one is not a slave to anything, it also keeps one from thinking too highly of oneself and of one's own beliefs or opinions. From Socrates' advice to Alcibiades, it should be clear that the practices around which the exercise and training of the young should be organized are designed as preparation for the subsequent rule of a household and, by extension, to prepare them for future leadership within the city. In contrast, the tyrannical person is unable to rule himself or herself and, therefore, is unable to resist the licentious indulgences and despotic abuses of power made possible by rulership of the city. Since it is necessary for the ruler to display self-control in the power wielded over others, no reasonable person would (or should) entrust the rule of others to people who manifest inferior capacities of self-rule, acting like slaves in their own lives. It is a recurrent theme in the dialogues that the tyrant shows himself to be a slave, precisely because he is unable to rule himself, therefore he is unable to act justly and temperately in ruling over others. Hence, many discussions in the dialogues depend upon the distinction between free man and slave, which Socrates employs to examine the proper ordering of the human *psuchē*. Throughout their conversation, Socrates has been trying to show Alcibiades that there is no difference in type between governing oneself, managing a household, and ruling over others in the city. Since all three require the exercise of *sophrosunē*, Plato's audience is invited to witness that Socrates' refutation of Alcibiades in conversation aims to introduce him to the virtue he will need most in his life, and the one he turns out to most desperately lack. (Notice what form Socratic "corruption" takes with handsome, capable youths such as Alcibiades and Lysis.)

Now it turns out that training in the practices by which one takes trouble over oneself is not only a precondition for formal education, it also is held to be antecedent to any eventual qualification for civic responsibility. Socrates has told Alcibiades that he must take trouble over himself *first*, prior to entering political life. It will not be possible for him to skip over the preparatory training and to advance directly to civic rule, so proper self-care is the prerequisite for the care of others. With both Lysis and Alcibiades, we have seen the gadfly philosopher asking these aspiring rulers how they know what is best for the city when they do not even know what is best for themselves. He wondered how these future statesmen could propose to rule the city when they could not yet rule themselves, and how they hoped to take care of its citizens—which is a ruler's primary function—when they had not yet taken sufficient care of themselves. Against those who would construe Socrates as positively Christian, it is important to notice that the philosopher's message to these youths is that the care of the self must precede the care for others, and most assuredly, the care of the self must precede the care for the city.[47] Hence, in exhorting them to take care of themselves, Socrates is insisting that the care of the self must precede the care of others, because it is only in and through caring for oneself that one properly cares for others.

The practices that comprise the proper self-care are the "first step in the overall *paideia* of a free citizen," as Werner Jaeger puts it, who will eventually assume his rightful place in the city and perform well his civic obligations. Once adequately trained, the exercise of citizen duties continues the development of one's character and excellence. Socrates has given Alcibiades a recipe for self-knowledge that promises to advance both his individual excellence and his political success. In fact, these two objectives, according to Socrates, will be achievable by the same means. The practices by which Alcibiades might "exercise himself" are thought to develop the very same qualities he will need in order to rule the city. One sees here that the philosopher is indeed offering an alternative *paideusis* suitable for the requirements of *politikē*. In their present condition, young men such as Alcibiades are vulnerable from two sides: on the one side, they risk remaining slaves to their desires, unable to rule themselves properly; on the other side, they will be tempted toward despotic abuses of power, unqualified to exercise properly the rule over others. In both an interpersonal and intrapersonal sense, then, they would remain unfree. Socrates is not only trying to teach them the art of governing, which for Plato's contemporaries would have been synonymous with having free status, he also is trying to show them how to become ethical citizens through a deliberate practice of freedom, a practice that has been shown to contrast sharply in places with the conventional ethos of late fifth-century Athens. And it would have been through some kind of practical activity that human freedom would have been thought by Plato's contemporaries to be concretely expressed.

Jaeger emphasizes that *paideia*, for Socrates, was always political *paideia*. He writes: "Socrates represents the classical ideal of permanent citizenship, and holds that his political mission is to educate his pupils to be rulers, through voluntary *askēsis*."[48] It is clear from what he says to Alcibiades that Socrates does not set such practices apart, relegating them to a separate domain of the soul; for Socrates, ethical training is inherent in, and derived from, the practical art of self-care. That it is a practical art, a *technē toū biou*, implies that Socratic gymnastics will make use of the same kinds of practices for the training in the other excellences that shape and perfect every citizen's civic excellence within a Socratic *paideusis*.

It seems important that Plato does not have Socrates justify this *askēsis* of freedom by appealing to his rights as a free citizen; rather, like Antigone, he justifies them by appealing to a higher authority—his service to the god. That Socrates is cloaked by Plato in a divinely ordained vocation augurs heavily against viewing him as conceiving his freedom in terms of a personal conviction thought to supersede the city's authority. This is a crucial distinction, one that grounds the contention that Socratic freedom can never be conceived as freedom from all constraints; Socrates does not pretend for long that his young associates can cast off every yoke of authority.[49] Instead, as we have noted, Plato has him illustrate how to make their best part ruler and the other parts subject. This means that rather than holding out to these young men an ideal of absolute emancipation or liberation, Socrates instead strives to show them that they will, in effect, be replacing the enslavement of their best part by the enslavement of their worst.

Hence it also is important that the path to self-knowledge that Socrates presents is not merely a solitary, inward turning one. For it will be dialogue with others, as we have seen, that serves to reflect oneself to oneself. Self-knowledge is only possible, according to Socrates, in community with others. It is suggestive that in two other contexts (*Theaetetus* 189e–190a and *Sophist* 63e–64b) thinking is defined as a kind of conversation one has with oneself. Given this metaphor for thinking, even solitary contemplation must be thought to consist of the same kind of interrogatory regimen through which Socrates leads Alcibiades, and in which he instructs him, here. It seems that, for Socrates, thinking is best characterized as a self-examination in which one puts questions to oneself and tests one's ability to supply adequate answers or plausible hypotheses. One forms a belief or an opinion, or one decides on an appropriate course of action by coming to agreement with oneself (*homologia*) about the matter under deliberation. Deliberation terminates when one comes (at least temporarily) to be of one mind about something. Clearly then, he is not recommending an *askēsis* based upon a model of idle contemplation or solitary introspection; it is instead a kind of political paradigm for self-knowledge, founded upon a poignantly erotic image. As their question shifts from "What does it mean to take trouble over oneself?" to "How can the self itself be grasped?" to "Who are we ourselves?" Socrates is seeking to provoke Alcibiades to appropriate the lesson still further. He is forcing him to ask, "What is distinctive about human beings?" and, by implication, "What am I?" Once he is equipped with the apparatus for self-examination with which Socrates attempts to arm him, Alcibiades should be able to carry out this philosophical inquiry on his own initiative.[50]

Hence, it is in dialogue that the practices defining proper self-care, for Socrates, are developed and displayed. Recalling how the *Lysis* showed dialogue also to be a way of exploring, expanding, and even transgressing one's limits, we might rightfully conclude that dialogue, for Socrates, is an activity with the power to shape and reshape human character. Through exercising oneself in thought, one transforms and perfects oneself as a person. Dialogue is one important, perhaps the most important, tool for developing one's character into the most virtuous or excellent character possible. The emphasis throughout the dialogues on the activity of *dialegesthai*, of *dokimasia*, of *elenchos*, and of *exetasis* and dialectic, coupled with the weighty evidence supplied by Plato's choice to write the kinds of dialogues he writes, provides grounds for concluding that it is the development of virtuous character, far more than the development of a positive moral doctrine, that Socrates wishes to bring about in his interlocutor and which Plato is attempting to engender in his audience.

In other contexts, such as the *Republic* and *Laws,* gymnastic training is said to also include exercises that develop physical endurance, courage, and self-restraint; various forms of musical education, training in the "manly arts" of hunting and combat; and trials aimed at inculcating the appropriate public demeanor. Yet in the present context, the only specific training that Socrates explicates is the one he demonstrates with Alcibiades: the training in conversation. It is significant that two things Socrates had utilized in his preliminary argument about the nature of humankind are reintroduced as part of his prescriptive formula for Alcibiades' self-improvement. Speech and the body were both held to be things human beings use but are not of the essence of being human. Once human beings are defined as essentially *psuchē*, speech and the body reappear as the loci of gymnastic attention. Socrates certainly knows that human beings do not use speech or inhabit a body in the way an artisan uses a tool from the toolbox. Through his subsequent inclusion—albeit subtly and without justification—of what he seemed to dismiss previously, Socrates secures the ineffable connection between being embodied, using logos to retool one's character, and having access to one's *psuchē*.

It becomes increasingly noticeable near the end of the dialogue that Socrates is distancing himself from Alcibiades and the city. Although he will offer the same forecast for himself and the youth at the hands of the city in the dialogue's closing lines, Forde observes that Socrates (after 134d) speaks in the second-person plural, setting himself apart from Alcibiades and the city.[51] He suggests several reasons for this: perhaps there never was any real bond between Socrates and Alcibiades, nor a common basis for the friendship upon which he swears (109d1); perhaps Eros is no more adequate a basis for community than was spiritedness; or perhaps the philosopher dissolves the bond of community just when it seems Alcibiades is inclined to become a disciple, placing him in the role of the "stork" and pledging to follow him faithfully. If so, then it is only fitting that Socrates should shift the focus of Alcibiades' pledge from himself to his god.

Section 3.d.2 Learning What Needs to Be Learned

Socrates gives Alcibiades fewer details about what has to be learned than he does about the kinds of exercises the young man should undertake to advance his goals. Nor is it clear how this learning should proceed. He says only that the youth should learn what needs to be learned. The Royal Tale had valorized both wisdom and skill in conjunction with taking trouble. This formula for self-knowledge may be inferred to lead to wisdom, and it can be supposed also that the vital first step to Alcibiades' acquisition of wisdom will be the knowledge of his own ignorance, since this first stage is the necessary precondition for any subsequent learning, and Socrates has to work hard to secure it fully and sincerely in the dialogue. From the substance of their conversation, it also is apparent that Alcibiades will have to learn about the nature of justice. Socrates brings him to realize that the affairs of the people qua citizens are the business of the political art.

Alcibiades defines this art of rulership first without naming it, saying, "I, at least, mean ruling those in the city who have a part in the regime and engage in dealings with respect to one another" (125d7–9). Socrates leads him through argumentation that foreshadows the broad lines along which an eventual definition of justice might be formulated. Justice will have to do with achieving a harmony among the various components of something by ensuring that each part performs the function for which it is best suited. The principle of order among the different parts is highlighted, not only by the explicit argumentation but also by Socrates' account of the "cosmos," or "order," found in the great Spartan and Persian cities. Socrates provides two other indications of the curriculum to be followed by Alcibiades' education: the analogy to the "ship of state" and the example of a chorus leader. Both analogies indicate that what Alcibiades needs to learn resembles a certain kind of art.

Socrates introduces the ship of state analogy at the precise moment in their conversation when Alcibiades supposes himself most able to overcome his rivals in Athens. With this analogy, the philosopher accomplishes two things: he incites Alcibiades' ambition to pilot a warship—in much the same way that he used the chariot example with Lysis—thereby utilizing the future commander's own latent desires as a way of inspiring his attention toward what needs to be learned, and he illustrates for Alcibiades that it is not enough to possess *relative* wisdom which, in the case of the sailing analogy, only required that one be the most able sailor among crewmen, all of whom lack the pilot's art. Now the possession of this wisdom will determine the success or failure of the battleship's voyage. Possession of such an art, in the case of navigation, is proved only by ensuring the ship's safe passage. Socrates directs the young man to look toward his true competitors, those who really understand the art of piloting, instead of resting complacently in the presumption that he has only to be superior to his present rivals.

The chorus leader example furnishes Alcibiades with another analogy to the art of rulership. This should be a particularly instructive metaphor for him, since it was the answer—music—that the youth was repeatedly unable to furnish when Socrates questioned him at the beginning of the dialogue. Neither the choral director nor the pilot is a political ruler per se, so it is not exactly their art that Alcibiades should learn; but theirs is an art analogous to that of the political ruler. Both must possess what Alcibiades calls "good counsel" (125e6). But it quickly becomes apparent that the education of Pericles' nephew can get underway only after the prerequisite trouble has been taken to improve himself. When Alcibiades is unable to apply the other two models of stewardship to politics, Socrates has to cease educating him about justice in order to speak to the preliminary matter of "taking trouble." This further confirms that the kind of exercises that "gymnastics" includes provides the antecedent training for more formal, general education. The dramatic movement of this dialogue supports the interpretation that gymnastics develops the proper disposition through habitual practices and routine exercises. Until Alcibiades becomes a competent interlocutor, for example, Socrates will be unable to utilize dialogue to teach him about more advanced subjects.

One other issue in the background of Socrates' attempt to persuade Alcibiades to prepare himself properly for political life needs to be investigated. This issue points to a problem that will become increasingly important in the next chapter in the examination of the results of Socrates' efforts at remaking Alcibiades. Here the problem arises through a comparison of the effectiveness of Alcibiades' two pedagogues, Socrates and Pericles, in improving Alcibiades. Socrates invokes the name of Pericles in his first speech to Alcibiades (104b) and attributes to his supreme power and reputation the most dominant source of Alcibiades' self-confidence. Socrates (at 124c) brazenly declares that if he is different from his young companion at all, the difference is that his guardian is superior to Alcibiades' guardian, Pericles. In all, Plato has Socrates invoke the name of Pericles seven times in this dialogue, chiefly to contrast the inability of Alcibiades' guardian to improve those closest to him with the envisaged benefits of Socrates' proposed curriculum.

The key exchange over Pericles begins at 118c, where Socrates and Alcibiades are attempting to identify teachers of excellence among those who concern themselves with the things of the city. An illuminating discussion ensues when Socrates begins to evaluate whether Pericles succeeded in making those around him wise.[52] Ironically, Socrates applies the same standard to evaluate the great Athenian leader that will later be used to judge his own philosophical practice when he is put on trial. Socrates had just summarized his position, stating that both the arguments and Alcibiades' own admissions lend credence to the accusation that the future statesman has been wallowing in the midst of the most extreme stupidity. Proclaiming that Alcibiades is not alone in this condition, and that, in fact, only a few can be noted as exceptions to the rule, Socrates allows that perhaps Alcibiades' guardian is one of the exceptions.

Alcibiades takes the bait and begins praising Pericles' acquisition of wisdom through association with Anaxagoras and two renowned teachers of music.[53] Socrates seizes the opening and moves in for the kill, asking Alcibiades, "Have you ever seen any wise man who was unable to make another wise in the same way as himself?" (118c7–9). Alcibiades asserts that, as he himself has been so improved, he will be able to confer this wisdom, in turn, upon others. Socrates draws in the unsuspecting youth by saying that it is surely good evidence that someone is indeed wise when they can teach what they know to others. Alcibiades is now asked to say whom Pericles has made wise, "beginning with his own sons." Socrates suggests that Pericles' two sons (Alcibiades' cousins) were "born fools" and that Alcibiades' brother is a madman. Resisting the implication of Socrates' slanders against his family, Alcibiades answers the question concerning how he came to be in his present condition by blaming himself for not paying sufficient attention. Socrates does not leave the matter here but instead broadens his inquiry. "But tell me," he says, "if there is anyone among the rest of the Athenians or foreigners, slave or free, whose becoming wise was held to have been caused by association with Pericles" (119a1–3). To dramatize his point, Socrates claims, uncharacteristically, to know of two people who became wise after paying Zeno a fee of 100 minae.

It is precisely after Alcibiades declares, by Zeus, that he does not know of any such people whom Pericles made wise, that Socrates asks Alcibiades for the first time whether he is ready to give up his misplaced confidence and begin taking trouble over himself. Since Alcibiades had no teacher who was capable of making him wise, and since he did not learn from the demos, and since moreover he has not investigated for himself the matters under consideration, perhaps he will at last be ready to entrust his training and education to the philosopher. But, of course, another possible loophole still needs to be plugged by Socrates before Alcibiades will finally be subdued. This is because implicit in the discussion of Pericles is a criticism that only becomes concrete at the very end of the dialogue. If it is the mark of a good statesman to impart excellence to those over whom he rules, and Pericles was judged to have improved no one, then Socrates' final argument to Alcibiades indicts Pericles retrospectively as a poor leader. It would seem from the conclusion of this dialogue that the opposition between Plato and Pericles goes much further than the direct contrast here between Socratic and Periclean *paideia*.

SECTION 3.E CONCLUSION: THE OMINOUS END OF THE *ALCIBIADES I*

It may be no wonder that Alcibiades abandons Socrates' counsel sometime between their conversation in *Alcibiades I* and his encomium of Socrates in *Symposium* seventeen years later.[54] Socrates has thoroughly dampened his future plans with the formula he has laid down. Alcibiades must give up relying on all of the natural gifts and conventional excellences with which he has been endowed—his nobility, his beauty, his money, and his manliness—and must begin to rely only upon a regimen of self-care and the pursuit of wisdom. But this wisdom is not an easy thing to attain, in Socrates' view. Moreover, it was suggested that he needs to already have this wisdom in some sense in order to attain it, and yet for Alcibiades to recollect this knowledge, he will have to draw himself away from the noise of the crowd and engage in rigorous gymnastic preparations, beginning the lifelong process of molding and retooling his basic character. Socrates expresses doubts that the young man will be able to resist the powerful allure of the demos, the corruption of Alcibiades that Socrates had already said (at 132a) he fears most, and the dialogue ends with the philosopher ominously voicing his suspicion that both of them may be overcome by the city (135e7–8). Thus, at the end of the conversation in which Alcibiades submits to the grueling and sometimes humiliating interrogation, Socrates voices doubts that the young man will be able to carry out his self-reform, making light of his pledge to attend upon him. Nothing in anything Alcibiades says at the end of the dialogue supplies a reason for Socrates' judgment about him; the philosopher's doubts are based solely on his keen insight into Alcibiades' character and the many difficulties he knows to be inherent in his prescription for the youth.

Socrates has told him that before he can enter politics, Alcibiades must first take trouble over himself and learn the things that need to be learned. But this might just be a never-ending task, and Socrates himself may be proof of this fact. Socrates has told Alcibiades that he will be a good leader only by making himself excellent and having the ability to impart that excellence to the people he rules. But even the greatest leader of the day, Pericles, is hardly up to the task of making Alcibiades or anyone else better, in Socrates' view. Given the doubts the philosopher expresses in his parting remarks, the present moment may be the perfect time for Alcibiades to rectify his wayward condition, but Socrates evidently does not believe it is likely that he will do so.

Chapter 4

The *Symposium:* Eros, Truth Telling, and the Preservation of Freedom

The speech of Alcibiades in the *Symposium* confirms that the doubts Socrates expressed at the end of the *Alcibiades I* were more than well founded; they were prophetic. Many historically significant events occurred between 433 and 416 B.C.E., the seventeen years separating the dramatic dates of these two dialogues, a period during which Athens found itself almost continuously at war. Alcibiades' appearance and testimony at the end of the *Symposium* is important for the study of Socrates' educational approach, because Plato has him express the frustrations of perhaps Socrates' most promising pupil. In his speech, Alcibiades details his consternation over Socrates' erotic aloofness, his annoyance over Socrates' ironizing posture toward others, and the fact that Socrates has the exceptional and vexing power to make a great man like him feel shame.

Alcibiades is an important figure in any study of Socrates' educational methods too, because he may be the pupil who receives the most attention from Socrates in the dialogues. He is described as Socrates' lover in *Protagoras* (306a–b, 316a, 317e, 320a, 336b) and *Gorgias* (418d, 519a). He also is mentioned in the *Euthydemus* (275a). Most decisively, two entire dialogues are devoted to Socrates' conversations with him, in addition to their infamous encounter in the *Symposium*.[1] The space Plato allots to the legendary Athenian commander combines with Alcibiades' historical renown to suggest that he was the member of Socrates' circle who was believed to embody the greatest promise and who was thought to exemplify the most grave disaster of any of Socrates' "projects."

This chapter examines the reasons for Socrates' failure to turn around Alcibiades and then elaborates on the broader implications of this glaring failure for Socratic education and for Socrates' practice of philosophy. In order to lay the groundwork for these broader issues involving him, I first analyze Alcibiades' encomium of Socrates, and I do so in three steps: first, by disclosing the primary motive for Alcibiades' strategy toward Socrates, a motive that will be shown to be exposed in Socrates' response to him at 218e7–219a4; second, by examining the means that Alcibiades employs to attain his objective, that is, his infamous sexual solicitation; and third, by scrutinizing their disagreement throughout the speech about what constitutes telling the truth as a way of clarifying Alcibiades' charge against Socrates' ironical manner of speaking. This will permit us to contrast their respective kinds of Eros. Let us first set the scene for Alcibiades' speech.

The *Symposium* reaches its dramatic climax with the entrance of Alcibiades, just after Socrates has finished recounting the teaching of the priestess Diotima. At the time of this symposium, Alcibiades would have been at the height of his brilliant career, perhaps already preparing to lead the Athenians on the expedition to Sicily. The figure of the drunken Alcibiades contrasts sharply to the rarified heights reached at the pinnacle of Diotima's speech, and his encomium of Socrates has the dramatic effect of making Socrates replace, or instantiate, Eros, enacting in deed the central tenet of Socrates' "speech": that the truest lover is the philosopher, a philosopher such as Socrates, who is positioned in between complete wisdom and sheer ignorance. Diotima had even described this hybrid erotic in characteristics such as those commonly associated with Socrates. Alcibiades gives voice to the quandary in which all of those noble, promising, and (usually) handsome youths who spend their time in the company of this curious erotic find themselves.[2]

Perhaps nowhere is the vexation felt by these young men made more explicit than in the characterization that Alcibiades presents in his speech. The speech articulates several reasons for his frustration with Socrates: the repudiation he encountered when he finally was willing to submit to Socrates as his beloved; Socrates' rebuff of him—couched in the philosopher's typical ambiguous, ironic manner—which did not discourage him from climbing right into bed with Socrates; the way that Socrates' words enchanted and lured him while producing in him a feeling of intense shame; and the agonizing choice he faced between his attraction to the demos and his attraction to the philosophic life, exemplified by Socrates.[3]

The entrance of Alcibiades also accomplishes at least two other important things for the dialogue as a whole: it makes concrete and particular the Eros that had become quite abstract in Diotima's speech, and it returns the conversation to the everyday world of human concerns. The speech, moreover, is one of many examples of the way in which this dialogue artfully blends tragedy and comedy. Despite its importance, the driving force behind Alcibiades' speech too often has been misidentified. Hence, this chapter shall attempt, first, to clarify the motive for Alcibiades' reported actions toward Socrates. It will accomplish this by focusing upon the specific aspects of the speech that are set in relief by the philosopher's response to it. It will not be long, however, before Alcibiades himself divulges his barely concealed motive for the proposed exchange with Socrates, a motive made even more explicit to the audience by Socrates' immediate reaction to the proposal. The discovery of Alcibiades' motive leads directly to questions about how he plans to implement his strategy, and it will be necessary to examine two specific fronts on which Alcibiades hopes to carry out his plot. This will show how Alcibiades' attempted exchange would undermine the freedom of this unlikely paragon of Eros. It will be necessary to differentiate the nature of their respective Erotes in order to support the claim that Socrates' Eros is compatible with Plato's conception of freedom, while Alcibiades' Eros is not. It turns out that Alcibiades' speech discloses much more than one might expect, given the character of the messenger. The analysis that follows will show how the speech reveals things of which the speaker himself seems unaware. Ironically though, because it divulges more than the messenger might be thought to grasp, Alcibiades' speech serves, finally, to acquit Socrates of the very charges that it brings against him, as the last part of this chapter will show. Thus his testimony simultaneously indicts and exonerates Socrates, while acknowledging that the blame for the speaker's condition rests squarely on his own shoulders.

Section 4.a Alcibiades' Motive in the *Agōn* with Socrates

It is well known that Alcibiades offers his body to the older philosopher in exchange for the wisdom he hopes to obtain, but the impulse propelling this attempted exchange still remains somewhat murky. The language Plato uses to frame their contest makes plain that Alcibiades desires to dominate Socrates, and it is this underlying intention that leads to Alcibiades' plot to seduce him. In fact, his specific motive dictates the means that he will use, leading him to suppose that he can come to possess Socrates through some form of exchange. His speech, and the bi-play with Socrates that borders it on both sides, reveals his intent to get the better of Socrates, and his bid to transact a "sex for wisdom" exchange turns out to be just an ancillary tactic in pursuit of this driving desire. While there are only a few pieces of evidence for his chief motive, these few indications Plato does provide are clear enough.

Proof that Alcibiades seeks to possess Socrates in some way and hints that he conceives of their relationship within a market economy is woven throughout his encomium of the philosopher. When Socrates repudiates him for attempting such a "bronze for gold" trade, however, this announces to everyone that the younger man's proposition involves a kind of transaction, conceived as his proposition is within the framework of exchange. When Socrates points out the speech's market conception of human relations in his ironical rejoinder, this has the effect of unveiling both Alcibiades' true motive and his modus operandi. Alcibiades himself will testify to this motive, as we shall see. Still other decisive clues are embedded in the speech and in the narrator's comment that follows it. Most important, we shall see below that it is Alcibiades' impulse to dominate him that Socrates identifies as the driving force behind the sexual solicitation. The philosopher's immediate reaction has a different ring to it, once this motive for the foiled seduction has been unveiled. Any interpretation of Socratic Eros, in general, and of the *Symposium* as a dialogue about Eros will need to pay close attention to the leading motive at the heart of Alcibiades' speech. Failing to do so may lead one to misconstrue the Socratic admonishment of him. The tenor of Socrates' response can be properly heard once Alcibiades' motive has been exposed. I shall first examine Alcibiades' motive in greater detail before attending to the ways in which his actions would constrain Socrates.

I will show that Socrates resists Alcibiades' advances not because he is asexual, as some commentators have argued,[4] and not merely because he is incapable of love for particular persons, as others have suggested.[5] Rather, it will become clear that Socrates must resist his solicitations in order to preserve his freedom. Socrates' behavior here need not be interpreted as a general disavowal of the physical Eros. In fact, his reproach does not suggest that philosophers should be asexual, and because Alcibiades gives an encomium of Socrates rather than Eros as the others had done, the philosopher is made to stand in for Eros, exemplifying Eros incarnate. Rather than signifying his (or Plato's) negative judgement on the physical Eros, Socrates resists Alcibiades' attempt to possess him and to "get the better of," or to dominate, him in the exchange of their respective beauties as a way of maintaining his freedom in the face of Alcibiades' challenge to it. But lest we suppose that Socrates has to renounce his erotic nature in order to perfect his freedom, the analysis that follows will show that Socrates' Eros turns out to be what sustains this philosopher's novel practice of philosophy and keeps it free.

In the dramatic action of the *Symposium*, Alcibiades' arrival alters immediately the direction of the proceedings. Already intoxicated, he insists that the consensus to imbibe temperately be abandoned for serious drinking. Filling the large wine bowl with undiluted wine, he drains it once himself, has the slave refill it, and orders everyone to drink, beginning with Socrates. This dramatic interlude permits him to comment for the first time on Socrates' seeming imperviousness to the effects of alcohol (a theme that will be developed in Section 4.c.2). More important, his behavior demonstrates that he is a man who is accustomed to dictating the terms of every situation he enters. In *Symposium*'s dramatic situation, Alcibiades takes over the proceedings in the single act of appointing himself "symposiarch," or "leader of the drinking" (213e9–10).[6] The Greek word for the leader of the symposium, *symposiarchos*, contains the same root as the word for the holder of a public office (*archon*).[7] The audience's awareness of his tumultuous political career would have made Alcibiades' autocracy here suggestive. In a manner that foreshadows his subsequent fate, Alcibiades comes close to inaugurating himself as dictator of this symposium.

His decision to seduce Socrates follows immediately upon his confession, "I felt I should obey him in everything" (217a2–4). Realizing that Socrates has not fallen for his charms, Alcibiades plots to conquer him instead of obeying. He makes clear that he initiates the attempted seduction (a curiosity that will be developed in section 4.b in connection with the general reversal of roles between lover and beloved, highlighted in this speech). It is the younger, more beautiful Alcibiades who invites Socrates to dinner, organizes the bouts of wrestling, draws Socrates into conversation, and suggests that the lateness of the hour makes the philosopher's departure imprudent. It is, moreover, Alcibiades who decides to divulge his thoughts when he and Socrates spend their night alone. Recalling his plot against Socrates, the clever Alcibiades says that he suspected Socrates was in love with him. In this calculating way, he shrewdly attempts to impute to Socrates the initiative for their encounter.

But his speech discloses that the plot to seduce the philosopher is motivated by a desire for possession; sexual seduction was simply a means to this end. Since Plato's contemporary audience would certainly have done so, it is worth recalling here that the historical Alcibiades was notoriously promiscuous. His sexual appetite and his penchant for seduction led him to violate one of the most sacred bonds for a Greek when he seduced the wife of his guest-friend, King Agis, while exiled in Sparta. Moreover, it is widely believed that his death in Phrygia in 403 was the result of the outrage of a well-known family whose daughter he had seduced. Although he was reputed to have collected lovers like a prototypical Don Juan, the audience of his *Symposium* speech may have surmised that his desire to possess Socrates issues, at least in part, from a somewhat different source—the shame he admits to feeling in Socrates' presence. He imagines that if he can shift the balance of power in their relationship, gaining in some way the upper hand with Socrates, he may be able to reclaim his self-respect. Alcibiades confesses:

> I heard Pericles and other good orators and I believe they spoke well, but I was not affected at all like this, nor was my soul disturbed and angered at my being in the position of a slave; but due to this Marsyas here I've often been put in that position, so that it seemed to me it was not worth living to be as I am. And this, Socrates, you will not deny to be true. And still even now, I am conscious that if I were willing to give ear I could not hold out against him; I would suffer the same things. For he compels me to agree that though I am myself much in need, I neglect myself and attend to the affairs of Athens. So I stop my ears by force as if against the Sirens and run away, in order that I may not grow old sitting here beside him. Before him alone among men I suffer what one might not have supposed is in me—shame before anyone. Before him alone I feel ashamed. For I am conscious that I cannot contradict him and say it isn't necessary to do what he bids, but when I leave him, I am worsted by the honors of the multitude. So I desert him and flee, and when I see him I am shamed by my own agreements. (215e4–216a6, Allen trans.)

The express desire to possess Socrates comes on the heels not only of both this admission of shame and his acknowledgment that he should obey Socrates in everything, but it also follows his repeated threat to pay back Socrates for his earlier remarks (213d7–8; 214e1–3). Though Alcibiades attributes his ability to speak "frankly" to his inebriation, and though he divulges to the other symposiasts the motivation that drives his attempt to ensnare Socrates, it is not until Socrates chastises him that his underlying impulse is fully disclosed.[8] Socrates knows, and states forthrightly, that Alcibiades is trying to get an advantage over him. Proof that the street-wise Socrates sees right through the unsubtle ploy is supplied by what he says in his rebuttal prior to declaring that the proposed exchange would be of bronze for gold: "If you then try to make a deal with me that involves trading our respective beauties, then you're planning to gain an advantage (*pleonektein*) over me" (218e3–5).

Alcibiades does not just want to get even with Socrates, he wants to get the better of him in a relationship that he can only conceive of as competitive. This revelation about the younger man's motive supplies the clearest, most important reason for the philosopher's resistance, justifying perhaps his ironical stance in the struggle against the young man's aggression. Plato allows the various audiences—of Alcibiades, of Apollodorus, and of his dialogue—to see clearly here the acquisitive tendencies that suffuse both Alcibiades' attraction to Socrates and the other objects at which the young man's Eros aims. What Alcibiades admits that he wants, ultimately, is to possess Socrates, or failing that, to sully him, because he believes that such a conquest would relieve his dissatisfaction with his own life. Only by knocking down the indomitable Socrates a notch or two, arousing him and bringing him to desire his beauty and other gifts, does Alcibiades think he can cleanse himself of the shame he says he feels in Socrates' presence. He wants to demonstrate that the philosopher too is human and has human desires. If he can bring Socrates to desire him, then he would not have to feel so badly about his own runaway desires and weak character. Alcibiades attests to a classic case of *akrasia:* he establishes a good for himself, and then he cannot bring himself to follow it. He "knows" what is best for him, but he cannot do it. Hence, even better than having Socrates dead—which he says he sometimes wants—would be for the unruly Alcibiades to knock this seemingly insuperable philosopher off of his pedestal and show him to be as corruptible as is Alcibiades himself. It is to accomplish this objective that the proudly handsome Alcibiades deploys his beauty to gain erotically the mastery he has been unable to secure in any other way.[9] When Socrates exposes the sexual offer as an outgrowth of the impulse to *pleonektein* over him, that is, to get the better of him, this makes explicit to everyone (except perhaps Alcibiades) the chief reason for the philosopher's behavior. (Alcibiades, of course, pretends to be shocked and embarrassed by this turn of events.)

The key word in Socrates' rejoinder is *pleonektein.* For Plato, *pleonexia* (or *pleonektia*) denotes a natural human desire for "the more" (*to pleion*). In political contexts, he frequently ascribes to *pleonexia* the insatiable appetites undergirding Athenian imperialism. These appetites feed the lust for power, inciting deceitfulness in political leaders. Such boundless desire to get more than one's fair share is epitomized in Glaucon's speech in *Republic* II. It also forms the locus of Callicles' argument in the *Gorgias* (*Gorgias* 483c*ff*). Here, in the *Symposium's* climactic scene, Plato illustrates how Alcibiades' kind of individualism usurps the freedom of others as the natural outgrowth of unrestrained spiritedness coupled with appetitiveness. In the character of Alcibiades, as in Athens itself by the end of the Peloponnesian War, there appears to be no limit to the appetite for domination.[10] It is therefore likely that Alcibiades' attempt to gain the advantage over Socrates stems from the same corrosive impulse that, for Plato, is symptomatic of the acquisitive Eros and its insatiable appetite for possession.[11] (The specific character of this acquisitive Eros, driven by unbridled spiritedness, will be explored in greater detail in Section 4.b.1.)

Thucydides, in his *History*, also pinpoints the desire to get more than his fair share at the expense of others as Alcibiades' chief character trait. He regularly describes him with words such as *pleonektein* and the noun *pleonexia* in connection with love of honor (*philotimia*). Alcibiades' "daring" (*tolma*), in Thucydides' view, goes far beyond ordinary courage or manliness (*andreos*).[12] Steven Forde has called this feature of Alcibiades' character a "specifically imperial or imperialistic quality."[13] For Thucydides, this imperialistic quality, this lust for power, becomes the fatal flaw of the Athenian spirit, and, as its boldest leader, Alcibiades seems to personify that spirit completely. This ambition is tragic, above all, because it results finally in the elimination of the political freedom that it sets out to safeguard, if this ambition is not subordinated to any end beyond the desire for power for its own sake. Alcibiades is like the "democratic man" in the *Republic*, representing the degeneration of the Periclean ideal of honor and glory into an admixture of sophistry, a deadly, endearing charm, and overreaching political avarice.[14] In Thucydides' view, this daring ambition contains the seeds of its own eventual destruction.[15]

SECTION 4.B ALCIBIADES' ATTEMPT TO DOMINATE SOCRATES

His immediate reaction to the seduction scheme underscores how Alcibiades' approach appears to Socrates an attempt to dominate him and undermine his practice of freedom. The philosopher's infamous objection, that Alcibiades is trying to exchange bronze for gold and opinion for truth, recalls an essential constituent of Socratic education, perhaps the one that keeps it most free.[16] Whereas Socrates makes it a policy to keep himself and his practice of philosophy free from market relations, Alcibiades seems to conceive of all human relations as some kind of exchange. Within such a matrix, even his body is something to be offered for a price. The disgruntled Alcibiades thinks that he can pull off some sort of barter with Socrates, evincing the philosopher's corruptibility by showing that he too has his price. Alcibiades therefore moves to dominate Socrates by attempting to sabotage his practice of freedom. He does this in three related ways: (1) by getting the better of or gaining an advantage (*pleonektein*) over him; (2) by luring him into an exchange economy with his proposed "sex for wisdom" transaction, thereby showing that Socrates too can be bought; and (3) by causing Socrates to desire him as a traditional *erastēs*, or lover, would. Through these three modes of constraint, Alcibiades seeks to assimilate Socrates' Eros to his own acquisitive Eros and undermine the philosopher's practice of freedom. In the process, he hopes to enslave the only man who has ever made him feel ashamed and caused the noble Alcibiades to act like a runaway slave.

The first way in which Alcibiades seeks to dominate Socrates has already been broached in the previous section. Socrates knows that Alcibiades is trying to swindle him, thus he exposes Alcibiades' offer as an act of acquisitiveness rather than as a genuine desire to attain wisdom. Alcibiades thinks that he can dominate or gain an advantage over Socrates by offering his body to him, thereby placing the incorruptible philosopher in his debt. Recalling the logic of the benefactor/beneficiary relation for Aristotle in Section 1.c should help clarify the rationale behind this strategy. If Alcibiades could confer a benefit upon Socrates, this would result in a kind of indebtedness of the philosopher to the no longer shamed Alcibiades. Such a benefit would obligate Socrates to him (at least until an equal or a greater benefit could be given in return), in which case the younger man would have accomplished a very important shift in the balance of power between them, a shift perhaps sufficient to alleviate the intense shame that he currently feels whenever he encounters Socrates.

This first way Alcibiades would dominate Socrates emerges after he tells Socrates that it would be stupid not to gratify him or give him whatever his friends have in return for his assistance in becoming good (218d). Socrates deftly refuses his offer of both money and sexual favors. Rather than being a flat rejection, however, his response is steeped in irony.[17] He counsels Alcibiades to take a closer look so that he will not be deceived into thinking that the philosopher possesses something he does not really have.[18] Unshaken, Alcibiades reiterates his intention to become the acquiescent beloved. But he defers to Socrates for a final decision on his offer, mustering what remains of his self-respect.

Yet not even his praise of Socrates for saving his life in battle escapes the logic of exchange. Once more, it is evident that Alcibiades conceives of their relationship on a creditor/debtor model when he says, "Then there's his behavior in combat; I owe him an account of this, to cover my debt" (220d6–7). He explains how Socrates saved his life in battle, but he places the greatest emphasis on the fact that the philosopher allowed the honor lover, Alcibiades, to claim for himself the resultant glory. It is deeply ironical then that he should accuse Socrates of one-upmanship in the tug of war for Agathon's attention following his speech. Like a spoiled child, the ambitious Alcibiades complains, "He thinks he always has to go one better than me" (222e7). In fact, it is Socrates who eschews the cycle of escalation throughout the story of their encounter by refusing to be lured into the potlatch model of human relations into which Alcibiades has sought to entice him.

One of the leading virtues of Alcibiades' speech is the way in which it calls attention to the critical components of the Socratic practice of freedom.

Alcibiades gives numerous examples of Socratic *sophrosunē* in the encomium, one of the cardinal features of freedom as Socrates practices it. And without explicating the connection between the various components that he highlights, Socrates is depicted in the speech as exercising unflinching self-mastery in every situation, exhibiting extreme power (*dunamis*) over necessity, and displaying unshakable independence and superlative self-sufficiency. Despite his repeated attempts to fulfill his own desires at the expense of Socrates' freedom, it cannot have escaped Alcibiades' notice that this principled philosopher habitually refuses fees or payments from anyone.[19]

We have seen that the refusal to accept a fee is a crucial tenet of Socrates' philosophical practice and an essential hallmark of his freedom. Socrates often demonstrates his unwillingness to be placed in another's debt, and he testifies to this practice in the *Apology*, as Chapter 1 established. This practice was shown to have the effect of keeping Socrates free to converse with whomever he wishes, without being forced to talk to anyone. Unlike the Sophists, who were obliged by their fee-based services to satisfy their customers in the intellect business, Socrates, to recall Teloh's apt point, did not have to pander to his interlocutors. By eschewing payments, gifts, bribes, honors, and now even sexual favors, the philosopher preserves his freedom to tell the truth to those with whom he converses (which will be examined in detail in Section 4.c).

Insofar as to be free in Socrates' Athens implied the capacity for beneficence, not being in a position to display one's beneficence or magnanimity would cause one to be regarded as a virtual slave. To be in another's debt also is a form of slavishness, as the citations from Aristotle illustrated. Hence, being indebted to "clients" for their fee payments would not simply have obligated Socrates to talk to certain people; fee taking would have made him a slave in a broader sense, someone beholden to his customers and dependent on the same kinds of payments that corrupted his intellectual competitors. This is why instead of simply trying to maintain the upper hand in benefaction, by conferring more than he receives, Socrates opts out of market exchange altogether. Throughout the dialogues, he consistently avoids any involvement in a market economy, because this would constrain his teaching, and he stresses this stance when he appeals to his poverty as an emblem of his independence.[20] He may be poor, but he does not owe anyone anything, and in an economy such as that pervasive in fifth-century Athens, this relative self-sufficiency would have been paramount to the ethos of freedom.[21]

Alcibiades' speech reveals that his insight into Socrates' character does not prevent him, at the same time, from badly misreading Socrates. In the story of his attempted seduction, it is evident that Alcibiades imagines that becoming Socrates' beloved would entitle him to receive from Socrates everything the philosopher knows (217a). Heir to a theme that hearkens back to the incident on the couch with Agathon upon Socrates' belated arrival to the party,

Alcibiades appears to think that knowledge can be obtained by just such a transfer. He thinks knowledge will follow automatically from coming into contact with Socrates and from hearing what the wise man knows. Recall that Agathon, likewise, appeared to think that knowledge could pass from one to another, like some kind of fluid. Moreover, Alcibiades' behavior shows that he assumes Socrates will speak or act differently in private than he does in public, something that the Sophists did, but something that Socrates, at his trial, vehemently denies doing, as *Apology* 33a attests. Socrates, of course, has no formulaic knowledge to lavish upon Alcibiades, and he has already vitiated the "knowledge-transfer" or "additive" conception of learning, teasing, "Wouldn't it be nice if wisdom were like that, Agathon?" Would that knowledge could "flow by contact from someone who had more of it into someone who had less of it" (175d3–5). But of course, for Socrates, not every form of knowledge can be rightly conceived on this hydraulic model. Yet it is just such a transfusion of wisdom that Alcibiades hopes will be the solution to his dissatisfaction with himself.[22] Admitting that Socrates' exhortations affect him only as long as he remains in the philosopher's company, Alcibiades is hoping that the contagion of wisdom will truly take hold of him once he comes to possess Socrates' body. But wisdom too would be merely a means to greater power for him. By possessing Socrates in this way, Alcibiades seeks both to mitigate the influence the philosopher has over him and to acquire this kind of power himself in the most expedient, painless manner possible.

Increasingly evident throughout his speech is the fact that Alcibiades knew full well the futility of his attempts to bribe Socrates. In his most revealing admission, he declares, "I was well aware that you'd be more likely to get a weapon through Ajax's guard than you would money through Socrates', and now he'd escaped the only trap I thought stood a chance of ensnaring him" (219e1–5).[23] Here the audience is given conclusive evidence that Alcibiades knew for sure that his calculated efforts at seduction were motivated by the desire to bribe Socrates, which he perceives as a shortcut to self-improvement. So the second way in which Alcibiades would dominate Socrates is closely linked to the first. A close reading of the phrasing of his proposition and the language in which Socrates rebukes him supplies clear proof that the philosopher resisted the younger man's sexual solicitation chiefly because he was unwilling to compromise the quintessential dimension of his character, namely, his inveterate practice of philosophy by which his freedom is exercised. It is through his practice of freedom that Socrates seeks to contravene not only the subjugation/domination model of human interaction and its connection to the benefactor/beneficiary relation—both of which underwrite Alcibiades' attempted transaction—but also the conventional roles of *erastēs* and *eromenos*, lover and beloved. His attempt to get Socrates to desire him (in the way in which Hippothales desired Lysis) according to a traditional *sunousiastic* model is thus the third and most overt way in which Alcibiades would dominate Socrates and sabotage his freedom.

The conventional Athenian view of the lover/beloved relation finds perhaps its noblest justification in the "good Eros," the "Aphrodite Ouranios," valorized in Pausanias' speech. (180c–185c). There the love of boys is justified as an exchange of wisdom and truth for sexual gratification. The *Symposium*'s early speeches in praise of Eros each presented a kind of defense of *sunousia* from either the standpoint of the beloved or the lover.[24] One important implication here of the practice of *sunousia* for the prevalent Greek understanding of social roles is that, in Greek homoerotic practices, we can again see a striking example of the extent to which, even among citizen-men of relatively equal wealth and social standing, distinctions such as lover and beloved in *sunousia* are used constantly to assess one's relative rank, power, and freedom. In other words, even where one expects to find relations of greatest equality, a tendency persists to conceive of human relationships as asymmetrical in various ways.[25] This is evidenced by the use of the model of *sunousia* to frame the relationship between Alcibiades and Socrates, who are in their thirties and fifties, respectively.

Against this background, Socrates' behavior in the story that Alcibiades tells can be better understood. His resistance to Alcibiades' overtures follows from his usual way of inverting these conventional dichotomies and of undermining philosophically such simple binaries. But the way in which Socrates subverts the prevalent dichotomy between an active, older lover and a passive, younger beloved proves most crucial for his erotic approach to his young, impressionable interlocutors. With Lysis and Alcibiades, Socrates made these customary roles and the practices traditionally associated with them the linchpin of his philosophical approach. We saw how he undermined traditional assumptions in an elaborate game of seduction, first inverting and then completely doing away with the conventional model, while seeming to be merely taking up his conventional *sunousiastic* role with them.[26] How Socrates employs his distinctive kind of Eros in conversation to arouse his target interlocutors and bring them to desire what he has in store for them has already been shown. This strategy was further shown to be carried out as a way of mobilizing the unsuspecting youths, pointing the way to their freedom. Just as Socrates supplanted the beautiful Lysis and Alcibiades as the prized object of pursuit during his first conversation with each boy,[27] here Alcibiades describes his attempt to consummate and complete this reversal. The younger Alcibiades admits to chasing the older, notoriously ugly Socrates.

Alcibiades (217c) shamelessly notes the irony of the reversal of gender roles, exclaiming, "As if I were the lover and he were the boy." What is unique about this reversal in the present context is that a more or less passive role is ascribed to Socrates. From Alcibiades' speech in the *Symposium* alone the audience would not have learned of the arousal with which Socrates had previously enticed Alcibiades. Showing only a latter phase in the relationship may be Plato's way of calling attention here to events that have come before, in other conversations to which Alcibiades alludes and to which he seems to be explicitly referring in his mention of "past agreements."[28] Socrates' usual tool for setting the reversal in motion in these erotic dialogues was shown to be a calculated arousal of the youth's deep-seated desires. The penetrating philosopher senses that the passive youth takes for granted that the world will be effortlessly his as a result of his beauty, intelligence, and noble birth. Once he detects such conceits, the crafty Socrates inflames the desires of the promising youth to provoke him to take trouble over himself. In the *Lysis*, we saw how the erotic arousal is followed almost immediately by a powerful chastening. The two primary elements of his strategy function in tandem. Here Plato's audience must look to the dialogues dramatizing the previous conversations between Alcibiades and Socrates to verify that such a Socratic arousal has indeed taken place.[29]

Alcibiades admits to being the initiator of the plan that would force Socrates either to "put up" or be guilty of teasing these boys through his frivolous flirtations, something he accuses Socrates of in his speech. It also becomes evident from his speech that the self-centered Alcibiades is not accustomed to yielding to any lover as a merely passive object. He tries on this role with Socrates only because he supposes that he will be able to win the larger war through his momentary submission in this particular battle. Hence, the reversal of roles here suggests more than simply Socrates arousing Alcibiades at some other time and place; it signals also that Alcibiades is a different kind of character than Lysis is, more bellicose and conniving. Alcibiades is not nearly as naively innocent as Lysis was. His report of the failed seduction divulges that something other than purely erotic desire motivates him. He relies upon his ability to gain supremacy in what he sees as a contest for domination. Lacking any appreciation for reciprocal Eros, there is really no room in Alcibiades' schema for Socrates to respond positively toward him.

Section 4.b.1 Eros and *Thumos*

The plot to gain an advantage over Socrates reveals how Alcibiades' Eros is driven by spiritedness (*thumos*) bound up as his Eros is with ambition, pride, and *pleonexia*. His Eros is the Eros that seizes upon its object as something to be acquired or assimilated. He not only confuses the object of desire with the aim of that desire,[30] which Socrates had taken pains to distinguish through his recollection of Diotima's teaching, but his fixation upon any object leads to the appetite for possession of it. Ultimately, Alcibiades desires to appropriate the object of his Eros which, on the evening he recalls in his speech, is Socrates.

Diotima had already forewarned of this kind of Eros, intertwined with *thumos* (spiritedness). In Socrates' recollection of her teaching, Diotima had remarked, "If you will look to the love of honor among men, you'd be surprised by the unreasonableness of which I've spoken, unless you keep in mind and reflect on how strangely disposed men are by Eros to make a name and 'lay up store of immortal glory for everlasting time' " (208c1–5; Allen trans.). Such an Eros mistakes the real aim of the striving for immortality—which Diotima says is happiness (*eudaimonia*)—for the desire to dominate or possess its object forever, an unsatisfying substitute for immortality. The problem here is analogous to the problem encountered in Chapter 2 in connection with Hippothales' attraction for Lysis. Since the ultimate object of all desire—including the desire for goodness, wisdom, friendship, or love—cannot be possessed, Socrates had shown Lysis and Menexenus a way of conceiving desire that does not fixate on objects intermediate to the ultimate aim of desire but that rather aims constantly at the eventual goal of desire without ever being able to possess it completely.

Alcibiades clearly has not learned this lesson. He imagines that he can come to possess both Socrates' wisdom and his goodness, as though these were themselves material belongings. He confesses to thinking that Socrates himself is the ultimate object of his longing. This reveals that he knows only what might be called the "terminal Eros." This terminal Eros can be directed at inappropriate objects or directed inappropriately toward what should otherwise be its proper object. Plato's equation of this Eros with the other appetites, such as hunger and thirst, draws attention to the way in which this "misguided Eros"—to borrow John Brentlinger's phrase[31]—fastens upon its object. The proclivity toward escalation and excess in appetitive desire arises from the sense of dissatisfaction that this Eros suffers once it gains hold of its misidentified object. And all intermediate objects of human striving, if regarded as the ultimate aim of that striving, are, for Socrates, objects misidentified. Dissatisfaction is caused by the fact that in possessing any object, this terminal, acquisitive Eros clutches only what is intermediate to its elusive, inarticulate aim. In Alcibiades' case, he is unable to grasp that the Eros that initially impelled him toward Socrates' guidance has given way to the unbridled desire to possess Socrates himself. When viewed through the lens of his frank expressions of hostility and recrimination, Alcibiades' plot to seduce Socrates can be seen for what it really is: a transparent attempt to dominate the philosopher. Hence, it is to preserve his freedom that Socrates resists being overpowered.

It is to highlight that Alcibiades' plot is contrived to undercut Socrates' practice of freedom—and not merely to exemplify his already legendary self-control or to show that Socrates has renounced all sexual desires—that Plato has the philosopher resist Alcibiades. This is not to say that Socrates' reaction does not also serve as another example of how the philosopher manifests just the right desires in every situation. It does, and it might in fact be the perfect example of this. But if it *does* provide a paradigmatic example of Socratic *sophrosunē*, then in the same way that Socratic irony works, this dramatic example leaves unclear whether Socrates did, then or ever, desire Alcibiades in the way in which Alcibiades wanted, and whether he, then or ever, engaged in the more conventional forms of *sunousia*.

Even if one construes his rebuff of Alcibiades as celebrating the virtues of self-mastery or soundmindedness, the choice to act or not to act upon a specific desire needs to be distinguished from the demand to rid oneself completely of such desire. Socrates is not depicted as struggling to control himself in the face of Alcibiades' offer; likewise, he is widely portrayed in the dialogues as having just the appropriate desires in every situation. It is worth recalling here that Alcibiades follows Eryximachus in reminding the audience that Socrates is equally good at drinking and not drinking.[32] That Socrates can go either way and is ready for whatever the occasion demands supplies additional evidence for the kind of soundmindedness implied by Socrates' refusal to consummate a sexual relationship with Alcibiades.[33]

The problem with Alcibiades' Eros is that it operates only within the dialectic of subjugation and domination. It is too closely tied to spiritedness to be compatible with either philosophy or philosophical freedom, as these are exemplified by Socrates. Misunderstanding both the nature of Eros and what David Halperin calls "erotic reciprocity,"[34] Alcibiades knows only the dynamic of rivalry (*antierastēs*) and not mutual eroticism (*sunerastēs*). His speech makes manifest that he conceives of all relationships in terms of the dialectic of master and slave, subjugation and domination. By having Alcibiades follow the speech of Socrates, Plato invites his audience to consider the profound, disparate consequences of the acquisitive Eros in full career.

From the historical example of Alcibiades, it can be adduced that the Eros driven by an unbridled *thumos, pleonexia,* and *philotimia* may combine to create a highly volatile political force. Left unharnessed, it may produce disastrous effects in social and political relations. Thucydides' *History* is, in many respects, a critique of this naked egoism and the sociopolitical relativism that it breeds. When one is visited by its powers, this spirited Eros can appear indistinguishable from Eros directed toward its proper aim (happiness); and to the untrained eye, Alcibiades' Eros may resemble the genuine desire to gratify a lover. But Plato unmasks it as the moving cause of the impulse to dominate and the tendency to conceive of all human relations in terms of such a domination/subjugation model. Forde underscores the fact that in his personal relations, as in his political dealings, Alcibiades manifests his belief that only by expansion and aggression can greatness be achieved. His speech to the Athenian assembly in favor of the Sicilian expedition in Thucydides' *History* argues for such aggrandizement in the guise of his "dominate or be dominated" logic. The same self-interested versatility guides his personal relationships. A recent article describes him as one who "collected lovers as part of a power game." The author goes on to say, "Their [Alcibiades' lovers] flattery and importunity confirmed the irresistibility of his attraction and the finality of his hold over their minds."[35]

Many clues to his warring impulses are submitted by his seemingly rambling speech. Yet for all of his scheming devices, Alcibiades confesses that, "no slave has been utterly more in the power of any master than I was in his" (219e3–5). He takes Socrates' inactivity toward him as an insult, and he appears to understand his freedom in the same terms in which he understands his relations with others: if he is not the master then he must be the slave. Supposing that one either rules another or is ruled by him, and that all relations between human beings involve a struggle for victory or gain in the quest for rulership, Alcibiades maneuvers to dominate Socrates.

Section 4.b.2 The Vindication of Socrates' Approach to Others

I have attempted to show that the contest between the enigmatic philosopher and the notoriously ambivalent political leader is, at bottom, a struggle over freedom that Plato dramatizes to illuminate the difference between two divergent trajectories of Eros: one the acquisitive, competitive Eros, personified in Alcibiades, which Socrates repudiates, and the other the Socratic-philosophic Eros, toward which the speech of Alcibiades can only point with anecdotes and examples.[36] Alcibiades' Eros threatens the freedom of others, while Socrates' distinctive Eros is compatible with, and even productive of, their freedom, notwithstanding Alcibiades' feeling in Socrates' presence that he is no better than a slave. Socrates can be seen repeatedly attempting to free his interlocutors from their present constraints. We saw this in the cases of both Lysis and the young Alcibiades. He was shown striving to disabuse these boys of the presumption that all forms of limitation entail constraints upon their freedom, introducing them to a new understanding of limits compatible with the proper ethos of freedom. When given the opportunity to exploit his advantage by seizing upon the vulnerability of his trusting, young pupils, Socrates refused to do so, striving instead to point the way to their increased self-sufficiency through his own paradigmatic example, as the *Lysis* and *Alcibiades I* illustrated.

Much of what Alcibiades says in his *Symposium* speech seems to outdistance his own understanding. He functions like a messenger or a medium: he does not always seem to be the author of his own thoughts. His speech is filled with rich symbolism, allusions to the later charges against Socrates, and comments that are unintentionally revealing, such as when, in describing Socrates' formidable performance in battle, he remarks, "Here was a man who would resist an attack with considerable determination" (221b4–6). As he spins his tale of the awe-inspiring *sophrosune* that Socrates exhibits, the analogy of this battle imagery to the thwarting of his own plot becomes increasingly poignant. Additionally, his testimony acquits Socrates of the kinds of charges to be levied against him seventeen years later. The speech refutes the formal charges against which Socrates makes his own defense in *Apology of Socrates:* it answers the charge of impiety by describing the strange function of Socrates' *daimonion* and by praising the god-like qualities of this exemplary human being; it answers the charge of corruption by offering testimony that places the blame on Alcibiades, not on Socrates, for the character shortcomings of this brilliant disappointment (and others like him). Furthermore, the speech highlights the vexation others feel upon witnessing the philosopher's incorruptibility and upon his regular displays of self-mastery, self-sufficiency, and soundmindedness. Threatening to call up witnesses to confirm his account of Socrates, Alcibiades speaks to the gathering as to a jury, even calling them "gentlemen of the jury" (219c). Serving as the ultimate jurist, Plato's audience is invited to judge between the two lives, assessing the differences between their respective ways of speaking, their respective Erotes, and the very different grounds on which each man in turn was charged with impiety and corruption.

Paradoxically, the speech, which Alcibiades delivers in the manner of an accusatory indictment, ends up exonerating Socrates of any responsibility for the speaker's character. Socrates' failure to improve Alcibiades, the failure of his Eros to reproduce itself in the young man who was perhaps his most promising associate, is disclosed as resulting from Alcibiades' lack of discipline, the fact that what self-knowledge he has is only intermittent, and from his admitted habit of "plugging his ears with wax" and running away from Socrates. It bears recalling that Alcibiades had lamented: "As soon as I'm away from him, I get seduced by the adulation of the masses. So I act like a runaway slave and keep away from him" (216b). The same testimony that relieves Socrates of responsibility for his pupil's subsequent career, then, indicts the demos for the way it encourages the honor-love of ambitious youths such as Alcibiades, inciting their pleonexic aspirations.[37] In the end, the *agōn* enacted between Socrates and Alcibiades in *Symposium* forces Plato's audience to recall the political fates soon to befall the two combatants. At the end of their very first conversation, Socrates confessed his doubts about the future of the gifted young man he has grown to love. These doubts persisted at the end of that dialogue, in spite of Alcibiades' vows to follow Socrates' prescription for him. The final exchange in the *Alcibiades I* adds to the ominous sense of foreboding on *Symposium*'s political horizon, making it clear that Socrates understands that his destiny as a teacher is bound up inexorably with this brilliantly flawed pupil (and others like him). That colloquy underlined the precarious position of both Socrates and Alcibiades vis-à-vis the city, deepening the significance of their contest in the *Symposium*. The dialogue concludes as follows:

> *Soc.* And are you now conscious of your own state? And do you know whether you are a free man or not?
>
> *Al.* I think that I am very conscious indeed of my own state.
>
> *Soc.* And do you know how to escape out of your present state, which I do not even like to name when imputing it to beauty?
>
> *Al.* Yes, I do.
>
> *Soc.* How?
>
> *Al.* By your help, Socrates.
>
> *Soc.* That is not well said, Alcibiades.
>
> *Al.* What ought I to have said?
>
> *Soc.* By the help of God.
>
> *Al.* I agree; and I further say, that our relations are likely to be reversed. From this day forward, I must and will follow you as you have followed me; I will be the attendant, and you shall be my master.
>
> *Soc.* O that is rare! My love breeds another love: and so like the stork I shall be cherished by the winged creature whom I have hatched.
>
> *Al.* Strange, but true; and henceforward I shall begin to think about justice.
>
> *Soc.* And I hope that you will persist; although I have fears, not because I doubt you, but because I see the power of the state, which may be too much for both of us. (*Alc. I* 135d–e, Jowett trans.)

In addition to foreshadowing the fates of the two lovers, the closing lines of the *Alcibiades I* reflect Socrates' disdain for disciples. Socrates responds sarcastically to Alcibiades' pledge to follow him. Chapter 3 exhibited how the philosopher gradually transfers the responsibility for Alcibiades' success from his own shoulders to the god's during the course of their first conversation, incrementally retracting or qualifying in the process his more outlandish claims regarding his own ability to help Alcibiades attain his ambitious political goals. Yet at the end of the conversation, Socrates still has to correct the youth when he erroneously states that it will be with the philosopher's help, rather than with the god's, that Alcibiades will improve himself. And Alcibiades immediately follows this corrective with a pledge to attend to Socrates.

Not incidentally, these final lines of their first conversation also bring into focus the problem of freedom. Socrates clearly attempts to direct Alcibiades toward the cultivation of his own freedom. Alcibiades seems to acknowledge his present slavishness and to understand the crucial connection of justice, as a principle of order, to his eventual liberation from his turbulent, chaotic impulses. Yet the audience of the *Symposium* might wonder what has become of this prescription for freedom. We have seen that the three cardinal features of Socrates' novel practice of freedom—*sophrosunē*, self-mastery, and self-sufficiency—are each highlighted in Alcibiades' encomium. We also have seen that, rather than simply accepting the model of political liberty as the basis for his conception and exercise of freedom, Plato has Socrates insist upon a different kind of isomorphism between the freedom of the city and the freedom of the individual. This new notion of freedom is not simply concerned with the absence of external constraints, rights of citizenship, freedom of movement, and access to legislative and juridical institutions. These external freedoms are considered secondary to the ability to rule oneself, the capacity for cultivating just those desires that one deems appropriate, and the degree of one's relative independence. Beyond the external freedoms, Socrates insists on the close relation between self-knowledge and soundmindedness, which again connects justice to his view of freedom. Moreover, we have seen that the philosopher's erotic conversations attempt to illustrate how this relation to oneself is best cultivated and strengthened in dialogue. The entire *Alcibiades I* tried to exhibit how dialogue becomes a way of forming one's character, of testing one's beliefs and opinions, and of continually refashioning oneself. Plato permits his audience to judge from Alcibiades' own testimony the extent to which he has adhered to the conversational regimen that Socrates prescribed for him seventeen years earlier.

Section 4.c Irony and Inebriation: Two Ways of Telling the Truth

We have noted that Alcibiades seems to function in the *Symposium* as a messenger or herald for many truths about Socrates and that he is perhaps even more forthcoming with respect to his own failures. Yet, the careful reader will notice that Socrates and Alcibiades hold fast to radically divergent conceptions concerning what constitutes telling the truth. My aim in this section is to clarify their vastly different views. This will necessitate, first, a close examination of the disagreement over truth telling preceding Alcibiades' speech (214e–215b). Then, the repeated emphases upon truthfulness throughout the speech will be explored in turn. The *Symposium*'s numerous allusions to drinking, which serve to contrast Alcibiades' drunkenness with Socrates' sobriety, help frame the contrast between intoxicated free speech and Socratic irony, which is at the heart of their disagreement. A final clue to their respective views is obtained from the narrator's use of the word *parrhêsia* (frankness) to describe Alcibiades' encomium. This contest over the meaning of truth telling serves to differentiate Socrates' irony from Alcibiades' inebriated frankness, or to put it another way, Socrates' ethical exercise of truth telling from Alcibiades' function as a political *parrhêsiast*.

Commentators have sometimes cited the explicit promise to "tell the truth" that precedes Alcibiades' speech as evidence that his unabashed, uncensored discourse is intended as the truest part of the *Symposium*.[38] To be sure, it is the only speech in the dialogue so distinguished. But, surprisingly, the precise sense in which Alcibiades' encomium is true, and why he repeatedly stresses its truth at key places, has not yet been adequately clarified. To assume that Alcibiades' professions of truthfulness are designed merely to underscore the de facto verity in his speech is to miss a crucial difference being emphasized. Inebriated free speech—that is, saying whatever one wants, regardless of its offensiveness—is counterpoised to Socrates' ironic and, to some, perhaps equally offensive way of speaking. Neither is this the only feature of truth telling about which the two disagree. Alcibiades announces his quarrel with Socrates' brand of truthfulness by declaring, "The truth is exactly the opposite of what he said" (214d1–2). That each accuses the other of jealousy bordering on physical assault, and that Alcibiades prefaces his speech by attempting to dissuade the others from believing the philosopher, draws attention right away to their profound disagreement.

The tension at play between the two senses of telling the truth in this exchange establishes a contrast between very different ways of speaking. In fact, neither interlocutor is able to fulfill the requirement that the other regards as mandatory for speaking truthfully: Alcibiades does not fulfill the conditions that Socrates considers necessary, which would require him to be consistent in his speech and aware of the interplay between his words and his deeds; Socrates does not satisfy Alcibiades' essential requirement that he shed his ironical mask and reveal his true self to others. One important effect of the disagreement over Alcibiades' truthfulness, then, is to underscore a problem that some of his interlocutors find with Socrates' own way of speaking. Socrates is always ready to insist that his unsuspecting interlocutor tell the truth. We have seen that this generally means that one should be sincere, forthright, and disclosive in conversation—the aspect Vlastos called the "say what you believe" requirement of Socrates' conversational practice.[39] It means also that one should speak consistently and be self-aware. Yet, according to Alcibiades, there is something equally wrong with Socrates' customary manner of telling the truth.[40] From the point of view of certain interlocutors, the philosopher seems to fulfill the second part of the "say what you believe" requirement without really satisfying the first. He may speak consistently and be aware of the relation between his speech and his deeds, but Alcibiades will supply reasons for wondering whether Socrates ever really says what he believes. Plato has Alcibiades exercise the political right of *parrhêsia*, using extraordinary frankness, to accuse the paradigmatic truth teller of not speaking the truth.

After Alcibiades' outburst at discovering Socrates on the couch next to Agathon (213b6–c5), Socrates asks for Agathon's protection, complaining that Alcibiades gets "so jealous and resentful that he goes crazy and calls me names and comes close to beating me up" (213d2–4). Alcibiades responds, "There's no chance of peace between us," threatening to pay back Socrates later for his remarks. The verbal jousting between them continues once Eryximachus has objected to simply gulping down wine without so much as conversation or song. Proposing to praise Socrates rather than Eros in his encomium, having missed the six previous speeches, Alcibiades protests that it is really Socrates who would beat *him* up were he to give a eulogy of anyone else, human or god, while Socrates is around (214d3–4). The ensuing clash over truthfulness will prove crucial for an interpretation both of Alcibiades' speech and for the dialogue as a whole. That Alcibiades' encomium of Socrates is framed by this struggle over the question of truth needs to be taken into account when unpacking the eulogy of this philosopher, who dramatically comes to stand in for, or incarnate, Eros as the object of praise in the dialogue.

When Alcibiades again threatens to pay back Socrates "in front of everybody," Socrates asks, "What are you planning to do—deliver a kind of mock eulogy of me?" (214e4–5).[41] Alcibiades replies, "I'll tell the truth—if you'll let me do that." "Of course I'll let you tell the truth," says Socrates, "In fact, I insist that you do" (214e6–8). Alcibiades announces, "Here I go then" (214e9).[42]

Now the audience will surely wonder why Alcibiades imagines that Socrates will not let him tell the truth and why he phrases his intention to do so as a threat to Socrates. Expressly stating that Socrates may interrupt if anything in his speech is not true, Alcibiades adds that he does not intend anything he is about to say to be false (*pseudos*). He assures those gathered that the images he will use are intended to elicit the truth of Socrates' character and not to mock him. No fewer than six times during his speech Alcibiades renews his offer, encouraging Socrates to rectify the account if he disagrees with any part of it, but Socrates just sits in silence. There is good reason for inquiring about the source of Socrates' disagreement with Alcibiades' speech, since he voices no objection to its depiction of him at any of these opportunities. What is wrong with Alcibiades' manner of telling the truth? Let us examine the six points that Alcibiades considers contentious. Perhaps by unearthing the reasons for Socrates' silence, it will be possible to ascertain what is distinctive about the philosopher's conception of truth telling.

Section 4.c.1 Six Points of Emphasis in Alcibiades' Speech

Alcibiades invokes two rich images for comparison to Socrates (215b). He first recalls the image of the little snub-nosed Dionysian statues with protrusive eyes, and he then likens Socrates to Marsyas, adding (with emphasis), "Even *you* can't deny that you *look* like these figures, Socrates." Alcibiades explains that when they are opened up, the plain-looking little replicas (of the head priests of the Dionysian mysteries) reveal a myriad of tiny images inside, all intricately carved.[43] Plato also employs the characteristic snub-nose and bulging eyes to indicate the likeness between young Theaetetus and Socrates (*Tht.* 143e). The image of Socrates as Marsyas, seeming to mock him while intimating that he is both musical and iconoclastic,[44] appears a faithful representation of how Socrates looks, and the silent Socrates does not object.

Alcibiades has not yet fully elaborated the meaning of the satyr images when he interrupts his account for a second time to certify the truth of a statement in an aside with Socrates. He says to Socrates, almost parenthetically, "You treat people hubristically." He goes on to challenge him: "Don't try to deny it— if you do, I'll call up witnesses" (215b7–8). This charge sounds like a legal indictment, backed as it is by the threat of deposing witnesses. Surely Socrates cannot be guilty of the kind of brutalizing hubris for which the satyrs were notorious, that is, drunken rape. Nor is it easy to reconcile his resolute ignorance with the hubris common to the tragic heroes, the arrogant hubris of claiming to know more than is humanly possible, violating mortal limits and encroaching on the province of the gods. In what, then, does Socrates' hubris consist?

From what we already know about their relationship, Socrates would have legitimate grounds for insulting Alcibiades: Alcibiades attempted to dominate him by attempting to get the better (*pleonektein*) of him in a mercenary exchange. Under these circumstances, one might be led to suppose that Alcibiades' accusation of hubris is merely an example of how loosely and widely this charge was applied. Hyperbole notwithstanding, however, there is a wealth of evidence throughout the dialogues of three kinds of hubris that can justifiably be attributed to Socrates. One of these in particular may justify Alcibiades' outrage; all three are related to his erotic method of practicing philosophy and, more precisely, to the breaking down of his interlocutors' unexamined opinions and beliefs. I shall call the first type of hubris "verbal assault," the second "false pretensions," and the third "mock humility." It will be this third kind that Alcibiades finds most offensive.

The first and most obvious kind of Socratic hubris can be seen in the way in which Socrates often upbraids his interlocutors, showing them the woeful inadequacies of their present opinions and telling them that they are no better than slaves. We have seen that to bring someone to admit ignorance often requires a powerful chastening under Socrates' stewardship, and examples of such verbal assaults, in which the philosopher drives someone to the brink of shame or humiliation, can be found throughout the dialogues. Socrates' tactics might be perceived by its victims as violating the protections against public shame afforded to the citizens of Athens by the hubris laws (discussed briefly in Chapter 2, see especially, Note 17.) But this is not the only kind of outrageous behavior to which Alcibiades objects. The kind of hubris primarily at issue here is more complicated and less transparent than this.

The second variety of Socratic hubris is the penchant for hyperbole that Socrates regularly demonstrates, utilizing false pretensions to inflame the passions of his interlocutors. He often targets inarticulate desires, arousing the interlocutor's ambitions, by resorting to patently outrageous claims. Often these claims implicitly or explicitly are based upon the condition that one engage in philosophy and acquire knowledge. Socrates commits this hubris of "false pretensions" most noticeably when he asserts that only with his assistance can the interlocutors attain their grandiose aspirations. When Socrates told Lysis (*Lys.* 210b*ff*) that on the day the boy acquires the kind of good sense that Socrates claims is necessary not only will his father, his neighbor, and the Athenians turn over their affairs to him but so will the Persian king, he may have been guilty of this kind of hubris. Socrates later (*Lys.* 218c) admits to having employed his hyperbolic example to "capture" Lysis and to (boastfully) enchant him with philosophy. Likewise, when he told Alcibiades, "All these designs of yours cannot be accomplished without my help; so great is the power which I believe myself to have over you and your concerns,"[45] these pretensions push Socrates perilously close to overstepping his limits. He surely appears to overstate his efficacy, since Alcibiades' "concerns" have just been disclosed to be political, and even imperialistic, ones. Of course, Plato usually has Socrates qualify (or even retract later) his inflated statements, as we saw him do in both the *Lysis* and *Alcibiades I*, although it seems unlikely that the affected interlocutor will have as clear a view as Plato's audience does of these later, often subtle retractions or qualifications.[46] Yet this is still not the variety of Socratic hubris that Alcibiades appears to find most offensive.

It is during his explanation of the way in which Socrates' words disturbed him and made him dissatisfied with himself that Alcibiades insists for the third time that he is being truthful: "You can't deny the truth of this, Socrates" (216a2). On the most literal level, Alcibiades accuses Socrates of leading on the beautiful young men he will later drop. More important is the less obvious accusation: Alcibiades is charging that Socrates' chief instrument of seduction is his manner of speaking; it is irony that allows this Marsyas' charms to work. This is what, in Alcibiades' view, makes Socrates' speech both more beguiling and more humiliating than that of "Pericles and other good orators" (215e4–5). His seemingly crude examples which, like the Sileni, are coarse and plain on the outside, reveal the presence of divinity within them, as Alcibiades tells his audience, naming all of the other speech makers (218b) as fellow sufferers who have experienced the divine allure of Socrates' philosophical discourse.

When Socrates occupies an ironic position with respect to his interlocutor or to their shared situation, then his manner of speaking cannot help but be unsettling to others. This ironical posture toward others provokes their greatest anger. On this other level, then, Alcibiades is accusing Socrates of using his irony as a weapon, a mask, or a trope, of hiding behind the veneer it affords him, and of spending his whole life, as Nehamas puts it, "ironizing and playing with people." The problem with Socrates' irony is not only that it obscures and complicates the meaning of words, as is readily apparent from the effect produced by his statement in the rebuff of Alcibiades' sexual solicitation[47] (proof of this is Alcibiades getting into bed with him right after Socrates had apparently rebuked him for his proposition[48]), what makes his ironizing posture so offensive to others is that irony insulates and detaches Socrates from others; hence, many characters do not feel that they can ever truly connect with him, and this causes them to regard Socrates as arrogant and condescending.

In contrast to Socrates' opacity about what he really believes, the brutal honesty in Alcibiades' speech is evident from its unflattering admissions about his own character. He is forthright about the compromising position in which he found himself as Socrates' beloved, and he complains that Socrates' way of speaking lacks an equivalent degree of forthrightness. By employing *parrhēsia*, the offended Alcibiades is free to express these complaints to Socrates.

Nehamas argues that Plato's emphasis on his inebriation underscores Alcibiades' incapacity to deceive by donning a mask, which is "a privilege afforded the sober Socrates through irony."[49] Yet it must not be assumed that Socrates merely *uses* irony when it befits the situation; rather, as we shall see later, Socrates *is an ironist*. And the possibility of this kind of irony inheres in his stature as a literary character; it is one of the principal devices Plato employs to allow the dialogues to function and "make sense" or "be true" on several levels at once.

Nehamas emphasizes that in charging him with irony, Alcibiades is charging Socrates with "arrogance and haughtiness." It is this "air of superiority," according to Nehamas, that here provokes the accusation of hubris. This "mock humility" is most obvious to Plato's audience whenever Socrates pretends to regard a clearly hostile or disingenuous interlocutor with great esteem.[50] His reasons for doing so, and his assessment of his interlocutor, may not be apparent to the interlocutor, however. This is because of the way in which irony masks what is meant. Irony is most vexing to the interlocutor when it takes the form of this mock humility, or self-deprecation. Twice in his speech, Alcibiades accuses Socrates of hubris for his customary mock humility (216e, 218d).

In *The Concept of Irony*, Kierkegaard locates the ironist on the threshold of the aesthetic and ethical realms, suggesting that irony displaces and disenfranchises the ironist while at the same time securing for him a calculated detachment. That Socrates preserves such detachment through what Alcibiades regards as his disdainful attitude toward others is precisely what permits him to ridicule his interlocutor while hiding his own true thoughts and feelings behind an ironic shield. This is the main point of the Silenus image. Yet, unlike the Sileni, whose intricate inner images are readily perceptible when the statues are opened up, Socratic irony obscures precisely to what extent the great gadfly knows or does not know such and such, is or is not serious, does or does not have the answer to his own question, and so on. Irony even obscures what part of the matter is being hidden from view. Alcibiades provokes doubt about whether anyone has ever succeeded in uncovering Socrates' innermost beliefs and feelings, since his manner of speaking so skillfully masks at the same time as it reveals. Like a tragic hero, Socrates remains aloof and cold, Alcibiades is charging. Robert Eisner nicely expresses this insulating power of irony implicit in Alcibiades' accusations. He writes, "Irony is a thinner disguise than Odyssean beggary, but it has the advantage of being even more impenetrable."[51]

Nehamas argues that in the erotic encounter with Alcibiades, Socrates is dissembling, and this involves Socrates in a double dissimulation: erotically, he both is and is not a lover, and discursively, he both does and does not reject Alcibiades. In general, his irony allows Socrates to both say and not say what others take him to be saying. It is the ambiguity that irony affords him that enables Socrates to preserve the fluidity in his precarious roles as lover, knower, teacher, believer, and political actor. So irony may function to bridge the differences between the conventional and philosophical meanings of the various roles that Socrates takes in the dialogues, while conjoining the dialogues' two levels. Here again, on the charge of hubris, Socrates presents no objection to Alcibiades' characterization of him as ironically dissembling.

Just before and just after Alcibiades' story of his foiled attempt to seduce Socrates, he pauses for the fourth and fifth times to allow Socrates to dispute the truth of his claims. Alcibiades builds up to his disclosure of "the whole truth," explaining, "There I was, alone with him." Then, as though to preempt exclamations of incredulity from the other symposiasts that he would go this far, he says, "I know, but I'm committed to telling you the whole truth. And Socrates, you're welcome to point out any time I stray from the truth" (217b1–3). Socrates does not interrupt. Alcibiades weaves his tale of the infamous night and concludes, "I put my arms around this remarkable, wonderful man—he is, you know—and lay there with him all night long. No, you can't deny the truth of this either, Socrates" (219b6–c2). What would Socrates be expected to deny? Is it that he lay with Alcibiades at all, or that he *only* lay there with him? From Alcibiades' point of view—and, judging from the speeches of the others,[52] from their perspectives as well—Socrates should be ashamed of himself for failing to take advantage of the opportunity to have this dashing Dionysos. Plato leaves deliciously ambiguous what inference his audience is to draw about the nature and direction of any possible objection.

Alcibiades accents for the sixth time the candor that drives his eulogy of Socrates (220e). Saying that he owes Socrates an account of these events to cover his debt to him, he testifies that the philosopher saved his life in battle and eschewed the resulting glory. Alcibiades immediately taunts, "Socrates, you won't find anything to tell me off for here, or any reason to claim I'm lying either." If this story is true, then Alcibiades owes Socrates a debt he cannot repay, a debt for his very existence, his *bios*. Why would Socrates, the benefactor in this relation, be expected to register any objection to this report? At first glance, Socrates is simply eschewing the love of honor. But if one recalls Aristotle's discussion of greatness of soul in *Nicomachean Ethics* IV.3, another reason for Alcibiades' stress here can be found. Anyone with a great soul should readily accept honors when they are deserved. In his refusal of rightful honors, Alcibiades perceives another example of Socrates' vexing self-deprecation. Mock humility, for Aristotle, is not appropriate to the great-souled person. It is exceedingly suggestive that Aristotle specifically mentions Socrates' mock humility, *eirones*, as a blameless vice.[53] It certainly falls wide of the mean of truthfulness but, for Aristotle, it is understandable, given the precarious place that Socrates occupies vis-à-vis his interlocutors and the city as a whole. Perhaps we should add, toward Plato's audience. For one last time, Socrates remains uncharacteristically silent.

Socrates' silence on these six points forces the audience to conclude that these statements about him are true. Accuracy must not be the aspect of Alcibiades' truth telling that the philosopher disputes. His failure to refute any of the possible points of contention underscored by Alcibiades has at least these two effects: it confirms the veracity of Alcibiades' portrayal and it provokes the audience to look elsewhere for the source of their disagreement. Socrates *does* look like the Sileni; he *does* verbally work his interlocutors over; he *did not* do anything to, or with, Alcibiades during that fateful night alone; and he both *saved* Alcibiades' life and *refused* the honors that he could have had in a vexing display of indifference to the good that drives Alcibiades. The behavior that Alcibiades describes illustrates, once again, how Socrates turns key aspects of conventional notions upside down: the distinction between what is *aiskros* (ugly) and what is *kālos* (beautiful);[54] the notion that the opinions and status of citizens were inviolable; the idea that wisdom could be purchased, traded, or otherwise transferred between two people on the basis of some form of exchange, such as that which he refuses with Alcibiades, and the meaning of the love of honor. But it is not only to contravene traditional practices and ideas that Socrates keeps silent.

Section 4.c.2 Inebriation and *Parrhēsia* in Truth Telling

To understand what Socrates says immediately following Alcibiades' speech, some additional background is needed. This will clarify further the role that intoxication plays in Alcibiades' kind of truthfulness. Throughout the *Symposium*, auspicious references are made to Socrates' legendary imperviousness to alcohol (see Note 32 in this chapter). In contrast, Alcibiades makes a great deal of his own drunkenness from the moment he arrives. He begs admission by asking, "Will you let someone who's drunk—very drunk, actually—join your party?" (212e3–4). He exclaims, "I suppose you'll laugh at me because I'm drunk" (212e9). When it is his turn to speak, all of the others having given their speeches on Eros, Alcibiades pleads, "I don't think it's fair to pit someone who's drunk against speeches delivered by sober men" (214c7–8). He prefaces his long attestation to the power of Socrates' enchanting manner of speaking with the prologue, "If it weren't for the fact that you would put it down to the drink, gentlemen" (215d6–7). Finally, Alcibiades enlists the proverb "Truth Comes From Wine" to redouble his claim of truthfulness (217e3–4). He ascribes to his inebriation his willingness to tell the whole truth, even though what he is about to say may seem unbecoming or overly personal. This proverb cements the connection that Alcibiades believes to obtain between inebriation and truth telling.

Alcibiades also remarks twice about Socrates' capacity for drinking without becoming drunk (214a, 220a). Curiously, Socrates mentions wine or drinking only once in the entire dialogue. When Alcibiades finishes his speech, Socrates exclaims, "It's *you* who are sober, I think" (222c). Socrates explains that only a sober man could have concealed his underlying motives so cleverly throughout his speech. Feigning indignation, the philosopher claims that Alcibiades' hidden motive is to scare off Agathon, warning the young and beautiful poet of the adder's bite that this curious lover is capable of inflicting. He accuses Alcibiades of telling Agathon not to let himself be moved by Socrates, lest he too be hurt before he understands the strange way in which this lover operates. Socrates pretends not to notice Alcibiades' more covert motive, an impulse most conspicuous to Plato's audience: his patent desire to possess, and even to dominate, the indomitable philosopher through the seemingly sincere attempt at seduction. I have demonstrated that this desire to get the better of Socrates permeates the encomium and surely would have remained its animating principle whether or not Agathon was present.

Although he may not be making Alcibiades' truest motive obvious, Plato does have Socrates warn the audience that there is both an explicit and an implicit dimension to the speech. Socrates' immediate reply signals one primary sense of its truthfulness: the speech divulges much more than Alcibiades imagines. Its various audiences are left to determine whatever more it reveals and to evaluate the degree to which Alcibiades himself grasps the more oblique truths of which he is the herald. A further indication of the kind of truth telling in which Alcibiades is engaged is provided by the dialogue's narrator. When Apollodorus highlights Alcibiades' "candor" and draws attention to the fact that the other symposiasts found his frankness amusing, Plato has him use the word *parrhêsia* to do so (222c2). That it is the narrator who uses this word means that this is a clue that Plato has written into the dialogue at the level of the narrative, and not at the level of the action and speeches within the frame. None of those present at the original symposium would have been privy to it. Neither Socrates nor Alcibiades need have conceived their conflict in these terms. Apollodorus is characterizing the speech for *his* audience, and we are permitted, as it were, to "listen in" on this second rehearsal of the framed story in three days. But an examination of Plato's use of the word *parrhêsia* here may shed light on what the audience is supposed to conclude from the contrast being drawn. *Parrhêsia* is a term Plato uses sparingly in his dialogues, and although I do not believe that he uses words in any highly technical sense, the use of the term *parrhêsia* here, like the use of the term *pleonektein* in Socrates' rejoinder to Alcibiades, is imbued with great signification.

Parrhêsia (literally, "outspokenness" or "frankness") originally named the democratic practice of free speech.[55] It referred, in general, to the activity of disclosing one's opinions completely and accurately in speech, without holding back anything. Michel Foucault's study of the problem of *parrhêsia* showed that achieving such frank expression required that one strive for a direct showing of one's mind, unencumbered by any rhetorical devices. In its political form, *parrhêsia* was available only to citizens; typically it was exercised by a person of lesser power toward someone of greater standing. For this reason, as Foucault points out, the one using *parrhêsia* must be courageous, since speaking frankly could involve considerable risk. The term *parrhêsia* would not apply where subordinate persons are spoken to—for example, when parents chastise their children, or when citizens speak to noncitizens—no matter how candidly they speak, because to be an act of *parrhêsia*, there must be an element of danger.[56] One citizen could use *parrhêsia* to speak to another in the agora, or one could engage in *parrhêsia* to speak to the demos as a whole. In Periclean Athens, this freedom of speech was one of the most cherished ideals, fundamentally intertwined with political liberty. In his famous funeral oration in Thucydides' *History*, Pericles valorizes Athens as a city in which all citizens are capable of judging for themselves what is best and voicing their opinions in the political arena.[57] The duty incumbent upon citizens in a participatory democracy could not be delegated, since only through direct participation could the benefits of citizenship thought to be derived. The critical assessment of values and institutions expressed through *parrhêsia* was a paramount feature of that duty.[58] Hence, Foucault shows, *parrhêsia* was an activity especially prized in Athens, associated with its free institutions and thought to be one of the distinctive qualities that differentiated Athenians from other Greeks.[59] To be unable to use *parrhêsia* was referred to as having a "slave's mouth."[60] The earliest extant occurrences of the word are found in Euripides' *Hippolytus*, where it carries a wholly positive connotation.[61] However, after fifteen years of war (c. 416 or 415), and probably not incidental to the crisis in Athenian democracy, Foucault argues that both the positive, or "critical" sense of *parrhêsia* and a pejorative sense of the political truth-telling activity could be identified.[62]

It is the negative sense of *parrhêsia* that is being used to characterize Alcibiades' speech.[63] But although he is intoxicated and uses the degenerate form of *parrhêsia*, Alcibiades qualifies as a truth teller because he fully believes what he says, unlike the mere rhetorician, who does not have to be sincere.[64] Plato has Apollodorus describe Alcibiades as having used *parrhêsia* in order to contrast one kind of telling the truth with another—the proper use of free speech, in ethical *parrhêsia*, with its abusive, political form. I suggest that the term and practice is invoked in the *Symposium* to denigrate Alcibiades' way of speaking, contrasting Socrates' truth telling as a way of life with its episodic invocation through *parrhēsia* by Alcibiades. To demonstrate this necessitates that we examine briefly the difference between the right way and the wrong way to employ *parrhēsia*.

We have already identified its proper employment by citizens to assess and critique civic institutions and people of greater standing. The misuse of frank speech, however, was widely thought to have a deleterious effect on democracy. Theognis complains that some people do not know when to ventilate their opinions or how to delimit their own affairs from the affairs of others.[65] Those who talked incessantly were known as *athuroglottos*,[66] that is, speakers who show no regard for *logos* as a means of exhibiting the truth. Plutarch compares the mouths of such talkative people to storerooms without doors and purses without clasps.[67] In contrast, the good *parrhēsiast* uses *logos* without being garrulous. The intemperate speech of the bad *parrhēsiast* often is connected in Greek literature and oratory to brash displays of daring, to impudence of the most outrageous kind, and, not surprisingly, to drunkenness.[68] Socrates himself makes this latter connection at *Phaedrus* 240e, where he refers to the "wearisome and unrestrained frankness (*parrhēsia*)" that a beloved boy has to endure from his intoxicated older lover.[69] The connection of these traits to Alcibiades' character and to his inebriation in the *Symposium* would not have been lost on Plato's contemporaries.

In "The Education of Children," Plutarch links *mathēsis* (learning) to genuine *parrhēsia*.[70] Without *mathēsis*, free speech would simply be mere babbling or a cacophony of words. If citizens abuse their duty to speak critically, or if they speak without the proper education, they harm the city. Considered in this light, Socrates' silence may signify that he is holding back from saying what he might want to say in order to set himself apart from Alcibiades' kind of truth telling. What Socrates means in his admonition of Alcibiades, when he accuses him of trying to obtain truth in exchange for opinion (218e6), now becomes luminous. Socrates had accentuated this point just prior to unveiling Alcibiades' scheme with the infamous charge that he is trying to exchange bronze for gold (218e6–219a1). The reference here to Alcibiades' *parrhēsia* further illuminates this contrast between opinion and truth. The use of the term *parrhēsia* underscores that Alcibiades is just expressing his opinions, opinions in which Eros and venom are mingled with his strangely revealing admission that he is unable to do what he knows is best for himself. We can only suppose how far his self-understanding really goes, and to what extent he is speaking without knowledge, but only from a kind of inspiration provided by wine that allows him to function as a messenger. He is perhaps a truth teller in the manner of the poets in the *Apology*, who seem to fare no better in giving a *logos* of their words than the average pedestrian. The messenger fails to grasp the message he delivers.

Plato surely knew that his audience would wonder to what extent Alcibiades' acknowledgment of what is good for him has been actually taken to heart. In his previous conversations with Socrates, recall that Alcibiades had agreed to take more trouble over his way of living and to learn (*mathē*) what needs to be learned through proper self-care. Socrates seemed to have persuaded him that he must take care of himself before attempting to rule the city, or anything else. From his speech here, it becomes increasingly obvious that he has not followed Socrates' prescription for him. But the speech also attempts to attribute partial responsibility for this failure to Socrates. Indeed, Plato has Alcibiades give voice to the most powerful critique of Socrates and one of the most damning criticisms of philosophy to be found anywhere in the dialogues. And Socrates' silence throughout the speech leaves Plato's audience to decide: is Alcibiades a good truth teller, or is his use of *parrhēsia* merely attributable to the wine? Is he a good *parrhēsiast*, or is he an *athuroglottos*? What is the point of this contrast between two different ways in which one is supposed to get at the truth of oneself and disclose it to others? In Alcibiades' view, Socrates should desist from using irony and must reveal his true self; for Socrates, Alcibiades' failure to adhere to his regimen has resulted in a glaring discrepancy between what he says and who he is, between his *logos* and his *bios*.

In making Alcibiades the champion of free speech,[71] Plato once again makes him the symbol of Athens,[72] of democracy, and of the democratic man. The invocation of this most democratic ideal of political *parrhēsia* here forces the audience to reflect upon the dissimilitude of the two senses of telling the truth surrounding Alcibiades' speech. While truth may be found in wine for Alcibiades, his lack of inhibition is not a sufficient warrant for the truth of what he says. In the last analysis, his speech ends up imparting to his audience truths of which he himself is not even aware. His revealing remarks reflect the upsurge of words propelled by inebriation, words that portend his eventual fate to the audience while bypassing his own self-awareness. In contrast, I argued earlier that the importance Plato places upon Socrates' imperviousness to wine should not be taken as a sign either of a mere physiological immunity to alcohol or a deeper asceticism, since it has been emphasized by the doctor, Eryximachus, that Socrates is equally good at drinking and not drinking (176c). Focusing on the perceptible symptoms of inebriation reinforces the fact that Socrates speaks no differently with the aid of wine than he does stone-cold sober.

In contrast to Alcibiades' manner of truth telling, Socrates' words are marked by a harmony of his beliefs and his character, a consistency between what he says and who he is. Anyone who knows him well seems to understand that a conversation with Socrates will directly test the character of the interlocutor in relation to his *logoi*. Submitting to a probing cross-examination by this relentless diagnostician requires a kind of courage, perhaps the courage hardest to muster in a human being. Nicias, at *Laches* 187e–188a, explains to Lysimachus that anyone who comes into close contact with Socrates will be led to give an account of the kind of life he has lived and to subject all of his habits to inspection. No matter what topic initiates the conversation, says Nicias, "I knew ... that our argument would not be about the boys if Socrates were present; but about ourselves."[73]

Whereas Alcibiades' encomium is anything but consistent, Socrates' words are further characterized by their consistency. Socrates, at *Gorgias* 482a, explicitly cites the "son of Kleinias" (Alcibiades) as one who says "now this and now that," a condition he referred to in the *Alcibiades I* as "wandering about in one's soul." He goes on to tell Callicles, "I ... should rather choose to have my lyre, or some chorus that I might provide for the public, out of tune and discordant, or to have any number of people disagreeing with me and contradicting me, than that I should have internal discord and contradiction in my own single self" (*Grg.* 482b–c). In his speech in the *Symposium*, Alcibiades is clearly dispossessed of equanimity; his speech exhibits the struggle between love and loathing, attraction and repulsion, submissiveness and the desire to dominate. In fact, he is so manifestly ambivalent that his decision to attempt to seduce Socrates, as we have seen, follows directly his pledge to obey the philosopher's counsel.

To illuminate further what Socrates means by telling the truth, it will help to recall once more the inaugural conversation between Alcibiades and Socrates. Socrates had insisted that Alcibiades tell the truth so that their first conversation would not be pointless (110a).[74] When the youth failed to maintain a consistent position in argument, Socrates chided him for wavering and for contradicting himself. And when Alcibiades retreats to a former position after Socrates had already refuted an analogous one, the philosopher says, "What a way you have! When you make a mistake which might be refuted by a previous argument, you insist on having a new and different refutation; the old argument is a worn-out garment which you will no longer put on, but someone must produce another which is clean and new" (113e5–114a1, Jowett trans.). When Socrates finally reduces him to perplexity, this prompts Alcibiades to confess to the confusion of being "of different minds in successive instants" (116e3–4). Socrates explains that this inconsistency is what engenders perplexity, and perplexity results from the conceit that he knows when he does not know. Alcibiades admitted that he is not perplexed about many things of which he is ignorant, and Socrates explained that this is because he is aware of his ignorance in these matters. Nor would he be perplexed about the things he truly knows. So one plausible explanation for Alcibiades' checkered speech in the *Symposium* is that he has become oblivious to the need for perplexity; his lack of self-knowledge is so great that he is unaware even of being in conflict with himself, of being of different minds at successive moments. It would seem that Alcibiades has recuperated his old conceits some time between the inaugural conversation with Socrates and his appearance in the *Symposium* seventeen years later.

This counsel regarding how to dialogue, which Socrates gives to Alcibiades in the first *Alcibiades*, parallels crucial aspects of his exchange with Callicles in the *Gorgias*. The most suggestive parallel occurs at *Gorgias* 486d, where Socrates says, "If my soul were gold, Callicles, don't you think I'd delight in finding a touchstone (*basanos*) to put that gold to the test?" (Allen trans.). He elaborates by saying that whoever would test the good or bad life of the soul must possess three qualities: "knowledge, kind regard, and frankness" (*Grg.* 487a).[75] Socrates declares that many people are not able to test him, because they lack one of these qualities. Some are not wise, and others are not well disposed toward him. But in many ways, the most indolent are those, Socrates says, whose modesty is so great "that they are driven to contradict themselves in the face of a large company, on matters of the highest moment." At least one of the essential requirements for telling the truth, then, in Socrates' view, is that one be shameless enough to be consistent, adhering to the consequences that follow from what one "really" believes. Professing irreconcilable views out of an anticipatory sense of shame is as detrimental to a discussion as refusing to admit, from a parallel sense of shame, that one holds fundamentally incompatible beliefs. Socrates always seems willing to allow his interlocutor to modify his position if the aim is to get at the truth and to bring his position into greater consistency (see, for example, *Tht.* 154c–e). Both waffling or wavering and intransigence are marks of an inadequate interlocutor. Just as Socrates will not stand for Callicles' refusal to declare what follows from his contention that doing injustice is preferable to suffering it, he will not tolerate Alcibiades' proclivity for saying one thing and doing another. One cannot say one thing and then another without violating the most rudimentary principle of human discourse and reason, the principle of non-contradiction.[76] And one cannot say one thing and do another without such hypocrisy undermining one's integrity—not only the integrity of the argument on its own but of the argment applied *ad hominem*, to the way the speaker lives.[77] Alcibiades admits, both in the *Symposium* and in the *Alcibiades I*, to feeling shame in the presence of Socrates, arising from his inability to follow the path that he himself agrees would be best for him (216b). But, like Callicles, the irrepressible Alcibiades takes this shame to be a constraint upon his nature, a wholly unnatural impulse that drives him into contradictions. He acknowledges what would be best for him, but his acquisitive Eros, intertwined with his driving love of honor, will not permit the ever-uncowed Alcibiades to take this counsel to heart and to rectify his situation. Lacking *sophrosunē*, Alcibiades' Eros incapacitates him from remaining firm in the knowledge of what is really good for him. His inebriation affords him sufficient shamelessness to admit the shame he experiences in Socrates' presence, but not enough shamelessness to remain consistent within himself, and so he is wrought with discord, unable to reconcile his conflicting impulses.[78]

SECTION 4.D CONCLUSION: ADJUDICATING THE *AGŌN* OVER TRUTH TELLING

The foregoing analysis has attempted to clarify the crucial disagreement between Socrates and Alcibiades about truth telling. Alcibiades' speech, like the lack of discipline to which he confesses, is an example of his waffling, intermittent self-awareness, a self-awareness that leads him one minute to assert confidently that Socrates can assist in his improvement, and the next minute to plug his ears, to run away from the philosopher, and to wish him dead. In his encounter with Callicles, Socrates explained what he means by truthfulness, and what he says there bears on the present problem. It also supplies one final reason Socrates remains silent throughout the speech rather than seizing the opportunity to reprimand the recalcitrant Alcibiades:

> And of the frankness (*parrhêsia*) of your nature and freedom from diffidence I am assured by yourself, and the assurance is confirmed by your last speech. Well then, the inference in the present case clearly is, that if you agree with me in an argument about any point, that point will have been sufficiently tested by us, and will not require to be submitted to any further test.... And therefore when you and I are agreed, the result will be the attainment of perfect truth.... And if you find me assenting to your words, and hereafter not doing that to which I assented, put me down for an utter fool, and never again admonish the worthless creature. (*Grg.* 487d7–488a3, Jowett trans.)

"Telling the truth" for Socrates means adhering to the *logos*, and this is exactly what Alcibiades, on his own account, lacks the self-discipline to do.[79] He is an *agumnastikos* character, and admits to being shamed by his own agreements. He fulfills the *Laches*'s requirement of engaging Socrates, of coming close enough to the philosopher to experience the effect of the Socratic "sting"—he experiences the arousal and provocation for which the philosopher is called a gift—but this only makes him aware of his slavish nature, without causing him to change. His speech admits that he fails to develop the antidote that Socrates prescribes for him, the regimen for self-care which would enable him to bring his practices into accord with his innermost beliefs. The speech celebrates his inability to modify his behavior and thereby to survive the assay provided by Socrates' erotic engagement. But his propensity for self-destruction, through acting in a manner contrary to what is best for him, is thereby made transparent. Viewed in one way, his speech discloses more about the speaker than it does about Socrates. For it is his own undisciplined, audacious character that is most embarrassingly unmasked by Alcibiades' encomium of Socrates, while it positions him, at the same time, as a harbinger of the political fates soon to befall both men.

In his quarrel with the Socratic way of telling the truth, however, Alcibiades professes that there is another side to the story, when perceived from the standpoint of Socrates' interlocutors. His encomium announces a rampant vexation, widespread among his interlocutors, with Socrates' manner of speaking. How is the present interpretation to adjudicate this *agōn*? When viewed most charitably, Alcibiades' speech exposes the underside of Socrates' approach. But what might Socrates have said to Alcibiades in response to these charges? Surely the audience will not be hoodwinked into taking the insolent Alcibiades' acknowledgment of shameful actions as honorable, or even as fully honest. Socrates might answer, in his defense, that if Alcibiades really felt ashamed, he would change his ways, and if he really were powerless over his own behavior, he would not flaunt his weakness with such casual disregard.

Yet the frustration to which Alcibiades attests also recalls what Nehamas calls the "unassailable reserve" that Socrates projects through his ironical attitude. Because he never completely abandons his ironical bearing, says Nehamas, others are provoked to wonder whether the philosopher has any feelings at all toward them or any beliefs of his own. For this posture, Socrates incites widespread indignation. We have seen that his interlocutors often experience him as less than forthcoming. Hence, Alcibiades' speech alerts the audience to something that would have been painfully obvious to many interlocutors—the fact that the *quid pro quo* for saying what they believe to Socrates is sometimes far less than they think is fair in return for their vulnerability.

There are no simple formulas that Socrates could give to his interlocutors and, likewise, becoming an attentive member of Plato's audience entails doing considerable work, only to have ends left open and questions unanswered. Alcibiades' drunken speech is at least extraordinarily forthcoming about his own foibles. His indictment charges that Socrates, on the contrary, is like the reticent Apollo in Euripides' *Ion*, when the god refuses to tell Creusa the truth, even though she uses *parrhēsia* to attempt to force it out of him.[80] Never revealing the "true" self Alcibiades expects him to divulge, Socrates' reticence, in Alcibiades' opinion, keeps the philosopher at arm's length from others. Hence, the speech expresses the frustration of all those interlocutors who have experienced a conversation with this artful dodger as a kind of shadowboxing.

We have seen that, for Socrates, dialogue is a way of forming and testing oneself, of maintaining a heightened self-regard and a distinctive self-relation in the practical exercise of *logos*. As an activity, Socratic truth telling requires more than simply a thorough self-examination, an uninhibited forthrightness, and an element of risk; it demands further that one maintain oneself in a constant relation to oneself, in and through the *logos*. Again we see why self-examination cannot be understood merely as a process of introspection, for it is not just a reflexive, inward turning, as might seem to be implied by the image of the examination of one's *psuchē* or by the metaphor of the soul as a mirror of the self offered in the *Alcibiades I*. Rather, for Socrates, self-examination is a cross-examination between two people. Put otherwise, the activity of truth telling is a testing in dialogue, a scrutiny in the face of others who provide the necessary forthrightness to function as the mirror to one's character. Moreover, Socrates requires that one's character be constantly related to the *logos* in the act of truth telling. This constant self-scrutiny makes Socratic truth telling a distinctively ethical activity, built around conversation as an *askēsis*, that is, a set of practices organized into a coherent, philosophical way of life.

How does this practice of ethical truth telling vindicate the philosopher of the charges Alcibiades brings against him? We have seen already that, for Socrates, telling the truth requires consistency. The meaning of the consistency demand can now be explicated more fully. One's speech is consistent when all of the principles derivable from one's statements are compatible. Consistency here means simply non-contradiction. On grounds of consistency, Alcibiades fails as a truth teller. Like Callicles in the *Gorgias*, Alcibiades does not even agree with himself; the lack of harmony his speech reveals confirms his conflicted condition. What is more, however, Socratic cross-examination tests not only one's statements but one's character, assaying the interlocutor's statements for their adequacy as an account of his way of living. In his demand that consistency apply not only to one's various statements but to the relation of those statements to the speaker's actions, Socrates inaugurates the distinctive legacy of the philosopher. Here consistency entails the concurrence of one's discourse with one's way of living, and, *ex hypothesis*, Alcibiades is unable to meet this standard. It is not his *logos* that is wanting; it is his *bios* that falls short of the

Socratic truth standard. His own behaviors entail contradictions that diminish the benefit to Alcibiades of his role as a truth teller; despite his speech's factual accuracy, he is unable to keep his own life on course.

Adopting *parrhêsia* reinstalls the spirited Alcibiades temporarily in the role of truth teller, positioning this consummate politician as someone sworn to speak the truth. Socrates is obliged to listen to the encomium for this reason; but the speech itself reveals that the notoriously ambivalent commander has not maintained himself in a steadfast relationship to truth. Indeed, it positions him in an inferior place to that of Socrates' along the scale of truthfulness. This underscores that the Socratic standard of truth telling requires a consonance with one's way of living, a harmony between one's *logos* and one's *bios*. The great political and military leader is no match for Socrates on this scale.[81]

Socrates' exposure of his calculating attempt to reverse the balance of power between them exacerbates Alcibiades' need to adopt *parrhêsia*. But this pose confirms that, for Alcibiades, *parrhêsia* is merely an episodic activity underwritten by his status as a free citizen and reinstated through intoxication; it is neither an ongoing activity nor a particularly ethical one. Hence, Alcibiades must be seen as only *using parrhêsia*, whereas Socrates *is* a truth teller; for Socrates, telling the truth is an essential constituent of the philosophic life. In Plato's dramatic portrayal, the freedom to speak truthfully to others in conversation has been shown to be assured by his refusal to accept gifts or fees, or indeed to engage in any form of market exchange.

There is still another reason Alcibiades' *parrhêsia* cannot be validated by Socrates. If, for Socrates, a person's character is determined, first, as the relation between one's various beliefs or opinions and, second, as the relation of one's speech to one's deeds, then any dissonance between these coordinates suggests the presence of unexamined beliefs or the influence of a covert desire-structure. Implicit in the process of examining the *bios*, either of oneself or others, is a presumption that one can be brought into accord with oneself. Unlike political free speech, the Socratic mode of truth telling necessitates that the exercise of oneself in conversation be guided by the ongoing, reflective relation of the self to itself, and this would seem to be a relation that Alcibiades has failed to cultivate.

In his revealing speech, Alcibiades acknowledges that he has been disrobed by Socrates. What Foucault calls "the *parrhêsiastic* contract" provides him with the warrant he thinks he needs to speak the truth, even though he has not maintained himself in the truth, that is, in a steady, harmonious relationship to himself. It is toward the cultivation of a more resolute relationship to himself that Socrates' *logos* aims. Socrates, at *Charmides* 166c*ff*, tells Critias that his refutations of others are aimed chiefly at clarifying his own beliefs, for they allow him to test what he thinks he knows. The peculiar relation to himself that Socrates secures through dialogue—through his style of interrogation and cross-examination, through his friendly inquiries, and through dialectical argument—is his only counterweight to the conceit of wisdom about things of which he is, in fact, ignorant. For those who have not yet attained Socrates' degree of *sophrosunē*, however, dialogue is an indispensable way of bringing beliefs, opinions, and desires into increasingly greater harmony.

Through *parrhēsia*, Alcibiades is able to underscore an unsettling problem with Socrates' ironical manner of speaking, yet his accusation entails the troubling assumption that if there is a "true self" behind Socrates' mask, then this character should appear and speak the same way in every situation. Alcibiades seems to think that this "true self" must be manifest in exactly the same way in every appearance, throughout its ongoing alterations. But if Socrates really does not possess the wisdom that he professes to seek, then his present self-knowledge and present character are merely provisional. And if closure in any Socratic examination is only a presumptive closure—since the great inquirer seems to be willing to reopen any investigation again and again[82]—then Socratic irony serves to announce that behind Socrates' ironical standpoint there is only another ironical standpoint. This posture too will be replaced later as Socrates undergoes further self-transformation.

That Socrates speaks ironically does not mean that he intentionally conceals himself from Alcibiades. It is consistent with Socrates' kind of truth telling to emphasize different aspects of the same topic as he tailors an approach specific to different interlocutors in particular contexts. Embedding what his characters say within a narrative is one way in which Plato's dialogues capture the richness and complexity of life and the world, in which things are not always clear and unequivocal. That Socrates is ironic does not prove that the philosopher dissembles, as long as Socrates can ultimately be judged to be sincere about what he does and does not know. And this sincerity is not necessarily inconsistent with the audience's being unable to determine what precisely Socrates knows or does not know.

If he is not withholding what he knows, and if his methods are judged to be more just than other approaches, then his irony is not a mask donned to shield others from who Socrates *really is;* irony is constitutive for what and who he is. To the attentive reader of the dialogues, Socrates' practices are thoroughly transparent, on one level, and his deepest beliefs are exemplified in, and through, these practices. But the harder one looks at what seems transparent, the more complex and multifaceted it becomes, or the less it seems has been said, in other cases. Still, in the characterization of Socrates, what you see is what you get. He is continuously testing and exercising himself in conversation, and he makes this constant, discursive relation to himself central to his ethical practice of philosophy.

Paradoxically, then, Alcibiades' use of *parrhēsia* to vent his opinions turns out to be a way of holding Socrates' feet to the fire of absolute truth, confining philosophy to a standard of eternal, immutable truth that would permit Socrates to speak with only one voice, no matter what the context demands. Through such a standard, Alcibiades hopes to require the philosopher, and philosophy itself by implication, to speak in precisely the same, univocal way to every interlocutor in every situation, stripped of the "plurivocity" with which irony equips him.[83] This standard implies, as we have seen in Chapter 3, the Socratically pernicious conviction that one's present self is one's "true self," because it presumes that the philosopher already possesses wisdom and therefore no longer needs to search or examine. By imposing such a standard on Socrates, Alcibiades would transform truth telling from an essentially conversational, ethical activity into a quasiscientific, dogmatic one.

Chapter 5

Dramatic Failure and the Gift
in Socratic *Paideusis*

That Plato has Socrates approach youths such as Lysis and Alcibiades at pivotal moments in their lives in an attempt to unsettle them confirms his belief that people with philosophical potential must be gotten hold of at the right time and nurtured in the right direction, or there is a risk that they will be corrupted by a more tyrannical way of life. It is the impulse to tyranny, far more than the impulse to hedonism, that seems mainly to concern Plato in his dialogues. This emphasis seems well placed in light of subsequent historical events, for it has not been chiefly mankind's desire for pleasure that has threatened to cause its destruction but its tendencies toward tyranny, especially when coupled with a fanatical devotion to a particular hegemonic belief or ideology. Throughout history, it has been these tyrannical impulses that have wreaked havoc in social and political relations. Plato's dialogues may be read as a partial corrective to these tyrannical tendencies, for they aim to nudge the bivalent character of their audience toward philosophy rather than tyranny and to nurture it along the path to self-improvement, depicted and discussed in these dialogues.

From the foregoing examination of both the content and the method of Socrates' approach to Lysis and Alcibiades, we have seen that he attempts to educate both boys to be rulers by teaching them the form of right management, which necessarily begins with self-management, through a voluntary regimen designed to reform and redirect their behaviors and practices. This approach has been shown to be based upon the principle that it is the one who takes the trouble over himself that will know best how to govern his household and his city. And this teaching is entirely compatible with Socrates' own example, one consistent in certain basic respects throughout the dialogues. To the extent that this *askēsis* by which one cares for oneself involves a radical change for Socrates' young targets, this means that they have not taken sufficient trouble over themselves in the past, hence their self-improvement will have to begin with the cultivation of greater concern.[1]

I have attempted to show that the two young men studied here are uniquely capable prospects for the turnaround that Socrates sets out to initiate. In addition to the qualities already stressed, they have access to political power and the opportunity to achieve greatness. We saw that when Socrates first encountered them, these two characters were ready to come of age, but their lives had not yet been informed by the love of wisdom. Since they were not predisposed toward philosophy, Socrates appealed to their desires for power and dominion, linking their aspirations to freedom and making a heightened self-care, accompanied by some kind of knowledge, a condition for the attainment of their goals. In these conversations, knowledge was stressed by Socrates not as the end toward which his counsel points but as a means to the ends his interlocutors already cherish. With these ambitious young men the philosopher was seen to build upon the latent desires the youths had already, instead of explicitly emphasizing the need for a complete turnaround in character or the redirection of their desires toward different aims. He surely hoped that the process he initiated with them would change them, reorienting them toward different goals than the ones they brought into the conversation; but he did not make it obvious to them that such a reorientation of their lives would be the likely outcome of sincere adherence to his prescriptions for them. Plato leaves it to his audience to apprehend these subtleties and to adduce their implications.

Because of their natural gifts and the propitious conditions under which he approached them, both Lysis and Alcibiades appeared capable of the philosopher's proposed character transformation. Due to their age and possibilities, the characters of these youths appeared the least stable, or fixed, of any of Socrates' interlocutors in the dialogues, thus they may still be amenable to change. Plato's desire to depict his paradigmatic philosopher in conversations under the best of circumstances and with the best and brightest youths led him to devote approximately one-third of his Socratic dialogues to dramatizations of Socrates on the hunt for such promising, teachable youths.[2] These conversations provide an important, interesting counterweight to the numerous cases in which Socrates fails because his interlocutor's character is already hardened, whether he is portrayed as a Sophist, a soldier, a businessman, or merely a self-assured citizen such as Euthyphro or Meno. In the encounters that we have examined, it was their apparent susceptibility to alteration, combined with their natural gifts and the exceptional circumstances in which the philosopher encounters them, that made Lysis and Alcibiades ideal candidates for Socrates' remedial strategy.

The potential for improvement that these two characters manifested at the outset of these dialogues was validated by the fact that, as the foregoing analysis has attempted to demonstrate, at the end of their first conversations with Socrates, these special interlocutors also appeared to be amenable to the philosophical process by which the initial turnaround begun by him will need to be sustained. Socrates was shown to provoke in these characters a moment of crisis, analogous to that which arises in tragedy as the result of some unexpected intervention from the gods to embroil a tragic hero in a predicament of epic proportions. We saw how Socrates, in his usual way, agitated these young men by confronting them with the conceits he took to be implicit in their aspirations and by disclosing to them the problems he anticipated in their impending political careers. That Lysis and Alcibiades responded positively to the provocation indicates a measure of success. Socrates did succeed dramatically in turning around each boy within the scope of their first conversation. Yet Plato's choice to use historical figures as the basis for his characters is one way he invites his audience to also bring history to bear on its evaluation of the ability of philosophical instruction to transform people such as Lysis, Alcibiades, Phaedrus, and Charmides.

From the standpoint of history, Plato's dialogues leave us, finally, uncertain about the long-term effect of Socrates as a *paideutēs* in the case of Lysis and pessimistic about the effectiveness of Socratic *paideusis* in the other cases. Although Lysis and Alcibiades noticeably benefitted from their initial conversation with him, their long-term commitment to the Socratic way of life remains doubtful at best. We have only this one conversation from which to discern improvement in Lysis. And one conversation alone supplies little evidence about the depth and permanence of changes in human character. With Alcibiades, for whom we have an important follow-up case, the philosopher was shown to provoke shame, but this shame only produced violent outrage toward Socrates.

Despite the sleight-of-hand tactics with which he equips him, Plato never seems to permit Socrates to succeed, or to succeed for long, with his target interlocutors. Yes, there are some modest successes, and to the first conversations with Lysis and Alcibiades we could add quite a few more limited successes, including at least every case in which a character is brought to admit perplexity, inasmuch as an admission of ignorance or perplexity represents the important first step in the Socratic turnaround and is thus itself a kind of turnaround. One can perhaps infer additional successes from Socrates' naming, at *Apology* 33d–34a, of nine men present at his trial who had associated with him since they were young, and whose fathers, uncles, older brothers would not testify that he had corrupted them.[3] Did Plato want his audiences to infer some de facto success for Socratic pedagogy from this minimal, largely implicit evidence? Finally, if all of the members of this group of nine (plus the "many others besides" who, Socrates says, were not in the courtroom that day) are not also members of the group of followers he describes as associates who enjoy using his style of cross-examination on prominent Athenians, then might not some of these constant companions of Socrates furnish additional examples of the philosopher's success as a *paideutēs*? Why does Plato leave these cases in the background? Why does he force his audience to adduce any success Socrates might be thought to have achieved from mere hints or only implicit evidence?

On the whole, one is bound to come away from the dialogues with the impression that his Socrates is not very effective as a teacher or a midwife. Although the *ad hominem* philosopher always meets his interlocutors on their own terms, beginning with them wherever he finds them and tailoring an approach particular to each of them, even this customized educational approach is not portrayed as overly efficacious. Judging from his overall portrayal of Socrates, one is forced to conclude that Plato appears quite pessimistic about the likelihood that philosophers will engender offspring, people worthy of carrying the torch of Socratic philosophizing. Neither of the two hopeful characters studied here furnishes convincing proof, and we have discussed several other promising characters who turned out to be rogues. Plato attributes these failures to different things in different dialogues—sometimes to a genuine *aporia* or confusion about the topic, sometimes to the limitations of Socrates' interlocutors, sometimes to Socrates' own shortcomings, and at other times to the weakness of some aspect of the way in which the interlocutors proceed in the conversation. In the *Lysis*, Socrates attributed the conversation's shortcomings to the confusion that the search for the friend produced in all concerned and to the inadequacies attributable to dramatic circumstances.[4] In the *Alcibiades I*, he pinned his doubts on the power of the state, though Alcibiades testifies later that it was really the allure of the demos that caused his downfall. (Of course, this insinuates that the real source of the problem is located in Alcibiades' honor-love, that is, in the young man's ambitious character itself.[5])

Now clearly the uncertain case of Lysis is different from the cases of Alcibiades, Phaedrus, and Charmides. And although the examination of Alcibiades' encomium in Chapter 4 attributed to the errant pupil responsibility for the failure of Socrates' counsel to improve him, it remains for us to ask, does Socrates corrupt or harm Alcibiades in any way? His extreme case furnishes a partial answer to the larger question, namely, what other reasons might Plato have had for downplaying Socrates' success with promising youths such as Alcibiades? The answer that emerges from our close study of the *Alcibiades I* and the *Symposium* is that Alcibiades does not fail because he perverts Socrates' lessons or because he appropriates the philosopher's techniques for his own selfish advantage; nor does his failure result from the Socratic arousal of his spiritedness, as though the young man's *thumos* had been first sparked by the philosopher's inflammatory approach to him. Rather, Alcibiades' failure was shown to be due to his inability or unwillingness to follow Socrates at all.[6] Characters such as these possess the full complement of qualities that would seem a prerequisite for learning from the Socratic method, and yet Plato portrays them as unanimously incapable of sustaining the practice for any length of time. Socrates can only indicate the general direction to be taken. And because his targets will only go so far with him, he can only go so far with them. Hence, an important first answer to the question concerning why Socrates generally fails to transform his interlocutors is that the success of his project with them depends largely upon their skills and intentions as interlocutors and as human beings. To this extent, the young characters studied here are no different from the other people the philosopher encounters in the dialogues. Many people experience the Socratic exhortation, and many also receive his provocation, in the form of a direct cross-examination and refutation. Yet it is not possible to point to any one of them as an unqualified and a lasting success. I will suggest later several reasons for Plato's decisions to depict Socrates' failures, to allow him only modest, and sometimes implicit, victories, and to leave out of his portrait some of the historical Socrates' most resounding successes.

 What needs to be underscored here is that in light of the historical facts surrounding characters such as Alcibiades, Charmides, and even Phaedrus, it is not that Socrates' teaching corrupts these young men but rather that he is unable in the end to change them at all. They never complete the crucial shift from carelessness to caring, or from caring about conventional goods to caring about the philosophical goods that Socrates thinks should come first. They all fail to undertake seriously the care of the self. And completing this turnaround is a prerequisite for any further change. Hence each proves unworthy of the teacher's attention, reluctant as each is to allow himself to be dissuaded or diverted from his original desires. Socrates is unsuccessful as a teacher, primarily because his interlocutors never fully relinquish their hope of attaining their original desires. When they come to realize that a continued association with Socrates is more likely to sour them on their original aspirations than to assist them in the attainment of these aims, these youths give up on Socrates rather than on their desires, as Alcibiades admits in his *Symposium* speech. As a consequence, Socrates would say, these characters remain unfree, not only because they lack the knowledge necessary to become truly powerful but also because they never abandon their former way of life and thus are unable to be transformed by the knowledge that they have already gained through their brief association with philosophy. They never learn to rule themselves, hence they are bound to remain tyrannized by their passions, and Plato's audience will be led to conclude that it is precisely these tyrannical tendencies that lead the likes of Alcibiades, Charmides, and Critias to violent, premature deaths.

Just because he chose to depict Socrates in conversation with characters such as these, however, Plato's audience might justifiably conclude that he appears to have been more anxious to understate than to overstate the efficacy both of Socrates in the dialogues and of philosophy in general. For not only does he portray Socrates as, at best, only marginally successful with his target interlocutors—even with those interlocutors who seem to be most teachable and even when he engages them under the most propitious conditions—and not only do the minimal successes of his Socrates contrast sharply both with the obvious successes of the historical Socrates and with the success that Xenophon's Socrates enjoys in his Socratic conversations, but Plato also is willing to allow the philosopher's successes to remain largely implicit while making his failures more explicit. Sometimes these phenomena occur in the very same dialogue. We can see an example of just such an explicit failure and an implicit success in the *Phaedrus*.

It is generally agreed that the dramatic date of the *Phaedrus* cannot be later than around 415, when Phaedrus was banished from Athens (to return only after Socrates' death at the turn of the century). The dialogue probably takes place even before that, since Isocrates, who was born in 436, is called "beautiful" by Phaedrus (278e) and "young" by Socrates (279a). At the very end of the dialogue, Socrates tells Phaedrus what he foresees for Isocrates, who went on to enjoy considerable prominence as an orator and a teacher of rhetoric. Since Isocrates would have barely reached the age of majority when Socrates and Phaedrus are discussing him, Socrates could not have known (at the dramatic date of the *Phaedrus*) what Plato would have known about the young man's later career when he wrote this dialogue some half-century later, by which time Isocrates would have been dead or an old man.[7] So when Plato has Socrates predict what he foresees for his beautiful young friend, he allows Socrates to fail explicitly as a prophet concerning the future of this character. Whatever reasons Plato might have had for having Socrates predict wrongly that Isocrates would become a philosopher—something that never, of course, happened—what Socrates proclaims at 279a–b is as follows:

> It seems to me that by his nature he can outdo anything that Lysias has accomplished in his speeches; and he also has a nobler character. So I wouldn't be at all surprised if, as he gets older and continues writing speeches of the sort he is composing now, he makes everyone who has ever attempted to compose a speech seem like a child in comparison. Even more so if such work no longer satisfies him and a higher, divine impulse leads him to more important things. For nature, my friend, has placed the love of wisdom (*philosophia*) in his mind (*psuchē*). (Nehamas & Woodruff trans.)

What is most interesting about this apparent failure on Socrates' part to predict correctly Isocrates' future way of life is that this glaring failure occurs later in a dialogue in which Socrates had earlier notched a significant, if only a tacit, success for himself and for philosophy. Recall that Socrates' second speech, complete with its imagery of the charioteer and two horses, is delivered as an atonement for the first speech that Socrates had given. The first speech had portrayed Love as something bad which, because Love is the child of Aphrodite, amounts to an offense against the gods. After Socrates is restrained from crossing the river by his divine sign, the challenge in his second speech is either to deliver a show-stopping speech to redeem himself or cause Phaedrus to go back to Lysias to get him to write another speech in an ongoing contest of speeches. That Phaedrus decides to remain with Socrates and engage in philosophical discussion for the duration of the dialogue rather than returning to the city to obtain the better speech from Lysias implicitly represents a moral victory for philosophy within the dramatic action. And this victory becomes, in fact, the condition for the possibility of the conversation that Phaedrus and Socrates later have concerning Isocrates, in which the prominent misdiagnosis occurs (see *Phdr.* 242d–e). So not only does Plato leave his audience to deduce the philosopher's victory by leaving it implicit, but the dialogue draws to a close with Socrates erroneously forecasting Isocrates' future, thereby accentuating the fallibility of Socrates as its parting shot.[8]

Why does Plato so qualify the successes of his protagonist-philosopher, even under the very best circumstances with the very best characters? Why does he depict Socrates' successes as so modest and short lived? Why does he often show the philosopher failing in some way? Assuming that he could have portrayed his Socrates any way he chose, why did he choose to depict him as such a failure in the dramatic action of his dialogues? It seems to me that there is a complex set of reasons for Plato's decision to fashion the dialogues in the way he does, and the remainder of this chapter will attempt to enumerate and clarify these reasons. Some have already been broached, but drawing them together here will allow them to be connected to his portrait of Socrates as a gift, as a final clue about Plato's overall characterization of Socratic *paideusis*.

The first and perhaps most obvious reason that Plato shows only limited successes in the dramatic action of the dialogues has to do with his general concern for literary verisimilitude. Since the most important beneficiary of Socrates' approach to any interlocutor is surely the audience for which Plato was writing, it is constantly necessary to ask, what is the relationship between the failure of the philosopher in the drama of a dialogue, on the one hand, and the success of Plato's pedagogical effort with his audience, on the other hand? I have argued that Socrates generally fails at the level of the drama, not, of course, that Plato's dialogues are failures with *their* audience. There is a need for the dialogues to "work" on at least these two levels at once. The consequences of his concern for literary verisimilitude can be seen in several ways. Plato certainly knew that what Socrates strives to engender in the characters he encounters is likely to precipitate an extreme fracture in the continuity of their lives. He also surely knew that Socrates' ability to convince or persuade youths such as Lysis and Alcibiades would depend crucially upon their own skills, and he wanted his dialogues to ring true to his audience with respect to the odds against the philosopher's success. In his appeal to these best and brightest youths, Plato does not allow his audience to minimize or underappreciate how radical the demand is that Socrates is making on them. Ultimately what is being asked of someone like Lysis or Alcibiades when Socrates challenges his most fundamental beliefs and closely held convictions is surely nothing less than that he relinquish his careless self and follow the *logos*. Socrates is challenging such characters to risk being fundamentally changed beyond recognition through adherence to the *logos*. And we have seen that his regimen for them mandates that they abandon their customary moorings for the radically uncertain replacement that the *logos* is supposed to supply for them. Additional obstacles stand in the way of their success.

In all learning, the burden of completing the mandated pedagogical tasks by which one learns rests entirely on the student. Plato allows his audience to see, at least in the case of Alcibiades, that it is his inability to follow through on what he knows to be best for him that causes the failure. Now although character transformations of all kinds also can occur throughout time in subtle, incremental ways, just as molecular and cellular changes are occurring constantly at the level of one's *bios*, radical change also can happen through the most jolting life experiences. An encounter with Socrates may have been just such a jolting experience, capable of altering a person's life indefinitely. It is no small challenge to ask young and ambitious men—especially those who enjoy the gifts and opportunities that privilege would have afforded them in classical Athens—to enter into a relationship in which the *logos* alone will function as a mirror to their identity and a constant reminder of their every conceit or pretense, every contradiction between their words and their deeds, and everything that they would disregard or be unconcerned about. To enter into such a relationship to the *logos* would already amount to an affirmation of one's readiness to be transformed into a new person.

Plato's audience is brought to see that by inducing a crisis of character, Socrates besets these youths in much the same way as a decisive dilemma or tragic vision descends upon a mythical hero. We see also that in place of their present conceits, Socrates offers to youths such as Lysis and Alcibiades something strange and unfamiliar, something that appears at times to be quite ridiculous. In return, he prescribes for them an ethic of self-care, but the condition for getting started in the care of the self seems, at least to the interlocutors, to be that they let go of their former selves, relinquishing the identity they presently have. Nearly all of the philosopher's interlocutors prove by their actions in response to him to be well satisfied with their present circumstances and with their prospects for pursuing a different kind of career than the one Socrates has in mind for them. The concern for literary verisimilitude that leads Plato to depict dramatically the overall failure of this barren midwife to improve others in a sustained, demonstrable manner serves importantly to caution the audience against construing such metamorphoses as either simple acts of choice or as wholly epiphanic experiences. What Socrates offers to Lysis and Alcibiades as tools for self-transformation entails a fundamental, comprehensive alteration in their behaviors and practices. This must be spurred by a love of wisdom and an ongoing commitment to examining their lives.

Hence, it is not simply the formulation of a positive ethical doctrine that Socrates is exhorting these characters to acquire, and which, likewise, Plato might like to foster in his audience, but an excellent character. And Plato does not seem to allow the possibility of a sudden, complete "conversion" of human character. To the extent that modifications in one's character are possible at all after basic habits and proclivities have been formed, they will be the result of gradual, vigilant, and sustained exercise, necessarily supported by a critical examination of one's beliefs and an alteration in the present structure of one's desires. On the one hand, this philosophical practice, this regimen of self-care and self-transformation, requires perseverance and courage; on the other hand, success in the program will depend upon the ability of its most talented pupils to resist the distracting enticements of money, power, honor, and ordinary pleasures. Socrates is wise to the extent that he knows that the human preoccupation with these conventional goods usually displaces what he thinks should be the fundamental human good, namely, the care taken over oneself required to develop the practices through which one truly acts like a good, free person.

Plato portrays Socrates' practice as having yet another important function, which we discussed in Chapter 4 in connection with the philosopher's kind of truth telling. Through his relentless exercise of himself in conversation, Socrates was seen to bring his deeds into harmony with his words. Dialogue was thus shown to function as a means of harmonizing or fine-tuning oneself. And in Socrates, this harmony has become practically perfect. In the persona of Socrates, Plato creates the exemplary character for whom the *logos* is sovereign and whose deeds harmonize with the *logos*. The philosopher's self-mastery is both refined and displayed through exercise in relation to the *logos*. In a sense, then, since the *logos* speaks through this paradigmatic philosopher, Jaeger is right in saying that Socrates, in Plato's powerful characterization, has *become* the *logos*. However, Socrates is himself a conversation and so he is not always of one mind and he does not speak with only one voice throughout the dialogues. It is a plurivocal, that is, a dialogical or polylogical, rather than a monological or univocal *logos*, that courses through the persona of Socrates in these dialogues.

Furthermore, as the dramatic embodiment of the *logos*, Plato's philosopher is a paradox. Since he is the one stationed by the god to roam the streets of Athens, ceaselessly exhorting others to take care of themselves, Socrates is positioned as the consummate philanthropist, the one who is most concerned for the care of others. Socrates assumes the daunting task of caring for the care of others, exhorting his fellow citizens to exercise concern for the most important things. If they respond to his exhortation by claiming that they do care, then he tests them in conversation. In this way, he carries out his vocation as a benefactor, occupying himself with his mission in the city to the neglect of his own affairs and in general disregard for the good things that people ordinarily seek. Whether this philanthropic mission is motivated primarily by his divine calling, or whether it is driven chiefly by the fact that Socrates has taken such trouble over himself that he has already perfected himself, his gadfly role in the city makes his fundamental concern the care of others. In this dramatic way, Plato provides, through the concrete example of Socrates, an enactment of how the care of others might be optimally undertaken. Socrates' own example teaches that it is only because this philosopher has tended to his own affairs—and continues to tend to them by ruthlessly testing himself in conversation and striving to harmonize further his words and deeds—that he is the one most capable of serving as the city's caretaker, the one who cares for the care of others, as Jaeger and Foucault stressed.

Dramatic Failure and the Gift in Socratic *Paideusis*   169

Now if Plato had portrayed Socrates as a glowing success in producing offspring and reproducing philosophical types, the philosopher would then at least have had to admit to being a teacher and perhaps the founder of a philosophical school or practice.[9] Instead, he disclaims disciples with the same fervor with which he disclaims certainty; anything less would be unpardonable hubris and pedagogically irresponsible.[10] So while philosophy, Socratic freedom, and proper self-care may appear at first available to everyone, the overall conclusion that the audience will undoubtedly draw from the fate of the characters in the dialogues is that these are congenial only to the rarest individuals. Not requiring prior training, wealth, or nobility, the simplicity of Socrates' philosophical practice belies its ultimate difficulty and camouflages its potential perils. Hence it is a peculiar benefit indeed that Socrates claims to have conferred upon his fellow citizens, at *Apology* 35d, after explaining that he surely would have been killed long ago if he had led a more public life. He says:

But I went to each of you privately and conferred upon him
what I say is the greatest benefit, by trying to persuade him not to
care for any of his belongings before caring that he himself should
be as good and as wise as possible, not to care for the city's
possessions more than for the city itself, and to care for other
things in the same way. (Grube trans.)

We also saw that at *Apology* 30d–e, Socrates boldly warned his jury against mistreating "the god's gift" to them by prosecuting the case against him. In having Socrates declare himself the god's gift to the city and its greatest benefactor, Plato is going out of his way to position his philosopher in a distinctive gift economy instead of a market economy based upon exchange, as Section 1.c attempted to show in connection with the preliminary discussion in *Republic* 1 between Socrates and Thrasymachus. Taking seriously this gift image helps make sense of many enigmatic features of the philosopher's character that otherwise would remain merely odd, idiosyncratic quirks.

Richard Kraut noted the peculiarity of this gift in his 1984 book *Socrates and the State*. Kraut writes, "Just as ordinary moral education, with all its limitations, is a great gift we receive from our parents and the city, so moral perplexity, with all its painfulness, is the gift Socrates thinks he is giving Athens."[11] What seems clear is that Socrates claims to be a great benefactor through the provocation he carries out with others. His testimony in the *Apology* confirms that he is interested in provoking people to move from carelessness to caring about how best to live, from being absorbed exclusively in worldly concerns to being concerned primarily with the best possible state of their *psuchē*. The gadfly's sting is designed to turn them around, to reorder their concerns, and to introduce them to a regimen of self-care, that is, to a set of practices organized around conversation (and through this, self-examination), which might best enable them to live good and happy lives.

Though it almost never happens that Socrates' sting produces a clear, measurable, and lasting benefit for the life of his target interlocutor, one must remember that, according to Socrates, the benefit he gives others on behalf of the god is conferred whenever he has had the opportunity to exhort and examine someone. Kraut stresses that Socrates does not portray himself as one who "tried to give a gift but failed." This would suggest that Socrates conceives of his uniqueness as consisting chiefly in his divinely sanctioned task of disabusing others of the conceit of wisdom, after his protreptic first step has aroused his fellow citizens like a gadfly rouses a sleeping horse. This is precisely the process the philosopher describes in his mission statement at *Apology* 29d–30b. That Socrates believes he has conferred such a benefit upon those he has engaged would explain also why he does not appear to regard his practice as tarnished in any way by his concrete failures to turn around the lives of those he targets or by the celebrated misdeeds of some of his close associates.

Examining the kind of gift that Socrates confers upon others will illuminate important principles that make Socratic philosophizing unique for Plato and that distinguish Socrates' curious gift from other kinds of gifts. This will show why the image of Socrates as a gift is more than just a case of forensic hyperbole. And it begins to furnish reasons for Plato's choice to use the gift image as the context within which to have his own philosophical exemplar act and speak. The focus on the image of Socrates as a gift also may shed greater light on the complex relationship between Plato, the author, and Socrates, the character. That Plato's dialogues consistently position Socrates as someone who stubbornly refuses to "transact" philosophy for any price supplies good evidence for maintaining that he considered keeping Socrates scrupulously free from a market or an exchange economy essential to the proper practice of philosophy, hence Socrates is always depicted as incorruptible.[12] Socrates, moreover, seems to conceive of his benefaction as being essential to his independence (see Chapter 4, Note 20). Although some attention has been paid to the explicit occurrences of the "gift" image in the *Apology*, Socrates' testimony to his jury about the policies upon which his practice is built is only the most prominent context in which this image is utilized by Plato. The connection between two essential characteristics of Plato's Socrates—the notion of the philosopher as a benefactor and the characterization of his gift as being incomparable with the kinds of goods that can be exchanged—underwrites the contrast that Plato is drawing between Socrates' behaviors and practices, on the one hand, and prevalent conventions, on the other hand.

Plato forces his audience to ask, how are we to understand the seeming paradox of the poor philosopher as the greatest benefactor? Besides delineating philosophy from sophistry, allowing Socrates the freedom to talk with whomever he chooses and enabling him to speak the truth to his interlocutors, what else does the portrait of the philosopher as an incorruptible benefactor signify, and what does it secure for Plato? What is the meaning of this image of Socrates as the consummate philanthropist, someone who can only be described as a gift? What precisely is the nature and function of the gift that Plato thinks he confers upon others?

To answer these questions fully would require a much more detailed examination than can possibly be carried out here, but I offer some preliminary reflections and suggest a few topics for further study. Recall the logic governing the benefactor/beneficiary relationship in Aristotle's account, discussed in Section 1.c. In contrast to the way the gift functions in that economy to oblige the other or render him indebted, Socrates' gift requires no repayment, since for the most part it is not even recognized by its recipient as a gift. In general, it is fair to say that practically all of the characters who converse with Socrates either do not recognize what he is offering them or they misconstrue or misappropriate the gift he gives them. The philosopher can nonetheless claim, however, that he has conferred upon Athens the greatest benefit, because the gift he gives his fellow citizens is not improvement but perplexity, as Kraut noted. It is provocation and not salvation that this curious benefactor claims to be giving his countrymen. In bestowing this peculiar benefit upon others, the philosopher casts himself as a gift to the city, dispatched to this service by the god. His gift is a gift of self, and it is so in two senses: first, Socrates gives himself as a gift to the city by neglecting his own affairs in order to do the god's work. By exhorting and examining his fellow citizens, functioning within the city as a social critic or as the city's collective conscience, the philosopher is the one who cares for the care of others. Second, he gives his interlocutors a gift of self by providing the occasion for them to take charge of themselves and thereby to win themselves. What is more, at the same time Socrates is conferring his gift, and through the very same activity, the philosopher claims to be benefitting himself. This is one sense in which Plato's depiction of Socrates as a gift may seem paradoxical.[13]

Unlike the way in which the gift functions in Aristotle's account, Socrates' gift is designed to liberate and empower rather than to enslave its recipients. This further distinguishes it from gifts in potlatch economies. Throughout the dialogues, this unlikely philanthropist consistently avoids becoming enmeshed in the prevalent forms of market exchange, a policy which the examples of his encounters with Thrasymachus and Alcibiades dramatized and which his testimony in *Apology* made explicit. At the same time (and with his author's help), Socrates somehow always manages to gain the upper hand in the dialogues within the conventional ethos governing gift relations.[14] By this I mean that he is consistently positioned as a benefactor and not as a beneficiary of others. He maintains this precarious posture in two main ways: (1) by giving rather than by receiving; and (2) by giving a gift of wholly indeterminate value. Like any other self-respecting benefactor within a restricted gift economy (as Aristotle's analytic matrix helps illustrate), Plato's Socrates eschews honors and accepts no gifts or payments in return for conferring his unique kind of gift upon those he targets. He prides himself on the freedom that this posture secures for him, and many of his interlocutors express the offense they feel at Socrates' "air of superiority." So far, Socrates would seem to be positioned simply as an insuperable benefactor within a restricted gift economy, the paragon of greatness of soul in the passage from Aristotle, cited in Section 1.c.

But because it is of the nature of Socrates' gift to be incommensurable with the kinds of gifts that can be exchanged, and that often mask a kind of warfare, Plato forces his readers to go beyond the traditional tension between self-regard and other regard, and beyond the exchange framework of the conventional ethos of benefaction, to grasp the nature and function of Socrates' gift. We have seen that this gift is not well construed within a restrictive or limited economy such as that which underwrites Aristotle's account of benefaction and Mauss's description of potlatch. This gift does not oblige its recipient to make an equal or a greater return to the giver. One obvious reason for this is that it is not recognized as a gift by most of his interlocutors. Is Socrates' gift then a "pure" gift, an act of pure generosity that carries with it no implied obligation to reciprocate because it goes unrecognized by its recipients and because Socrates expects nothing in return? If so, then Socrates' gift might then be conceived of within a general or an unrestricted economy. Construed in this way, one wonders whether the failure of Socrates' interlocutors to recognize that a gift is being given is evidence of a fault or a misuse of Socrates' gift, as Nietzsche charged, or whether this is rather its necessary condition.[15] Is the purity of Socrates' "stealth" gift diminished by his own acknowledgment of it? Is it enough to make Socrates' gift a pure gift that the recipient alone fails to recognize it?

That it is only in the *Apology* that the explicit image of the gift is employed to characterize Socrates' peculiar philosophical vocation and his unique stance toward pecuniary affairs might be intended partly to explain why Socrates' gift goes largely unnoticed. Considered dramatically, his remarks to his jury present Socrates' self-characterization at the end of his life's work. The divinely appointed philosopher offers the notion of the gift as part of his retrospective on his entire career, and it is supposed to substantiate his claim that he has been stationed in the city by the god. It is reasonable to assume, judging from Plato's other Socratic dialogues, that the contents of this self-assessment were never made quite so explicit to his interlocutors in other contexts. Socrates is here announcing publicly for the first time what had previously been unexpressed in his daily practice. Given the late dramatic date at which the declaration is made—only the *Crito* and *Phaedo* are set later than the *Apology*—we are led to conclude that only at the end of his career did Socrates characterize himself in these terms, making explicit the gift image. It should not be surprising then that most people Socrates exhorted and examined throughout the dialogues did not recognize that a gift was being given to them because these conversations occurred prior to Socrates' declarations at his trial. It also is perfectly consistent with Socrates' contention in his defense that he has given a gift to Athens to say that others do not recognize his gift for what it is. We have said that it is the nature of the purest kinds of gifts to go unrecognized by their recipients. So to this extent, Socrates' gift might be construed as circulating within a general, unrestricted economy. But a pure gift within a general economy, as Derrida and Bataille have stressed, must be an act of excess, of pure squandering.[16] For his gift to be conceived of within a general economy then, Socrates would have to be regarded as not caring about any of the possible effects that might be produced by his gift. He could not care in the least whether or how his provocation affects its recipient, either in individual cases or with the city as a whole. He would not be able to engage in protreptic discourse, because he could not be seen encouraging others to follow his path. Nor could he consistently even be seen conducting his routine conversations, since this practice makes him dependent upon the participation of others. For Socrates to be Socrates, he needs interlocutors. Now if his gift is meant to be construed as a pure gift, in Derrida's and Bataille's sense, then Socrates should have no need for his interlocutors or his associates, and he should not care about how any of them choose to live. Plainly then, Socrates' gift cannot be a "pure" gift in this sense.

Thus there are weighty reasons for rejecting both a restrictive and a general economy as fitting frameworks within which to understand Plato's portrait of Socrates' gift. A *tertium quid* emerges from the notion of a circulating gift, a gift that arises neither from an act of squandering nor from the desire to enslave another, but rather from the gift's own intrinsic powers. This is the notion of the gift as something that must be shared with others, something sacred that one must pass along for one's own good. Alan Schrift points out that second-generation commentators on Mauss have focused more closely upon the spiritual significance of the gift and the idea of a circulating gift than on the practice of potlatch. This shift in focus provides an important clue for our investigation here.[17] In the case of Socrates, a circulating gift would be the gift that truly keeps on giving. Socrates does not want his target interlocutors to give anything back to him, but he does wish for something to be appropriated by them and passed on to others. Socrates wants his gift to circulate as far as possible within his city. This way of construing his gift also is consistent with the Socratic understanding of freedom, justice, and excellence, as being strengthened through their practice and spread through their exercise. In a parallel way, Socrates' gift is meant to be passed on by its recipients to others. He does not want to be repaid, but neither is he unconcerned about the effects of his gift. His is not an act of squandering or of superabundance.

Now given Plato's portrayal of his Socrates as the greatest benefactor to Athens, and as a man who neglects his own affairs in order to care for the care of others without accepting payments or honors in return, it may be surprising that at the same time Plato portrays this larger-than-life character as being so enormously unsuccessful in the pedagogical or psychagogical project that unfolds through the action of many dialogues. Though Kraut is correct to note that Socrates does not cast himself as a failure, Plato seems to want to cast him as one. I noted in the Introduction that it is extremely odd that the Socrates who speaks and acts in the conversations that Plato immortalizes is so much less successful as a pedagogue or psychagogue to others than the historical Socrates was. And Plato's Socrates is shown failing, despite the fact that no mere mortal philosopher could be as adept in argument, incisive in character assessment, and clever in deed as this literary Socrates is. Is there additional proof that Plato wants to cast Socrates as a failure, or at least as less successful than the historical Socrates was? There is the matter of the most famous protégés of the historical Socrates (both Plato's and the historical Socrates'), which Plato chooses not to stress or even mention at all. His dialogues do not show Socrates conversing with either of the historical figures whom we know went on to become writers of Socratic dialogues, namely, he and Xenophon. And although Plato mentions himself three times in the dialogues, if he means for us to count his own loyalty as a success story, he also means for us to adduce it ourselves, because he never makes it explicit.

So why does Plato portray Socrates in the way that he does? Pointing out the hazards of the Socratic education must have been calculated to communicate something important about his own conception of education and his own vision of philosophy. While Socrates is busy conferring the benefit of provocation upon those he engages in conversation, Plato wants to confer upon the larger audience of his dialogues something quite different. He seems strongly to want to produce in his audience the experience of being in a conversation with Socrates but, importantly, he also guides and shapes that experience by the way that he writes his dialogues. Composing his dialogues to keep alive rather than flatten the many voices audible in them is Plato's way of mediating, while preserving through his style of writing, the experience of engaging in a conversation with Socrates. Those who are smitten with this vision of philosophy will want to pass this gift along to others. They are likely to model their way of teaching after Socrates', but they also will be duly cautioned as a result of Plato's circumspect mediation.

This way of construing Socrates' gift as a circulating one allows us to recapitulate, in conclusion, several reasons Plato seems to have written his dialogues in the way that he did. First, I have suggested that Plato is mindful of the odds against turning souls toward philosophy and a life of self-examination. Perhaps the primary reason Plato depicts Socratic *paideusis* as a failure at the level of the dramatic action is not just to disclose the odds against success, however, but also to illustrate that, in a sense, no one ever really "teaches" anyone anything. Just as no one is able to communicate anything the other is not disposed to hear, just as no one can be made to "see" anything she or he is not able (or willing) to see, and just as no one can really "convert" another, so no one can teach another something she or he is not ready to learn.

Plato seems to have been well aware that the ideas people hold are intimately related to their particular characters, and only if something the teacher says resonates with the student is the student likely to learn or remember it. When teaching is understood as this kind of shared activity—rather than as an activity only on the part of the teacher—there is a further implication, namely, that the teacher cannot really be said to teach if the student does not learn. In a sense then, it is true that, at bottom, all learning ultimately requires a kind of self-teaching too, because for learning to take place, the pupil must appropriate or incorporate the teacher's lessons. Consequently, it is too much to suppose that anyone, even the seemingly superhuman Socrates, can "convert" another to a new way of life. Given the concern for literary verisimilitude, the dialogues must, in fact, depict Socrates failing if Plato truly wants to distinguish his kind of intellectual from those irresponsible competitors. Philosophers should know the limits of philosophy, and teachers should know the limits of teaching.

Second, the dialogues work simultaneously on two levels. The failure of Socrates with his target, on one level, may have seemed the best way for Plato to succeed in presenting his conception of philosophy to his audience. Given the above reflections on how learning occurs, the dialogues must teach in a way that harmonizes with the admission that learning takes place *within the pupil.* The dialogues must provoke as Socrates provoked, if his gift of provocation is to keep circulating. And it is Plato's audience that is always the ultimate audience for the philosophical dramas that he creates; indeed, his audience alone is privy to Socrates' encounters with certain solitary interlocutors in dialogues such as the *Ion, Crito, Euthyphro,* and *Alcibiades I.* And his audience is the only one that could possibly benefit from the information supplied by the narrative frame in those dialogues that employ this device. What is going on at the level of the dramatic action must then be continually examined for the possible effects that it might be expected to produce in Plato's audience. When an interlocutor's mistake provides an occasion for us to learn, this is an essential, and not an accidental, way that the dialogues function.[18] When they function in this way, Socrates' gift continues to circulate to ever-new recipients, like a perennial chain letter of provocation. Viewed in this way, Socrates' gift circulates far beyond the confines of the dramatic conversation that he is portrayed as having with a target interlocutor, and this is sometimes even captured in a dialogue itself. In the *Symposium,* Apollodorus is recalling the framed conversation as recollected for him by Aristodemus more than a decade later, and within the frame, Socrates recalls what he learned from Diotima a quarter-century earlier when he remembers a series of conversations that he had with his teacher about erotic matters.

A third reason Plato does not depict Socrates as being more successful is because he seems well aware of the dangers inherent in presenting philosophical viewpoints through endearing characters, even (or especially) superlative philosophical characters who make well-reasoned arguments. His dialogues betray his acute awareness of the pitfalls of a method that depends so heavily upon the character and example of Socrates himself. The followers of such characters become like disciples, proselytizing for the master, falling in love with the messenger instead of with the message. Plato appears doubtful that another Socrates can be found. This poses a danger that the message will be lost entirely, dying with the messenger. The critique of discipleship that he builds into his portrayal of Socrates underscores the risks of using charismatic figures and methods that rely heavily upon imitation and upon *ad hominem* argumentation. Perhaps this also is the main reason, in dramatizing more than two dozen of Socrates' innumerable conversations, that Plato shows the philosopher succeeding only momentarily or in some small measure with select interlocutors. More pronounced success might not only trivialize what is at issue in his approach to these youths and lead readers to underestimate the odds against the popularization of philosophy, it also might minimize the risks of misappropriation to which even Socrates, who proclaims not to teach, nevertheless remains vulnerable. Time after time his interlocutors are shown falling in love with the philosopher instead of with philosophy. This is perhaps a problem endemic to the role of philosophical exemplar, in which Plato casts him; but it also is a problem that threatens all teachers and mentors in the process of nurturing others. Plato wrote these dialogues in such a way as to illuminate the problem we now call "transference" and to show how closely the Eros that can lead one to philosophy is related to honor-love (*philotimia*), spiritedness (*thumos*), and the desire to get more than one's fair share (*pleonexia*).

The fourth reason is connected to the third. By depicting the widespread failure of Socrates as a teacher, Plato provides his audience with an important antidote to the effects of Socrates' dominance as a persona in the dialogues. Now in spite of the fact that the disciple types Plato portrays appear unenviable, even laughable, the most seductive effect that Socrates' dominance produces in readers is the tendency to think that we are closer to Socrates than we are to the interlocutors. From the privileged standpoint we enjoy as members of Plato's audience, we may be tempted to scoff at a character's mistakes in argument and feel confident that we ourselves would have been more circumspect and clever as interlocutors than are the sometimes hapless partners of Socrates. It is sobering to realize that Socrates fails with these characters, no matter how persuasive we find him. The audience is brought to witness the failures of Socratic teaching, even though no flesh-and-blood interlocutor could possibly be either as prescient or as clever as Plato's character. He is unparalleled in dialogue, at least in part because he is unequalled as a diagnostician. He knows what the interlocutor desires before, and better than, the interlocutor himself; and he seems to know this prior to discussion with them in many cases.[19] Now even though this acuity in diagnosis is more plausibly to be ascribed to his author's genius than to any actual trait of the historical Socrates, we are led to conclude that his uncanny acumen for diagnosing his interlocutor and then crafting a personalized strategy for unsettling him falls short of knowing which, if any, of the people he approaches will be capable of carrying forth the turnaround that the philosopher has begun with them. This seems designed to humble Plato's audience and to temper its infatuation with Socrates.

In addition to explaining why Plato portrays Socrates as a general failure in the dramatic action of the dialogues, the final reason Plato seems to have chosen to portray him as he does also may explain why he did not ascribe more positive, fully elaborated, and authoritative views to Socrates. This goes a long way toward explaining why Plato wrote dialogues, and more precisely why he wrote *the kinds* of dialogues he did. Consider for a moment how different the effects on their audience would have been had Plato provided more positive, fully articulated views for Socrates than he did. Socrates is already a character insuperable in word and deed. Had his author given him more positive, authoritative views, the dialogues would have been much more susceptible to uncritical appropriation. Audiences would find it very difficult to avoid merely taking Socrates' words as authoritative and final. Thus the dialogues would have functioned to put an end to their audience's questioning rather than inspiring such questioning in them as they now do.[20] If Socrates were portrayed as more authoritative, and the dialogues were not so open-ended, Plato's Socratic dialogues would have then been merely veiled treatises and the dialogue form simply a literary cloak for the straightforward, monological presentation of their author's views. In that case, Plato's writings would resemble Bishop Berkeley's dialogues between Hylas and Philonous, in which the author's own deeply held philosophical beliefs are manifestly obvious. Instead, he has given us richly textured conversations in which his own deeply held views remain latent, often debatable, conversations in which the philosophical issues discussed are not fully resolved for us. These are what we have come to appreciate as Plato's dialogues. If Plato had not written his dialogues in such a way as to carefully and subtly undermine the claims to authority made by his philosophical characters, as he did, his own deeply held views would, at the same time as they put an end to questioning, be just that much more susceptible to uncritical appropriation by his devoted students, who would fasten on the master's doctrines without being at all familiar with the long, difficult process through which his views were shaped and tested.[21] In the end, the dialogue form of these Socratic *logoi* would be undermined by the monological views of their dominant philosophical protagonists, now speaking as the voice of authority.

How different the tenor of such dialogues would be from Plato's works, which indeed present several dominant, favored philosophical characters—most notably Socrates, but also Diotima, Timaeus, the Athenian Stranger, the Eleatic visitor, Parmenides, and so on—but which depict them as masters of placing in question, of proposing hypotheses, and of exposing the shortcomings in the views of others on an endless quest for wisdom. To be sure, Plato wrote open-ended dialogues so they would serve a vital pedagogical function, but it also must have been a matter of great importance to him that they, like Socrates himself, do not teach by being didactic. Plato makes sure that philosophy does not die with Socrates, but to accomplish this he seems to have considered it necessary to take a vow of silence, sacrificing his right to appear and speak as a character himself in the dialogues that he wrote. Perhaps it was only by removing his dominant, authorial voice from the dramatic conversations that present his philosophy that Plato could best ensure that any disciples he engenders will fall in love with his vision of philosophy, and not with Plato the man.

NOTES

INTRODUCTION

1. I will always specify "the historical Socrates" when I mean the historical Socrates rather than Plato's Socrates. It should be clear from the outset that this is a study of Plato's Socrates. I do not think that we will ever have answers to many important questions concerning the historical Socrates, because access to him has been closed off, so it seems fruitless to attempt to reconstruct him.

2. They are "would-be" in a dual sense: many of them are reluctant participants who would not class themselves as students of Socrates; and Socrates claims to be unable to teach anybody anything. It remains a disquieting fact that Socrates rarely, if ever, seems to enjoy long-term success in his project of improvement, even if the only explicit goal is to get others to examine themselves. In his account of his role as a midwife (*Tht.* 150c–151b), Socrates ascribes his gift to the god, beginning his speech by saying that the god determines which ideas will live and which will be stillborn. And it is those people favored by the god, he says, who encounter Socrates and make progress in conversation with him.

3. Plato does not show Socrates advising anyone to enter political life, and Xenophon shows his Socrates advising only Charmides to do so. He was the nephew of Critias, with whom he appears in the *Charmides* and under whose influence he became one of the Thirty Tyrants. He was a relative of Plato and was killed in the Piraeus in 403. Alcibiades was one of the greatest political leaders of his time, but his legacy is tainted by several irregularities. He was accused of defiling the Herms and of profaning the sacred mysteries just after his departure as a co-commander of the Sicilian expedition. When he was called back to Athens to answer the charges against him, he defected to Sparta and aided Athens' bitter enemy.

4. Gerald Press has argued that the dialogues are enactments that "make" or "show" as much as they assert. See Gerald A. Press, "Plato's Dialogues as Enactments," in *The Third Way: New Directions in Platonic Studies*, ed. Francisco J. Gonzalez (Lanham, Md.: Rowman & Littlefield, 1995), 133–152. Press believes, as I do, that since Plato presents his philosophy in conversational dramas, it is not possible simply to extract propositions or arguments from their context when examining them. Since they are propositions or arguments advanced by a specific character for some particular purpose in the context of a larger conversation, it may not always be obvious whether the speaker *believes* what he says, to say nothing of what Plato might think of the statement. Now since Plato does not speak as a character in the dialogues he writes, it is necessary to provide justifications when ascribing views to Plato. See also J. J. Mulhern, "Two Interpretive Fallacies," *Systematics* 9 (1971): 168–172. Mulhern coins, what he calls, the "Plato says" fallacy.

5. Which is precisely what he does at 505c–d, where he tells Socrates to carry on the argument by himself. Callicles had previously professed his friendship and good will toward Socrates (see, for example, 485e and 486a). In turn, Socrates addresses him as "friend" (499c4) and begins his severest chastisement of the Sophist's position with the entreaty, "In the name of friendship . . . " (500b6). The existential contradiction involved in Callicles' desire to dominate Socrates in argument at the expense of friendly relations illustrates the other side of his claim at 492b, that only the strong man will be in a position to give gifts to his friends. Socrates concludes his refutation of Callicles by insisting that the strong (immoderate) man can be friend neither to men nor gods, because such men exhibit no willingness to share. Without *sophrosunē*, a human being is incapable of community, and one who is not capable of community is incapable of friendship (see *Grg.* 507e).

I am drawing here upon Roger Duncan's short but insightful piece, "*Philia* in the *Gorgias*," *Apeiron* 8 (1974): 23–25. Duncan's clues provoked me to consider the broader relation between *philia* and *pleonexia* in Plato. Duncan shows that Callicles' desire to win the argument and to dominate Socrates conflicts with the friendly tenor that initially frames their conversation. It is noteworthy, though, that Socrates never seems to lose his friendly demeanor toward his interlocutors. Chapter 4 shall attempt to develop the wider implications of Duncan's insight while analyzing another example of Socrates' resistance to a character's attempt to dominate him.

6. These youths may still be benefited in some way by their engagements with Socrates, but there is no hard evidence that they are. The exclusion of young women from the philosopher's enterprise is a reflection of the times in which Socrates and Plato lived. I shall argue that Plato subverts conventional assumptions and uses traditional models as a way of criticizing them, and this is especially true with respect to women, but I do not defend this thesis at any length here.

7. Catherine Osborne makes the novel assertion that Apollodorus and Aristodemus are depicted as further along the path of philosophy than others, and she claims that, in the *Symposium*, Aristodemus is ahead of Socrates on the philosophical path. In fact, she claims that Aristodemus "has already arrived." See Catherine Osborne, *Eros Unveiled: Plato and the God of Love* (Oxford: Clarendon Press, 1994), 98. Despite the richness of her analysis of the imagery of guides and followers, and of the

activity of philosophy as being on a road or a path, Osborne fails to convince with her claim about the depiction of Aristodemus.

At a minimum, it would seem that Plato intends for such characters to be regarded as caring less for Socrates' concerns than for Socrates himself (*Symp.* 173d). In addition, Apollodorus is less than estimably portrayed in the *Phaedo*, when he is first named (at 59a) as the most passionately devoted person in Socrates' circle, and at 117d he is said to have never stopped weeping throughout the conversation Socrates has been having with Simmias and Cebes. And in the *Symposium*, Aristodemus is described as a "real runt of a man" (173b). It seems to undermine the rank and credibility of both narrators that: (1) there are admitted gaps, memory lapses, and editing in their narrations (cf. 178a, 180c); (2) Aristodemus falls asleep during the important debate over tragedy and comedy (223b–c); and (3) Apollodorus insults his audiences (at 173a and 173d), as Agathon will insult one of his guests later. Together these examples exhibit a general lack of care for the handling of the narration. Various clues seem to point us to the shortcomings of these fawning followers of Socrates, even while they are indispensable to us as narrators of the dialogue. (And perhaps Plato undermines the completeness and exactness of their account as a way of acknowledging that he is recreating the *spirit* of a Socratic conversation and not its *letter*.) Crito too is depicted in the *Crito* and *Phaedo* as having missed the point of some of Socrates' most important teachings: about past agreements in the *Crito* and about Socrates' body in the *Phaedo*.

8. Allan Bloom, *Love and Friendship* (New York: Simon and Schuster, 1993), 448.

9. Ruby Blondell has recently argued—convincingly, I think—that the striking similarities—physical, circumstantial, intellectual, moral, and methodological—between Socrates and Theaetetus in the *Theaetetus* suggest that Plato makes Socrates the symbolic father of Theaetetus (and not just a midwife for ideas). In Blondell's view, Theaetetus is the heir to Socrates' philosophical practice, and the hope that he will one day equal or surpass Socrates in wisdom is hinted at *Theaetetus* 165b and dramatized by the "coming of age" motif in the dialogue, which ends with Socrates commenting on the progress the boy has made. She deftly contrasts the fatherhood model for the pedagogical relationship between Socrates and Theaetetus with two other possible models—a homoerotic one of *sunousia* and one based on philosophical *philia*—to show that the parental model best suits the relationship between Socrates and Theaetetus in this dialogue. See Ruby Blondell, "Reproducing Socrates: Dramatic Form and Pedagogy in the *Theaetetus*," *Proceedings of the Boston Area Colloquium in Ancient Philosophy* 14 (1998): 21–38.

10. I shall not use the terms *method* or *methods* as technical expressions. Socrates does not seem to regard himself as having a single, overarching method, if method means a set of techniques or predetermined procedures that can be uniformly applied with any and every interlocutor. There is no specific formula or single strategy behind what Socrates does, and neither he nor Plato christens his approach with any label. Brickhouse and Smith argue eloquently against a method, as thus defined, in the first chapter of *Plato's Socrates* (New York and Oxford: Oxford University Press, 1994), 3–29. Since the most important questions Socrates puts to his interlocutors always seem to refer back to their character, his method cannot be invariable. Unlike an ordinary *technē*,

Socrates' educational strategy would be a bad one if it could not respond to the unique tendencies of each interlocutor. Hence, his reflections on method in the dialogues seem to be quite local and case specific. Socrates does, however, seem to think certain aspects of his cross-examinations can be imitated and practiced by others (see *Ap.* 23c, 38a, 39c–d, and 41e–42a). Moreover, Plato also appears to think that there is something special about Socrates' approach to others, even though it cannot be reduced to a *technē*. But he leaves his audience to determine what is most distinctive about this way of philosophizing.

11. Greek homoerotic practices have been the focus of much scholarly attention in the last two or three decades. Eva Keuls attributes this recent interest to two events: (1) the fact that many fifth-century and fourth-century Attic red and black figure vase paintings were first made widely accessible by the museums that owned them; and (2) the translation into English of the pathbreaking study by Paul Brandt (first published in German in 1932 under the pseudonym Hans Licht), entitled *Sexual Life in Ancient Greece*. See the Introduction to Eva C. Keuls, *The Reign of the Phallus: Sexual Politics in Ancient Athens*. 2d ed. (Berkeley: University of California Press, 1985), 1–15. My analysis in this study has been informed by the work on this issue by many other authors listed in the bibliography, including Cohen, Cole, Dover, Foucault, Golden, Halperin, Saxonhouse, Winkler, and Zeitlin.

12. If this is correct, then it is probably not an accident that in the *Lysis* Plato will have Socrates take the place of Lysis' and Menexenus' hired pedagogues for the duration of the dialogue. That Socrates stands in dramatically for the boys' pedagogues parallels what Socrates sets out to do in the arguments to follow.

13. Alcibiades' report in the *Symposium* of his attempt to ensnare Socrates takes even further the reversal of conventional roles Socrates began in the first *Alcibiades*. Throughout this study, many other dialogues, notably the *Charmides, Meno, Republic, Gorgias, Alcibiades Minor, Laches, Phaedrus,* and *Apology of Socrates*, will provide illuminating examples to supplement the primary textual evidence under consideration.

14. Vlastos identifies what he calls a "last zone of frigidity in the soul of the great erotic" (Vlastos, "The Paradox of Socrates," in *The Philosophy of Socrates: A Collection of Critical Essays*, ed. Gregory Vlastos (Garden City, N.Y.: Anchor Books, 1971), 16. Nussbaum follows Vlastos in espousing the view that Socrates is incapable of love for particular persons. See Martha C. Nussbaum, "The Speech of Alcibiades: A Reading of the Symposium," in *The Fragility of Goodness: Luck and Ethics in Greek Tragedy and Philosophy* (Cambridge, Mass.: Cambridge University Press, 1986), 165–199. See also Vlastos, "The Individual as an Object of Love in Plato," in *Platonic Studies*, ed. Gregory Vlastos (Princeton, N.J.: Princeton University Press, 1973), 3–11.

15. See the end of Vlastos's essay, "The Paradox of Socrates," 19–21.

CHAPTER 1

1. Nehamas argues that what Socrates denies having is the kind of "technical or expert knowledge" of *aretē*, which the Sophists claim to have. This knowledge, says

Nehamas, which the Sophists "can articulate and transmit to others with a reasonable assurance of success," is being contrasted with Socrates' "common, nontechnical, nonexpert knowledge of *aretē*." See Alexander Nehamas, "What Did Socrates Teach and To Whom Did He Teach It?" *Review of Metaphysics* 46, No. 2 (1992): 293–294. Despite his supple analysis of the "profound irony" in this and other Socratic statements, consistency should require also that we take at face value Socrates' assertion at 19d–e (cited above) that it is a "fine thing to be able to teach," as the Sophists do, a statement that *prima facie* conflicts with many other things Socrates says about the Sophists. For Nehamas, teaching can mean only one of two things: (1) "One may in fact know (or claim to know) what the good and successful life is, and one may be able (or claim to be able) to transmit that knowledge to others." Or (2) "One can set oneself up as an example, perhaps as the only example, of what it is to lead a good and successful life" (284). Nehamas holds that Socrates is not a teacher in either sense, though he thinks Plato engages in teaching by depicting the philosopher as an exemplar of the good and happy life. Yet Socrates does encourage others in the dialogues to do as he does, using himself as an example. He does valorize the life spent in examination of *aretē*, and he does make some sweeping remarks about how all humans shall live braver and freer and more just lives by engaging in the practice of philosophy as he does.

2. Gerald Press has argued persuasively for such a conception of the dialogues in his "Knowledge as Vision in Plato's Dialogues," *The Journal of Neoplatonic Studies* 3, No. 2 (Spring 1995): 61–90.

3. Commentators have interpreted this statement in one of two main ways: one either takes Socrates' denial here as an example of complex irony (construing the statement as true in a sense and not true in another sense), or takes Socrates' words "at face value," as Nehamas and others claim to be doing. However, if one were really taking Socrates' denial at face value, it should not require seventeen pages of critical exegesis in a scholarly journal to explain what the statement means. I would argue that the first alternative glosses too readily over the complex ambiguities inherent both in Socrates' claim and in his role in the city; the second alternative fails to account for the degree to which Socrates is educating or engaging in teaching in the dialogues, even while eschewing the conventional label *didaskalos*. Whereas the latter view, as section 1.d argues, adheres to a quite narrow (possibly bankrupt) definition of "teaching" and accords little interpretive weight to the overall context of Socrates' statement, the too-hasty conclusion that Socrates is *merely* being "ironic" short-circuits the perplexity about these matters that Plato seems to want to provoke in his audience.

4. David Blank argues that payment alone obligates the seller of a product or service to "deliver the goods" under Athenian law. He cites F. Pringsheim, *The Greek Law of Sale* (Weimar, n.p., 1950), whose study argues that, "Greek law of sale seems to have recognized transfer of ownership of goods only upon payment of the price, irrespective of the physical transfer or nontransfer of possession. It is probable that the provider of a service was legally obligated to provide that service only if he accepted the fee in advance." Blank shows that this principle helps clarify both Xenophon's and Plato's characterization of Socrates' policy to refuse payments for conversing with others. See David Blank, "Socratics versus Sophists on Payment for Teaching," *Classical Antiquity* 4, No. 1 (1985): 11. See especially note 45.

5. Xenophon asserts that according to the accusers of the historical Socrates, it was Socrates' associations with Alcibiades and Critias that swayed the city against him. That Socrates was believed to have taught them politics, and that their political careers hurt Athens so much, according to Xenophon, caused blame to focus on Socrates. (Xenophon, "Memorabilia," I.2.12*ff*, in Xenophon, *Conversations of Socrates*, trans. Hugh Trieadnick and Robin Waterfield [London: Penguin Classic Books, 1990]).

6. Gregory Vlastos, *Socrates: Ironist and Moral Philosopher* (Ithaca N.Y.: Cornell University Press, 1991), 110.

7. Nehamas, "What Did Socrates Teach?," 299–303. There also are strong undercurrents of elitism in discussions outside of the *Apology*. I agree with Nehamas in concluding that, far from talking to "all and sundry," Socrates is really quite selective. ("These are . . . all special people.") He points out that Plato's Socrates talks to three different kinds of people: (1) acknowledged experts; (2) self-proclaimed experts; and (3) handsome (I would add, noble and promising), young men (299). Socrates' claim to talk to all comers may be designed to address the suspicion that he, refusing to work through conventional political channels, elected to work selectively upon the best and brightest of Athens' youth in the hope that their ascension to power would secure for the philosopher the influence he truly wanted all along. And the results of this choice on Socrates' part, the charge would go, have been disastrous for the city. Examples of acknowledged experts would be Nicias, Laches, Euthydemus, Dionysodorus, Ion, Protagoras, Gorgias, and Hippias. Examples of the self-proclaimed experts would be Meno, Euthyphro, Agathon, Anytus, Thrasymachus, and Critias. Besides Lysis, Alcibiades, and Charmides, the class of handsome and promising youths might also have included Menexenus and Phaedrus.

8. It seems right to conclude, as Nehamas does, that Socrates' leading aim in his divinely appointed role in the city is to identify people who believe they are wise when they are not, and to attempt to expose this vain conceit. However, he does not include the conversations with these young and beautiful boys in either his class of "acknowledged experts" or "self-professed experts," placing them instead into a third category of Socratic interlocutor. And this type of interlocutor does not fit so well within the mission statement that Socrates presents to his jury (*Ap*. 29d–30b). In those dialogues in which Socrates confronts some kind of acknowledged or self-proclaimed expert, his primary objective appears quite straightforward: to purge these characters of their conceit of wisdom, or failing that, to make their arrogance and inconsistencies painfully obvious to them and to anyone else who might be listening in on the conversation. The philosopher's objectives with the handsome, nobly born, and well-educated youths with whom he loved to spend time in conversation are not nearly as transparent.

9. Nehamas argues that, "If there ever was a sense, any sense, in which Socrates did think of himself as a teacher of *aretē*, he would never have disavowed this central responsibility" (Nehamas, "What Did Socrates Teach," 299). This may be true. But besides disavowing the narrow and bold claim that he is a teacher of human excellence, I hope to show that there are several other important entailments that Socrates seeks to avoid in denying to be anyone's *didaskalos* (of anything).

10. Socrates' stipulation at *Republic* 540a, that training in dialectics should commence only from age fifty for those select few guardians who have proved themselves

to be the best in every respect, is worth recalling in this connection. This statement may be interpreted in one of several ways: (1) Socrates could be expressing that he considers the failures of his efforts with the best and brightest youths to be due primarily to their youth, just as any inadequacy in the arguments of the *Lysis* will be seen in Chapter 2 to be due to the youth of Socrates' interlocutors. Yet this only begs the question, "Why does Plato use such young characters?" and the question, "Why does Socrates waste his time on them?" Socrates' remark in the *Republic* also may be taken as Plato's sharp criticism of Socrates' pedagogical methods, although the theory that Plato is critical of Socrates seems difficult to support for very long. (Two commentators who have advanced this argument are cited below in Note 17.) Or Socrates' statement may be taken to apply only to "training in dialectic," therefore, it may not be a criticism of Socrates at all.

11. Nehamas analyzes the similarities and differences between Socrates and the Sophists in his "Eristic, Antilogic, Sophistic, Dialectic: Plato's Demarcation of Philosophy from Sophistry," *History of Philosophy Quarterly* 7 (1990): 3–16.

12. And they are successful at least in exposing the conceit of wisdom in those they cross-examine. For evidence that in Socrates' own time there were others who could employ *elenchos* successfully, see *Apology* 38a, 39c–d, and 41e–42a. Socrates describes these imitators in all-too-familiar terms at *Republic* 538b–c, expressing just how great a role he thought these followers played in causing charges to be brought against him.

In a sense, Socrates' denial that he has ever been anyone's teacher stakes out a contrary position to the one maintained by Charlie Brown in a classic Peanuts cartoon strip in which Charlie Brown boasts to Lucy that he "taught Snoopy to whistle." Lucy retorts, "I don't hear him whistling," to which Charlie declares indignantly, "I said I *taught* him; I didn't say he *learned* it." Socrates is saying, "I said he *learned* it; I didn't say I *taught* him."

13. At 23e, Socrates says Meletus is in court on behalf of the poets, Anytus on behalf of the craftsmen and politicians, and Lycon on behalf of the orators.

14. Blank surveys in considerable detail the kinds of criticisms directed at the Sophists by other Athenians ("Socratics versus Sophists," 2–6). Legends concerning the more exorbitant fees paid seemed to have circulated widely in Socrates' time, but in Kerferd's study of the Sophists, he argues that, "To many it was the mere fact that they took fees, not the size of the fees, which was objectionable." G. B. Kerferd, *The Sophistic Movement* (Cambridge: Cambridge University Press, 1981), 25.

15. This is especially the case as a result of the general slander against him that was propagated by Aristophanes in *The Clouds*. Socrates knows, and says explicitly at 18b, that these largely nameless accusers will be the hardest to refute. Aristophanes' caricature of Socrates gave rise to the widespread belief in Athens that Socrates was some kind of marginal Sophist crossed with a natural philosopher. In Aristophanes' comic rebus, Socrates' practice entailed "making the worse argument the stronger," speaking against justice, discussing things in the heavens and beneath the earth, and, in general, teaching people to deceive, while picking bedbugs off of his skin or while suspended above the stage by a crane. For a thorough examination of how Socrates' defense in Plato's *Apology of Socrates* is responding to the various images used to caricature

Socrates, as fashioned by Aristophanes in *The Clouds*, see Elinor J. M. West, "Socrates: Aristophanes and Plato's Old Quarrel" (1998, Typescript).

It has been noted already that the unspoken charge against which Socrates seems to be defending himself, both by insisting that he is not a teacher and by explaining his brand of knowledge, is that he is a teacher of virtue. An Athenian gentleman would have believed that it is the job of one's father and one's city to mold one's natural gifts and provide a good upbringing into virtue. Hence, Athenian gentlemen would have believed that virtue requires no teacher, and certainly that it cannot be acquired for a price.

16. This formulation is indebted to the generous, most helpful comments on an earlier version of this chapter offered by Mauro Bottalico. I am grateful to Mauro for reminding me of this discussion in the *Republic* and for providing several other rich suggestions that have been incorporated into this chapter.

17. David Hansen concludes his careful, penetrating examination of Socrates' self-reflections in the *Theaetetus* by stating that the answer to the questions "Can or will Socrates teach Theaetetus?" and "Is Plato presenting a critique of Socrates?" remains ambiguous. David T. Hansen, "Was Socrates a 'Socratic Teacher'?" *Educational Theory* 38, No. 2 (1988): 224. Anne-Marie Bowery has argued that Plato is indeed critical of Socrates' methodology. That Socrates seems so vulnerable to discipleship suggests to Bowery that Plato is critical of what she calls "self-oriented narration." Anne-Marie Bowery, "Looking Beyond the Elenchus: On the Possibility of a Platonic Critique of Socrates," *Southwest Philosophy Review* 14 (1998): 157–68.

18. For example, at *Charmides* 166c–d, Socrates says:

> How can you think that I have any other motive in refuting you but what I should have in examining into myself? This motive would be just a fear of my unconsciously fancying that I knew something of which I was ignorant. And at this moment, I assure you, I pursue the argument chiefly for my own sake, and perhaps in some degree also for the sake of my other friends. For would you not say that the discovery of things as they truly are is a good common to all mankind? (Jowett trans.)

And, at *Meno* 86b–c, Socrates tells Meno:

> Some things I have said of which I am not altogether confident. But that we shall be better and braver and less helpless if we think that we ought to inquire, than we should have been if we thought that there was no knowing and no duty to seek to know what we do not know; that is a belief for which I am ready to fight, in word and deed, to the utmost of my power. (Jowett trans.)

See also *Grg.* 486d and *Ap.* 28e in this connection.

19. A student taking my Classical Philosophy course as an introduction to philosophy put this frustration most eloquently when she wrote out the following reading question: "I was reading the *Meno*, and I have to admit I was becoming more and more

annoyed with Socrates. After a point, I just really wanted him to give a definition of virtue. His method of conversation is tiresome, in some ways, because it seems as though he doesn't really have an answer and that he is dancing around Meno trying to aggravate him. What does he really think? Why doesn't he ever just say what virtue is? It is surprising to me that no one ever seems to notice that he is being mocked in some ways by Socrates!"

20. See Blank, "Socrates versus Sophists," and West, "Socrates."

21. After Socrates' death, his poverty was increasingly mythologized. In fact, the historical Socrates came from a moderately well-to-do family. Since Socrates served as a hoplite soldier, a station assigned only to property holders, he had to have come from what would now be called an upper-middle-class family. However, since the philosopher did not accept money for his work on behalf of the god, whatever money he inherited was probably gone by the time of his trial. Plato's Socrates does not display any of the outward trappings of wealth, but he evidently has plenty of leisure.

22. Nehamas and Press are among the contemporary commentators who have made this point. The claim is based on the scarce usage of the term *philosophy* prior to Plato and on the degree to which Plato, in the dialogues, seems to be carving out a distinct, quasi-specialized meaning for "philosophy" (although it is clearly not nearly as specialized as it is today). In doing so, he aims to distinguish philosophy from both sophistry and rhetoric. For this reason, Werner Jaeger and Eric Havelock claimed earlier in this century that Plato "invents" philosophy. A version of this claim has been reiterated most recently by Andrea Nightingale in *Genres in Dialogue: Plato and the Construct of Philosophy* (Cambridge: Cambridge University Press, 1996), 14. Nightingale thinks Plato regards himself as having invented philosophy (cf. 67, 73, 133). See also Werner Jaeger, *Paideia: The Ideals of Greek Culture*, trans. Gilbert Highet (Oxford and New York: Oxford University Press, 1971 [1943]), Vol. 3, Book 4, Ch. 2; Eric A. Havelock, *Preface to Plato* (Cambridge and London: Harvard University Press, 1963); Nehamas, "Eristic, Antilogic, Sophistic, Dialectic" and Press, "Plato's Dialogues as Enactments," 133–52. For a discussion of Plato's role in "creating" the Sophists, see G. B. Kerferd, *The Sophistic Movement*. For a comprehensive study on the use of the term *philosophy* in Plato's dialogues, see Monique Dixsaut, *Le Maturel Philosophe: Essai sur les Dialogue de Platon* (Paris: 1985). Dixsaut's book studies Plato's use of the terms *philosophia, philosophos,* and *philosophein*.

23. Two notable exceptions to this oversight are Christopher Smith and Andrea Nightingale. See P. Christopher Smith, "Not Doctrine but 'Placing in Question': The 'Thrasymachus' (*Rep.* I) as an Erôtêsis of Commercialization," in *Who Speaks for Plato?: Studies in Platonic Anonymity*, ed. Gerald A. Press (Lanham, Md.: Rowman & Littlefield, 2000), and Nightingale, *Genres in Dialogue*. Another important predecessor who examined the image of Socrates as a gift is Richard Kraut. See Kraut, *Socrates and the State* (Princeton, N.J.: Princeton University Press, 1984), esp. Chapter 8 on democracy.

24. It is worth noting that, to Plato's contemporaries, being "corruptible" means literally being "conquered by money," and so they would have thought that a poor person is more easily corrupted than someone of means. See Dover, *Greek Popular Morality in the Time of Plato and Aristotle* (Indianapolis and Cambridge: Hackett Publishing Co.,

1994), 125. Here Dover quotes Thucydides' Pericles expressing this view. Also see Dover, page 34, note 1 on the view that a poor person is more easily corrupted than one with money.

25. Two people might even be thought of as exchanging sex for wisdom, if one is to believe the rationale in Pausanias' *Symposium* argument for the Heavenly Aphrodite (cf. *Symp.* 180c–185c).

26. Marcel Mauss, *The Gift: Forms and Functions of Exchange in Archaic Societies*, trans. Ian Cunnison (New York: W. W. Norton and Co., 1967). Mauss studied American, Pacific Island, and New Zealand cultures, and his ethnographic evidence derives from the practices of "potlatch," "*kula*," and "*hau*" in the three cultures, respectively. See also Lewis Hyde, *The Gift: Imagination and the Erotic Life of Property* (New York: Vintage Books, 1983). After reading Mauss, it may be difficult to read Plato's Socratic dialogues without noticing the extent to which similar conceptions of the gift are operative in them.

27. Xenophon, more than Plato, highlights the principles underwriting such a matrix of gift relations and stresses the connection between Socrates' refusal to accept fees or gifts and his independence, as David O'Connor, following Blank, has emphasized. Xenophon claims that Socrates nicknamed those who took fees "self-enslavers," because taking payment obligated them to talk to anyone who paid. Xenophon, "Memorabilia," I.2.6, in Xenophon, *Conversations of Socrates*, 51–215. In his version of Socrates' defense, Xenophon has Socrates say, "Do you know anyone less a slave to the appetites of the body than I? What man is freer than I, since I accept no gifts or pay from anyone?" (Xenophon, *Ap.*, line 16). The interpretation offered here argues that the same cultural milieu serves as the context for Plato's dialogues, and that Plato appropriates certain aspects of it for his own purposes while criticizing some of its other dimensions. O'Connor has argued also that Xenophon's view of Socrates is close to that of the Cynics' view. David O'Connor, "Socrates and the Gift," lecture delivered at the 12th Annual Meeting of the SAGP/SSIPS, Binghamton University, Binghamton, N.Y. October 30, 1993.

28. I take the main points of Aristotle's account to be supported also by Xenophon's Socratic conversations and the work of K. J. Dover, in addition to the ethnographic evidence of gift-giving practices in other cultures analyzed by Mauss.

29. While I am sympathetic to Adkins' criticism of the idea of "popular" morality, Dover's analysis does help illuminate various aspects of the ethos operative in Plato's time. See A. W. H. Adkins "Problems in Greek Popular Morality," *Classical Philology* 73 (1978): 155–57. Dover emphasizes that many people confuse the Socratic view with the prevalent Athenian view, and one of the aims of his study seems to be to differentiate between the two. See, for example, Dover, *Greek Popular Morality*, 125.

30. All citations from Aristotle, unless specifically noted, are from *The Complete Works of Aristotle*, 2 vols. ed. Jonathan Barnes (Princeton, N.J.: Princeton University Press, 1984). Consider also two similar passages:

> This is why it would not seem open to a man to disown his father (though a father may disown his son); being in debt, he should repay, but there is nothing by doing which a son will have done the equivalent of what he has

received, so that he is always in debt. But creditors can remit a debt; and a father can therefore do so too. (*Nic. Eth.*, Bk. viii, Ch. 14: 1163b19–22)

But the friendship of man and wife is a friendship based on utility, a partnership; that of father and son is the same as that of god to man, of the benefactor to the benefited, and in general of the natural ruler to the natural subject. (*Eud. Eth.*, Bk. vii, Ch. 10: 1242a32–35)

31. Consider also what he says in *Rhetoric,* Book I, Chapter 11:

Conferring and receiving benefits belong to the class of pleasant things; to receive a benefit is to get what one desires; to confer a benefit implies both possession and superiority, both of which are things we try to attain. It is because beneficent acts are pleasant that people find it pleasant to put their neighbours straight again and to supply what they lack. (1371a34–1371b4)

32. The relation between being in another's debt and being a slave is discussed more explicitly in recent works such as Dover, *Greek Popular Morality*, 298. To be in debt is the social equivalent of being a slave, because in either condition one is constrained by mere survival needs. Should one's debt grow too large, loss of citizenship privileges could occur. Xenophon's Socrates regularly speaks in the language of benefaction and exchange, making it somewhat easier to see the prevailing culture in which Plato too has Socrates act. We shall see that Aristotle conceives of the benefactor as analogous to the gods in relation to mankind or a father in relation to his children.

33. James T. King, "Nonteaching and Its Significance for Education," *Education Theory* 26 (Spring 1976): 223–230.

34. In the *Protagoras,* Socrates criticizes the Sophists for disseminating their lessons so indiscriminately, without regard for the effect these will have upon different kinds of characters, or souls (see especially 313d). And in the *Hippias Major,* Socrates ironically applauds the Sophists for being wiser than the Seven Sages, since the old wise men did not realize how valuable money is (*Hi. Ma.* 282dc). In other contexts, the Sophists are characterized differently, though the specific context and a statement's tone must be taken into account. Socrates suggests (most assuredly with tongue in cheek) that Meno should be sent to a Sophist to learn virtue (*Meno* 91b). At *Euthydemus* 271d, the Sophist brothers Euthydemus and Dionysodorus are said to be able to teach a specific skill, namely, fighting in armor.

35. He does claim to have knowledge on one occasion, and he attributes this knowledge to a woman's teaching. In the *Symposium,* Socrates tells the gathering that he learned about *ta erotika* (matters of love) from Diotima (201d–212c, see especially 201d–e, 206b, 207c, and 212b–c). See also what he learned of rhetoric from Aspasia in the *Menexenus* (especially at 236a–b and 249d).

36. Here again, it would seem that the real problem is the tendency to frame the matter as an "either/or": King will conclude that Socrates does not give speeches, he does not speak to a crowd, he does not profess to have knowledge, and he "serves no personal purpose" through his practice (224–225). But none of these statements is

unambiguously true. Counterexamples can be found for each point. In the view of many interlocutors, Socrates is speech making, and the *Phaedrus, Symposium,* and *Apology,* at least, give examples of occasions when, albeit uncustomary, speeches are required of Socrates. Despite his habitual disclaimers about his own knowledge, if one considers knowing *what is not* a good answer to be a kind of knowledge, Socrates is a genius. Finally, while he may derive no conventional benefit from his practice, Socrates does indeed believe that he is living the best possible life and that his practice improves him. See *Meno* 86b–c and *Charmides* 166c–d (cited in note 18 above).

The fact is that Socrates clearly and often *uses* rhetoric, but to nobler ends and through more highly-varied means than the Sophists do. Some of his rhetorical devices will be examined closely in chapters 2, 3, and 4. Perhaps Socrates is the "true rhetorician," described at *Gorgias* 504d–e and *Phaedrus* 269d–274b. He may be the one who uses rhetoric to aim at the truth. While Socrates "is not a rhetorician"—because he does not behave like other "rhetoricians" or "teachers" of the day—he *does* engage in all the classical forms of rhetoric, just as he engages in some kind of teaching in the dialogues.

37. But a conversation with Socrates would not be experienced as painful if the philosopher were talking with people who possessed the kind of character for whom philosophical inquiry and self-examination would be attended by pleasure rather than pain.

38. The same two positions may be found in attempts to explain the origin of the human brain. One view of the modern human brain sees philo-genetic heritages as buried deep inside the brain and more recently evolved features, identified with the neo-cortex, are conceived of as layered over the older parts. The other view sees the modern human brain as fundamentally reconstructed, incorporating or blending in such a way as to fundamentally reconstitute it, rather than conceiving of the brain's evolution as a matter of piling recent evolutionary advances on top of the brain's philo-genetic past.

39. And he ultimately concedes: "I think we shall not go wrong if we loosen up our language and assert Socrates to be a teacher, not of doctrines, but of the philosophic form of life" ("Nonteaching," 228).

40. "Pander" is Teloh's term. See Henry Teloh, *Socratic Education in Plato's Early Dialogues* (Notre Dame: University of Notre Dame Press, 1986), 109. Teloh seems to notice only this one implication of Socrates' circumvention of the prevalent exchange economy, however. He does agree that, for Socrates, the art of conversation is an end in itself and not merely a means to a fee. By taking a fee, says Teloh, the Sophists denigrate their art and reveal that they do not really care for the *psuchē* of their interlocutor (8, 105–106).

41. The discussion to follow draws upon several textual sources for this composite sketch. Most notably, see the discussions in *Republic* I (348a–b) and in *Protagoras* (329a–b and 334c–338e) about why the question-and-answer method is preferred over giving set speeches. Hence, the *Apology, Phaedrus* and *Symposium* are somewhat anomalous dialogues in that Socrates is required by the contexts to give a speech. We shall see that Socrates does use cross-examination to refute Meletus and advance his *ad hominem* counterclaim that Meletus (whose name is cognate with the Greek word for

care or concern) does not really care either about the gravity of the charges or the improvement of the young. And in the *Symposium,* Socrates uses his recollection of a series of conversations he claims to have had with Diotima to refute Agathon's view of Eros through the question-and-answer method. But in both cases, this method is "smuggled in" by Socrates, which is at least partly to subvert the required form of speaking. The cross-talk comprises only a small part of each dialogue.

42. In his paper "Not Doctrine but 'Placing in Question' " (cited in Note 23 above), Christopher Smith uses Aristotle's distinction between dialectical and demonstrative arguments in the *Prior Analytics* (24a22–25) to show that the aim of the "What is X?" dialogues is precisely to interrogate both sides of a contradiction rather than to stake out a position and adduce grounds as premises in support of it.

43. Interpreting the passage with which this chapter began, Vlastos writes,

> In the conventional sense, where "to teach" is simply to transfer knowledge from a teacher's to a learner's mind, Socrates means what he says. But in the sense which he would give to "teaching"—engaging would-be learners in elenctic argument to make them aware of their own ignorance and enable them to discover for themselves the truth the teacher had held back—in that sense of "teaching" Socrates would want to say that he is a teacher, the only true teacher: his dialogue with his fellows is meant to have, and does have, the effect of evoking and assisting their efforts at moral self-improvement. (Vlastos, *Socrates: Ironist,* 32)

I follow Nehamas in holding that Plato writes his dialogues in such a way as to make it impossible to know whether Socrates knows what he claims not to know. And his only claim to knowledge, repeated several times in the *Symposium* (at 201d–e, 206b, 207c, and 212b–c), to know about matters of love turns out to be a much less surprising claim than at first it appears to be, because Eros is desire for what one lacks, thus Socrates' assertion to have knowledge of Eros is another way of saying that he knows what he lacks. Put otherwise, he is Socratically ignorant, driven to seek wisdom by this knowledge of his lack.

There are good reasons for rejecting a view that makes Socrates dogmatic. As Nehamas has pointed out, Socratic irony, at its most complex, leaves unclarified—both for his interlocutor and for Plato's readers—the extent to which Socrates himself knows the answer or believes he does. Nehamas has stressed the difference between regarding Socrates as merely *using* irony, as Vlastos does, and *being* an ironist. Nehamas conceives of Socrates as being profoundly ironical, and he underscores how this ironical posture of Socrates' gives rise both to the frustration experienced by various interlocutors at what they perceive as Socrates' willful manipulation of them, and to the offensive air of superiority that the philosopher sometimes projects toward others in the dialogues. So while his reticence may have the positive benefit of drawing out an interlocutor and assisting in the birth of his own ideas, it should not be assumed that Socrates could just as easily have supplied a predetermined answer himself. We shall return to the role of irony in Chapter 4.

44. Don Adams has formulated this procedure as Socrates' "evidentialism." See Don Adams, "Elenchos and Evidence," *Ancient Philosophy* XVIII, No. 2 (Fall 1998): 287–307. Mark McPherran also has made much of Socrates' use of induction. See Mark L. McPherran, "Elenctic Interpretation and the Delphic Oracle," in *Rethinking Socratic Method: Essays in Dialogue with Gregory Vlastos's "The Socratic Elenchus"*, ed. Gary Alan Scott (University Park: Pennsylvania State University Press, Forthcoming). My remarks in this section have been greatly enriched by numerous discussions with Bill Welton.

CHAPTER 2

1. The *Lysis* was, for a long time, regarded as either wholly aporetic or as only propadeutic to Plato's more mature dialogues, *Phaedrus* and *Symposium*. Lamb, Cornford, Bluck, and Grote all held it to be wholly aporetic, and Guthrie, Grube, Vlastos, and Taylor all concluded that the *Lysis* was incomplete and, therefore, merely a primer to the *Phaedrus* and *Symposium*. Guthrie thought so little of the *Lysis* that he concludes, "There are many opinions about this dialogue, and I must confess to my own, which is simply that it is not a success. Even Plato can nod." W. K. C. Guthrie, *A History of Greek Philosophy*, Vol. 4, *Plato, The Man and His Dialogues: The Earlier Period* (Cambridge: Cambridge University Press, 1978), 143. Beginning with Friedländer, Gadamer, and especially David Bolotin's 1979 translation and commentary, readers have begun to rediscover the *Lysis*, and several recent interpreters—especially Gonzalez and Tessitore—have found a way to reconcile the *Lysis'* argumentation with its dramatic action.

2. The argument begins at *Lysis* 217b1, where Socrates leads the boys through a discussion of instrumental and final goods (relative and ultimate ends), for which certain things are desired as means. The results of this part of the argument will be examined in Section 2.c.

3. As a noun, *philia* means "love" or "affection"; as an adjective, it is used like the English word "dear." *Philos* means friend. H. G. Liddell and R. Scott, *An Intermediate Greek-English Lexicon*, founded upon the seventh edition of *Liddell and Scott's Greek-English Lexicon* (Oxford: Clarendon Press, 1994), 862–866. Commentators generally agree that the *Lysis* does a better job of delineating a model or an outline of human relationships than it does of supplying a definition of the friend. One recent author argues that the *Lysis* does provide a model of friendship, if not a simple definition. See Amy Coplan, "Tri-partite Friendship in Plato's Lysis," *Aporia* (1995): 37–47.

4. Many recent interpreters have stressed the need to take seriously the dialogue form in which Plato presents his philosophy, arguing that the form is inseparable both from the content of Platonic philosophy and from Plato's conception of how philosophy, in general, should be practiced. Francisco J. Gonzalez has argued persuasively that interpreters must strive to account for both the argumentation and the dramatic action navigating a "third way" between dogmatism and skepticism. He writes: "The skeptical interpretation can account for the form of Plato's writings only by minimizing their

positive philosophical content, while the 'doctrinal' interpretation can uncover their content only at the cost of considering their form little more than a curiosity and even an embarrassment." See Gonzalez, "A Short History of Platonic Interpretation and the 'Third Way,'" in *The Third Way: New Directions in Platonic Studies*, ed. Francisco J. Gonzalez (Lanham, Md.: Rowman & Littlefield, 1995), 13. The dramatic form of the *Lysis* is more than simply a fancy package within which Plato presents argumentation intended to convey his own deeply held beliefs about the issues discussed. Since readers often have disregarded the dialogue's dramatic, or extraargumentative, features, and therefore the interplay between the action of the dialogue and what is said by the characters in it, it is little wonder that some have failed to discover its highly rewarding teachings.

5. That Lysis is probably the youngest interlocutor of Socrates is indicated by several pieces of evidence. We are told that Lysis still goes by his father's name (204e3–4) and that he is accompanied by his pedagogue to the Palestra (208c3–4). One learns also that a pedagogue still accompanies Lysis to and from school, and that he is not yet "of age" to do the things Socrates enumerates in their first exchange. Vlastos points out that the interlocutors' young age necessitates a milder form of questioning than is found in other dialogues. Perhaps it would be more apt to say "less deep" instead of "milder". Yet Socrates does not permit these boys to answer open-ended questions, presenting several alternatives instead from which they must merely choose. This leads Vlastos to conclude that there is no genuine *elenchos* in the *Lysis*, a contention that presupposes a quite narrow conception of Socratic cross-examination and refutation since both boys are chastened by Socrates and each becomes perplexed about the issues discussed. Though Socrates may not truly force these young interlocutors to put forth answers themselves without any prompting from him, and although Lysis seems quite willing to be refuted, this only suggests that *elenchos* may not be the only tool that Socrates employs to accomplish a refutation. What Vlastos notices about the *Lysis*, I would argue, is apropos of many conversations in which genuine inquiry actually gets underway. These cooperative conversations—for example, in the *Republic* and *Phaedo*—are not characterized in major part by the contentious, competitive cross-examination typical of *elenchos*. They are not aimed at shaming anyone, rather they are characterized by a friendly mode of inquiry.

In the *Lysis*, the philosopher's prodding and leading appears to lay the groundwork for the arguments that follow. To be sure, the approach tailored to these youths engenders a distinctive pace of "dialectics" in the *Lysis*, but it should not be supposed from this, I think, that his refutation of Lysis or Menexenus is any less complete than it is in the case of his refutation of Meletus, Polemarchus, or Agathon. What is more, the refutation of Menexenus, quite unlike the humbling that Lysis experiences, is very similar to the kind of cross-examination that Socrates carries out with his more contentious interlocutors. This is precisely because Menexenus is a lover of disputation and a neophyte in rhetorical practice, so a more standard *elenchos* is used with him, and the verb *elenchein* is used at 211b7 to refer to the threat of being refuted by Menexenus.

6. Plato seems to have inserted two kinds of precaution into the *Lysis* to guide his audience: *narrative*, or *literary*, clues and *dramatic* ones. Clues on both levels provide essential information for Plato's audience, and the first type of clue would not have

been recognized by the participants in the original conversation, because they are given only outside of the framed conversation between Socrates and the boys. The *narrative*, or *literary*, clues include the carefully placed and explicit warnings throughout the dialogue about its argumentation, Plato's use of Socrates' inner monologue to supply information about the philosopher's motives, intentions, and judgments about the boys, and the dialogue's employment of names and its use of characterization. The *dramatic* clues include the extreme youth of Socrates' interlocutors, the setting, the pretext for Socrates' meeting with the two boys, and the movement within the dramatic action of their conversation. So in addition to the age of the boys, Plato constructs additional, more restrictive, boundaries to the discussion of friendship in the *Lysis*.

For Plato's audience, signposts warning of difficulties with *Lysis*' argumentation are well placed throughout the dialogue. After the opening scene outside of the Palestra and Socrates' first exchange with Lysis, the arguments begin, with Socrates telling Ctesippus a little lie (211d). The spontaneous alliance through which the older philosopher and promising pupil conspire to deceive Menexenus' uncle about what they had been planning to do strengthens the newly formed bond between them. The lie is harmless enough, but because Plato involves Socrates in this little deception, this serves to differentiate the tenor of his relationship with Lysis from that of his relationship with Menexenus. That Socrates dramatically sides with Lysis affirms that he will approach the two boys differently. It also, of course, serves to enhance Socrates' ongoing seduction of the youth and to drive a further wedge between the two friends, a process that began earlier when Socrates asked them who, between them, was older, nobler, and more beautiful (207c).

Socrates underscores other inadequacies in the arguments at key points in the discussion. Their line of argument is said to lead them first to seek "in an altogether incorrect fashion" (213d–e), then it reportedly leads the discussion astray (215c), and finally the line of inquiry provokes Socrates to exclaim, "I am really dizzy myself from the perplexity of the argument" (216c). The most revealing qualification that Plato inserts into the dialogue is conveyed in Socrates' suspicion "that the things we had agreed to were not true." He declares, "I'm afraid it was a dream that we've been wealthy" (218c), later calling the three of them drunk with argument (222c). This is an indication that the quasi-eristic argumentation risks producing in the interlocutors, at worst, total confusion and, as a result, the cynicism or skepticism of the misology that Socrates warns against in the *Phaedo* (89d–91b). At the other extreme, it risks producing an intoxication with words that could override the genuine desire to ascertain the truth about the friend. Finally, Socrates explains that he was about to continue the discussion with older interlocutors (223a), confirming the reasons for the inadequacies the attentive reader will have already discerned. Recapitulating its roundabout course, Socrates himself claims to be unable to recall the many twists and turns the argument has taken (222e). His admission here underscores his earlier precautions about the merit of the argumentation. Perhaps Plato intends to supply a further indication that the arguments about friendship are of secondary importance to the philosopher's psychagogical project with the youths when he has Socrates claim to be merely weighing their pros and cons like those in the law courts do (222e). It is the balance sheet for the value of the arguments, in terms of their adequacy in pinpointing what a friend is, that Socrates is reconciling.

7. Readers of Dover might suppose that these boys are too young to be the objects of this kind of attention, but this would seem to be disproved by the fact that the whole pretext for Socrates' conversations with the boys was not to engage them in philosophical argument but to show Hippothales how a lover should properly approach his beloved (cf. *Lys.* 206c).

8. A host of compound words are formed in Greek from the verb stem *lusi* or *lysi*. The phrase *lysis kreiōn* means liquidating a debt, and *lysi* can be combined with other words to connote the power of releasing or loosing. *Lysigamos* means "dissolving a marriage"; *lysikakos* eliminating evil; *lysimakos* "ending strife"; *lysipothos* to be "delivered from love"; and *lysiponos* being free from toil. *Lysiteleō* means both to pay dues or tributes to another and "being useful." And *lysiphron* connotes "setting free the mind." Plato presumably chose to feature a character named Lysis in this dialogue because his name reveals something important about the dialogue's goal. The word *lysis* in standard Greek usage also can mean "a ransoming," or "a deliverance from an oppressor," in the case of slaves. See Liddell and Scott, *Greek-English Lexicon*, 480–481. Plato seems to be playing with the three meanings of *lysis:* "cutting-loose," being useful, and profiting.

9. This also is one of many examples of Plato utilizing a historical figure as a character in one of his dialogues. Though what is known about the historical Lysis is minimal, we know that he came from an illustrious family, that he was the son of Democrates of Aixone and father of Timocleides, and that he lived to an old age. Lysis' tomb was discovered in 1974, as was the tomb of his son. It is on display in the Piraeus museum. His daughter's grave was discovered in 1912. Stroud suggests that its modesty and simplicity would lead one to conclude that the family's wealth had declined by the time of Lysis' death. See Ronald S. Stroud, "The Gravestone of Socrates' Friend, Lysis," *Hesperia: Journal of the American School of Classical Studies at Athens* 53 (1984): 355–360. See also J. K. Davies, *Athenian Propertied Families 600–300 B.C.* (Oxford: Oxford University Press, 1971), cited by Stroud. (Thanks to François Renaud and Frank Gonzalez for these references.) Stroud argues against the view that Lysis' grandfather is the "Lysis kalos" depicted on several red-figure vases. Even though Plato often assigns to his characters the names of real, historical figures, there is no reason to suppose either that his choice of characters is accidental or that he will be constrained in his own use of such characters by their actual, independently verifiable words and deeds. This interpretation assumes that Plato chose the characters he wished to place in each dialogue, and that he also made countless decisions concerning the way in which he would portray the historical figures he used as the basis for one of the seventy-one characters in his dialogues.

10. The Greek word for freedom (*eleutheria*) becomes *liberalis* in Latin, connecting the senses of freely giving, on the one hand, and being a generally educated non-specialist, a layman rather than a professional. Liddell and Scott indicate an analogy: the Latin word *liberalis* is to *eleutherios* as *liber* is to *eleutheros*. *Eleutherios*, like *liberalis*, describes the way one acts when one is free. It also means liberal, freely giving, the way a free man acts toward others. The sense of freedom operative in classical Athens was primarily negative: freedom means, first and foremost, not being a slave. Moreover, it is the freedom from constraint, need, bondage, blame, and so on. The word *eleutheron*

means "a setting free," as does the word *lysis*. See Liddell and Scott, *Greek-English Lexicon*, 249.

11. The problem of limitless freedom, characterized by a lack of self-restraint and self-knowledge, not only provides the wedge for Socrates' initial cross-examination of Lysis, it is the proleptic conclusion of his argument to Alcibiades at the end of the *Alcibiades I*, as Chapter 3 will show. See *Alc. I.* 134c–135c.

12. This neglect may be traceable to the authors of Socratic dialogues. At the beginning of his "Memorabilia" where Xenophon lists the topics that Socrates regularly discussed, freedom (*eleutheria*) is not among them. Even here, however, the question of freedom looms in the background. (It is noteworthy, also, that Xenophon's *Cyropaideia* begins with a discussion of freedom.) Nor does Plato make freedom the express theme of any of his dialogues, though he devotes whole conversations to justice, Eros, piety, *sophrosunē*, friendship, pleasure, courage, duty, knowledge, rhetoric, beauty, names, and legislation. Some scholars explain the absence of a direct treatment of the problem of freedom in the Socratic dialogues by suggesting that its ordinary political sense was so widely accepted that most ancient thinkers did not take up the topic explicitly. This is the view, for example, of Pohlenz. See Max Pohlenz, *Freedom in Greek Life and Thought: The History of an Ideal*, trans. C. Lofmark (New York: Humanities Press, 1966). Pohlenz rightly holds that the commonsense idea of freedom, as doing whatever one pleases, unchecked by any limits, would be anathema to Socrates' view (63–64). He goes on to say, "Socrates was really free because he was master of himself" (88), but the implications of this insight are not pursued.

13. To say that freedom is often overlooked as a Socratic or a Platonic theme is not to claim that no one has ever paid attention to Plato's conception of it. A few commentators have pointed out that freedom is an important concern for Platonic political philosophy, and some have even argued that he advances a new political theory of freedom. Julius Moravcsik, for one, has written that Plato's chief disagreement with Periclean democracy stems from their fundamental "disagreement about freedom." Moravcsik, "Plato and Pericles on Freedom and Politics," *Canadian Journal of Philosophy* 9, Supplemental (1983): 7.

Plato's dialogues offer greater insight into the topic than may be apparent, because debate in the secondary literature on Plato about the Platonic conception of freedom has frequently been confined to the direct discussions of liberty in the political dialogues. This approach tends to ignore the dramatic examples of freedom that the dialogues themselves supply. The dialogues adumbrate an example of the proper exercise of freedom in the character and behavior of Socrates. In this way, I would argue, they exhibit the concrete practices through which Plato thinks freedom is best developed, exercised, and preserved.

14. In the *Alcibiades I*, Socrates provides a reason for the inability to act: action implies confidence in one's knowledge. Since both Lysis and Alcibiades are brought to an awareness of their ignorance through Socrates' chastening, the fact that his questioning is also capable of forestalling action should not be surprising. See *Alcibiades I* 117d–e.

15. Given the possibility of such a humbling under the duress of Socratic cross-examination, Vlastos notes that submitting to Socrates' probe requires courage. He

says: "The search for moral truth that may prove your own life wrong takes humility that is not afraid of humiliation" (Vlastos, "Paradox," 20).

16. *Autarchia* is one of the two conditions that happiness fulfills in Aristotle's account in *The Nicomachean Ethics* I.7. He stipulates that the "final good must be a thing sufficient in itself" (1097b9). Aristotle continues immediately after introducing this condition for happiness by insisting that this does not imply a life in isolation, because "man is by nature a political being." Liddell and Scott define *autarchia* as "sufficiency in oneself; independence" (see Liddell and Scott, *Greek-English Lexicon*, 133). The full pertinence of such self-sufficiency to Socrates will be developed throughout this book. More than simply the "freedom from" constraint implied by *eleutheria*, self-sufficiency connotes what is generated from out of oneself, requiring little to be imported from the outside. Socrates regards his self-sufficiency, especially with respect to the market economy, as the mark of his independence, not only because he is able to rule himself but because this self-sufficiency signifies that he possesses enough of the goods that humans desire, and this realization helps him modulate his appetites.

17. It was Hippothales' hubris that made him appear ridiculous to Socrates at the beginning of the dialogue. Socrates had chastised Hippothales for not realizing that his praises of Lysis were, at bottom, praises of himself. Here it is necessary to ask whether Socrates' own hubris has led him to overstep appropriate boundaries in his approach to Lysis. In his chastening of the boy, Socrates comes perilously close to the shaming kind of hubris. Athenian law prohibited certain kinds of shame, rage, or assault against citizens. (Of course, since Lysis has not yet reached the age of majority, his inviolability as a citizen would not yet be fully protected under the hubris laws.) If it can be shown that Socrates really shames Lysis by reducing him to the level of a slave, then this humbling will qualify as the ordinary legal sense of hubris. If, however, Socrates does not enslave Lysis through his questioning, he will be vindicated. For an excellent discussion of the relationship of political, economic, and sexual hierarchies in classical Athens, and for a more detailed explication of the hubris laws, see David Halperin, *One Hundred Years of Homosexuality and Other Essays on Greek Love* (New York: Routledge, 1990), 88–112; Mark Golden, "Slavery and Homosexuality in Athens," *Phoenix* 38 (1984): 308–24, and "*Pais*, 'Child' and 'Slave,' *L'Antiquite Classique* 54 (1985): 91–104; and David Cohen, "Law, Society and Homosexuality in Classical Athens," *Past and Present* 17 (1987): 3–21. The question of Socrates' hubris will be explored further in Section 4.c.1.

18. This confession occurs just after Socrates has presumed to show conclusively that only the philosopher, who is neither wholly good nor wholly bad, can truly be called the friend. Socrates says:

> I rejoiced greatly myself, as if I were a hunter and had, to my satisfaction, what I had been hunting. But then some most strange suspicion came over me—from where, I don't know—that the things we had agreed to were not true. (218c4–7).

All passages from the *Lysis* cited in this chapter are from the Bolotin translation. David Bolotin, *Plato's Dialogue on Friendship* (Ithaca and London: Cornell University Press,

1979). Socrates continues by saying that he is afraid that they have come across some false arguments about the friend, "false like boastful human beings" (218d2–4). Perhaps Socrates is acknowledging the kind of hubris of which he is guilty here. He clearly seems to intimate to Lysis that he can give him the knowledge needed to attain his ambitious aspirations. Paradoxically, those who would spend time with Socrates may end up realizing that they no longer aspire to the same things they did before they met him, in which case Socrates' boastful claim would not be quite so implausible.

19. Burnyeat has called self-knowledge "the benefit peculiarly associated with the Socratic method." Myles Burnyeat, "Socratic Midwifery, Platonic Inspiration," in *Essays on the Philosophy of Socrates*, ed. Hugh H. Benson (New York and Oxford: Oxford University Press, 1992), 60. It is difficult to locate this self-knowledge within the framework of traditional epistemology. Plato does not really explain how, within the traditional categories supposed to elucidate his conception of knowledge, the soul can have knowledge of itself. Instead, he has Socrates introduce the image of two persons looking into each other's eyes and conversing soul to soul in the *Alcibiades I*.

A kind of tension or circularity runs throughout ancient thought with respect to the problem of self-knowledge: on the one hand, there is the ancient belief in the principle of affinity, and on the other hand, there is the principle that dialogue is a fundamental mode of human existence and an activity by which human cognition will be defined. (The idea of thinking as a conversation will be discussed briefly in Section 2.b.1.) But then coming to any opinion or belief about anything will entail reaching agreement (*homologia*) within oneself, so that one comes to be of one mind about something. This same circularity appears in Aristotle's discussion of friendship. For while the true friend is a second self, all friendship is modeled on self-love, since like is attracted to like.

20. Throughout the dialogues, Socrates is concerned, at least implicitly, with the problem of self-knowledge. Two examples seem especially pointed. At *Charmides* 164d and following, *sophrosune* and self-knowledge are directly linked. Self-knowledge is invoked as the essential condition for discriminating between what one knows and does not know at *Charmides* 167a, and Socrates raises the issue again in the discussion of first and second order *technai* at *Charmides*. 169d–170a. In the *Phaedrus*, Socrates disparages abstract, theoretical knowledge and attributes hubris to a lack of self-knowledge, saying:

> I myself have certainly no time for the business, and I'll tell you
> why, my friend. I can't as yet "know myself," as the inscription
> at Delphi enjoins, and so long as that ignorance remains it seems
> to me ridiculous to inquire into extraneous matters. Consequently
> I don't bother about such things, but accept the current beliefs about
> them, and direct my inquiries, as I have just said, rather to myself,
> to discover whether I really am a more complex creature and more
> puffed up with pride than Typhon, or a simpler, gentler being
> whom heaven has blessed with a quiet, un-Typhonic nature.
> (*Phdr.* 229e–230a; Hackforth trans.)

21. It is noteworthy that Plato often chooses to feature a main character with a name related in some way to the issues under discussion. Meletus is cross-examined by Socrates in the *Apology*, perhaps because the fact that his name is cognate with the Greek word for care or concern allows Socrates to play on his name while questioning him as a witness and accusing him of lack of care for the grave matters under deliberation. Likewise, it is Charmides who needs the charm with which Socrates can provide him. And whereas Meno's name betokens someone who remains in the same place, Lysis' name announces the kind of setting free that the boy is about to undergo at the hands of Socrates ("saving-power") to illustrate the contrast with Hippothales ("asininity") and his methods. A close look at the *Lysis* will determine whether the promissory note tendered by Plato's choice of main character can be redeemed.

22. Compare 223b1–2. The Hermea were rites in celebration of the god, Hermes, observed in *palestrae* and connected with athletic competition. In addition to being the patron god of young men in competition, and the agon in general, Hermes is also connected with Aphrodite, inasmuch as the two are united in the figure of the Hermaphrodite. Gonzalez cites Burkert who calls Hermes "the god of boundaries and their transgression," since the Herms were stones stacked on top of one another to mark boundaries. Francisco J. Gonzalez, "How to Read a Platonic Prologue", (1999, Typescript). See also Walter Burkert, *Greek Religion* (Cambridge, Mass., Harvard University Press, 1985), 158. Finally, it is noteworthy that Hermes, somewhat like Eros in Diotima's *Symposium* account, was known by the Greeks as both preserving and transgressing the boundaries between mortals and gods.

23. The *Lysis* is one of four Platonic dialogues that are set in wrestling schools; the others are *Euthydemus*, *Charmides*, and *Theaetetus*. The *Lovers* is set in a class taught by Dionysos, and it is unclear precisely where the *Sophist* and *Statesman*, thought to be set dramatically on the same day as the *Theaetetus*, occur.

24. Compare 216d. These claims require clarification. Brickhouse and Smith have argued that Socrates' claims to possess knowledge in these matters do not entail a claim to know *why* or *how* he is able to divine such knowledge; and Socrates' knowledge, here, remains thoroughly human, even though he attributes it to a kind of divine inspiration. See Brickhouse and Smith, *Plato's Socrates*, 38–45.

25. It may be enlightening to read the *Lysis* as an elaborate example of the solution to Meno's so-called paradox. The crucial turn in the roundabout discussion of the friend, the lover, and desire in the general terms of the *Lysis* will be shown below (in Section 2.c) when Socrates suggests that their "false" arguments failed to note a distinction between the *like* (*homoion*) and the *akin* (*oikeion*). Near the close of the dialogue, at 222b–c, Socrates indicates that the arguments must be reexamined, substituting *akin* for *like*. The kindred and the absolutely identical are clearly not the same and should not be conflated. Clarified in this way, desire, which is for a lack, can nevertheless be for what is, in some sense, akin. The dialogue, here, seems to propose a way of responding to Meno's paradox. Desire and trust have in common that they are both for what is kindred. Trust, which is always in the familiar, comes out of the past to presage one's future likes and dislikes. In this way, human beings are always already predisposed to trust what is akin. Eros, likewise, draws one toward what one lacks, but

this is nevertheless akin. It has to be in some sense familiar, or it would not even be recognizable as something desirable. This is how the *Lysis* parallels the "in-between," spoken of in Diotima's speech in the *Symposium*, while providing Plato's answer to Meno's "paradox."

26. Socrates ironically claims just this kind of faith in Protagoras in order to broach his patented "one little question": "Now I, Protagoras, have almost all I need, and shall have everything if you will answer me one question. You were saying that virtue can be taught—that I will take upon your authority, and there is no one to whom I am more ready to trust" (*Prot.* 329b–c; Jowett trans.).

27. One could reasonably argue that Socrates has many companions but no real friends. None of his interlocutors seems like a genuine friend to Socrates. Even his longtime companion Crito, who plays a vital role in the dialogues surrounding Socrates' death, does not seem to be enough of an equal to Socrates to be a friend in the philosophic sense. There is a limit beyond which their friendship does not go. Even though Crito is the prime mover in offering to post the thirty minae at Socrates' trial, and even though he is the one instructed to take Xanthippe home, before returning to cry for Socrates in the *Phaedo*, in the dialogue *Crito* he is rendered unnecessary. Though he is the one willing to risk himself to rescue Socrates, he is shown to be unnecessary in two ways: first, Socrates' dream conveys the news that Crito has come to tell him, and then the laws replace him as an interlocutor in the dialogue. From 51c–54b, Crito speaks only three times to ratify Socrates' monologue. Whether or not the historical Socrates had friends, Plato's Socrates does not appear to have one in the dialogues. In the *Lysis*, Plato uses "companion" (*heteira*) and "friend" (*philos*) almost interchangeably. He maintains no precise distinction between them.

28. This might be the clearest evidence in any dialogue for holding that Plato means to position Socrates as an alternative kind of teacher.

29. Mitchell Miller identifies another "structural moment" in Plato's dialogues in which the philosophical character, such as Socrates, offers a "reorienting insight that shows a path through the aporia." See Mitchell Miller, *Plato's Parmenides: The Conversion of the Soul* (University Park: Pennsylvania State University Press, 1991), 7. Miller claims that the interlocutor always fails this test, a test ultimately for "philosophical kinship." Miller notes that no dialogue ever ends here, at the point at which the philosopher makes his most significant contribution. Rather, the fourth step Miller identifies entails a "return" to the level of discourse prior to the reorienting insight being offered (8).

30. One notable implication of this process of limiting one's desires is made evident to Plato's audience even though it may not be grasped by Socrates' interlocutor. When Socrates exhorts someone to learn what needs to be learned in order to attain his lofty desires, the audience might rightly suspect that the limit introduced by knowledge upon those presently insatiable desires will have the eventual effect of transforming the nature of those desires.

31. In fact, though, he does show this in his own, deceptively philosophical way. His immediate reply to Hippothales' request is, "It's not easy to say" (206c4).

32. One of several things that makes Socrates an unusual hunter is that instead of "capturing" his prey through the hunt, he sets him loose. Whereas the lovesick trouba-

dour Hippothales only makes Lysis harder to catch through his endless flattery, the way Socrates "gets hold of" the boy simultaneously (and paradoxically) liberates him.

33. Besides the trust in people, trust can be placed in other things. The dialogues often focus on instances where such overt trust is misplaced—in rulers (*Grg.* 525d–526b), arguments (*Phd.* 89d–e), names (*Crat.* 440a–d), and pleasures (*Phil.* 67b–c).

34. Socrates will call disregard of one's character "carelessness" (*ameleta*) in the *Alcibiades I*. See *Alcibiades I* 120b5–6. It is extremely interesting, also, that Plato gives this name to the river that runs through the plain of *Lethē* in the Myth of Er. (see *Rep. X*, 621a5). This is the disposition most anathema to the philosopher's counsel to "take care of oneself."

35. He will use various forms of this word, however, in the *Alcibiades I* to elicit precisely the kind of trust at issue in the *Lysis*. See especially his use of forms of *pistis* in the so-called Royal Tale, *Alcibiades I* 123c8, 123d3, and 123e3.

36. The meaning and function of *pleonexia* in Plato will be developed in greater detail in Section 4.b.1 in connection with Alcibiades' *Symposium* speech.

37. Socrates' use of this tactic is more forthright with Alcibiades in the *Alcibiades I*, a dialogue in which Socrates' strategic use of exaggerated pretensions closely parallels the *Lysis*. There Socrates tells Alcibiades, "All these designs of yours cannot be accomplished without my help; so great is the power which I believe myself to have over you and your concerns" (105d). Here Socrates intimates the same thing by speaking about what he and Lysis would be permitted to do, if only Lysis acquires *phronesis*.

38. The philosopher's failure to teach is not a failure to try, and although a character such as Meno may not be teachable, Lysis surely is. It is interesting that another meaning of the word *lysis* is "redeemable."

39. See *Republic* 340d*ff*. This principle has been discussed many times, most recently by Teloh, who calls this the "bivalence principle," and views it as being essential to Socratic psychagogy. See Teloh, *Socratic Education*, 19.

40. As Bolotin claims he does. In his interpretive essay, Bolotin remarks that the age of Socrates' interlocutors in the *Lysis* helps "to explain what might otherwise be a serious omission from the dialogue. . . . In particular, the *Lysis* contains no mention of trust (*pistis*)" (*Plato's Dialogue*, 67–68). Bolotin contends that Eros "aims at the now" and argues from this premise that trust ultimately turns on the promise to remain alive forever, which is, of course, impossible. This analysis seems to misconstrue the temporal modalities of both trust and Eros. Eros is a striving for what one has not or is not at present, that for which one is *endees*. This "not-yet" at which Eros "aims" stretches the one who desires toward the future, even if the desire contains within it the anticipation of fulfillment. Trust seems to have the past as its predominant temporal modality. Trust is primarily for the familiar and, as I have argued, what is most familiar is that upon which one implicitly relies. This is why trust is an obstacle to change; it roots one to the past and to the taken for granted. My argument is that Plato, by having Socrates seem to beg the question, forces his audience to think about the implicit and overt levels of trust that subtend all entrusting.

41. The relation between *pleonexia* and *philia* in Plato needs to be explored further. The *Gorgias* may provide the clearest indication that Plato considers these to be two possible directions of spiritedness: one direction respects boundaries and recognizes

limits as arising from the natural human desire for sociality, and the other oversteps all limits and ignores boundaries out of the natural human desire for "the more" (*to pleion*). Duncan brings out this connection without developing it fully (see Note 5 of the Introduction). The *Lysis* contains an undeveloped counterweight to this side of *thumos* in its presentation of *philia* as involving the recognition of necessary limits.

42. In his seminal essay "The Individual as an Object of Love in Plato," Vlastos argues that the connotation "being useful" is not to be understood in the narrow sense and that the beloved's utility is not *to* the lover but is indiscriminate, that is, being useful as such, in the sense of "good-producing." This helps clarify why Socrates intertwines being useful and being loved. Vlastos will hold that the individual is not the object of love in Plato at all. He argues, from his reading of Diotima's speech in the *Symposium*, that love of an individual is only a vehicle for pure love.

43. This chastening of Lysis seems to argue, against Vlastos, that Socrates does in fact carry out a refutation with Lysis, thoroughly and systematically humbling the boy through his argument. And he brings Menexenus to an admission of *aporia* at 213c9. Surprisingly, some interpreters maintain that Socrates' refutation of Lysis is "mild." See, for example, Henry Teloh, *Socratic Education*, 18. Though the relationship between Lysis and Socrates is not adversarial, and although the presumptions of Lysis that are refuted are proportional to his years, Socrates' refutation of the boy is nonetheless complete and devastating to the boy's prior conceits. Socrates ends up telling him that he has no right to think highly of himself since he is, as yet, thoughtless, showing him why he is still shepherded around like a child.

44. Plato employs the phenomenon of blushing at critical junctures in many other dialogues (see *Charm.* 158c; *Prot.* 312a; *Euthyd.* 275d and 297a; and, most famously, *Rep.* 350c). He sometimes uses the blush in a figure of speech to signify shame (such as *Grg.* 522c; *Phdr.* 243d and 255a; *Ap.* 17b; *Symp.* 217e; *Rep.* 566c and 606c; and *Laws* 819d, 819e, and 820b). In the *Lysis*, he uses a blush on three occasions: with Hippothales, 204b5 and 204c3, and, in the present context, 213d3.

45. Lysis responds "perhaps" to Socrates' question concerning whether the poets tell the truth. This measured response is a sign of maturity. In his study, Dover notes that such answers were viewed by the young in Athens as the typical way in which old people equivocate. See Dover, *Greek Popular Morality*, 104. See also Aristotle's comment at *Rhetoric* 1389b18-22, that the old become cynical and always add "perhaps" to their statements. I would claim that far from intimating cynicism, here, Lysis' use of "perhaps" indicates his increased circumspection in the wake of the humbling that he has suffered at Socrates' hands.

46. This also is translated as "stingray." It is how Meno describes Socrates' effect on him (*Meno* 80a*ff*), charging that he makes anyone who comes close to him feel numb.

47. There are other justifications for the practice of *sunousia*, including: (1) securing the protection of the beloved by the lover; and (2) a kind of initiatory role the lover performs for the beloved. The first three speeches in the *Symposium* probably advance the better contemporary Athenian arguments for the practice. Bloom makes clear the paradox inherit in the rationale for construing *sunousia* as an exchange of sex for wisdom: the younger boy, who is supposed to lack the wisdom he hopes to receive from the older man, must display the wiser, more noble aim in the relation, while the puta-

tively wiser partner is revealed to be only interested in the boy for sex. For an elaboration on this paradox, see Allan Bloom, *Love and Friendship*, 466–468.

48. Paradoxically, though, Socrates also is dependent on his interlocutors for his vocation. Theirs is a symbiotic relationship, because it is always over and against these others that Socrates ranks as wisest and most free. In fact, he could not practice philosophy as he does without them.

49. See Bloom, *Love and Friendship*, 439–442.

50. Whereas the physical violence committed in rape is done without the victim's consent, seduction requires only words. Hence, the victim must bear some responsibility for yielding to the seducer. Euripides trades on the ambiguity that enshrouded the difference between the two acts for his contemporaries. It is not clear from Hermes' prologue to the *Ion* whether Apollo has seduced or raped Creusa. For a survey of the attitudes toward rape in classical literature, see Froma I. Zeitlin, "The Configurations of Rape in Greek Myth," in *Rape*, eds. S. Tomaselli and R. Porter (Oxford: Basil Blackwell, 1986), 122–51.

51. Dover explains: "To seduce a woman of citizen status was more culpable than to rape her, not only because rape was presumed to be unpremeditated but seduction involved the capture of her affection and loyalty; it was the degree of offense against the man to whom she belonged, not her own feelings, which mattered" (146). See K. J. Dover, "Classical Greek Attitudes to Sexual Behavior," in *Women in the Ancient World: The Arethusa Papers*, eds. John Peradotto and J. P. Sullivan (Albany: State University of New York Press, 1984), 143–58. He makes substantially the same point elsewhere (*Greek Popular Morality*, 147). This difference is examined further by Susan G. Cole in her informative study "Greek Sanctions against Sexual Assault," *Classical Philology* 79 (1984): 97–113. Cole cites evidence from the orators for the different penalties and attitudes toward rape, which fell within the general domain of the laws against violence (*bia*) and seduction, which was classified in general with the laws governing adultery (*moikeia*). The penalty for the woman caught having sexual relations in her home with someone other than her "guardian" (and this applied equally to wives and concubines) was exclusion from public ceremonies. It would have brought shame both upon her and any children she might have. For the offending man, the penalty could include death and would not have been less than disenfranchisement. In the case of rape, either of a boy or a woman whose guardian enjoyed citizenship status, the penalty was only a fine. Cole explains that the difference seems to have been partly due to the fact that rape was not thought to be premeditated, the woman or boy certainly lent no volition to the act, and it did not involve any intent to shame the family or the guardian as did *moikeia* in one's house.

52. The political problem for Lysis will be the problem facing all Athenian citizens. It does not so much concern the casting off of any particular yoke as much as it does the obligation to exercise self-rule in the absence of external constraints. More precisely, given that citizenship was restricted to propertied, male Athenians, an important question of limits may be the one regarding the citizen's self-restraint vis-à-vis wives, concubines (*heteira*), prostitutes (*porna*), slaves, and, most problematic of all, boys. Practices involving boys must have presented a somewhat unique problem for Athenian citizens, because these boys are vulnerable disproportionately to the older

men, and yet boys such as Lysis will soon grow up to become full citizens in the city and the equals of these men.

53. The two main lines of interpretation taken by many have already been noted. A few more recent interpretations deserve mention here. Umphrey, in his review of Bolotin's book, suggests provocatively that the *Lysis* may not be a dialogue primarily about friendship at all but may be trying to focus on the impulse to friendship, or "friendly feeling," that is, to distinguish Eros from *thumos*. But Duncan ("Philia") is right to claim that the *Gorgias* offers a much clearer look at the relation between *philia* and *thumos* than does the *Lysis*. See Stuart Umphrey, "Eros and Thumos," *Interpretation* 10 (1982): 352–422. This relation will be discussed more fully in Section 4.b.1 below.

Hyland suggests that the *Lysis* may be attempting to delineate the salient differences between Eros, *epithumia*, and *philia*. But Plato does not adhere to any strict, technical definitions of these terms, and Hyland's reading leads to the conclusion that the *Lysis* offers nothing not offered in the *Symposium*. See Drew A. Hyland, "Eros, Epithumia, and Philia in Plato," *Phronesis* 13 (1968): 32–46.

54. Two early modern commentators on the *Lysis*, Ast and Socher, for example, came to this conclusion. See the discussion of the Pohlenz-von Arnim debate over the *Lysis*, included as the appendix to Bolotin's translation of the dialogue, pp. 201–226.

55. To this list could be added Lysis' trust in the rewards he expects to follow automatically from two of his natural gifts: his noble rank and exceptional beauty. Socrates, at 209a, seems to be telling Lysis that he has no right to prance and preen, holding his body out as a kind of prize, since he does not possess the requisite independence himself. Lysis is still shepherded around by others, and since he does not rule over his own body, his beauty is of no use to him. Chapter 3 will show how Socrates utilizes the same approach with Alcibiades, telling him that his body is a worthless commodity.

56. The question that inaugurates Socrates' contest with Menexenus typifies the kind of question one finds in eristic disputation. The best example of this kind of argumentation in the dialogues can be found in the *Euthydemus*. The sharp distinction between lover and beloved is a quasi-technical one, common to discussions about homoerotic relations, as can be seen clearly from the speeches of Phaedrus, Pausanias, Eryximachus, and Agathon in the *Symposium*. The inaugural question of the discussion with Menexenus also resembles the questions that propel the speeches in the *Phaedrus*, such as the one regarding whether the lover is better off becoming involved with a beloved who does not reciprocate love in return or with one who does. Socrates, at *Lysis* 212b, asks Menexenus, "When someone loves someone, which one becomes a friend of the other, the one who loves of the loved or the loved one of the lover?" The phrasing of this question in the *Lysis* goes straight to the heart of the problems posed by asymmetrical relationships, which are, after all, more common than the reciprocal and equal type. Perhaps this is why, in Aristotle's treatments of friendship (*Nic. Eth. VIII–IX; Eud. Eth. VII*), there is far more discussion of the friendships based on utility and pleasure than of those more equal, but rare, friendships of character. And this is true even though Aristotle takes the friendship of the good to be the model for the other two types.

57. This section has pieced together some of the lines of argument not further explored by the interlocutors themselves. But the main point he appears to make plain for these youths is that while Socrates had denied previously that the bad can be a friend to the good, and he had introduced desire as being essential for explaining how people become friends or lovers, now he ties together these two threads by showing that the intermediate and not the bad is truly friend to the good, as Gonzalez notes.

58. This is a central thesis of Tessitore's "Plato's *Lysis*." Gonzalez follows Tessitore in making this a central theme in his interpretation of the *Lysis*. See Francisco J. Gonzales, "Plato's *Lysis:* An Enactment of Philosophical Kinship," *Ancient Philosophy* 15, 1 (1995): 69–90, especially p. 78. Tessitore holds that Socrates' teaching threatens the friendship between the two boys by the end of the dialogue. Although his reading of the *Lysis* is careful and sensitive, I am not convinced that Lysis' relationship with Socrates is exclusive of others. After all, they have only one brief conversation. In practice, even the philosopher will sustain many nonphilosophic friendships of the sort experienced by Lysis and Menexenus. See Aristide Tessitore, "Plato's *Lysis:* An Introduction to Philosophic Friendship," *The Southern Journal of Philosophy* 28, 1 (1990): 115–32. The analysis in this section has benefited especially from Gonzalez' article. I had the opportunity to read an earlier version and discuss these issues with him. Particularly helpful has been his effort to offer a coherent interpretation of the argumentation in the *Lysis*, which illustrates that the *aporia* experienced by Socrates' young interlocutors does not leave Plato's audience at an impasse or a dead end.

59. Gonzalez, "Plato's *Lysis*," 83.

60. I am thinking here of Heidegger's distinction between two modes of "solicitude" in Section 26 (Div. 1, Chap. 4) of *Being and Time*. He calls the first, inauthentic sense of solicitude "leaping-in," in which one person intervenes for another, disburdening him or her of the responsibility to act upon his or her possibilities; he terms the other, authentic mode of solicitude "leaping-ahead," in which the one who is "ahead" of the other in some respect uses this superiority to disclose to the other his or her own possibilities, thereby enhancing the other's freedom. Martin Heidegger, *Being and Time*, trans. John Macquarie and Edward Robinson (New York: Harper & Row: 1962), 158–159.

61. Gonzalez, "Plato's *Lysis*," 86; Tessitore, "Plato's *Lysis*," 127.

CHAPTER 3

1. Friedländer claims that in antiquity, this dialogue enjoyed special status among Plato's works. He cites Alfarabi, who considered the *Alcibiades I* the capstone of the Platonic corpus, containing all of the seeds of Plato's philosophy in an embryonic form. See Paul Friedländer, *Plato,* trans. Hans Meyerhoff (Princeton, N.J.: Princeton University Press, 1973), 2: 233. This dialogue was included among the thirty-five dialogues and thirteen epistles comprising the nine tetralogies of the Thrasyllus canon of the Platonic corpus, and early scholars who expressed doubts about other dialogues in

the canon do not appear to have found fault with the *Alcibiades I*. The tendency to discount it as spurious began in the early nineteenth century with Schleiermacher and his pupil Ast. See Friedrich E. D. Schleiermacher, *Introduction to the Dialogues of Plato*, trans. William Dobson (New York: Arno Press [Reprint of translation of 2d German edition of 1836], 1973).

The conclusions of Schleiermacher and Ast are frequently supported by stylometric considerations, about which there is growing disagreement. Stylometry attempts to solve both the mystery of the order in which Plato wrote the dialogues and the disputes regarding the authenticity of certain dialogues on the basis of statistical evidence of the relative frequency of linguistic peculiarities. Some stylometrists themselves regard with skepticism this effort, partly for its subjectivity and partly because this method has failed to solve the important problems of authenticity and interpretation. In his Introduction to *The Roots of Political Philosophy*, Thomas Pangle quotes Gomperz, who reports that:

> Three of [Plato's] latest works (*Timaeus, Critias,* and *Laws*) contain
> nearly 1500 words which are absent from his other works, and some,
> indeed, from the whole of the literature of his time. What, then, is
> proved if in a particular dialogue we detect a small number of words or
> phrases not met with elsewhere in Plato, or even if we find a few thoughts
> which have no close parallels in his other works? Indeed, we must
> be prepared to encounter serious contradictions, not only in thought,
> but in that which lies deeper and should therefore be less subject
> to change—in tone and sentiment.

See Thomas Pangle, ed., "Editor's Introduction," in *The Roots of Political Philosophy: Ten Forgotten Socratic Dialogues* (Ithaca, N.Y., and London: Cornell University Press, 1987), 15.

With few exceptions, modern scholars are much less familiar with the language and its conventions than were the early commentators, most of whom found nothing unauthentic in the *Alcibiades I*. That this dialogue was considered for 900 years to be not only genuinely Platonic but the crown jewel of the Platonic corpus by ancient and medieval commentators, and because its authenticity was not really questioned until the nineteenth century, places the burden of proof on those who wish to undermine its status as a Platonic text. There is so little independent evidence about any of these dialogues that the same reasons that cause scholars to dismiss one dialogue as spurious could lead to the questioning of all of them. Some argue that there is certainty only about those dialogues specifically mentioned by Aristotle, but he mentions very few of them. Ironically, the recourse to Aristotle has led most commentators to accept as genuine, for example, the *Hippias Minor*, despite prior scholarly conviction that its style and content is anomalous. To address this problem fully would take us too far afield. For the most comprehensive recent analysis of attempts to determine the order in which Plato is supposed to have written his dialogues, see Debra Nails, *Agora, Academy, and the Conduct of Philosophy* (Dordrecht: Kluwer Academic Publishers, 1995), especially Part II: "The Developmental Hypothesis." See also Nails, "Problems with

Vlastos's Platonic Developmentalism," *Ancient Philosophy* 13 (1993): 273–291; Jacob Howland, "Re-reading Plato: The Problem of Platonic Chronology," *Phoenix* 45, No. 3 (1991): 189–214; and Charles Young, "Plato and Computer Dating," *Oxford Studies in Ancient Philosophy* 12 (1994): 227–250.

2. *Alcibiades I* 103a*ff.* Friedländer sees this dialogue as further distinguished by the fact that the final exchange reveals Socrates' premonition that his newly formed bond with Alcibiades may be threatened by future events (2: 233).

3. Just how closely Socrates has monitored the movement and development of this young man becomes evident during their conversation. He tells Alcibiades that he could not have left his home "by night or by day" without being detected because of Socrates' constant surveillance (106e8–9). Socrates reports, at 110b, "I often heard you when a child, in your teacher's house or elsewhere, playing at dice or some other game ... crying and shouting that one of the boys was a rogue and a cheat, and had been cheating."

4. Socrates says, "Then if, as you say, you desire to know, I suppose that you will be willing to hear, and I may consider myself to be speaking to an auditor who will remain, and will not run away?" (104d6–8). The first prerequisite for Socrates to be successful is that the interlocutor must be willing to come close enough to him to receive his sting. Just how the philosopher stings him will be quite case specific. Jaeger explores the analogy between Socratic questioning and stripping naked for examination before a trainer or a doctor. He cites *Charmides* 154d–e and *Gorgias* 523e in eliciting the features common to the two activities. See Jaeger, *Paideia*, 2: 34–35.

5. Friedländer is not alone in noticing the intimate setting of the dialogue. In his interpretive essay "On the *Alcibiades I*," the main lines of which are sketched in this chapter, Steven Forde calls this "a very private dialogue" in which Socrates and Alcibiades are "very pointedly alone." Forde, "On the *Alcibiades I*," in *The Roots of Political Philosophy: Ten Forgotten Socratic Dialogues*, ed. Thomas Pangle (Ithaca, N.Y. and London: Cornell University Press, 1987), 222. Besides the two *Alcibiades* dialogues, a number of other conversations take place in an intimate or a private setting, featuring Socrates and his interlocutor as the only characters. These include the *Euthyphro*, *Hippias Major*, *Hippias Minor*, *Ion*, *Phaedrus*, *Crito*, *Menexenus*, *Hipparchus*, *Minos*, and *Cleitophon*. We should expect the tenor of these conversations to differ from occasions on which Socrates speaks before a large crowd (*Apology*) or a handful of third parties.

6. Friedländer, *Plato*, 2: 240. Friedländer continues by elaborating on the many crucial parallels between the *Gorgias* and *Alcibiades I*.

7. Forde concludes, "There is no question that, over the course of this dialogue, the character and convictions of Alcibiades undergo a great transformation." He cites Cicero, who refers to a tradition that reports that Alcibiades broke down in tears at the end of his first conversation with Socrates, realizing his present ignorance and imploring the philosopher to help him. Forde sees the transformation in Alcibiades as occurring on two levels, "both from a change in heart and from a change in his understanding of the political categories" (Forde, "On the *Alcibiades I*," 238).

8. Though the word *epimelesthai* means "to care for" or "to be concerned with," Carnes Lord's translation (in Pangle, *Roots*, 175–221) "taking trouble over" or "taking pains about" reminds us that Socrates is not talking about a passive interest or a distant

concern; nor does his idea of self-care imply the mere emotional attachment customarily signified by the modern sense of caring for something. Whether one uses "taking trouble" or "taking care," it must be remembered that Socrates means to describe a set of exercises or practices, a regimen of self-examination capable of molding one's character and beliefs.

9. It is interesting that Socrates uses a form of the word *tolma* (daring, bold) here. This is the word Thucydides takes to be the emblematic quality of Alcibiades' nature. Socrates says, although "it is difficult for a lover to come to grips with a man who never succumbs to lovers, I must be bold (*tolmateon*) all the same and tell you my mind" (104e4–6). In Section 4.b.1, it will become clear what makes Socrates' use of the word *daring* here so appropriate with reference to Alcibiades.

10. The issue of Alcibiades' trust—that is, what he relies upon most fundamentally and most unreflectively—is addressed directly by Socrates in the myth he fashions for the youth in the middle of the dialogue. This excursus shows how Socrates' method narrows in on the putative good that his interlocutor relies upon and takes for granted. His strategy for unsettling Alcibiades' trust includes at least four steps: (1) enumerating in his opening speech those excellent things Alcibiades assumes he possesses; (2) attacking the sufficiency of those qualities directly in argument; (3) declaring explicitly that action implies the presumption of knowledge (and, by implication, certain deep-seated beliefs, such as a concern for justice, that support this presumption); and (4) completing the refutation of his old conceits and exhorting him to new standards by fashioning a mythical tale that highlights the inadequacy of his present education and training in preparing him to meet his ultimate rivals. We shall see that Socrates tells the story of the education and training of Alcibiades' "true rivals," the great kings of Persia and Sparta, and this story climaxes with the imaginings of the Queen about an Alcibiades who believes himself capable of challenging her son. Socrates says:

> She would wonder what this Alcibiades could ever be trusting in to have the intention of competing against Atarxerxes, and I suppose she would say that there is nothing else this man could be trusting in to attempt this except taking trouble and wisdom, these being the only things worthy of account among the Greeks. But if she should learn that this Alcibiades is now attempting it, in the first place, before he is twenty years old, and at that is completely uneducated, and in addition to these things, in spite of his lover telling him he must first learn and take trouble over himself and practice before going to compete against the king, he is unwilling, and asserts that even his present state will suffice, I suppose she would wonder and ask: "Whatever is it, then, that the lad trusts in?" If, then, we should say that it is beauty and size and lineage and wealth and nature of the soul, she would think us mad, Alcibiades. (123d–e)

11. Socrates addresses Alcibiades' inflated self-image in his opening remarks, saying, "As for the reason that made you think excessively of yourself, I would like to explain it." This will be a recurrent motif of the dialogue. Alcibiades' conceit is so entrenched that Socrates must push beyond his first admission of ignorance, essentially refashioning the same arguments in the form of a *muthos*, forcing Alcibiades to undergo

a second refutation and to reiterate his perplexity. That Alcibiades is brought to admit total ignorance a second time before the more constructive third part of the dialogue can get underway suggests how much more rigidly Alcibiades is ensconced in his conceits at nineteen than Lysis was at twelve or thirteen.

12. The meaning of Socrates' offer here seems to be that Alcibiades can speak, without the threat of interruption, in order to present a coherent argument that the just and the advantageous are not the same.

13. In the *Symposium*, the bi-play between Socrates and Agathon at 194a–c leads the careful reader to conclude that it would be less intimidating to perform in front of a crowd of 30,000 people than to be subjected to direct cross-examination by Socrates. Socrates draws the audience's attention to the difference here, reminding us that the two activities entail very different kinds of courage.

14. This tactic, and Socrates' clarification about which one of them is saying something, makes plain the fact that Socrates wants his interlocutor to give voice to his own beliefs and opinions. Implicit in this demand is Socrates' presumption that only by acknowledging to himself what he truly believes will an interlocutor become responsible for a position as his own. This demand will be further elaborated on in Section 3.d.1 (see also Note 34 below).

15. Forde makes the important point in his commentary that Socrates is seeking to place Alcibiades' self-image on a new foundation, one that rekindles a sense of excellence in him, but a sense of excellence more appropriate to Socrates' teaching. The analysis in this section owes much to Forde's interpretive essay, as well as to his book on Alcibiades, cited often in Chapter 4.

It is important to see that the Royal Tale constitutes a Socratic refutation. Socrates is refuting Alcibiades, even though it is not a refutation accomplished through argument, or in the form of argument that Vlastos (following Grote and Robinson) dubbed "the Socratic Elenchus." The Royal Tale illustrates that a Socratic refutation can take different forms. Here it takes the form of a myth designed to refute Alcibiades' conception of his rivals in the political arena and to bring him to see the need to undertake a regimen of self-care.

16. At *Alcibiades I* 112b and following. Forde (226) thinks that Socrates' references to Homer, as the source of what the many think, is peculiar because it suggests that the conception of justice exemplified by Achilles and Odysseus is based on an erotic desire for possession. As the consummate diagnostician, Socrates may already sense that this will be the fatal flaw of Alcibiades' Eros, if indeed his ambition will ever allow him to rise beyond the love of winning honors. This problem will be examined in greater detail in Section 4.b.1.

17. Forde writes that if it is indeed Socrates' intention to test Alcibiades with the Royal Tale, the youth fails the test miserably, "in a way that jeopardizes everything Socrates has accomplished with him" (Forde, "On the *Alcibiades I*," 228).

18. The antithesis of "taking trouble" is indifference or heedlessness to these matters about which one should be concerned. Helen North argues that, for Xenophon, it was the lack of *sophrosunē* in the cases of Alcibiades and Critias that led to their failure to benefit in the long term from their associations with Socrates. Xenophon distinguishes the two antitheses of *sophron* that characterized Critias and Alcibiades: the first is "heedlessness" (*agnomon*) and the second is "profligacy" (*akrates*). See Helen North,

Sophrosyne: Self-Knowledge and Self-Restraint in Greek Literature (Ithaca, N.Y.: Cornell University Press, 1966), 124.

19. Alcibiades used exactly these words at 119b1. This image of "putting their heads together," as Lamb translates, pervades most of the remainder of the dialogue (compare 124c, 124e). This indicates two pivotal things: (1) Only here does the constructive search begin in earnest; and (2) Dialogue is capable of fostering a kind of community. Socrates follows this expression by including himself with Alcibiades as a seeker who needs to "take trouble" over himself as well so he too might become as excellent as possible. He asks Alcibiades later to "consider in common" with him (124d). Forde (237) points out that this would-be community is abandoned, however, after 134d.

20. The "perhaps" in Socrates' answer discounts the hyperbole of his claims about the god and about his ability to serve as the exclusive avenue to Alcibiades' success. The stamp of truth is put on the second part of his response.

21. Later Socrates effaces these hyperbolic claims still further. He tells Alcibiades that only if the youth pursues goodness and what is divine will he be dear to the gods (134d). And only if Alcibiades takes trouble and improves himself will Socrates be the guarantor of his happiness (134e). It is arguable that every hyperbolic claim that Socrates makes in the dialogues is somewhere quietly retracted in some way, though this subtlety is surely lost on most of the interlocutors, who are the targets of his inflammatory tactics. That Plato has Socrates find a way to take back later something he has knowingly used to arouse an interlocutor tends to be noticed only by Plato's audience and not by Socrates' young targets. This is one of those tools in the dialogues, like irony, that requires that an interpretation differentiate what is happening on the level of the drama from what Plato's audience is supposed to discern from the dramatic action.

22. Cf. 130c–d. Not only does this proof assume a hidden artisan within human beings instead of demonstrating it, as Forde (235) charges, but, as a proof, it rules out *a priori* one of the three possible alternatives: that human beings are both body and soul together. The argument fails to consider that the predicate, ruling, could be true of both body and soul together, but not of each on its own. In other contexts, Socrates makes further divisions to show that the soul and the body each have a ruling and a ruled element.

23. Mark McPherran has argued that the duty to philosophize implied by the oracle is "consequentially varient," which means that it is, in Kant's terms, an imperfect duty, and to what extent and in which way each person should undertake philosophy must vary. Mark L. McPherran, "Socrates and the Duty to Philosophize, *The Southern Journal of Philosophy* XXIV, No. 4 (Winter 1986): 555. In an attempt to account for the transformation in the conception of the soul from Homer to Plato, Jean-Pierre Vernant writes:

> A very different conception of the soul, opposite to this Homeric *psuchē*, is elaborated in the milieu of the philosophical-religious sects like the Pythagoreans and Orphics, and seems to be linked to spiritual exercises designed to escape from time, from successive reincarnations, and from death through acts of purifying and liberating the little particle of the

divine everyone carries within himself. . . . But it is with Plato that the inversion of the values attributed to the body and soul is finally completed. Instead of the individual being intimately bound to a living body and a *psuchē* presented like the *eidolon* of the body that is no longer here, its phantom or double, it is now the immortal *psuchē* that constitutes one's real being in the interior recesses of each and every individual during the period of one's life. The living body therefore changes its status: it now becomes a simple appearance, an illusory, insubstantial, fugitive, and transitory image of what we ourselves truly and always are. Jean-Pierre Vernant, "Psuche: Simulacrum of the Body or Image of the Divine?" in *Mortals and Immortals: Collected Essays*, trans. Froma I. Zeitlin (Princeton, N.J.: Princeton University Press, 1991), 190.

24. Socrates makes this connection explicit, not only in the present context but most notably at *Charmides* 164d, where the Delphic maxim is said to mean "Practice *sophrosunē*." At *Timaeus* 72a, Socrates also connects self-knowledge to *sophrosunē*. North's 1966 study remains the most comprehensive discussion of the relationship between *sophrosunē* and self-knowledge in Greek literature and thought. See, especially, Chapters 4 through 6 for her survey of its use in Xenophon, the minor Socratic schools, and Plato.

25. Compare *Gorgias* 506d–507d, where Socrates elucidates this connection for Callicles.

26. *Republic* 402d. Socrates goes on to contrast this beauty with the opposite excess and disorder that he likens to violence and lack of self-restraint (*hubris*).

27. Forde finds in Socrates' doubts the suggestion that perhaps the worst thing that can happen to Alcibiades is that he will be successful without the preparations the philosopher insists upon. That Alcibiades should succeed by trickery, through seduction, or through his endearing charm may be Socrates' greatest concern about him. Alcibiades' eventual fate in history seems to confirm that Socrates' worst fears came to pass, as we shall see in Chapter 4 (Forde, "On the *Alcibiades I*," 239).

28. In his essay "Socratic Midwifery," Burnyeat gives a succinct statement about this problem of circularity and its implications for self-knowledge. He writes: "Self-knowledge, then, is not only the goal of Socratic education. It is also, right from the beginning, a vital force in the process itself, which involves and is sustained by the pupil's growing awareness of his own cognitive resources, their strengths and their limitations" (60). This explains further the source of the circularity implicit in Socrates' lessons to Alcibiades.

29. As Lord notes in defense of his translation of 116b: "Whoever acts nobly, does he not also act well?" (in Pangle, *Roots*, 192, note 13.) Socrates had used a similar ambiguity (between "being useful" and "being profitable") in his first approach to Lysis. Of course, for Socrates, "acting well" simply *is* prosperity; there is no reward beyond the practices themselves, as dialogues such as *Euthydemus* seem to illustrate.

30. It is hinted that this counsel is supposed to be therapeutic for Alcibiades. At the end of the dialogue, Socrates responds ironically upon hearing that Alcibiades plans to attend upon him as he has followed Alcibiades all of these years. There he uses the

word *therapeustai*, in the sense of offering service, or attending upon (135e3). Socrates' antidote (*alexipharmaka*) was mentioned at 132b2.

31. He says:

> And when we want to make him rightly fearful, must we not introduce him to shameless pleasures, and train him to take up arms against them, and to overcome them? Or does this principle apply to courage only, and must he who would be perfect in valour fight against and overcome his own natural character—since if he be unpractised and inexperienced in such conflicts, he will not be half the man which he might have been—and are we to suppose that with temperance it is otherwise, and that he who has never fought with the shameless and unrighteous temptations of his pleasures and lusts, and conquered them, in earnest and in play, by word, deed, and art will still be perfectly temperate? (*Laws* 647c–d; Jowett trans.)

32. The full text of Socrates' response at 132b1–3 reads: "Train first (*gumnasai proton*), blessed fellow, and learn what needs to be learned in order to approach the things of the city, and do not do it before, so that you may have an antidote and suffer nothing terrible."

33. This question is reminiscent of the *Lysis* question. Notice that Socrates later reverses his description of their roles when, at 129b, he calls himself the speaker and Alcibiades the listener.

34. Vlastos coins this demand "the say what you believe" requirement of the Socratic *elenchos*. He explains that "Socrates wants them [the interlocutors] to tie their opinions to their life as a pledge that what they say is what they mean" (Vlastos, "The Socratic Elenchus," *Oxford Studies in Ancient Philosophy* 1 [1983]: 36). He argues that this requirement for a conversation with Socrates shows that Socrates examines "not just propositions but lives" (37). (For further evidence that this is Socrates' desired goal, see *Grg.* 482b and *Ap.* 39c.) But there is disagreement among scholars concerning whether Socrates really holds firm to this demand. In many cases, Socrates cannot get his interlocutors to state their sincerely held beliefs, as the examples of Callicles, Thrasymachus, and Protagoras seem to show, and yet the philosopher continues conversing with them anyway (see *Grg.* 505d*ff*, *Rep.* 350d*ff*, and *Prot.* 333c*ff*). It does seem clear that Socrates would at least like to be able to hold to this demand (see, for example, *Crito* 49c, *Euthyp.* 9d, *Grg.* 458a–b, 495a–b, 500b–c, *Prot.* 331c–d, and *Rep.* 349a).

35. See, for example, *Phaedrus* 230d, where Socrates uses the word *pharmakon* to refer to *logos*. Socrates seems to be suggesting the inexorable power of *logos* which, as a significant force not reducible to speech alone, impels those in its grasp toward the province of the gods. In his commentary on the *Phaedrus*, William S. Cobb concludes, "By hinting that Oreithuia was playing with logos when she became involved with the god, Socrates implies that logos is a power, even a magical power, that can work good or ill and also points toward themes that become more explicit later on in the dialogue about the power and significance of logos." See Cobb, *Plato's Erotic Dialogues* (Albany: State University of New York Press, 1993), 143.

36. Daniel Anderson makes a similar point regarding the self. What I am here calling the interlocutor's "present viewpoint," Anderson, drawing on the elaborate

guises that adorned the characters in Greek theater, refers to as "masks." He explicitly and interestingly connects self-determination to freedom when he writes, "For Plato, the *aretē*, the excellence, of the human is the human capacity to reserve to the self the power of defining the self; and ... to yield that power to others is the fundamental corruption out of which arise all other forms of corruption of the person." See Daniel Anderson, *The Masks of Dionysos: A Commentary on Plato's Symposium* (Albany: State University of New York Press, 1993), 22.

37. Anderson, *Masks*, 74.

38. Hugh Benson and Mark McPherran have each argued this point against Vlastos' claim that in a Socratic refutation Socrates proves the refutand false. Benson and McPherran argue that all Socrates ever claims to have proved is the inconsistency of the interlocutor's beliefs. See Hugh H. Benson, "Problems with Socratic Method," and Mark L. McPherran, "Elenctic Interpretation and the Delphic Oracle," in *Rethinking Socratic Method: Essays in Dialogue with Gregory Vlastos's "The Socratic Elenchus"*, ed. Gary Alan Scott (University Park: Pennsylvania State University Press, Forthcoming).

39. Brickhouse and Smith conclude that, "Any characterization of the purpose of the elenchus ... that conceives of it as prescriptive or proscriptive only with regard to beliefs or propositions is thus too narrow to accommodate all that Socrates hopes to do with the elenchus. Thomas C. Brickhouse and Nicholas D. Smith, "Socrates' Elenctic Mission," *Oxford Studies in Ancient Philosophy* 9 (1991), 155–156. What precisely Socrates hopes to accomplish through the use of cross-examination is shown through their analysis of Socrates' argument to Meletus in *Apology*. There, according to Brickhouse and Smith, Socrates uses *elenchos* with Meletus first to *diagnose* Meletus' character; second to *reproach* him for his carelessness in bringing the charges against Socrates (26e); third to *refute* the charges against him and, at a more basic level, the beliefs his jurors harbor about him; fourth to *expose* the contradictions or confusions in Meletus' opinions; and fifth to *exhort* Meletus, and by extension the jury, through his reproaches to act rightly and justly in the matter before them ("Socrates' Elenctic Mission," 154–155). They emphasize elsewhere that an interlocutor's *bios* is not all that is tested by *elenchos* (137).

In their chapter on Socratic psychology in *Plato's Socrates*, they argue that Socrates wants his interlocutors to say what they really believe and that their true beliefs need to be compatible with the aims of right living. But they note that if these characters were not intrinsically good, the exhortation to examine themselves might lead Socrates' associates to destructive, and therefore tragic, consequences. See *Plato's Socrates*, Chapter 3, especially pp. 73–79.

40. This is the case with Thrasymachus (*Rep.* 352d), Callicles (*Grg.* 487e–488a, 505e), Critias (*Charm.* 166c–d), and Meno (*Meno* 86b–c). The last two citations are quoted in Chapter 1, note 18.

41. Brickhouse and Smith, "Socrates' Elenctic Mission," 137. Socrates tells Callicles at *Gorgias* 505e:

> Not only I but all of us should have an ambition to know what is true and what is false in this matter, for the discovery of the truth is a common good. And now I will proceed to argue according to my own notion. But if any of you think that I accept from myself conclusions which are

untrue you must interpose and refute me, for I do not speak from any knowledge of what I am saying; I am an inquirer like yourselves, and therefore, if my opponent says anything which is of force, I shall be the first to agree with him. (Jowett trans.)

42. See, for example, Brickhouse and Smith, "Socrates' Elenctic Mission," 137.

43. Indeed, it is rare that Socrates is shown being questioned at length by others. There are only two such examples of the tables being turned in all of the dialogues: *Protagoras* 338c–d and *Gorgias* 462a–467c. He also tells in the *Symposium* of having submitted to the questioning of Diotima, but since the whole conversation is rehearsed by Socrates, and may well have been made up by him, this does not really furnish an example of the philosopher being examined directly. The same reasoning would apply in the *Crito*, where Socrates submits to questioning by the personified laws.

44. Burnyeat makes this point eloquently and concludes, "This is, of course, exactly what happens in a discussion conducted by the Socratic method, but, more than that, it offers a purchase for the somewhat elusive notion that the real reward of Socratic inquiry is a certain kind of self-knowledge." See Myles Burnyeat, "Socratic Midwifery," 59.

45. Michel Foucault, "The Ethic of Care for the Self as a Practice of Freedom," trans. J. D. Gautier, S. J., in *The Final Foucault*, eds. James Bernauer and David Rasmussen (Cambridge, Mass.: MIT Press, 1987), 7–8.

46. Foucault makes a great deal of this isomorphism in the interview cited in the previous note.

47. Foucault stresses that the ethic of self-care for Socrates has precisely the opposite trajectory of the care for self in Christianity. See "The Ethic of Care for the Self," 4–5.

48. Jaeger, *Paideia*, 2: 53.

49. He did pretend this for awhile with Lysis, as section 2.b.2 showed.

50. At *Lysis* 211a–b, Socrates seemed to suggest that Lysis is capable of cross-examining Menexenus in order to carry out on his friend the kind of humbling refutation that Socrates has just administered to him. Admittedly, Socrates implies that Lysis will be capable only of repeating the series of questions that Socrates has just put to him, but if Socrates truly believes his method can be employed by this youth after only one short conversation with him, then his method of interrogation would not seem unique (or necessarily proprietary). See also the following places in the *Apology*—discussed in Chapter 1—where Socrates tells his jury about his question-and-answer method and about how his associates imitate it (23c, 38a, 39c–d, and 41e–42a). That others might employ *elenchos* does not mean, however, that cross-examination and refutation are not used for distinctive (and presumably more constructive) purposes in Socrates' hands than in the hands of those who imitate him. And no other practitioner is armed with the arsenal of argumentation, the wealth of examples, and the well-honed ability to assess character with which Plato equips Socrates.

51. Forde, "On the *Alcibiades I*," 237. Forde emphasizes that the makeshift community established by this Socratic conversation does not last very long. Though the dialogue refers four times to "taking common counsel" or "deliberating in common," he thinks that good reasons have been given for supposing that this *ad hoc* community had

always existed more truly in speech than in deed. Forde concludes that Socrates' representations about a shared search are just aimed at securing intermediate agreements that solidify his position and allow him to take the next step with his less skilled debate partner. He is not convinced by the fact that Socrates begins his questions with "Come let us consider" several times or by the fact that he includes himself with Alcibiades as one who needs to take trouble over himself.

52. A similar discussion occurs at *Protagoras* 319e–320b, where Socrates argues, ironically, that virtue cannot be taught, because Pericles was unable to teach it to his own children, and at *Gorgias* 514c–519c, where Socrates expresses his low opinion of Pericles, denigrating him as a role model for virtue.

53. Damon and Pythokleides. Socrates recalls his own association with Anaxagoras and his eventual disappointment with the materialism that he discovered in the Anaxagorean notion of *nous* at *Phaedo* 97c–99c, a disappointment that led Socrates to embark on his legendary "second sailing."

54. The dramatic date of the first *Alcibiades* dialogue is 433 B.C.E. and *Symposium* 416 B.C.E. Also, Alcibiades is "not yet twenty" in the *Alcibiades I*, so he and Socrates have not yet fought together in battle. Alcibiades is age thirty-five or thirty-six in the *Symposium*, which would make Socrates about fifty-four.

CHAPTER 4

1. Besides Socrates and Alcibiades, twelve other characters appear or are named in at least three different dialogues. They are: Apollodorus, Chaerophon, Charmides, Crito, Ctesippus, Glaucon, Hippias, Menexenus, Phaedrus, Young Socrates, Theaetetus, and Theodorus.

2. Dover notices a pervasive tendency in Socrates to invert an important aspect of conventional Athenian morality by taking *kālos kāgathos* to mean "handsome" (*Greek Popular Morality*, 71). He attributes this penchant of Socrates' to "naivete," but this explanation misconstrues Socrates' erotic strategy. He does not even consider that Socrates knows full well what he is doing, and that Plato has every intention of deploying this aspect of Athenian custom for his own philosophical purposes. In seeming to confuse beautiful young men with Athenian gentlemen, as he did with Lysis, Socrates is exploiting prevalent conventions. Dover makes the same point in his introduction, but he does not elaborate on or justify it sufficiently in either place. In his review of Dover's book, Adkins is widely critical of his implicit methodology, and he is particularly critical of some of the inferences drawn concerning the meaning of *kālos kāgathos*. See A. W. H. Adkins, "Problems."

3. This choice itself is epitomized in the actions of the historical Alcibiades. The ambivalence of Plato's Alcibiades recalls the checkered career of the great Athenian commander and statesman.

4. Gagarin, for one, comes to the conclusion that Socrates has transcended the physical Eros and is no longer a lover. In a less dogmatic way, this also is the position of Allen, Dover, Vlastos, Nussbaum, and others, who make essentially the same claim, arguing that the philosopher has passed beyond the physical Eros. See Michael

Gagarin, "Socrates' Hybris and Alcibiades' Failure," *Phoenix* 31 (1977): 22–37; R. E. Allen, *The Dialogues of Plato*, Vol. 2 (New Haven, Conn., and London: Yale University Press, 1991); and K. J. Dover, *Plato: Symposium* (Cambridge: Cambridge University Press, 1980). Eisner holds that Socrates cannot "reciprocate love," because this would threaten his "impenetrability." See Robert Eisner, "Socrates as Hero," *Philosophy and Literature* 6, Nos. 1 and 2 (1982): 116. It is worth recalling here that Socrates fathered a son not long before his death at age seventy.

     5. See note 14 of the Introduction. The principal critics of Vlastos, Nussbaum, and others who hold this view—most notably, Price—hope to have found a way to avoid the problem by emphasizing that Eros in Plato is not aimed at individuals in their contingent particularity. See A. W. Price, "Martha Nussbaum's Symposium," *Ancient Philosophy* 11 (1991): 285–299. While it is dangerous to read modern expectations of "the person" into Plato, it seems that Eros can be aimed at individuals, as Allen suggests, in their status *qua* lovers. For the best overview of the scholarly debate over this aspect of Socrates' character, and of Alcibiades' speech in particular, see Christopher Gill, "Platonic Love and Individuality," in *Polis and Politics*, eds. A. Loizon and H. Lesser (Aldershor: Avebury, 1990), 69–88.

     6. Schein remarks on the homology between *tēs poseos* ("of the drinking") and *tēs poleos* ("of the city"). See Seth Schein, "Alcibiades and the Politics of Misguided Love in Plato's Symposium, *Theta Pi* 3, No. 2 (1974): 159. All citations of the *Symposium* in this chapter, unless otherwise noted, are from Robin Waterfield's translation (Oxford and New York: Oxford University Press, 1994).

     7. Schein's article "Alcibiades" calls attention to the political overtones of the language used here. His short article hints at much more than it can develop, and I have tried to adumbrate some of its possible implications. His article first provoked me to take a closer look at Alcibiades' motive.

     8. Plato's employment of the term *parrhēsia* differentiates political free speech, spurred on by inebriation, from ironic speech, which may describe Socrates' customary way of speaking. This contrast will be developed further in Section 4.c.2.

     9. Anderson makes a similar point in *Masks*, 122–24.

     10. This suggests that, for Plato, the Periclean kind of freedom is somehow connected to the impulse for domination. Although he would argue, as Chapter 3 illustrated, that the inability to rule oneself renders one incapable of ruling others, such inability in no way precludes the attempt to do so. Forde speaks in almost the same terms about Alcibiades' attempt to dominate the city as I am using to describe his attempt to dominate Socrates. He writes that Alcibiades "refuses to be anything less than honest about his ambitions in the city. Alcibiades wishes to dominate the city, but frankly and openly, as it were." See Steven Forde, *The Ambition to Rule: Alcibiades and the Politics of Imperialism in Thucydides* (Ithaca, N.Y.: Cornell University Press, 1989), 84.

     11. Finlay makes substantially the same point when he writes: "We see the same versatility in Alcibiades' political and his sexual lives.... He successively fitted into the democracy of Athens, the aristocracy of Sparta, and the despotism of Persia. He became a participant in whatever political philosophy he could use for his own machinations." See John Finlay, "The Night of Alcibiades," *The Hudson Review* 47, No. 1 (1994): 68.

12. Forde points out that Pericles is made to use the word *courage* only once in his speeches, employing *daring* at every other opportunity. The analysis of the role of daring in Thucydides' *History* is surely one of the highlights of Forde's book. He shows how inseparable this rash daring was from the Athenian character and its tendency toward seemingly boundless ambition. For Thucydides, according to Forde, daring supplants courage as the specifically Athenian virtue. See Forde, *Ambition*, especially pp. 13–15.

13. Forde, *Ambition*, 19. Forde reminds us that the majority of references to Eros in Thucydides' *History* occur in connection with the Sicilian expedition and Alcibiades' arguments for this extraordinary venture. Nicias, in his speech opposing the Sicilian invasion, criticizes what he sees as an "erotic passion" for faraway places, an erotic passion inspired chiefly in the Athenians by Alcibiades. I argue below that this "misguided Eros" is really a barely concealed *thumos*, because it is indistinguishable from the desire to outdo, even to dominate, others. Likewise, in his "Memorabilia" (I.2), Xenophon refers to Alcibiades and Critias as "the most ambitious persons in all Athens, determined to have personal control over all State affairs and to be famous above all others" (Treadnick and Waterfield trans.)

14. Of course, Alcibiades is much more ambitious than the democrat Socrates caricatures in Book VIII. There Socrates illuminates the correspondence between the decline of individual types and the degeneration of the states that produce them. The chaos and disorder he describes captures the wavering spirit that Alcibiades personifies in the *Symposium*:

> Yes, I said, he lives from day to day indulging the appetite of the hour; and sometimes he is lapped in drink and strains of the flute; then he becomes a water-drinker, and tries to get thin; then he takes a turn at gymnastics; sometimes idling and neglecting everything, then once more living the life of a philosopher; often he is busy with politics, and starts to his feet and says and does whatever comes into his head; and, if he is emulous of anyone who is a warrior, off he goes in that direction, or if of men of business, once more in that. His life has neither law nor order; and this distracted existence, which he terms joy and bliss and freedom, continues throughout his life. (*Rep.* 561c–d, Jowett trans.)

In his richly descriptive but philosophically flawed essay, John Finlay defends the view that Plato has Alcibiades in mind in this passage. He notes that no other prominent Athenian politician possessed both the brilliance and diversity that Plato describes. Alcibiades was so versatile and yet so unabashedly hedonistic that to drink the black broth and eat the stale bread of the Spartans while adorning himself in the coarse cloak of a Spartan aristocrat must have seemed to him, according to Finlay, "the last novelty" (Finlay, "Night," 59). Although the essay illuminates well the character of Alcibiades and its contrast to Socrates', there are no notes accompanying it, and the reader is left wanting to see the evidence mentioned without citation. More problematic, however, is that Finlay's treatment of the relation between Socrates and

Alcibiades suffers from an undue methodological reliance upon a kind of psychologism to make its case.

15. The best example of this can be found in Thucydides' account of the so-called Melian dialogue. In their cruel arrogance, the Athenians killed all adult males and forced the women and children of the tiny island of Melos into slavery for attempting to maintain their neutrality in the war. According to Thucydides, Alcibiades was a leading proponent for this course of action. See Thucydides, *History of the Peloponnesian War*, trans. Rex Warner (New York and London: Penguin Books, 1954), Sections 5: 84–116.

16. Socrates accuses Alcibiades with the phrase *anti doxes alethias kalon ktasthai epicheireis* (218e6). Section 4.c will clarify precisely how Alcibiades is attempting to exchange opinion for truth.

17. Anderson (*Masks*, 122–124) points out two important aspects of this encounter that bear repeating here: (1) Socrates does not, strictly speaking, reject Alcibiades. He neither leaves the bed nor forces Alcibiades to leave. This indicates that Socrates is not struggling with his own passions, renouncing his desires and resisting Alcibiades' attack in the same impulse; and (2) Alcibiades is patently duplicitous, and this forces Socrates to speak as he does.

18. Nehamas has argued that Alcibiades' characterization of Socrates here goes to the very heart of the frustration others feel at Socrates' superior stance toward them. Nehamas stresses that Alcibiades does not merely accuse Socrates of using irony; he charges him with *being ironical*, which for Nehamas means that he occupies an unassailable position vis-à-vis his interlocutors and companions. Socrates' ironical posture distances him from those around him and, in the present instance, would allow him, if pressed, to claim that he did not really mean what Alcibiades takes him to mean. That Socrates permits Alcibiades to misunderstand is evident from the fact that Alcibiades jumps into bed with the philosopher right after Socrates seems to rebuff him. This indicates that Alcibiades has not taken Socrates' repudiation as an outright rejection. The audience sees how Socrates' irony always leaves the door open. For Nehamas, Alcibiades' reference to "his ironical manner" suggests that the rebuff of Alcibiades is an example of Socratic irony functioning to dissemble. The nature and function of Socratic irony will be examined more closely in Section 4.c.2.

19. Xenophon's Socrates is motivated by the desire to maintain the upper hand in conventional roles without escaping the exchange economy. In his version of *Apology*, line 16, Socrates is reported as saying, "So, do you know anyone who is less of a slave to bodily desires than I am? Do you know anyone more free, since I accept no gratuities or payments from anyone?" The passage continues with Socrates asking: "Could you plausibly regard anyone as more upright than the man who is so in tune with the immediate circumstances that he has no need of anything extraneous?" (Treadnick and Waterfield trans.) I am arguing that Plato is going further than Xenophon does in his characterization of Socrates.

20. That Socrates' poverty is evidence of his benefaction is stated at *Apology* 23c and 31c. The connection of his poverty to his independence must be adduced from other evidence. Not accepting fees or gifts keeps Socrates free to talk to whomever he wishes; he is forced to talk to no one. And I have suggested that although he claims in

his *Apology* to go around exhorting whomever he meets, Socrates is, in fact, quite selective about his interlocutors, at least if we judge only from those conversations that Plato has chosen to dramatize. The freedom from pecuniary constraints allows Socrates to make speaking truthfully his primary concern. And because he does not profit from his practice, Socrates is always positioned as a benefactor and never as a beneficiary, and in the conventional Athenian ethos of freedom, such benefaction is a sign of a free man.

21. See Waterfield's note, *Symposium,* 94.

22. Socrates may be partly to blame for this expectation. We saw that in their initial conversation, Socrates does his part to arouse Alcibiades' passions (cf. *Alc. I* 105a–106a).

23. Notice how different Plato's portrayal of their relationship is on this point from Xenophon's. Xenophon shows his Socrates refusing large gifts from Alcibiades over the objections of Xanthippe. See Xenophon, "Oeconomicus," in *Xenophon in Seven Volumes.* Vol. 4: "Memoribilia" and "Oeconomicus," trans. E. C. Marchant (Cambridge, Mass.: Harvard University Press, 1968), 2.8.

24. In a sense, each speech gives a vision of the good social order within which their view of this relation, and thereby their views of Eros and beauty, might flourish. Each account stresses the particular excellences fostered by the interlocutor's conception of civil society. I would go so far as to say that every account offers a kind of *muthos* for the speaker's chosen way of life. In this view, not only would Aristophanes' speech but *every* speech in the dialogue needs to be interpreted as a *muthos,* including those of Socrates'/Diotima's and Alcibiades', insofar as neither speech is merely descriptive.

25. Since the younger man in a relationship of *sunousia* will become a citizen as soon as he attains the age of majority, both parties to the association occupy the status of free persons. Yet within the logic of the exchange economy, there will always be one person who acts *more* like a free man and the other who acts *more* like a slave, as one sees clearly from the way Alcibiades' speech employs this distinction. In this sense, the active, older, less handsome, and manly lover enjoys the additional freedom endowed with his liberty, while the passive, receptive, younger, more beautiful beloved may be dominated in a way that makes him closer to a slave than a free person. Even though the boy has not yet attained the full status of his free citizenship, however, he is never reduced to the status of a slave through *sunousia,* at least in its best case, because the imperative to act like a free person (and perhaps the threat of reprisals from the male relatives of the boy) limits the older man's prerogative with him.

26. When Socrates and the targeted interlocutors become joint lovers of wisdom, they become *sunerastēs,* companions in the striving after wisdom. Unfortunately, very few of the boys are capable of playing this role for very long.

27. I have tried to show that Socrates utilizes some of his most questionable tactics to effect these reversals. He is not above using outrageous examples that appeal to the fantastical desires of the youths, engaging in false pretensions that make his assistance key to the attainment of his interlocutors' desires, and constructing faulty, even eristic, arguments that rely more heavily upon seduction than induction or deduction. This strategy seems designed to prepare his interlocutors for the *paideusis* that will follow, once they experience an initial turnaround. Since, as Aristotle says with respect to the study of ethics, the beginning is more than half of the whole, the dialogues rarely

show Socrates getting beyond this first stage. It is because the dialogues predominantly portray the "negative" or "destructive" dimension of Socrates' approach to others that some commentators have been led to view him as being capable only of exhortation, or to regard him as a social critic, or to conclude that he is a "nonteacher."

28. Alcibiades, at 216b, speaks of the promises he made to Socrates. Another such prior agreement is mentioned at 219b. In the *Alcibiades I*, Alcibiades agrees to attend to the matter of his self-improvement and to follow Socrates' advice. But, of course, it becomes clear from his own admissions in the *Symposium* that he has failed to uphold these agreements.

29. Plato provides several clues, besides the references to past agreements, that indicate important connections to the two *Alcibiades* dialogues. Friedländer emphasizes this connection when he writes:

> To understand fully the speech of Alkibiades in the *Symposium*, we must look to the dialogue *Alkibiades* as its background and we must be aware constantly, in each dialogue, both of the extraordinary greatness and of the catastrophe of the historical Alkibiades. (*Plato*, 242–243)

That Plato had the *Alcibiades I* in mind, he says, is proven by the fact that Alcibiades' initial response to Socrates, upon discovering him on the couch next to Agathon, is parallel to his opening remark in the *Alcibiades I* (cf. *Symp.* 213b; *Alc. I* 104d). Friedländer cites further Alcibiades' emphasis in both texts on Socrates' strange nature (*Symp.* 215a; *Alc. I* 106a) and the fact that Alcibiades confesses in both dialogues to feeling shame in the presence of Socrates. Surprisingly, Friedländer does not mention the *Symposium*'s references to past agreements, therefore he does not explicate how the past agreements and oaths of the *Alcibiades I* illuminate the dilemma to which Alcibiades is referring in the *Symposium*.

30. David Halperin has developed this distinction. From Diotima's speech, the reader learns that the beautiful is not the ultimate object of Eros. Eros, at bottom, aims at happiness, the final good, to which the many instances of beauty are intermediate. For Halperin, Eros always longs for something beyond its immediate object, something transcendent to the particular object. The longing for immortality is shown, in Diotima's teachings, to give expression to this desire to attain (or dwell in) the beautiful forever. See Halperin's "Plato and the Metaphysics of Desire," *Proceedings of the Boston Area Colloquium in Ancient Philosophy* 5 (1989): 27–52. See also Nussbaum's critical commentary following Halperin's article. She offers a wide-ranging discussion in her strong disagreement with Halperin's reading.

31. John Brentlinger, "Introduction: The Cycle of Becoming in the Symposium," in *The Symposium of Plato*, trans. Suzy Q. Groden and John A. Brentlinger (Amherst: University of Massachusetts Press, 1970), 6. In the introduction, Brentlinger calls Alcibiades' fatal flaw "excessive love of self." But I think Alcibiades is driven by something more grandiose and less introspective than excessive self-love (compare Forde's explanation, cited in note 37 below). It is true that in his first speech before the assembly, in which he argues in favor of undertaking the ill-fated Sicilian expedition, Alcibiades unabashedly presents a conception of honor that no longer depends upon

doing service to the public good. Forde asserts that Alcibiades authors a conception of honor coextensive with the individual interests of great leaders (such as himself), and the people endorse him. But what might have begun as self-love is intensified, complicated, and ultimately transformed by the adulation that Alcibiades relied upon for validation. See Thucydides, *History*, VI: 16–18, and Forde, *Ambition*, 79–99.

32. After proposing that the guests forego the traditional practice of imbibing required amounts of wine in deference to those who were badly hung over from the previous night's excesses, Eryximachus says, "I'm not counting Socrates, since he's ready for either alternative: whichever of the two courses we follow will be all right with him" (176c). Alcibiades enters and insists that the participants begin the customary bouts of drinking, filling the large bowl that was normally used for diluting the wine. He consumes the first bowl himself and, as a slave is refilling it for circulation, says, "Not that this ploy of mine will do any good as far as Socrates is concerned. It doesn't matter how much you tell him to drink, he drinks it all down without ever getting drunk" (214a). Later in his speech, when recalling Socrates' feats at Potideia and Delium, Alcibiades says, "And especially when it came to drinking: he was reluctant to drink, but when pushed he proved more than a match for everyone. And the most remarkable thing of all is that no one had ever seen Socrates drunk" (220a). Socrates' imperviousness to alcohol is confirmed dramatically at the end of the dialogue, when Socrates is still drinking the next morning after most of the participants, including the dialogue's narrator, had passed out or fallen asleep (223c–d).

33. Socrates' presentation of Diotima's teaching is instructive here. In her account of the true lover's journey, the love of beautiful bodies is never denied its relative value. Therefore, when interpreting Socrates' refusal to take up Alcibiades' offer of his body, this should not be construed as a general renunciation of the physical expressions of Eros. Also noteworthy here is that Plato absents Socrates from the previous night's festivities—which likely included sexual activity—rather than having him attend the first night but not participate fully.

34. Halperin seems to see this reciprocity both in Socrates' term *antierastēs* and in the word *sunerastēs* in the *Phaedrus*. See Halperin, "Plato and Erotic Reciprocity," *Classical Antiquity* 5 (1989): 60–80. Plato's dialogue, called *Erastēs* (Lovers) in most manuscripts, appears in some variant manuscripts as *Antierastēs* (Rivals). Jeffrey Mitscherling's recent translation has combined the two titles (or captured its two senses) by translating the dialogue as "Rival Lovers." See *Plato: Complete Works*, ed. John M. Cooper (Indianapolis, Ind.: Hackett Publishing Co., 1997), 618–626.

35. Finlay, "Night," 60.

36. Adkins frames the contrast between philosophical and political values in Plato as a contrast between "cooperative" and "competitive" *aretai*. This begins to clarify the difference between Alcibiades' spirited Eros and Socrates' desire to have his interlocutors become *sunerastēs* in a conversational *agōn*. See A. W. H. Adkins, *From the Many to the One* (London: Constable Press, 1970), especially pp. 145–148. A notion of reciprocity, implying some measure of cooperation, can be found, if less prominently, in political and heroic traditions, and it may simply be that the goods for which Socrates and his companions compete, such as wisdom and virtue, are goods that can be shared. In fact, it may be that the competition for these goods itself enriches the competitors.

37. Near the end of his book, Forde succinctly summarizes Alcibiades' character. Recall Diotima's warning about the misguided striving for immortality and what has been exhibited of Alcibiades' thumos, which captures in a word what Forde refers to as his "political ambition." Forde writes:

> In the economy of Alcibiades' soul only one passion reigns supreme, that for political achievement and immortal glory, his political ambition. All his other inclinations are strictly subordinate to this—thus can Alcibiades claim that all his extravagant indulgences are subservient to his general project of garnering fame and honor. His argument becomes nearly circular, however, once it is understood that the standard Alcibiades implicitly uses for discerning what is honorable is to a large extent simply his own undisciplined nature. Rather than saying that Alcibiades' appetites are strictly subordinated to his political project, it is closer to the truth to say that they are all taken up into his political project, becoming part of his notion of what greatness and hence honor is. (Forde, *Ambition*, 205)

38. Nussbaum articulates this view in her essay on Alcibiades' speech. She appeals to the emphasis on truth telling to support her reading of Socrates as being unable or unwilling to accept the truth Alcibiades offers him. This is part of her larger criticism of Socrates for being closed off to the love of particular persons. She does not say why, in her view, Socrates fails to interrupt Alcibiades to assert his disagreement. Nor does her treatment of the political significance of Alcibiades' speech extend to their argument about truth telling. And she does not seem to think it matters that Alcibiades' speech confesses to his impulse for domination and his willingness to try to trap Socrates in any way he can in order to discharge the shame he feels in Socrates' presence.

39. Gregory Vlastos, "Socratic Irony," in *Socrates: Ironist and Moral Philosopher* (Ithaca, N.Y.: Cornell University Press, 1991), 35–38. We saw in Section 3.d.1 that Socrates conceives of his vocation as a matter of testing his interlocutor's way of living, most notably at *Apology* 39c, where he refers to his *elenchon toū biou*. On testing his interlocutor's character, that is, the relation of his beliefs and opinions to his way of living as the primary objective of Socratic cross-examination, see also *Gorgias* 482b.

40. Alcibiades can only be referring to Socrates' characteristic speech in general, that is, his customary manner of speaking. Since he arrived at Agathon's house after Socrates had given his encomium, he could not have heard Socrates' speech in this dialogue and cannot be referring to it. The descriptions and analyses of Socrates' life and practices in Alcibiades' eulogy lend credence to this interpretation.

41. The audience must wonder in what sense Alcibiades' speech might be a mock eulogy. This may be a reference to another sense of the speech's *parrhēsia:* the popular practice of lampooning the city, its leaders, or its customs. This was one kind of *parrhēsia*. Jaeger provides a perspicuous discussion of this form of *parrhēsia* in the context of evaluating Aristophanic comedy. He argues that such lampooning was driven largely by "personal invective" and that such personal attacks became "to some extent the medium of public criticism in the new liberty of the Ionian city-state." Jaeger, *Paideia*,

1: 364. Jaeger continues by saying that the new Attic comedy exceeded even the outrageousness of Iambic lampooning and was "a true product of democratic free speech." When the excessive liberty of Athenian democracy was replaced with a new tyranny, comedy disappeared. He argues that comedy did not merely coincide with democracy; it was produced by it "as an antidote to its own overdose of liberty, thereby outdoing its own excesses, and extending *parrhêsia*, its vaunted freedom of speech, to subjects which are usually tabu even in a free political system" (1: 364).

42. Compare this bi-play with lines 1046–1060 of Euripides' *Electra*, where Electra asks permission from her mother Clytemnestra to speak the truth. Foucault argues that the establishment of an explicit right to speak with *parrhêsia*—which he calls the *parrhêsiastic* contract—limits the risk of reprisals against the speaker. Clytemnestra tells Electra, "So, if you're anxious to refute me, do it now; speak freely; prove your father's death not justified." Electra follows the choral interlude by reminding her mother that she had given her permission to speak freely. "Mother, remember what you said just now. You promised that I might state my opinions freely without fear." Clytemnestra replies, "I said so, daughter, and I meant it." Electra is still fearful, however, that her mother will punish her once she has spoken, so she clarifies: "Do you mean you'll listen first, and get your own back afterwards?" Her mother assures, "No, no; you're free to say what your heart wants to say." Finally, Electra says, "I'll say it, then. This is where I'll begin." See Euripides, "Electra," in *Medea and Other Plays*, trans. Philip Vellacott (New York: Penguin Books, 1963), 141.

43. No examples of these statues of Silenus have survived.

44. Both of which were traits of Marsyas, the satyr who challenged Apollo to a flute-playing contest and was flayed alive upon losing.

45. *Alcibiades I* 105d. This assertion is repeated at 124c, when Socrates says that "through no other man but me will you attain to eminence."

46. At *Lysis* 218b (see Chapter 2, note 18). Socrates eventually qualifies his bold claims, but the caveat is not added until the end of the dialogue. He tells Alcibiades that if he and the city act justly and with *sophrosunê*, they will be dear to the gods (134d). He goes on to say that if Alcibiades continues toward these ends, he (Socrates) will stand as guarantor of his happiness (134e). Finally, Socrates enumerates the consequences of injustice and license, linking them to slavishness and godlessness. The dialogue ended with Socrates expressing profound doubts about the future for both himself and Alcibiades in the city. Socrates had attributed this initial conversation with the young Alcibiades to the permission of his *daimonion* and, thus, in a sense, it is the god who is the indirect guarantor of Socrates' hyperbolic promise to Alcibiades. Of course, this is certainly too subtle for Alcibiades to notice, and it treats uncritically Socrates' claims about his *daimonion*.

47. That Alcibiades qualifies his account of Socrates' repudiation with the adverb *ironically* confirms this point. Rather than being a fairly straightforward rebuff, as Vlastos takes it to be in his essay on "Socratic Irony," the modifier "ironically" accentuates the ambiguous meaning of Socrates' statements. Socrates' ironic way of deprecating himself as his preferred way of turning down Alcibiades' offer allows his meaning to remain ambiguous (cf. *Symp*. 218d).

48. Socrates' response to Alcibiades' offer is neither clear nor unequivocal; and some readers may find it difficult to agree with Vlastos that Socratic irony is always

designed to bring his young interlocutors into the truth. Kierkegaard had suggested that just as people can be deceived out of the truth, Socrates' irony may be designed, according to Kierkegaard, to deceive others *into the truth*. Vlastos follows Kierkegaard in arguing that Socrates is always concerned with the truth, but he disagrees with Kierkegaard that Socrates ever deceives.

In a lecture "Socratic Irony," delivered at the University of Pittsburgh on October 8, 1994, Alexander Nehamas argued, following Kierkegaard, that for the ironist, irony secures a kind of detachment, keeping him at a safe remove not only from others but also from being too closely identified with his own words. Dissimulation is the vehicle for this detachment, which disenfranchises the ironic standpoint from many forms of belonging. Nehamas also invokes Muecke to support his argument that, in the dialogues, Socrates' sense of superiority flaunts this detachment. This is vexing, because the philosopher's ironic standpoint allows him to ridicule his interlocutors from behind a shield. This frustrates them in at least two ways, according to Nehamas: (1) Socrates never has to reveal his truest thoughts and feelings; and (2) His insular remove, like a kind of guerilla warfare, makes it impossible for any interlocutor to land his arrows in return. Nehamas' penetrating and supple discussion of Socratic irony made plain that he does not agree with those more charitable interpreters, such as Vlastos, who find in Socratic irony nothing more than the use of a thinly veiled trope designed to bring an interlocutor into the truth. Much of Nehamas' 1994 lecture has been incorporated into *The Art of Living* (Berkeley and Los Angeles: University of California Press, 1998). See especially Part One.

49. Nehamas, in the lecture cited in the previous note. The treatment of irony in this section has been enriched by Nehamas' remarks, especially in clarifying the sense in which Alcibiades is charging Socrates with *being an ironist*. But because Nehamas does not see Socrates' behavior as an act of resistance to Alcibiades' attempt to dominate (*pleonektein*) him, and as something that must be done in order to maintain his philosophical practice, he does not seem to think, as I do, that Alcibiades' approach mandates and justifies Socrates' ironical standpoint toward him.

50. Perhaps the best, though certainly not the only, example of this mock humility occurs at *Republic* I, 336e–337a, where Socrates pretends to esteem Thrasymachus as someone truly clever, imploring him to take pity on the ignorant philosopher rather than to display anger. Socrates says:

> [I] said with a slight tremor, Thrasymachus, don't be harsh with us. If I, and my friend, have made mistakes in the consideration of the question, rest assured that it is unwillingly that we err. For you surely must not suppose that while, if our quest were for gold, we would never willingly truckle to one another and make concessions in the search and so spoil our chances of finding it, yet that when we are searching for justice, a thing more precious than much fine gold, we should then be so foolish as to give way to one another and not rather do our serious best to have it discovered. You surely must not suppose that, my friend. But you see it is our lack of ability that is

at fault. It is pity then that we should far more reasonably receive from clever fellows like you than severity. (Shorey trans.)

See also *Protagoras* 329b–c. In other cases, Socrates imputes to his inferior interlocutors an expertise that he claims he does not have. See, for example, *Lysis* 211d; *Apology* 17a–d.

51. Eisner, "Socrates as Hero," 115. Eisner argues that Socrates is given all of the attributes of a tragic hero by Plato. This is why, in Eisner's view, irony, more than dialectic, distinguishes the Socrates that Plato presents. He explains: "Upon irony centers the essence of his heroic coldness and no other tool could be more appropriate for the mythological exemplar" (115). Eisner goes too far, however, when he attributes to Socrates' desire for impenetrability his failure to "reciprocate" the love of his young associates (116).

52. This is especially true of the speeches of Phaedrus and Pausanias. But, it is noteworthy that seven of the eight named participants in this symposium were "coupled." Phaedrus is the beloved of Eryximachus, Pausanias is the lover of Agathon, and Socrates is linked to Alcibiades and Aristodemus. There are two curious aspects of Socrates' couplings: (1) the way in which Socrates unhinges himself before arriving at Agathon's house so that he can be alone in contemplation; and (2) the way in which Socrates pretends to compete with his beloved Alcibiades for Agathon's affections from the moment they all three share the same couch. The only named participant who is unattached is the comic poet Aristophanes. Of course, he will be the one to tell the tragic myth about the bisection of the originally doubled human beings.

53. Aristotle speaks of irony as "playing down" what one is or knows and contrasts it to boastfulness, where one exaggerates one's qualities. Both miss the mean virtue of truthfulness, though mock humility is said to be closer to truthfulness than boasting, since boasting involves embellishment. Aristotle does not consider mock humility blameworthy so long as no desire to harm is involved. He specifically names Socrates in *The Nicomachean Ethics* (at 1127b21–32). What is especially interesting in his treatment of the excess and deficiency of truthfulness is the way in which they are connected. Because irony in the form of mock humility involves an assumption or a pretense to superiority that dissociates the ironist from others, shielding him or her from scrutiny, this superiority makes irony a kind of hubris. Not surprisingly, detached superiority manifests itself to others as arrogance.

54. Socrates makes this point explicitly in his admonition of Alcibiades upon hearing of Alcibiades' proposed exchange, accusing him of trying to exchange true beauty, which Alcibiades supposes Socrates to have, for seeming beauty, the kind that Alcibiades can give Socrates in the form of his handsomeness (218d). Xenophon has Socrates compare beauty and wisdom, saying, "If one sells one's favors to anyone who wants them, one is a whore, but if one gives it to good people, one is judged to be a friend." See Xenophon, "Memorabilia" I.6.11 (Treadnick and Waterfield trans.). In the *Alcibiades I*, Socrates called himself the truest lover, the only one who remains with Alcibiades, and the only one who will remain after his good looks have faded (*Alc. I*, 104d and 131c–d).

55. In the last year of his life, Michel Foucault's courses at both the University of California at Berkeley and the Collège de France focused upon the ancient practice of *parrhêsia*. The lectures comprising the fall semester 1983 course at the University of California, Berkeley, have been collected under the title "Discourse and Truth: The Problematization of *Parrhêsia*." These notes to the seminar have been transcribed from tapes and annotated by Joseph Pearson with the help of John Carvalho (typescript). This course focused chiefly upon political *parrhêsia*. Foucault's last course at the Collège de France, in 1984, available only on tape in the Centre Michel Foucault in Paris, examined the shift that Foucault perceives from "political" to "ethical" *parrhêsia*. Ever interested in what he referred to as "games of truth," Foucault's study of Plato's use of *parrhêsia* centers, in the Berkeley seminar, around Socrates' role as a truth teller and, in the French lectures, around Plato's role in the transformation from political to ethical *parrhêsia*. While Foucault does not mention Plato's use of the term *parrhêsia* in the *Symposium*, my analysis of *parrhêsia* owes much to Foucault's research in these lectures, and I am indebted to him for alerting me to many of the textual sources cited in this section.

Outside of its political use, Foucault concludes that one finds "greater mutuality" in the act of truth telling. What Foucault calls the "*parrhêsiastic* contract" ensures that both parties will speak frankly and not be obsequious or cowardly. The risk here is that one will be told the truth in return, to be judged ruthlessly by the other. Alcibiades surely must have expected such brutal honesty from any engagement with Socrates. This risk helps explain the bi-play over who will tell the truth and who will beat up whom that precedes his speech.

56. Foucault makes this point in the lecture notes cited above.

57. Thucydides' Pericles says, "Even those who are mostly occupied with their own business are extremely well-informed on general politics—this is a peculiarity of ours: we do not say that a man who takes no interest in politics is a man who minds his own business; we say that he has no business here at all" (Thucydides, *History*, 2: 40, 147). He says later that, "No subject can complain of being governed by people unfit for their responsibilities" (2: 41, 148).

58. J. Peter Euben, professor of politics at the University of California, Santa Cruz, used to quip that, for a fifth-century Athenian, delegating the exercise of one's citizenship duties to another, such as happens in a representative democracy, would be like "paying someone to work out for you." Since something beneficial was thought to be gained from political participation in Periclean Athens, each citizen was obliged to undertake these activities for himself for the benefits of citizenship to redound fully to him.

59. Foucault points out that in actual practice, the right to speak freely appears to have been less rigorously policed. He cites Demosthenes, who treats it as a commonplace that an Athenian slave had greater liberty to speak freely than a citizen of any other city. He says, in his "Third Philippic," "In other matters you think it so necessary to grant (*parrhêsia*) general freedom of speech to everyone in Athens that you even allow aliens and slaves to share in the privilege." See Demosthenes, "Third Philippic," trans. J. H. Vince, in *Demosthenes I: Olynthiacs, Philippics and Minor Orations* (Cambridge, Mass.: Harvard University Press; London: Heinemann [Loeb Classical Library], 1962), Para. 1s 3–4, 227.

60. See, for example, Euripides, *Ion,* lines 670–672, and *The Phoenician Women,* lines 386–394.

61. In his *Ion,* Euripides will be seen to cast mortals in the role of truth tellers toward the gods (see note 80 below).

62. The best example of these two senses of *parrhēsia* can be seen in Euripides' *Ion* (c. 418–417). The concept of *parrhēsia* was appropriated by the Stoics and can still be found in the early Christian writers of the fourth century C.E. In fact, Foucault argues, something like the "parrhesiastic contract" still survives into the Middle Ages in the relationship of a messenger to a king. This is made explicit when the messenger says to the king, "Beg permission to speak freely sir."

63. Plato uses the term *parrhēsia* in his criticism of rhetoric in the *Gorgias* (461e, 487a–e, 491e) and in his first speech in the *Phaedrus* (240e).

64. Foucault takes Plato to be the one largely responsible for the transformation in the activity of *parrhēsia* from a merely political frankness, which one does not necessarily believe, to a primarily ethical sense of the term in which one must believe what one says. Thomas Flynn explains:

> But "democratic" parrhēsia was criticized by the aristocrats in fourth-century Athens because it gave freedom of speech to the masses, that is, to those who judged in view of the desires of the crowd, not in terms of what was best for the polis. Their opposition was not only an expression of class interest; it revealed a perceived structural incompatibility between parrhēsia and democracy that challenged Greek political thought for generations. One can recognize the plight of Socrates before the demos as Plato's example of the dangers of such false parrhēsia. Thomas Flynn, "Foucault as Parrhesiast: His Last Course at the Collège de France," in *The Final Foucault,* eds. James Bernauer and David Rasmussen (Cambridge and London: MIT Press, 1987), 105.

65. Theognis, *Elegies,* trans. Dorothea Wender, in *Hesiod and Theognis* (New York: Penguin Books, 1981), 111, lines 421–424.

66. The word *athuroglottos* means literally "one who cannot keep his mouth shut" or an "incessant babbler," according to Liddell and Scott in *Greek-English Lexicon,* 18.

67. Plutarch, "Concerning Talkativeness," trans. W. C. Helmbold, in *Plutarch's Moralia,* Vol. 6 (Cambridge, Mass.: Harvard University Press; London: Heinemann [Loeb Classical Library], 1962), 503c, VI: 403.

68. In Isocrates' speech *"Areopagitus"* (386 B.C.E.), he draws this connection: he tells the Athenians that whenever they seek counsel regarding the affairs of the city, they rely "on the most depraved of the orators who come before you on this platform; and you prefer as being better friends of the people those who are drunk to those who are sober" (*"Areopagitus:* On the peace," 2:13, trans. George Norlin, in *Isocrates,* Vol. 2 (Cambridge, Mass.: Harvard University Press; London: Heinemann [Loeb Classical Library], 1968), 15.

At least two other features of the *athuroglottos* person may apply to Alcibiades: (1) It was thought that the *athuroglottos* preferred the passive role in a homoerotic relationship, a role that Alcibiades was willing to assume with Socrates; and (2) Athenians thought that those who had "mouths like running springs" had acquired their citizenship rather than receiving it through birth. Though Alcibiades was a natural-born Athenian, the vacillation in his allegiances makes the question of roots most apt. His disloyalty to his native Athens was widely held to be bound up with its demise. We saw previously that in his speech in support of the disastrous Sicilian expedition in Thucydides' *History*, Alcibiades dissociates individual interests from the good of the community, arguing from a conception of honor that no longer depends upon service to a common good. So, in a sense, his political ambition transcends traditional ties to place, making him a resident alien even in his own city. Forde calls Thucydides' Alcibiades "the most uninhibited of the uninhibited" (*Ambition*, 68) and "the most immoderate of men" (*Ambition*, 156). These qualities make Alcibiades, in Thucydides' view, a man whose "ambition and talent have emancipated themselves from any ordinary attachment to city" (*Ambition*, 88). See also 111*ff.*

69. At *Phaedrus* 240e. Socrates is wondering what the younger, still beautiful, beloved gets out of all of the doting and fondling from his older lover who has passed his prime. The beloved, he summarizes, "is jealously watched and guarded against everything and everybody, and has to hear misplaced and exaggerated praises of himself, and censures equally inappropriate, which are intolerable when the man is sober, and, when he is drunk, become disgusting, as well as intolerable, in their wearisome and unrestrained frankness (*parrhēsia*)" (*Phdr.* 240c–e, Jowett trans.). This sheds light on another aspect of Plato's inversion of their respective roles in the *Symposium*.

70. Plutarch, "The Education of Children," trans. Frank Cole Babbit, in *Plutarch's Moralia*, Vol. 1 (Cambridge, Mass.: Harvard University Press; London: Heinemann [Loeb Classical Library], 1960), 11c, I: 52–53.

71. Thucydides, too, underlines the remarkable frankness of Alcibiades' speech, as Forde notes throughout his treatment of Thucydides' view of Alcibiades. Forde first argues that this frankness contributes to Athenian moderation, vis-à-vis other cities, since no attempt was made to conceal their true motives. The unabashed ambition and daring that their words exhibit helps readers comprehend the character of Alcibiades and his extraordinary frankness. See Forde's discussion of Athenian frankness in general (*Ambition*, 44–46 and 155). Also see his chapter "The Speeches of Alcibiades" for his treatment of Alcibiades' radical frankness. He refers to Alcibiades' "unabashed frankness" (71), to his "amazing frankness" (78), and to his "astonishing frankness" (97 and 124). Finally, see pp. 166–168 for his comparison of Alcibiades and Pericles on this point.

72. Alcibiades enters Agathon's house draped with ribbons, crowned with the ivy and the violets that Pindar's Ode made the unmistakable symbol of Athens. Martha Nussbaum is one of the few commentators who mentions the violets, and she has eloquently explicated this rich symbolism in her essay "The speech of Alcibiades," 194–195.

73. *Laches* 187e–188a. See also *Republic* 352d; *Apology* 29c–30a.

74. In their first encounter Socrates had commanded Alcibiades, "Answer with the truth, so that our conversations may not be to no point." This is a crucial condition of a fruitful conversation, a condition Socrates does not state when he first tells

Alcibiades that he can "prove the truth" of what he is claiming about Alcibiades' nature if Alcibiades "will grant him one little favor . . . answer some questions" (*Alc. I* 106b). Notice the parallel to Socrates' exhortations in other dialogues. At *Republic* 346a, Socrates says, "My good man, don't answer contrary to your real opinion so we may get somewhere." See also *Gorgias* 500b, *Crito* 49c–d, and *Protagoras* 331c.

75. Plato is using *parrhēsia* in a positive sense here, although Socrates is surely displaying irony by imputing these three qualities to Callicles at this juncture of the dialogue. Just as Polus is unable to remain consistent on account of his shame, Callicles has to be shamed into admitting what he "really" believes, as Richard McKim shows so clearly. See McKim, "Shame and Truth in Plato's Gorgias," in *Platonic Writings, Platonic Readings*, ed. Charles Griswold (New York: Routledge, 1988). Socrates ironically imputes these three qualities to Callicles, even though it is obvious that Callicles does not exhibit good will toward Socrates, is not being honest about what he truly believes, and does not even possess the knowledge of himself that would make these beliefs transparent to him. If Socrates is denigrating frankness, in this context, he is doing so only as it pertains to Callicles, who still refuses to say what he really believes.

McKim calls Socrates' method here "psychological, not logical." Socrates does not try to "argue them [his interlocutors] into believing it [that they really believe that suffering injustice is preferable to committing it] but to maneuver them into acknowledging that, deep down, they have believed it all along" (37). He calls shame the "chief weapon" in this "psychological warfare" in which Socrates engages with the three Sophists. McKim says Socrates takes shame to be a sign of the natural inclinations toward justice and *sophrosunē*, thus he does not see justice as simply a conventional constraint upon nature. Far from causing men to assert what they really believe to be false, as Callicles claims, Socrates believes that their natural sense of shame motivates people to say what they actually believe is true (40). Brickhouse and Smith (*Plato's Socrates*, 25) discuss shame as a feature of Socrates' method of interrogation that inspires interlocutors to act rightly. Their treatment of shame is restricted primarily to the shame one feels at the end of a Socratic refutation, the shame one feels after sober reflection upon the ignoble deeds of one's past, for example. This is not the only kind of shame at issue, however; it does not seem to be the type of shame under discussion with Callicles.

76. Socrates rebukes Thrasymachus for this kind of waffling at *Republic* 345b, when he says, "Heaven forbid! I said. Don't do that. But in the first place when you have said a thing stand by it, or if you shift your ground change openly and don't try to deceive us" (Shorey trans.).

77. This is the irreducible basis of every argument, and indeed of every discussion with Socrates. Socrates says this explicitly to Thrasymachus: "Our argument is over no chance matter but over what is the way we ought to live" (*Rep.* 352d, Jowett trans.). He makes a similar assertion to Callicles at *Gorgias* 487e. See also *Gorgias* 500c.

78. Socrates twice expresses to Callicles that his goal is to make "Callicles agree with Callicles," to bring him to "see himself aright" (*Grg.* 482b*ff*, 495e). It is this manifest discord that plagues Alcibiades too.

79. Jaeger phrases Socrates' message to others as follows: "'It is not I, Socrates, but the *logos* that says this. You can contradict me but you cannot contradict it'." Werner

Jaeger, *Paideia*, 71. Jaeger concludes Chapter 5 with the suggestion that Socrates and "the *logos*" may amount to the same thing.

80. Here Euripides casts mortals in the role of *parrhēsiasts* toward the gods. Creusa wants to know if Ion is her son, and Apollo, who seduced or raped her while she was sleeping and then stole away with the child, refuses to speak. Foucault stresses that her use of *parrhēsia* toward Apollo, who refuses to tell the truth, inverts the typical trajectory of truth telling at the Delphic oracle. See *Ion*, lines 859–922; 67–68.

81. In fairness to Alcibiades, no other mortal has the aid of Socrates' *daimonion* to help him perfect this accord.

82. Since he professes to lack certain knowledge (and the wisdom the gods have), Socrates is committed to examining others and questioning himself. He testifies in *Apology* to this daily practice. At *Gorgias* 508e–509a, Socrates tells Callicles: "This appeared true in our former discussion, as I say, and it is secured and bound fast, if it is not too rude to say so, with arguments of adamant and iron. So, at any rate, it would seem, and unless you, or someone younger and more daring than you, shall unbind and loose those arguments, it is impossible to speak well and yet say other than what I am saying now." (Allen trans.)

83. I am borrowing this term from William Desmond, who has argued that Plato is one of a select group of thinkers in the philosophical tradition who practices what Desmond calls "plurivocity." He contrasts these "plurivocal" (to be distinguished from "equivocal") thinkers with another tradition symptomatic of what he calls "univocity." See Desmond, "Comedy and the Failure of Logos: On Dialectic, Deconstruction, and the Mockery of Philosophy," in *Beyond Hegel and Dialectic* (Albany: State University of New York Press, 1992), 251–342.

CHAPTER 5

1. That this antagonism between caring and not caring is at the heart of Socrates' message to the city seems to be confirmed in his exchange with Meletus, whose name is cognate with the Greek word for care or concern, in the *Apology*. See especially *Apology* 24c. Heidegger's distinction between authentic and inauthentic modes of caring and his definition of the Being of Dasein as Care (*Sorge*) in Div. I, Ch. 6, of *Being and Time* is relevant in this connection.

2. The precise percentage depends on how one regards the dialogues considered by some to be spurious and upon whether one includes certain dialogues, such as *Theaetetus, Phaedrus,* and even the *Republic, Phaedo,* and the two dialogues with Hippias. These are dialogues whose dramatic movements are wholly unlike the dialogues exhibiting the erotic reversal (a list of which would include *Lysis, Charmides, Alcibiades Major,* and also perhaps *Euthydemus,* although Euthydemus is not Socrates' principal target).

3. They are: Critobulous, Aeschines, Epigenes, Nicostratus, Paralios, Adeimantus, Plato, Acantidorus, and Apollodorus. It is especially interesting that while six of the followers Socrates names here are mentioned in other dialogues as well, none

of them is ever made the direct target of his approach. Why does Plato avoid depicting the philosopher in conversation with this group of regular associates, the ones who would later become known as his "circle"? Could this be another clue concerning how we are to regard Socrates as a teacher? Does Plato want his audience to conclude that although Socrates does not teach those people he cross-examines en route to showing their conceit of wisdom to be unjustified, he does, however, teach those regular associates who observe him gathering inductive evidence from conversation after conversation, showing them how those who challenge their mentor always end up in more or less the same difficulties? Does Socrates' method teach *indirectly*, not only in the sense that it teaches through questioning rather than by arguing for the philosopher's own positive doctrines, not only in the sense that it seems to show only what answers are *not* suitable answers to his questions, and not only in the sense that indirect discourse ("Oratio Oblique") is widely used throughout the dialogues, but also in the sense that the ultimate targets of his method are not the people being directly refuted but rather the ones observing and listening to his refutations of others? What are we to conclude about the bystanders to Socrates' conversations, who might well have benefitted from listening to Socrates cross-examine other people and from imitating him? Should one conclude that the audience learns more from the lessons than the target interlocutors, just because the audience hears many conversations instead of only one, or does the audience learn more because its members are not as emotionally invested in the positions taken as Socrates' target interlocutors are?

4. At least in the *Lysis*, the audience is told quite explicitly at the end of the dialogue that the main shortcoming of the argument was imposed upon it by the youth of the interlocutors, as I noted in Section 2.b. If there is anything about his *logoi* in the *Lysis* that gives Socrates qualms, it is not his faulty or incomplete argumentation but the way in which his arguments have been designed to "capture" Lysis. But Brickhouse and Smith argue that Socrates' fallibility, in general, is confirmed by the fact that his inner voice, or *daimonion*, "is always opposing him because he is about to do something wrong" (*Plato's Socrates*, 21, note 35).

5. In the case of Alcibiades, of course, we also have his highly disclosive *Symposium* testimony concerning his choice against the philosophic life! This testimony provides the strongest attack but also the best acquittal of Socrates. In a similar way, Alcibiades' speech is deep in signification, which the speaker himself seems only partially capable of grasping, as Chapter 4 argued. For another interpretation of Alcibiades' speech that illuminates these two sides of it, see R. Rutherford, *The Art of Plato* (Cambridge, Mass.: Harvard University Press, 1995), 197–204.

6. Recall that Socrates ended their first conversation by expressing his doubts about the strength of Alcibiades' character to resist the power of the state. Although in these closing remarks he utilizes his familiar strategy of including himself with his disappointing interlocutor, we saw in Chapter 3 that Socrates conspicuously distances himself from his young associate near the end of the dialogue. The point is that what provoked Socrates' trouble with Athens was far different from what landed Alcibiades in difficulty.

7. I am grateful to David Wolfsdorf's article, "Plato and the Mouth-piece Theory" (*Ancient Philosophy* [special issue: Representations of Philosophy in the

Classical World, K. V. Rosenbecker and Jana L. Adamatis, eds.], 1999): 13–24, for calling my attention to the Isocrates reference cited here. Wolfsdorf points out that interpreters cannot merely dismiss Socrates' prophecy as an instance of a Socratic jest, since Socrates could not have known how Isocrates actually turned out. He is manipulated here for some purpose that Plato must have had, whether his aim was to poke fun at Isocrates, to show how difficult it is to detect a philosophical nature, to show how easily such a nature can be perverted, to accomplish some pedagogical aim with Phaedrus by using the Isocrates example to denigrate Phaedrus' idolization of Lysias, or to show that Socrates was a poor prophet.

8. Nietzsche accuses Socrates of misdiagnosing the character of his interlocutors and hence of misusing his gift. But it seems more likely that the people he targets appear teachable at first, and that Plato means to emphasize that there are long odds against transforming human character. See Friedrich Nietzsche, *Twilight of the Idols*, especially "The Problem of Socrates," in *The Portable Nietzsche*, trans. Walter Kaufmann (New York: Penguin Books, 1968).

9. Plato appears to have Socrates himself suggest reasons for his failure, as a teacher, as the long passage from *Republic* VI, cited at the front of the book, shows. See also the *Theages*. In Book I, Chapter 2 of his "Memorabilia", Xenophon takes up the failure, and the eventual prosecution, of the historical Socrates. He claims that the historical Socrates "rescued many" from their states of corruption. He had just questioned how someone who did not himself manifest the qualities of irreverence, criminality, greediness, licentiousness, and laziness could produce them in others. Assuming that his testimony about the historical Socrates is reliable, it is clear that Plato chose to depict his Socrates as being even less successful than the one who the Athenians put to death. In contrast, Xenophon goes out of his way to make Socrates seem good and beneficial to others. Again, Plato's answer is advanced only indirectly and implicitly.

10. Socrates would then be merely installing himself as an authority in place of established authorities, making him less and less distinguishable from the Sophists. That Plato portrays as laughable all of those characters in the dialogues who tend toward discipleship and the fact that he has Socrates disavow the kind of knowledge that might entitle him to the role of authority figure, I think, confirms this point.

11. Richard Kraut, *Socrates and the State* (Princeton, N.J.: Princeton University Press, 1984), 225.

12. This might be borne out further by the peculiar status of the philosopher-kings. (See also Chapter 1, note 24.)

13. I do not regard the charge of egoism, arising from Socrates' frequent claims to be benefitting himself by practicing philosophy in the way he does, as a fatal counterclaim against the purity of Socrates' gift. Socrates gives as much of himself as any human ever did, and the benefits he insists he receives redound chiefly from the activity of exercising himself in conversation, especially in the process of cross-examining and refuting others. I want to argue that Socrates' gift undercuts the (false) dichotomy between self-regard and other-regard, egoism and altruism.

14. On two occasions in the dialogues, Socrates comes close to becoming the beneficiary of his friends' economic assistance. In the passage cited from *Republic I*

(337d) in Section 1.c, Glaucon and Socrates' other associates mollify Thrasymachus by offering to cover for Socrates the fine or fee payment the Sophist continues to demand. The other occasion is at Socrates' trial, when Plato, among others, is named as one of the people willing to stand surety for a bond thirty times more than the one mina of silver Socrates himself initially proposes (*Ap.* 38b). In both instances, dramatic circumstances obviate the need for Socrates to be bailed out by his friends, and thereby to be positioned as a beneficiary of someone. In the first case, Thrasymachus is not able to give a better definition of justice than anyone else, therefore he does not even receive the praise he expects from Socrates. In the second case, of course, the jury votes for the death penalty instead of for the proposed fine.

15. This criticism of Socrates extends across several of Nietzsche's books, but it is perhaps most clearly presented in *Twilight of the Idols*, especially the section entitled "The Problem of Socrates." Nietzsche accuses Socrates of being a decadent, inasmuch as he needs followers to philosophize as he does. The adoration of these fawning disciples, Nietzsche would say, is what Socrates gets out of his philosophical practice. Relying on his reading of the *Phaedo*, Nietzsche accuses Socrates of seeking the gift of death, which is what he thinks the philosopher has wanted all along.

16. For critical analyses of the difference between "restricted" and "general" economies in recent philosophy, see Georges Bataille, *The Accursed Share: An Essay on General Economy, Vol. 1: Consumption*, trans. Robert Hurley (New York: Zoom Books, 1988) and "The Notion of Expenditure," in *Visions of Excess: Selected Writings, 1927–1931*, ed. Allan Stockl, trans. Allan Stockl, with Carl R. Lovitt and Donald M. Leslie Jr. (Minneapolis: University of Minnesota Press, 1985); and Jacques Derrida, "From Restricted to General Economy: A Hegelianism without Reserve," in *Writing and Difference*, trans. Alan Bass (Chicago: University of Chicago Press, 1978).

17. I would like to thank Alan Schrift for first suggesting this idea to me in his comments on an earlier paper entitled "On Plato's Portrait of Socrates as a Gift," presented at the Eastern Division Meeting of the American Philosophical Association in Philadelphia, on December 28, 1997.

18. Many have noticed this before. Alexander Nehamas, in *Nietzsche: Life as Literature* (Cambridge, Mass.: Harvard University Press, 1985), 29, for example, writes: "Yet it is just in being shown to fail to change the mind and life of those who talk to him that Socrates has succeeded in changing the mind and life of all those who have read the Platonic dialogues, and of many others besides." See also Helger Thesleff, "Looking for Clues: An Interpretation of Some Literary Aspects of Plato's 'Two-Level Model'" in *Plato's Dialogues: New Studies in Interpretation*, ed. Gerald A. Press (Lanham, Md.: Rowman & Littlefield, 1993), 17–46.

19. Lest his acumen for ascertaining a character's identity be wholly ascribed to his status as a literary character, however, it is clear that some foreknowledge of his interlocutor's aspirations would have been available simply from knowledge of the person's station: his profession, his family ties, his age, and his project at the moment when Socrates initially approaches him. The examination of the *Alcibiades I* in Chapter 3 provided evidence that, at least in the case of this extraordinary youth, Socrates spent years observing his behavior prior to approaching him. But he had never seen Lysis before

their one single conversation, hence much is inscribed in these characters by their author. Often Plato's characters seem to serve as "types," in the sense that all boys of good birth and education, for example, might be expected to desire power and honor.

20. Because the dialogue form lends itself to teaching through interrogation, these conversations raise far more questions than they answer. Griswold puts the point nicely when he says, "Plato structures the dialogues so as to cast doubt on any claims to completeness." See Charles Griswold, "Response to Kenneth Sayre," *Proceedings of the Boston Area Colloquium in Ancient Philosophy* IX (1993) eds. John J. Cleary and William Wians (Lanham, Md.: University Press of America, 1995), 201. On the previous page, Griswold writes:

> Indeed it eventually strikes just about every reader that closure on each of the important topics raised in the dialogues—the nature of the soul, virtue, the good life, politics, philosophy, and so forth—is never achieved therein, even when there is a prima facie claim to closure. That is, not only the aporetic dialogues are aporetic; superficially non-aporetic dialogues such as the *Statesman* and the *Republic* are also aporetic in that they raise important questions to which they provide no answers or at least no satisfactory answers. (200)

I prefer to say that Plato writes open-ended dialogues, for he does not leave his reader utterly perplexed or *without a way*, which is the root meaning of *aporia*. Elinor West has argued that Plato wrote his dialogues in such a way as to preserve the "spirit" of Socratic philosophizing and not to record the "letter" of his philosophy. See Elinor J. M. West, "Plato's Audiences, or How Plato Replies to the Fifth-Century Intellectual Mistrust of Letters," in *The Third Way: New Directions in Platonic Studies,* ed. Francisco J. Gonzalez (Lanham, Md.: Rowman & Littlefield, 1995), 41–60.

21. While I cannot argue for this claim here, I believe that this also is true of all of the other supposed authority figures in the dialogues besides Socrates. I have argued elsewhere that all seven of the so-called mouthpieces for Plato say things that downplay their claims to authority or are simply in tension with other things that they say. The "mouthpiece theory" furnishes no means of resolving these tensions and ambiguities, hence it is a useless device for the attempt to determine Plato's views. See Gary Alan Scott and William A. Welton, "Eros as Messenger in Diotima's Teaching," in *Who Speaks for Plato: Studies in Platonic Anonymity,* ed. Gerald A. Press (Lanham, Md.: Rowman & Littlefield, 2000): 147–159. For an excellent introduction to the problems entailed by the mouthpiece theory, see Wolfsdorf, "Plato and the Mouth-piece Theory."

Selected Bibliography

Adams, Don. "Elenchos and Evidence." *Ancient Philosophy* XVIII, No. 2 (Fall 1998): 287–307.
———. "The Lysis Puzzles." *History of Philosophy Quarterly* 9: 1 (1992): 3–17.
Adkins, A. W. H. *From the Many to the One.* London: Constable Press, 1970.
———. "Problems in Greek Popular Morality." *Classical Philology* 73 (1978): 143–158.
Allen, R. E. *The Dialogues of Plato.* Vol. 1. New Haven, Conn., and London: Yale University Press, 1984. [Cited "Gorgias."]
———. *The Dialogues of Plato.* Vol. 2: The "Symposium." New Haven, Conn., and London: Yale University Press, 1991.
Anderson, Daniel E. *The Masks of Dionysos: A Commentary on Plato's Symposium.* Albany: State University of New York Press, 1993.
Aristophanes. *The Clouds.* Trans. Kenneth McLeish. Cambridge, Mass.: Cambridge University Press, 1979.
Aristotle. *The Nicomachean Ethics.* Trans H. Rackham. Cambridge, Mass.: Harvard University Press, 1990 [1926].
Bacon, Helen. "Socrates Crowned." *The Virginia Quarterly Review* 35 (1959): 415–430.
Barnes, Jonathan, ed. *The Revised Oxford Translations of the Complete Works of Aristotle.* Princeton, N.J.: Princeton University Press, 1984.
Bataille, Georges. *The Accursed Share: An Essay on General Economy, Vol. 1: Consumption.* Trans. Robert Hurley. New York: Zoom Books, 1988.
———. "The Notion of Expenditure." In *Visions of Excess: Selected Writings, 1927–1931.* Ed. Allan Stockl, trans. Allan Stockl, with Carl R. Lovitt and Donald M. Leslie Jr. Minneapolis: University of Minnesota Press, 1985.
Benson, Hugh H. "Meno, the Slave Boy, and the Elenchos." *Phronesis* 35 (1990): 128–158.
———. "The Problem of the Elenchus Reconsidered." *Ancient Philosophy* 7 (1987): 67–85.

———. "Problems with Socratic Method." In *Rethinking Socratic Method: Essays in Dialogue with Gregory Vlastos's "The Socratic Elenchus."* Ed. Gary Alan Scott. University Park: Pennsylvania State University Press, Forthcoming.

Berti, Enrico. "Ancient Greek Dialectic as Expression of Freedom of Thought and Speech." *Journal of the History of Ideas* 39 (1978): 347–370.

Blank, David L. "Socratics versus Sophists on Payment for Teaching." *Classical Antiquity* 4, No. 1 (1985): 1–24.

Bloom, Allan. *Love and Friendship.* New York: Simon and Schuster, 1993.

———. *The Republic of Plato.* 2d ed. Trans. Allan Bloom. New York: Harper & Row, 1968.

Blundell, Mary Whitlock {Ruby Blondell}. "Reproducing Socrates: Dramatic Form and Pedagogy in the *Theaetetus.*" *Proceedings of the Boston Area Colloquium in Ancient Philosophy* 14 (1998), 21–38.

Bolotin, David. *Plato's Dialogue on Friendship.* Ithaca, N.Y., and London: Cornell University Press, 1979.

Bowery, Anne-Marie. "Looking Beyond the Elenchus: On the Possibility of a Platonic Critique of Socrates." *Southwest Philosophy Review* 14 (1998): 157–168.

Brandt, Paul (pseud. Hans Licht). *Sexual Life in Ancient Greece.* Trans. J. H. Freese, ed. Lawrence H. Dawson. New York: Barnes & Noble, 1953.

Brentlinger, John. "Introduction: The Cycle of Becoming in the Symposium." In *The Symposium of Plato.* Trans. Suzy Q. Groden and John A. Brentlinger. Amherst: University of Massachusetts Press, 1970.

Brickhouse, Thomas C., and Nicholas D. Smith. *Plato's Socrates.* New York and Oxford: Oxford University Press, 1994.

———. "Socrates' Elenctic Mission." *Oxford Studies in Ancient Philosophy* 9 (1991): 131–159.

———. *Socrates on Trial.* Princeton, N.J.: Princeton University Press, 1989.

———. "Vlastos on the Elenchus." *Oxford Studies in Ancient Philosophy* 2 (1984): 183–195.

Bruell, Christopher. "Xenophon and His Socrates." *Interpretation* 16 (1988–1989): 295–306.

Burkert, Walter. *Greek Religion.* Trans. John. Raffan. Cambridge, Mass.: Harvard University Press, 1985.

Burnet, John, ed. *Platonis Opera.* 5 vols. Oxford: Clarendon Press, 1900–1907.

Burnyeat, Myles P. "Socratic Midwifery, Platonic Inspiration." In *Essays on the Philosophy of Socrates.* Ed. Hugh H. Benson. New York and Oxford: Oxford University Press, 1992.

Cobb, William S. *Plato's Erotic Dialogues.* Albany: State University of New York Press, 1993.

Cohen, David. "Law, Society and Homosexuality in Classical Athens." *Past and Present* 17 (1987): 3–21.

Cole, Susan Guatel. "Greek Sanctions against Sexual Assault." *Classical Philology* 79 (1984): 97–113.

Cooper, John M., ed. *Plato: Complete Works.* Indianapolis: Hackett Publishing Co., 1997.

Coplan, Amy. "Tri-partite Friendship in Plato's Lysis." *Aporia* (1995): 37–47.
Cummins, W. Joseph. "Eros, Epithymia and Philia in Plato." *Apeiron* 15 (1981): 10–18.
Davidson, Arnold. "Ethics as Ascetics: Foucault, the History of Ethics, and Ancient Thought." In *The Cambridge Companion to Foucault.* Ed. Gary Gutting. Cambridge, Mass.: Cambridge University Press, 1994.
Davies, J. K. *Athenian Propertied Families 600–300* B.C. Oxford: Oxford University Press, 1971.
Demosthenes. "Third Philippic." Trans. J. H. Vince. In *Demosthenes I: Olynthiacs, Philippics and Minor Orations.* Cambridge, Mass.: Harvard University Press; London: Heinemann (Loeb Classical Library), 1962.
Derrida, Jacques. "From Restricted to General Economy: A Hegelianism without Reserve." In *Writing and Difference.* Trans. Alan Bass. Chicago: University of Chicago Press, 1978.
Desmond, William J. "Comedy and the Failure of Logos: On Dialectic, Deconstruction, and the Mockery of Philosophy." In *Beyond Hegel and Dialectic.* Albany: State University of New York Press, 1992.
Dixsaut, Monique. *Le Maturel Philosophe: Essai sur les Dialogue de Platon.* Paris: n.p., 1985.
Dorter, Kenneth. "The Significance of the Speeches in Plato's Symposium." *Philosophy and Rhetoric* 2 (1964): 215–234.
Dover, K. J. "Classical Greek Attitudes to Sexual Behaviour." In *Women in the Ancient World: The Arethusa Papers.* Eds. John Peradotto and J. P. Sullivan. Albany: State University of New York Press, 1984.
———. *Greek Homosexuality.* Cambridge, Mass.: Cambridge University Press, 1978.
———. *Greek Popular Morality in the Time of Plato and Aristotle.* Indianapolis and Cambridge, Mass.: Hackett Publishing Co., 1994; London: Basil Blackwell, 1974.
———. *Plato: Symposium.* Cambridge, Mass.: Cambridge University Press, 1980.
Duncan, Roger. "*Philia* in the *Gorgias.*" *Apeiron* 8 (1974): 23–25.
Edmunds, Lowell. "Aristophanes' Socrates." *Proceedings of the Boston Area Colloquium in Ancient Philosophy* 1 (1985): 209–240.
Eisner, Robert. "Socrates as Hero." *Philosophy and Literature* 6, Nos. 1 and 2 (1982): 106–118.
Euben, J. Peter. "The Battle of Salamis and the Origin of Political Theory." *Political Theory* (August 1986): 359–390.
Euripides. "Electra." In *Medea and Other Plays.* Trans. Philip Vellacott. New York: Penguin Books, 1963.
———. "Hippolytus." In *Three Plays.* Trans. Philip Vellacott. New York: Penguin Books, 1974.
———. "Ion." In *The Bacchae and Other Plays.* Trans. Philip Vellacott. New York: Penguin Books, 1973.
———. "The Pheonician Women." In *Orestes and Other Plays.* Trans. Philip Vellacott. New York: Penguin Books, 1972.

Finlay, John. "The Night of Alcibiades." *The Hudson Review* 47, No. 1 (1994): 57–79.
Flynn, Thomas. "Foucault as Parrhesiast: His Last Course at the Collège de France." In *The Final Foucault*. Eds. James Bernauer and David Rasmussen. Cambridge, Mass. and London: MIT Press, 1987.
Forde, Steven. *The Ambition to Rule: Alcibiades and the Politics of Imperialism in Thucydides*. Ithaca, N.Y.: Cornell University Press, 1989.
———. "On the Alcibiades I." In *The Roots of Political Philosophy: Ten Forgotten Socratic Dialogues*. Ed. Thomas Pangle. Ithaca, N.Y. and London: Cornell University Press, 1987.
Foucault, Michel. "Discourse and Truth: The Problematization of 'Parrhesia.'" Notes to the seminar given by Foucault at the University of California Berkeley." Ed. Joseph Pearson. Typescript.
———. "The Ethic of Care for the Self as a Practice of Freedom." Trans. J. D. Gautier, S. J. In *The Final Foucault*. Eds. James Bernauer and David Rasmussen. Cambridge, Mass.: MIT Press, 1987.
Friedländer, Paul. *Plato*, Vols. 1–3. Trans. Hans Meyerhoff. Princeton, N.J.: Princeton University Press, 1973.
Gadamer, Hans-Georg. "Logos and Ergon in Plato's Lysis." In *Dialogue and Dialectic*. Trans. P. Christopher Smith. New Haven, Conn.: Yale University Press, 1980.
Gagarin, Michael. "Socrates' Hybris and Alcibiades' Failure." *Phoenix* 31 (1977): 22–37.
Gill, Christopher. "Platonic Love and Individuality." In *Polis and Politics*. Eds. A. Loizon and H. Lesser. Aldershor: Avebury, 1990.
Glidden, D. K. "The Language of Love: Lysis 212a8–213c9." *Pacific Philosophical Quarterly* 61 (1980): 276–290.
———. "The Lysis on Loving One's Own." *Classical Quarterly* 31 (1981): 39–59.
Golden, Mark. "*Pais*, 'Child' and 'Slave.'" *L'Antiquité Classique* 54 (1985): 91–104.
———. "Slavery and Homosexuality in Athens." *Phoenix* 38 (1984): 308–324.
Gomperz, T. *Die Lebensauffassung der griechischen Philosophen und das Ideal der inneren Freiheit*. Jena: n.p., 1904.
Gonzalez, Francisco J. "How to Read a Platonic Prologue: Lysis 203a–207d." (Typescript).
———. "Plato's *Lysis:* An Enactment of Philosophical Kinship." *Ancient Philosophy* 15, No. 1 (1995): 69–90.
———. "A Short History of Platonic Interpretation and the 'Third Way'." In *The Third Way: New Directions in Platonic Studies*. Ed. Francisco J. Gonzalez. Lanham, Md.: Rowman & Littlefield, 1995.
Griffin, Drew. "Socrates' Poverty: Virtue and Money in Plato's Apology of Socrates." *Ancient Philosophy* 15, No. 1 (Spring 1995): 1–16.
Griswold, Charles. "Response to Kenneth Sayre." *Proceedings of the Boston Area Colloquium in Ancient Philosophy* IX (1993). Eds. John J. Cleary and William Wians. Lanham, Md.: University Press of America, 1995.
Guthrie, W. K. C. *A History of Greek Philosophy*, Vol. 4. *Plato, The Man and His Dialogues: The Earlier Period*. Cambridge, Mass.: Cambridge University Press, 1978.
Haden, James. "Friendship in Plato's Lysis." *Review of Metaphysics* 37 (1983): 327–356.

Halperin, David M. *One Hundred Years of Homosexuality and Other Essays on Greek Love.* New York: Routledge, 1990.

———. "Plato and Erotic Reciprocity." *Classical Antiquity* 5 (1989): 60–80.

———. "Plato and the Erotics of Narrativity." In *Oxford Studies in Ancient Philosophy.* Ed. Julia Annas. Oxford: Oxford University Press, 1992.

———. "Plato and the Metaphysics of Desire." *Proceedings of the Boston Area Colloquium in Ancient Philosophy* 5 (1989): 27–52.

———. "Platonic Eros and What Men Call Love." *Ancient Philosophy* 5 (1985): 161–204.

Halperin, David M., John J. Winkler, and Froma I. Zeitlin, eds. *Before Sexuality: The Construction of Erotic Experience in the Ancient Greek World.* Princeton, N.J.: Princeton University Press, 1989.

Hamilton, Edith, and Harrington Cairns, eds. *The Collected Dialogues of Plato.* Princeton, N.J.: Princeton University Press, 1971.

Hansen, David T. "Was Socrates a 'Socratic Teacher'?" *Educational Theory* 38, No. 2 (1988): 213–224.

Havelock, Eric A. *Preface to Plato.* Cambridge, Mass. and London: Harvard University Press, 1963.

Heidegger, Martin. *Being and Time.* Trans. John Macquarie and Edward Robinson. New York: Harper & Row, 1962.

Hoerber, Robert. "Plato's Lysis." *Phronesis* 4 (1959): 15–28.

Howland, Jacob. "Re-reading Plato: The Problem of Platonic Chronology." *Phoenix* 45, No. 3 (1991): 189–214.

———. "Socrates and Alcibiades: Eros, Piety, and Politics." *Interpretation* 18 (1990): 63–90.

Hyde, Lewis. *The Gift: Imagination and the Erotic Life of Property.* New York: Vintage Books, 1983.

Hyland, Drew A. "Eros, Epithumia, and Philia in Plato." *Phronesis* 13 (1968): 32–46.

Isocrates. "*Areopagitus* (On the peace)." Trans. George Norlin. In *Isocrates.* Vol. 2. Cambridge, Mass.: Harvard University Press; London: Heinemann (Loeb Classical Library), 1968.

Jaeger, Werner. *Paideia: The Ideals of Greek Culture.* Trans. Gilbert Highet. 3 Vols. Oxford and New York: Oxford University Press, 1971.

Jowett, Benjamin. *The Dialogues of Plato.* 4 Vols. Oxford: Oxford University Press, 1953.

Kahn, Charles. "Plato's Theory of Desire." *Review of Metaphysics* 44 (1963): 77–103.

Kerferd, G. B. *The Sophistic Movement.* Cambridge, Mass.: Cambridge University Press, 1981.

Keuls, Eva C. *The Reign of the Phallus: Sexual Politics in Ancient Athens.* 2d ed. Berkeley: University of California Press, 1985.

Kierkegaard, Soren. *The Concept of Irony with Continual Reference to Socrates.* Trans. L. M. Capel. New York: Harper & Row, 1965.

King, James T. "Elenchus, Self-Blame and the Socratic Paradox." *Review of Metaphysics* 41 (1987): 105–126.

———. "Nonteaching and Its Significance for Education." *Education Theory* 26 (Spring 1976): 223–230.

Kraut, Richard. "Commentary on Vlastos' 'Socratic Elenchus'." *Oxford Studies in Ancient Philosophy* 1 (1983): 59–70.
———. *Socrates and the State*. Princeton, N.J.: Princeton University Press, 1984.
Krell, David F. "Socrates' Body." *The Southern Journal of Philosophy* 10, No. 4 (1972): 443–451.
Kreutz, Arthur. "Dramatic Form and Philosophical Content in Plato's Dialogues." *Philosophy and Literature* 7 (1983): 32–47.
Lacey, A. R. "Our Knowledge of Socrates." In *Essays on the Philosophy of Socrates: A Collection of Critical Essays*, ed. Gregory Vlastos. Garden City, N.Y.: Anchor Books, 1971.
Lesses, Glenn. "Plato's Lysis and Irwin's Socrates." *International Studies in Philosophy* 18 (1986): 33–43.
Levin, Donald. "Some Observations Concerning Plato's Lysis." In *Studies in Ancient Greek Philosophy*. Ed. John Anton, with George Kustas. Albany: State University of New York Press, 1971.
Liddell, H. G., and R. Scott. *An Intermediate Greek-English Lexicon*. Founded upon the seventh edition of *Liddell and Scott's Greek-English Lexicon*. Oxford: Clarendon Press, 1994.
Lycos, Kimon. *Plato on Justice and Power: Reading Book I of Plato's Republic*. Albany: State University of New York Press, 1987.
Maier, Heinrich. *Sokrates*. Tübingen: n.p., 1913.
Mauss, Marcel. *The Gift: Forms and Functions of Exchange in Archaic Societies*. Trans. Ian Cunnison. New York: W. W. Norton and Co., 1967.
McKim, Richard. "Shame and Truth in Plato's Gorgias." In *Platonic Writings, Platonic Readings*. Ed. Charles Griswold. New York: Routledge, 1988.
McPherran, Mark L. "Elenctic Interpretation and the Delphic Oracle." In *Rethinking Socratic Method: Essays in Dialogue with Gregory Vlastos's "The Socratic Elenchus"*. Ed. Gary Alan Scott. University Park: Pennsylvania State University Press, Forthcoming.
———. "Socrates and the Duty to Philosophize." *The Southern Journal of Philosophy* XXIV, No. 4 (Winter 1986): 541–560.
McTighe, Kevin. "Nine Notes on Plato's Lysis." *American Journal of Philology* 104 (1983): 67–82.
Miller, Mitchell. *Plato's Parmenides: The Conversion of the Soul*. University Park: Pennsylvania State University Press, 1991.
Moravcsik, Julius. "Plato and Pericles on Freedom and Politics." *Canadian Journal of Philosophy* 9, Supplemental, 1983: 1–18.
Morris, T. F. "Plato's Lysis." *Philosophy Research Archives* 11 (1985): 269–279.
Mulgan, R. G. "Liberty in Ancient Greece." In *Conceptions of Liberty in Political Philosophy*. Eds. Z. Pelczynski and J. Gray. London: Athlone Press, 1984.
Mulhern, J. J. "Two Interpretive Fallacies." *Systematics* 9 (1971): 168–172.
Nails, Debra. *Agora, Academy, and the Conduct of Philosophy*. Dordrecht: Kluwer Academic Publishers, 1995.
———. "Problems with Vlastos's Platonic Developmentalism." *Ancient Philosophy* 13 (1993): 273–291.
Nehamas, Alexander. *The Art of Living*. Berkeley and Los Angeles: University of California Press, 1998.

———. "Eristic, Antilogic, Sophistic, Dialectic: Plato's Demarcation of Philosophy from Sophistry." *History of Philosophy Quarterly* 7 (1990): 3–16.
———. "Meno's Paradox and Socrates as a Teacher." In *Essays on the Philosophy of Socrates*. Ed. Hugh H. Benson. New York and Oxford: Oxford University Press, 1992.
———. *Nietzsche: Life as Literature*. Cambridge, Mass.: Harvard University Press, 1985.
———. "Socratic Irony." Lecture delivered at the University of Pittsburgh, October 8, 1994.
———. "What Did Socrates Teach and To Whom Did He Teach It?" *Review of Metaphysics* 46, No. 2 (1992): 279–306.
Nehamas, Alexander, and Paul Woodruff, trans. *Plato: Phaedrus*. Indianapolis and Cambridge, Mass.: Hackett Publishing Co., 1995.
———. *Plato: Symposium*. Indianapolis and Cambridge, Mass.: Hackett Publishing Co., 1989.
Nietzsche, Friedrich. *Twilight of the Idols*. In *The Portable Nietzshce*. Trans. Walter Kaufmann. New York: Penguin Books, 1968.
Nightingale, Andrea W. *Genres in Dialogue: Plato and the Construct of Philosophy*. Cambridge, Mass.: Cambridge University Press, 1996.
North, Helen. *Sophrosyne: Self-Knowledge and Self-Restraint in Greek Literature*. Ithaca, N.Y.: Cornell University Press, 1966.
Nussbaum, Martha C. "Commentary on Halperin." *Proceedings of the Boston Area Colloquium in Ancient Philosophy* 5 (1989): 27–52.
———. "The Speech of Alcibiades: A Reading of the Symposium." In *The Fragility of Goodness: Luck and Ethics in Greek Tragedy and Philosophy*. Cambridge, Mass.: Cambridge University Press, 1986.
O'Connor, David K. "Socrates and the Gift." Lecture delivered at the 12th Annual Meeting of the SAGP/SSIPS. Binghamton University, Binghamton, N.Y. October 30, 1993.
Osborne, Catherine. *Eros Unveiled: Plato and the God of Love*. Oxford: Clarendon Press, 1994.
Pangle, Thomas, ed. *The Roots of Political Philosophy: Ten Forgotten Socratic Dialogues*. Ithaca, N.Y., and London: Cornell University Press, 1987.
Penwill, J. L. "Men in Love: Aspects of Plato's Symposium." *Ramus* 7 (1978): 143–175.
Plato. "Alcibiades I." Trans. Carnes Lord. In *The Roots of Political Philosophy: Ten Forgotten Socratic Dialogues*. Ed. Thomas Pangle. Ithaca, N.Y., and London: Cornell University Press, 1987.
———. "Alcibiades I." In *Plato in Twelve Volumes*. Trans. W. R. M. Lamb. Vol. XII. Cambridge, Mass.: Harvard University Press, 1986; London: Heinemann (Loeb Classical Library), 1927.
———. *Symposium*. Trans. by Robin Waterfield. Oxford: Oxford University Press, 1994.
Plochmann, George. "Supporting Themes in the Symposium." In *Ancient Greek Philosophy*. Ed. John Anton, with George Kustas. Albany: State University of New York Press, 1971.

Plutarch. "Concerning Talkativeness." Trans. W. C. Helmbold. In *Plutarch's Moralia*, Vol. 6.Cambridge, Mass.: Harvard University Press; London: Heinemann (Loeb Classical Library), 1962.

———. "The Education of Children." Trans. Frank Cole Babbit. In *Plutarch's Moralia*, Vol. 1. Cambridge, Mass.: Harvard University Press; London: Heinemann (Loeb Classical Library), 1960.

Pohlenz, Max. *Freedom in Greek Life and Thought: The History of an Ideal*. Trans. C. Lofmark. New York: Humanities Press, 1966.

Press, Gerald A. "Knowledge as Vision in Plato's Dialogues." *The Journal of Neoplatonic Studies* 3, No. 2 (Spring 1995): 61–90.

———. "Plato's Dialogues as Enactments." In *The Third Way: New Directions in Platonic Studies*. Ed. Francisco J. Gonzalez. Lanham, Md.: Rowman & Littlefield, 1995.

———. ed. *Plato's Dialogues: New Studies in Interpretation*. Lanham, Md.: Rowman & Littlefield, 1993.

Price, A.W. "Martha Nussbaum's Symposium." *Ancient Philosophy* 11 (1991): 285–299.

Randall, John Herman, Jr. *Plato: Dramatist of the Life of Reason*. New York and London: Columbia University Press, 1970.

Robinson, Richard. *Plato's Early Dialectic*. 2d ed. Oxford: Clarendon Press, 1953.

Rutherford, Richard B. *The Art of Plato*. Cambridge, Mass.: Harvard University Press, 1995.

Saxonhouse, Arlene W. "Eros and the Female in Greek Political Thought: An Interpretation of Plato's Symposium." *Political Theory* 5 (1984): 5–27.

———. "The Philosopher and the Female in the Political Thought of Plato." *Political Theory* 4, No. 2 (1976): 195–212.

Schall, James. "The Death of Plato." *American Scholar* (1996): 401–415.

Schein, Seth. "Alcibiades and the Politics of Misguided Love in Plato's Symposium." *Theta Pi* 3, No. 2 (1974): 158–167.

Schleiermacher, Friedrich E. D. *Introduction to the Dialogues of Plato*. Trans. William Dobson. New York: Arno Press [Reprint of translation of 2d German edition of 1836], 1973.

Scott, Gary Alan, ed. *Rethinking Socratic Method: Essays in Dialogue with Gregory Vlastos's "The Socratic Elenchus"*. University Park: Pennsylvania State Universtiy Press, Forthcoming.

Scott, Gary Alan, and William A. Welton. "Eros as Messenger: Diotima's Teaching." In *Who Speaks for Plato?: Studies in Platonic Anonymity*. Ed. Gerald A. Press. Lanham, Md.: Rowman & Littlefield, 2000.

Sedley, David. "Is the Lysis a Dialogue of Definition?" *Phronesis* 34 (1989): 107–108.

Smith, P. Christopher. "Not Doctrine but 'Placing in Question': The 'Thrasymachus' (Rep. I) as an Erôtêsis of Commercialization." In *Who Speaks for Plato?: Studies in Platonic Anonymity*. Ed. Gerald A. Press. Lanham, Md.: Rowman & Littlefield, 2000.

Soble, Alan. "Love Is Not Beautiful: Symposium 200c-201c." *Apeiron* 19 (1985): 43–52.

Stroud, Ronald S. "The Gravestone of Socrates' Friend, Lysis." *Hesperia: Journal of the American School of Classical Studies at Athens* 53 (1984): 355–360.

Taylor, A. E. *Plato: The Man and His Work.* Cleveland: Meridian Books, 1963.
Teloh, Henry. *Socratic Education in Plato's Early Dialogues.* Notre Dame: University of Notre Dame Press, 1986.
Tessitore, Aristide. "Plato's *Lysis:* An Introduction to Philosophic Friendship." *The Southern Journal of Philosophy* 28, No. 1 (1990): 115–132.
Theognis. *Elegies.* Trans. Dorothea Wender. In *Hesiod and Theognis.* New York: Penguin Books, 1981.
Thesleff, Helger. "Looking for Clues: An Interpretation of Some Literary Aspects of Plato's 'Two-Level Model'." In *Plato's Dialogues: New Studies in Interpretation.* Ed. Gerald A. Press. Lanham, Md.: Rowman & Littlefield, 1993.
Thucydides. *History of the Peloponnesian War.* Trans. Rex Warner. New York and London: Penguin Books, 1954.
Tindale, Christopher. "Plato's Lysis: A Reconsideration." *Apeiron* 18 (1984): 102–109.
Umphrey, Stuart. "Eros and Thumos." *Interpretation* 10 (1982): 352–422.
Vernant, Jean-Pierre. "The Individual within the City-State." In *Mortals and Immortals: Collected Essays.* Trans. Froma I. Zeitlin. Princeton, N.J.: Princeton University Press, 1991.

———. *The Origins of Greek Thought.* Ithaca, N.Y.: Cornell University Press, 1982.

———. "Psuche: Simulacrum of the Body or Image of the Divine?" In *Mortals and Immortals: Collected Essays.* Trans. Froma I. Zeitlin. Princeton, N.J.: Princeton University Press, 1991.

Vlastos, Gregory. "Afterthoughts on the Socratic Elenchus." *Oxford Studies in Ancient Philosophy* 1 (1983): 71–74.

———. "The Individual as an Object of Love in Plato." In *Platonic Studies.* Ed. Gregory Vlastos. Princeton, N.J.: Princeton University Press, 1973.

———. "The Paradox of Socrates." In *The Philosophy of Socrates: A Collection of Critical Essays.* Ed. Gregory Vlastos. Garden City, N.Y.: Anchor Books, 1971.

———. *Socrates: Ironist and Moral Philosopher.* Ithaca, N.Y.: Cornell University Press, 1991.

———. "The Socratic Elenchus." *Oxford Studies in Ancient Philosophy* 1 (1983): 27–58.

———. "Socratic Irony." In *Socrates: Ironist and Moral Philosopher.* Ithaca, N.Y.: Cornell University Press, 1991.

———. *Socratic Studies.* Ed. Myles Burnyeat. Cambridge: Cambridge University Press, 1994.

Werner, Martin. "Dialectical Drama: The Case of Plato's Symposium." *Apeiron* 25, No. 4 (1992): 157–175.
West, Elinor J. M. "Plato's Audiences, or How Plato Replies to the Fifth-Century Intellectual Mistrust of Letters." In *The Third Way: New Directions in Platonic Studies.* Ed. Francisco J. Gonzalez. Lanham, Md.: Rowman & Littlefield, 1995.

———. "Socrates: Aristophanes' and Plato's Old Quarrel." (1998, Typescript).

White, F. C. "Love and Beauty in Plato's Symposium." *Journal of Hellenic Studies* 109 (1989): 149–157.
Winkler, John J. *The Constraints of Desire: The Anthropology of Sex and Gender in Ancient Greece.* New York: Routledge, 1990.

Wolfsdorf, David. "Plato and the Mouth-piece Theory." *Ancient Philosophy* [special issue: Representations of Philosophy in the Classical World. K. V. Rosenbecker and Jana L. Adamatis, eds.] (1999): 13–24.

Wolz, H. G. "Philosophy as Drama: An Approach to Plato's Symposium." *Philosophy and Phenomenological Research* 30 (1969–1970): 323–353.

Xenophon, *Conversations of Socrates*. Trans. Hugh Treadnick and Robin Waterfield. London: Penguin Classic Books, 1990.

———. *Cyropaideia*. Trans. Walter Miller. Cambridge, Mass.: Harvard University Press, 1960.

———. "Oeconomicus." In *Xenophon in Seven Volumes*, Vol. 4: "Memoribilia" and "Oeconomicus." Trans. E. C. Marchant. Cambridge, Mass.: Harvard University Press, 1968.

Young, Charles. "Plato and Computer Dating." *Oxford Studies in Ancient Philosophy* 12 (1994): 227–250.

Zeitlin, Froma I. "The Configurations of Rape in Greek Myth." In *Rape*. Eds. S. Tomaselli and R. Porter. Oxford: Basil Blackwell, 1986.

Index

Achilles, 89, 209n. 16
active learning, 45
Adeimantus, 3, 25, 230n. 3
ad hominem argumentation, 4, 151, 162, 176
Adkins, A.W. H., 215n. 2, 221n. 36
Agathon, 3, 127, 128, 129, 139, 146
akin or kindred (*oikos*), 20, 53, 57, 65, 68, 76, 78–80, 105, 199n. 25
akrasia, 125
Alcibiades, 11, 31, 44, 57, 59, 81–117, 119–64, 166–67, 171, 176
   and Athens, 19, 95, 113, 124–25, 149, 179, 184n. 5, 216n. 11, 217n. 13, 228n. 72
   and self-improvement, 112, 129, 152, 220n. 28
   Symposium speech of, 73, 85, 119–64
   See also Lysis and Alcibiades
Anaxagoras, 115, 215n. 53
Anderson, D., 103
Antigone, 111
Aphrodite, 82, 130, 165, 188n. 25, 199n. 22
Apollodorus, 3, 4, 23, 125, 146–47, 176, 180n. 7, 215n. 1

aporia (perplexity), 7, 39, 41, 45, 47, 63, 80, 82, 88, 89, 101, 150–51, 161–62, 169, 171, 183n. 3, 200n. 29, 202n. 43, 205n. 58, 209n. 11
aretē (virtue or excellence), 5, 6, 43, 73, 86, 89, 90, 92, 96, 98, 109–11, 115–17, 174, 182n. 1, 184n. 8, 209n. 15, 213n. 36
Aristodemus, 3, 4, 23, 176, 180n. 7
Aristophanes, 3, 185n. 15, 225n. 52
Aristotle, 42, 54, 197n. 16, 198n. 19; on benefaction, 33–36; on friendship, 33–35, 52, 74, 188n. 30, 198n. 19; 204n. 56; on irony, 144–45, 225n. 53; works by:
   Eudemian Ethics, 33, 34, 189n. 30, 211; *Nicomachian Ethics*, 34, 35, 52, 54, 144, 189n. 196n. 16, 30, 225n. 53; *Politics*, 35; *Rhetoric*, 190n. 31, 202n. 45; writings of (general), 9, 32, 206n
Aspasia, 28, 189n. 35
Athenian conventions, 10–12, 24, 63, 73–74, 104, 109–10, 130, 215n. 2, 219n. 20

245

Athenian democracy, 6, 19, 126, 147, 149, 217n. 14, 223n. 41, 227n. 64
Athenian laws, 141, 183n. 4, 197n. 19, 203n. 51
Athenian practices, 32, 104. *See also* sunousia
Athenian Stranger, 178
Athens, 18, 22, 33, 60, 66–67, 119, 141, 147, 164, 185n. 15, 195n. 10, 226n. 59, 227n. 64, 231n. 6; after Peloponnesian War, 6, 11, 13; Socrates' gift to, 35, 168–169, 171, 173–174; youth of, 15, 17, 20, 63, 167, 184n. 7
athuroglottos (intemperate free speech), 148–49, 227n. 66

Bataille, G., 173
Benson, H., 213n. 38
Berkeley, G., 178
Billings, J., 40
bios, 149, 154–155, 166, 213n. 39
Blank, D., 23, 185n. 14
Blondell, R., 181n. 9
Bloom, A., 29, 202n. 47
blush, blushing, 72, 202n. 44
Bolotin, D.,192n. 1, 201n. 40
boundaries and freedom, 55–6, 59–60, 69–70, 194n, 196nn. 11, 12, 201n. 41. *See* limits and freedom
Bowery, A., 186n. 17
Brentlinger, J., 132
Brickhouse, T. C. & N. D. Smith, 181n. 10, 199n. 24, 213n. 39, 231n. 4
Burkert, W., 199n. 22
Burnyeat, M., 198n. 19, 211n. 28, 214n. 43

Callicles, 3, 23, 83, 105, 125, 150–52, 154, 180n. 5, 229n. 78
care of the self (self-care), 12, 84, 89–92, 102, 104, 106, 110, 112, 116, 149, 153, 160, 163, 167, 169–70, 207n. 8, 214n. 47; and freedom, 102, 108–11

Cebes, 3
Chaerophon, 215n. 1
Charmides, 1, 4, 7, 19, 63, 82–83, 161–64, 179n. 3, 199n. 21, 215n. 1
Cobb, W., 212n. 35
Cole, S., 203n. 51
Coplan, A., 192n. 3
Critias, 19, 107, 155, 164, 179n. 3, 209n. 18, 217n. 13
Crito, 5, 181n. 7, 200n. 27, 215n. 1
Ctesippus, 60, 61, 64, 194n, 215n. 1

Delphic oracle, 14, 42, 230n. 80
Derrida, J., 173
Desmond, W., 230n. 83
dialectic, 104, 112, 133, 184n. 9, 193n. 5, 225n. 51
dialogue and self-transformation, 102, 106–8
dialogue form, 2, 44, 104, 178, 192n. 4, 234n. 20; drama of, 2, 3, 10, 53, 62, 80, 104, 120, 123, 139, 165–67
didaskalos (teacher), 16, 18–26, 30, 38, 105, 183n. 3, 184n. 8; definition of, 14–27
Dionysos, 144
Diotima, 14, 28, 36, 48, 76, 120, 121, 131–132, 176, 178, 189n. 35, 191n. 41, 199n. 22, 214n. 43, 220n. 30, 221n. 33
divination, 4, 93. *See also* Socrates' *daimonion*
Dixsaut, M., 187n. 22
Dover, K. J., 33, 74, 187n. 24, 188n. 29, 189n. 32, 195n. 7, 202n. 45, 203n. 51, 215n. 2,
Duncan, R., 180n. 5, 201n. 41, 204n. 53

education, 15, 36, 169, 174, 208n. 10, 211n. 28; additive vs. integrative models, 40–41; in *Alcibiades I*, 91, 99, 103, 109, 112–15; in *Lysis*, 51, 53, 58, 62–3; in *Symposium*, 120,

126, 148; Socratic vs. sophistic, 2–7, 11–2, 25–6, 30, 37–49
Eisner, R., 143, 216n. 4, 225n. 51
Eleatic visitor, 178
elenchon toū biou, 106, 222n. 34
elenchos, 106, 112, 185n. 12, 191n. 43, 193n. 5, 213n. 39
Eros, 51, 52, 61, 76, 139, 145, 148, 177, 199n. 25, 201n. 40, 217n. 13, 219n. 23; Alcibiades' vs. Socrates', 126–37, 221n. 36; philosophical, 10, 14 ; Socrates', 5, 8, 58–59, 82, 95, 120, 122, 221n. 33; Socrates' knowledge of, 61, 191n. 43; in *Symposium*, 14, 80, 119–53; and *thumos*, 87, 90, 112–13, 125–27, 131–37, 204n. 53, 209n. 16, 220n. 30
erotic reversal, 4–5, 7, 55, 72–4, 120–30, 230n. 2
Eryximachus, 3, 133, 139, 149, 221n. 32, 225n. 52
Euripides' works: *Electra*, 223n. 42; *Hippolytus*, 147; *Ion*, 154, 203n. 50, 227n. 60–2, 230n. 80; *Phoenician Women*, 227n. 60
Euthydemus, 184n. 7, 189n. 34, 230n. 2
Euthyphro, 3, 39, 161, 184n. 7
exchange economy, 31, 43, 54, 73, 126, 170, 190n. 40, 218n. 19, 219n. 25. *See also* market exchange

Finlay, J., 216n. 11, 217n. 14
Flynn, T., 227n. 64
Forde, S., 85, 89–90, 98, 112, 126, 133, 207nn. 5, 7, 209nn. 15–7, 210nn. 19, 22, 211n. 27, 214n. 51, 216n. 10, 217n. 13, 220n. 31, 222n. 37, 228nn. 68, 71
Foucault, M., 108, 147, 155, 223n. 42, 226nn. 55, 59, 227nn. 62, 64, 230n. 80
frankness, 138–39, 146–48, 151–52, 227nn. 61–4, 228n. 71, 229n. 75. *See also parrhēsia*

Friedländer, P., 82–83, 205n. 1, 207n. 6, 220n. 29
friend, the (*ho philos*), 57–59, 68, 75–80, 162, 225n. 54
friends, 57, 62, 80; Socrates and, 62, 76–79, 180n. 5, 200n. 27, 232n. 14
friendship, 12, 52–53, 72, 74–80, 90, 112, 132, 180n. 5, 193n. 6, 204n. 53, 205n. 57.; between Lysis and Menexenus, 53, 61–2, 72, 193n. 6, 205n. 58; *See also* Aristotle on friendship

Gagarin, M., 215n. 4
gift, 11, 31–36, 73, 153, 166, 169, 170–76, 179, 187n. 23, 188n. 28, 218n. 20, 219n. 23, 232n. 14
Gill, C., 216n. 5
Glaucon, 3, 29–30, 215n. 1, 233n. 14
Golden, M., 182n. 11
Gonzalez, F. 77–78, 192n. 4, 195n. 9, 199n. 22, 205n. 58
Gorgias, 25, 37–43, 184n. 7
Griswold, C., 234n. 20
Guthrie, W. K. C., 192n. 1

Halperin, D., 133, 182n. 11, 220n. 30, 221n. 34
Hansen, D., 186n. 17
Heidegger, M., 205n. 60, 230n. 1
Hermea, 59, 62, 199n. 22
Hermes, 61, 199n. 22, 203n. 50
Herms, 19, 179, 199n. 22
Hippias, 25, 184n. 7, 215n. 1, 230n. 2
Hippocrates, 4
Hippothales, 14, 52–3, 59–61, 63–4, 72, 79–80, 129, 132, 195n. 7, 197n. 17, 200n. 31, 201n. 32, 202n. 44
hubris, 58, 103, 108, 140–44, 169, 197n. 17, 198n. 18, 225n. 53
Hyland, D., 204n. 10

Ion, 184n. 7
Isocrates, 164–65, 232n. 7

Isocrates, *"Aereopagetis"*, 227n. 68
isonomia (equality), 9–10, 130

Jaeger, W., 110, 168, 207n. 4, 222n. 41, 229n. 79

Kerferd, G. B., 185n. 14, 187n. 22
Keuls, E., 182n. 11
Kierkegaard, S., 143, 224n. 48
kindred. *See* akin
King, J., 15, 37–41, 123, 189n. 33
Kraut, R., 169–171, 174, 187n. 23

Laches, 5, 184n. 7
Limits and freedom, 51, 53–61, 64–6, 69–70, 79, 103–4, 134–35, 196n. 12. *See* boundaries and freedom
logos, 102, 108, 112, 148–149, 152, 154–155, 166–168, 212n. 35, 229n. 79, 230n. 83
lover (*erastēs*)/beloved (*eromenos*), 4, 9–10, 53, 59, 61, 78–79, 120, 123, 126, 129–30, 148, 202n. 42, 204n. 56, 219n. 25, 225n. 52, 228n. 69; role in dialogues, 81–82, 84, 195n. 7
Lysias, 165, 232n. 7
Lysimachus, 150
Lysis, 11, 51–80, 83–86, 88, 101, 113, 129, 131–32, 134, 141, 161–62, 184n. 7, 209n. 11, 211n. 29, 214nn. 49, 50, 215n. 2, 230n. 2, 231n. 4, 233n. 19; age of, 15, 61–4, 184n. 10, 193n. 5; and Alcibiades, 4, 7–10, 12, 20, 31, 55, 58, 88, 109, 130, 135, 142, 159–61, 166–67, 196n. 14; and freedom, 52–66; and Menexenus, 13, 44, 52, 56–7, 61–2, 72, 79, 132, 205n. 58

market economy, market exchange, 8, 11, 30–32, 36, 122, 128, 155, 169, 171, 197n. 16
market relations, 11, 43, 126
Marsyas, 124, 140, 142, 223n. 44

Mauss, M., 32–33, 35, 172–73, 188n. 26
McKim, R., 229n. 75
McPherran, M., 192n. 44, 210n. 23, 213n. 38
Meletus, 40, 185n. 13, 190n. 41, 199n. 21, 213n. 39, 230n. 1
Melian dialogue, 218n. 15
Menexenus, 13, 28, 44, 52–53, 56–57, 61–63, 71–72, 74–76, 79, 132, 182n. 12, 184n. 7, 193n. 6, 202n. 43, 205n. 15, 214n. 50, 215n. 1
Meno, 3, 62–63, 70, 72, 96, 106, 161, 184n. 7, 187n. 19, 189n. 34, 199n. 21, 201n. 38, 202n. 46, 213n. 40
Meno's paradox, 96, 199n. 25
Meno's slave boy, 3, 62–63
Miller, M., 200n. 29
mock humility, 141, 143–44, 225n. 53. *See* Socratic irony

Nails, D., 206n
Nehamas, A., 19–20, 46, 48, 142–43, 153, 165, 182n. 1, 183n. 3, 184nn. 7–9, 185n. 11, 187n. 22, 191n. 43, 218n. 18, 224nn. 49–50, 233n. 18
Nicias, 5, 150, 184n. 7
Nietzsche's critique of Socrates, 172, 232n. 8, 233n. 15
Nightingale, A., 187n. 22
North, H., 209n. 18, 211n. 24
Nussbaum, M., 12, 182n. 14, 216n. 5, 222n. 38, 228n. 72

O'Connor, D., 188n. 27
Odysseus, 89, 209n. 16
oikos. *See* akin
Osborne, C., 180n. 7

paideia, 6, 59, 83, 99, 110, 116
paideusis. *See* education
paideutēs, 26, 31, 38–39, 161–62; true vs. *atopos*, 25–26
Pangle, T., 206n
Parmenides, 40, 178

parrhêsia, 138–39, 142, 145–49, 152, 154–57, 216n. 8, 222n. 41, 227nn. 61–64
parrhêsiastic contract, 155, 223n. 42, 226n. 55, 227n. 62
Pausanias, 3, 82, 130, 188n. 25, 204n. 56, 225n. 52
pedagogue, 3, 13, 41, 62, 65, 72, 89, 174, 193n. 5; definition of, 13
Peloponnesian War, 19, 125, 218n. 15
Periclean, Athens, 147, 226n. 58; freedom, 196nn. 11, 13, 216n. 9
Pericles, 2, 6, 28, 86, 92, 114–17, 124, 142, 147, 215n. 52, 217n. 12, 226n. 57; in Thucydides, 147
perplexity. See *aporia*
Phaedrus, 3, 161–65, 184n. 7, 204n. 56, 215n. 1, 225n. 52, 232n. 7
philotimia, 126, 133, 177
Plato's, conception of philosophy, 2, 6, 11, 23, 31, 44, 46, 161–71; dialogues: *Alcibiades I* (or Major), 4, 5, 9, 11, 58, 81–117, 135, 136, 37, 150, 151, 162, 163, 176, 196nn.11, 14, 198n. 19, 201nn. 34, 35, 37, 205–15, 220nn. 28, 29, 225n. 54; *Alcibiades II* (or Minor), 182n. 13; *Apology of Socrates*, 13, 14, 15–26, 30, 31, 36, 37, 38, 40, 42, 61, 86, 92, 107, 128, 135, 148, 162, 165, 169–73, 185n. 15, 190n. 36, 199, 213n. 40, 222n. 39; *Charmides*, 4, 9, 83, 107, 155, 186n. 18; *Crito*, 85, 173, 181n. 7, 200n. 27, 214n. 43; *Euthydemus*, 44, 83, 119, 189n. 31, 199n. 23, 204n. 56, 230n. 2; *Euthyphro*, 85, 176, 207n. 5; *Gorgias*, 14–15, 23, 36–43, 83, 85, 105–06, 119, 125, 150–52, 154, 190n. 36, 201n. 41, 204n. 53, 207nn. 4, 6, 211n. 25, 213n. 41, 214n. 43, 215n. 52, 222n. 39, 227n. 63, 229nn. 74, 77, 230n. 82; *Hippias Major*, 189n. 34, 207n. 5, 230n. 2; *Hippias Minor*, 206n, 207n. 5, 230n. 2; *Ion*, 176, 209n. 5; *Laches*, 5, 14, 85, 150, 152; *Laws*, 99, 112, 202n. 44, 206n, 212n. 35; *Lysis*, 4, 5, 9, 14, 49, 105, 112, 131, 141, 162, 182n. 12, 185n. 10, 192–205, 214n. 50, 223n. 46, 225n. 50, 231n. 4; and *Alcibiades I*, 81–2, 135, 142; *Menexenus*, 28, 189n. 35, 207n. 5; *Meno*, 40, 85, 104, 182, 186n. 18; *Phaedo*, 36, 173; *Phaedrus*, 9, 14, 19, 51, 148, 164–65, 189n. 36, 192n. 1, 204n. 56, 207n. 5, 221n. 34, 227n. 63, 232n. 7; *Protagoras*, 19, 27, 37, 119, 189n. 34, 190n. 41, 214n. 43, 215n. 52, 225n. 50, 229n. 74; *Republic* (general), 112, 182, 186, 230n. 2, 234n. 20; *Republic* I, 15, 28–36, 60, 169, 190n. 41, 201n. 39, 224n. 50, 228n. 73, 229n. 74, 232n. 14; *Republic* II, 78, 99, 125; *Republic* III, 95, 211n. 26; *Republic* VI, 25–6, 38, 232n. 9; *Republic* VII, 53, 184n. 10, 185n. 12; *Republic* VIII, 126; *Sophist*, 14, 71–72, 111; *Symposium*, 3, 9, 11, 14, 19, 23, 28, 36, 48–49, 51, 61, 67, 73, 76, 80, 82, 84–85, 116, 119–57, 163–64, 176, 180n. 7, 182n. 13, 188n. 25, 189n. 35, 190n. 41, 191n. 43, 192n. 43, 199nn. 22, 25, 202n. 47, 204n. 56, 209n. 12, 214n. 43, 215n. 54, 216n. 30, 231n. 5; *Theaetetus*, 20, 111, 140, 151, 179n. 2, 181n. 10, 186n. 17
pleonexia, pleonektein, 125–126, 131, 133, 177, 180n. 5, 201nn. 36, 41, 224n. 49
Plutarch, 148
poets, 4, 6, 72, 75, 105, 148, 185n. 13, 202n. 44
Pohlenz, M., 196n. 12, 204n. 54
Polemarchus, 28, 193n. 5
politicians, 6, 42, 185n. 13
Polus, 3, 229n. 75
Press, G., 180n. 4, 183n. 2, 187n. 22

Price, A. W., 216n. 5
Prodicus, 25
Protagoras, 16, 200n. 26, 212n. 34
proton philon argument, 52, 77
psuchē, 96, 109, 112, 154, 165, 169, 190n. 40;

question-and-answer method, 44–5, 87–8, 90, 107

rape, 74, 140, 203n. 51, 230n. 80
rhetoricians, 8, 14, 37, 43
roles, 2, 11, 15, 48, 67, 102, 129, 144, 212n. 33; gender, 9, 130. *See also* lover/beloved; reversal of, 8–10, 72, 81–4, 123, 127, 130–31, 182n. 11, 228n. 69
Royal Tale, 85, 89, 91, 113, 201n. 35, 209n. 17
Rutherford, R., 231n. 5

Saxonhouse, A., 182n. 11
say what you believe, 101–06, 139, 153, 209n. 14, 212n. 34, 213n. 39, 229n. 75
Schein, S., 216n. 6
Schrift, A., 173, 233n. 17
seduction, 5, 58, 73–74, 76, 80, 122–23, 126, 128–31, 142, 146, 194n, 203n. 51, 211n. 27, 219n. 27
self-care. *See* care of the self
self-deprecation, 143–44. *See also* mock humility
self-improvement, 5, 53, 57, 71, 97, 102, 159–60, 191n. 43
self-knowledge, 48, 54–5, 67, 84–5, 90, 94–8, 102–3, 110–11, 113, 135, 137, 151, 198n. 20, 211n. 28, 214n. 44
self-transformation, 102, 156, 167
sexual assault, 73. *See also* rape
shame, 119–20, 124–25, 127, 141, 151–52, 161, 197n. 17, 202n. 44, 220n. 29, 222n. 38, 229n. 75
Sicilian expedition, 134, 179n. 3, 217n. 12, 220n. 31, 228n. 68

Silenus, 143, 223n. 43
Simmias, 3, 181n. 7
Socrates, and fee taking, 25, 33, 43, 128; and freedom, 31, 54, 102–4, 137; as gadfly, 1–2, 30, 31, 86, 106, 109, 143, 168–70; and the gift, 31, 35–6, 73, 170–76, 232n. 13; and Gorgias, 37–43; followers of, 18–23; historical, 1–2, 20, 163–64, 174, 177, 179n. 1, 184n. 5, 187n. 21, 200n. 27, 232n. 9; as pedagogue, 62; and rhetoricians, 23, 39, 42, 189n. 36; as student, 1, 11, 15, 27–36
Socrates', *askēsis* of philosophy, 12, 55, 99, 107, 110–11, 154, 160; *daimonion* (divine sign), 82, 92–93, 135, 165, 230n. 81, 231n. 4; erotic approach, 53, 57–58, 70, 73–74; hubris, 141–44; poverty, 20, 30, 128, 187n. 21, 218n. 20; *pro bono* method, 25, 43; two pronged strategy, 57, 59, 101; arousal, 63, 131, 163; chastening (humbling), 7, 68–70
Socratic, conversations, 1, 10, 21, 164, 188n. 28, 214n. 31; cross-examination, 18, 21, 64, 71, 99–100, 106–8, 150, 154, 156, 162–63, 190n. 41, 209n. 13, 213n. 39, 214n. 50, 222n. 39; cross-examination and refutation, 21–22, 163, 193n. 5, 196n. 15, 214n. 50; eros, 8, 82, 122; ignorance, 46–8, 61, 78; irony, 45–6, 133, 138, 142–44, 156, 191n. 43, 218n. 18, 223nn. 47, 48; method, 21, 163, 198n. 19, 214n. 44; *paideusis* (education), 14, 22, 43–9, 55, 58–9, 84, 110, 159–78; refutation, 70–1, 88–9, 105; seduction, 4–5, 73, 142
Sophists, 5–6, 8, 11, 13, 15, 21, 23–26, 29–30, 32, 36–37, 42–43, 75, 103, 128–29, 182n. 1, 185nn. 11, 14, 189n. 34, 190nn. 36, 39, 229n. 75, 232n. 10
sophrosunē, 11, 59, 67, 71, 85, 90, 95–96, 98, 108–09, 128, 133, 135,

137, 152, 156, 198n. 20, 216m. 24, 223n. 46
Sparta, 6, 19, 123, 179n. 3, 208n. 10, 216n. 11
Stroud, R., 195n. 9
subjugation/domination, 67, 77, 104, 129, 133
sunousia, 9, 82, 130, 133, 181n. 9, 202n. 47, 219n. 25

Taylor, A. E., 192n. 1
taking trouble over oneself (*epimelesthai sautou*), 82, 85, 90–116, 207n. 8. *See* care of the self
teachers, 5, 15, 36–8, 90, 115, 175–76, 190n. 36
technē, 43, 67, 69, 91, 110
technē toū biou, 110
Teloh, H., 128, 201n. 40
Tessitore, A., 77, 192n. 1, 205n. 15
tethering philosophy to character, 46, 162
Theaetetus, 7, 71, 82, 140, 186n. 17, 215n. 1
Theodorus, 215n. 1
Theognis, 148
Timaeus, 178
Thirty Tyrants (or Thirty Oligachs), 6, 18–9, 179n. 3
Thrasymachus, 15, 28–31, 35–6, 169, 171, 184n. 7, 212n. 34, 213n. 40, 224n. 50, 229nn. 75, 76, 233n. 13
Thucydides, 126, 133–34, 147, 208n. 8, 217nn. 12, 13, 218n. 15, 221n. 31, 226n. 57, 228n. 71

thumos (spiritness), 58, 66, 87, 89–90, 112, 125, 131–33, 163, 177, 201n. 40, 204n. 53, 222n. 37
trust (*pistis*), 53, 56–60, 64–70, 91–3, 199n. 25, 201n. 40, 204n. 55, 208n. 10
truth-telling, 147, 150–55, 222n. 38, 226n. 55, 230n. 80. *See also parrhēsia*

Umphrey, S., 204n. 53

Vernant, J. P., 210n. 23
Vlastos, G., 12, 19–20, 46, 139, 182n. 14, 191n. 43, 192n. 1, 193n. 5,196n. 15, 202nn. 42, 43, 209,n. 15, 212n. 34, 213n. 38, 215n. 4, 216n. 5, 223n. 47

warranty of service (or implied warranty), 17–21, 24–5, 43
West, E., 186n. 15, 234n. 20
wisdom
  conceit of, 3, 39, 42, 62, 88, 89, 91, 108, 150, 156, 170, 184n. 8, 185n. 11, 230n. 3
  human, 14, 40, 47, 61, 199n. 24

Xenophon, 1, 35, 164, 174, 179n. 3, 184n. 5, 188n. 27, 196n. 12, 209n. 18, 219n. 23, 225n. 54, 232n. 9; *Apology of Socrates*, 188n. 27, 218n. 19

Zeitlin, F., 182n. 11, 203n. 50
Zeno, 115

www.ingramcontent.com/pod-product-compliance
Lightning Source LLC
Chambersburg PA
CBHW020645230426
43665CB00008B/323